THE AUTHOR

Luigino Caliaro is an acclaimed aviation photographer based in northern Italy. He has flown in the 'back seat' of many aircraft starting with an RAF Tucano in 1995. Since then he has flown numerous photo-sorties with many of the world's premier military aerobatic demonstration teams including the US Navy's Blue Angels, the Canadian Snowbirds, the Frecce Tricolori and the Red Arrows. He has photographed, air-to-air, many of the world's most advanced military jet aircraft including the F-15, F-16, F/A-18, Tornado, Mirage, MiG-29 and Harrier, and also flown a six-hour mission on board a B-1B 'Lancer'. He has visited US Navy and French aircraft carriers several times and he has made a landing and take-off in an Italian Navy Harrier from the deck of the aircraft carrier *Garibaldi*. In addition, he has flown photo-sorties with aircraft from several historical aviation collections and museums around the world.

Luigino is the author of several books on Italian aviation history and aviation photography, including the acclaimed *Savoia-Marchetti S.79 Sparviero – From Airliner and Record-Breaker to Bomber and Torpedo-Bomber 1934-1947* and *Aeronautica Macchi Fighters C.200 Saetta, C.202 Folgore, C.205 Veltro*, both published by Crecy. He has also written numerous magazine and journal articles published in the English language in *Aeroplane*, *FlyPast* and *The Aviation Historian*.

FIAT Fighters
© 2024 Luigino Caliaro and Paolo Waldis

First published 2024

ISBN 978-1-80035-312-1
Produced by Chevron Publishing Limited
Project Editor: Robert Forsyth
Book design: Mark Nelson

© Colour profiles: A. Brioschi
© Line artwork: A. Brioschi

The Editor wishes to thank Nick Beale and Mikael Olrog for their kind assistance during the preparation of this book.

Classic
An Imprint of
Crécy Publishing

All rights reserved. No part of this book may be reproduced or transmitted in any form or by any means, electronic or mechanical, including photocopying, recording, scanning or by any information storage and retrieval system, on the internet or elsewhere, without permission from the Publisher in writing.

© Crécy Publishing Ltd. 2024
Classic is an imprint of Crécy Publishing Ltd.
1a Ringway Trading Estate,
Shadowmoss Road, Manchester, M22 5LH
Visit the Crécy Publishing website at:
www.crecy.co.uk

Copyright Illegal copying and selling of publications deprives authors, publishers and booksellers of income, without which there would be no investment in new publications. Unauthorised versions of publications are also likely to be inferior in quality and contain incorrect information. You can help by reporting copyright infringements and acts of piracy to the Publisher or the UK Copyright Service.

Printed in Türkiye by Özlem Print

Contents

Acknowledgements
Author's Note
Glossary and Military Ranks

CHAPTER ONE	**A long and proud history**	9
CHAPTER TWO	**The Rosatelli biplane family**	21
CHAPTER THREE	**FIAT CR.32**	33
CHAPTER FOUR	**The *'Volo Folle'* years**	57
CHAPTER FIVE	**FIAT CR.42** *FALCO*	63
CHAPTER SIX	**FIAT G.50** *FRECCIA*	127
CHAPTER SEVEN	**FIAT G.55** *CENTAURO*	173
CHAPTER EIGHT	**The *Corpo Aereo Italiano* (C.A.I.)**	205
CHAPTER NINE	**FIAT fighters to the training schools**	223
CHAPTER TEN	**FIAT fighters in post-war service**	229
CHAPTER ELEVEN	**From G.55 to G.59 – a brief, but intense story**	239
CHAPTER TWELVE	**Camouflage and Markings** *by Paolo Waldis*	247
CHAPTER THIRTEEN	**The Survivors**	257
	Index	288

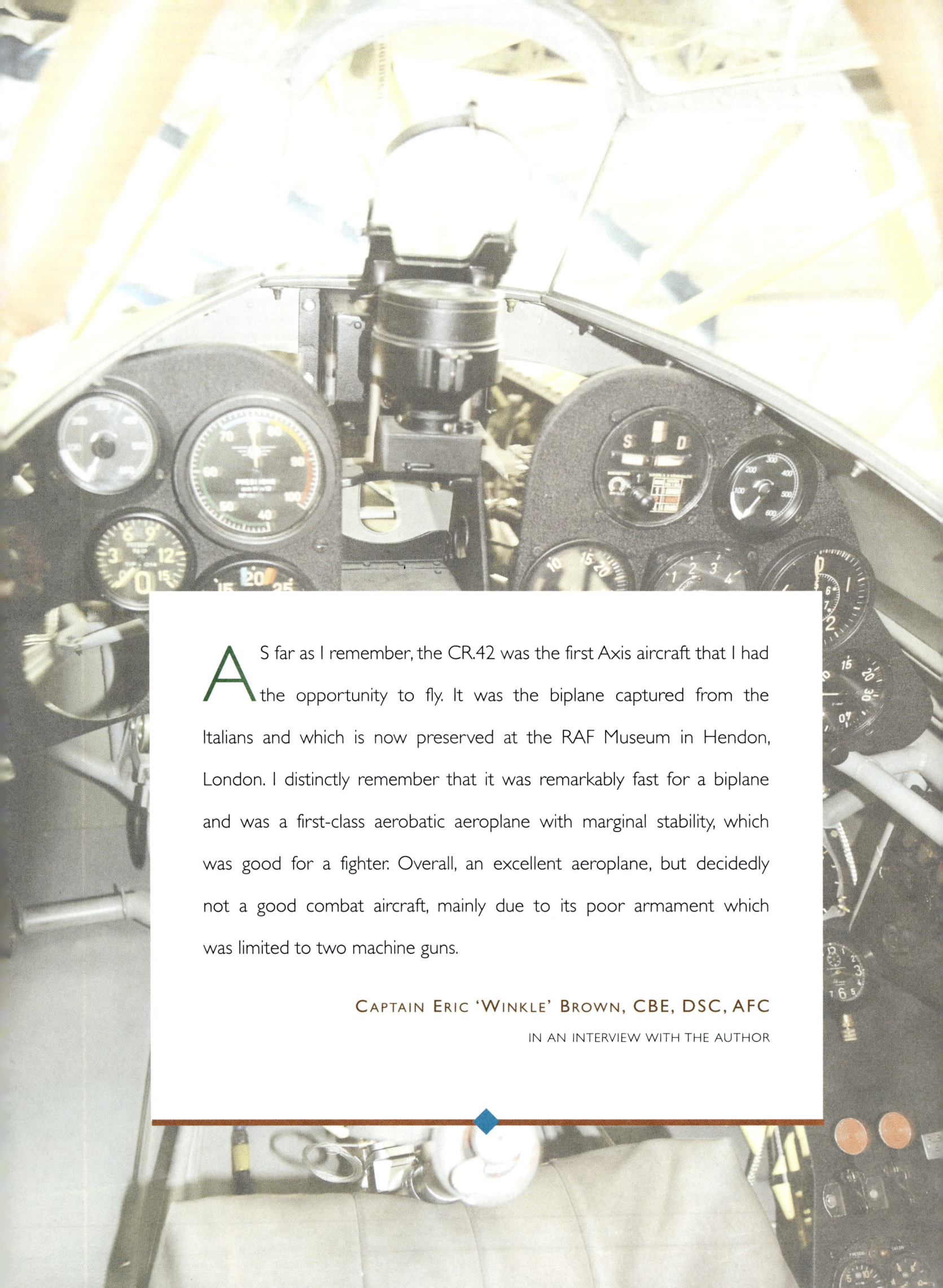

As far as I remember, the CR.42 was the first Axis aircraft that I had the opportunity to fly. It was the biplane captured from the Italians and which is now preserved at the RAF Museum in Hendon, London. I distinctly remember that it was remarkably fast for a biplane and was a first-class aerobatic aeroplane with marginal stability, which was good for a fighter. Overall, an excellent aeroplane, but decidedly not a good combat aircraft, mainly due to its poor armament which was limited to two machine guns.

CAPTAIN ERIC 'WINKLE' BROWN, CBE, DSC, AFC
IN AN INTERVIEW WITH THE AUTHOR

Acknowledgements

AMONG all the people who supported my work, I must extend a special thanks to my long-time friend, Giorgio Apostolo, to whom I am forever grateful for his continual help with my research and my books.

I also give a special thanks to Giulio Cesare Valdonio and Francesco Ballista; it is largely because of their generosity in making their photographic and document archives available to me, and because of their suggestions and advice, that I was able to assemble this work.

I am grateful to Paolo Waldis who provided the colour profiles and drawings of Macchi fighters created by the late Angelo Brioschi and who, thanks to his knowledge of modelling and history, provided the text for the chapter dedicated to FIAT fighter camouflage.

I am also particularly grateful to my friends Ludovico Slongo and Roberto Gentilli who provided me with documentation and gave me concrete help in verifying the correctness of the information contained in this book.

An important photographic contribution came from Mario Federighi of ASF (Archivio Storico Federighi).

Special thanks also for the support provided by my friends Boris Cilic, Enrico Leproni, Fabrizio Sanetti, Franco Storchi, Giovanni Massimello, Gyorgy Punka, Loris Meneghini, Massimo Amatiello, Paolo Monti, Paolo Borgonovi, Paolo Pesaresi, Pelle Lindquist, Roberto Gentilli, Santiago Rivas and to Frank McMeiken for the English translation support. Also to Nick Beale and Mikael Olrog for their assistance with specialist aspects of the text.

Finally, a special thought to my friend Nicola Malizia, recently passed away, who supported me with documents and photos.

LUIGINO CALIARO
JUNE 2024

PHOTO CREDITS

If not expressly indicated, the photographs in this book belong to the GAE – Giorgio Apostolo archive, via Caliaro, and to the author.

The author also thanks for the photographic material provided:

AM	fototeca Aeronautica Militare
AUSAM	Archivio Ufficio Storico Aeronautica Militare
AMAM	Archivio Museo Aeronautica Militare
ASF	Archivio Storico Federighi

Boris Cilic
Enrico Leproni
Fabrizio Sanetti
Federico Anselmino
Francesco Ballista
Franco Storchi
Gyorgy Punka
Giulio Cesare Valdonio
Ludovico Slongo
Nicola Malizia
Paolo Monti
Paolo Borgonovi
Paolo Pesaresi
Pelle Lindquist
Roberto Gentilli
Maurizio Di Terlizzi
Santiago Rivas
Tony Buttler

Author's Note

SINCE there is no official nomenclature style for fighter types, I have made the choice to identify aircraft using the original code of the project as shown in the official technical manuals and as used by FIAT Aeronautica d'Italia, placing before the project number the aircraft's main mission and the initial of the designer.

For example, using this method, 'CR.32' means *Caccia Rosatelli* Project 32 and 'G.50' means *Gabrielli* Project 50.

Furthermore, again for personal choice and in order to make the text more readable, I have decided in some cases to use the names *Falco* (CR.32 and CR.42), *Freccia* (G.50) or *Centauro* (G.55) that were applied for benefit of general use and the press, but rarely used by pilots to identify the respective aircraft types.

The name of FIAT is also maintained in the text for simplicity even though, in reality, the aeronautical activities of the Torino (Turin)-based company were carried out through Aeronautica d'Italia S.A., also known at the time as Aeritalia.

The author has also maintained the informal and unofficial denomination of officer '*Aeronautica Cobelligerante Italiana*' which, although not reflected in the documents of the time, was used in the post-war period by some historians and authors with the aim of clearly differentiating the pre-armistice Regia Aeronautica from the Regia Aeronautica which fought alongside the Allies after 8 September 1943. The Regia Aeronautica subsequently changed its name to the Italian Air Force on 18 June 1946.

The author has preferred to keep the names of units, departments, and military ranks as per their Italian style and nomenclature, referring the reader to the specific table for the respective identification in English.

REGIA AERONAUTICA FIGHTER UNIT STRUCTURE

The basic operational unit of the Regia Aeronautica was the *Squadriglia* (similar to the German *Staffel*), generally equipped with 12 aircraft, although this was more theoretical than practical as this strength was almost never achieved, especially in operational conditions. Usually, the *Squadriglia* was commanded by an officer with the rank of *capitano*. Three, or more rarely four, *Squadriglia* formed a *Gruppo* under the command of a *maggiore*. Two or three *Gruppo* made up the *Stormo* commanded by a *tenente colonnello* or *colonnello*.

Often, depending on particular operational activities, the *Gruppo* could operate autonomously and independently. In turn, two or more *Stormo* could be grouped under the control of a *Brigata Aerea* under the command of an Air Brigade General.

The units were controlled by senior commands such as the *Squadra Aerea*, the *Zona Territoriale* (ZAT) or by peripheral area commands or by specific *Corpi di Spedizione* (Expeditionary Forces). At the top of the chain of command was the *Stato Maggiore* (General Staff) of the Regia Aeronautica, also known under the name of *Superaereo* during the Second World War. Together with the *Supermarina* (Navy) and *Superesercito* (Army), it directly placed under the *Comando Supremo* (Supreme Command).

In addition to the main command in Rome, there were sub-commands in Italian East Africa until its fall, in North Africa, the Balkans and in Russia during the related campaigns in these Theatres. *Superaereo* remained in operation until 12 September 1943.

The numbering of the various units was individual and independent, assigned at the time of their establishment.

Personal aircraft assigned to wing commanders were usually operated directly by one of the squadrons.

LC
2024

Glossary

ITALIAN		ENGLISH
ANR	Aeronautica Nazionale Repubblicana	National Republican Air Force
ARM.I.R.	Armata italiana in Russia	Italian Armada in Russia
Aut.	Autonomo	Autonomous
B.A.	Brigata Aerea	Air Brigade
C.I.E.A.	Consorzio Italiano Esportazioni Aeronautiche	Italian Consortium of Aeronautical Exports
CT	Caccia Terrestri	Land-based fighter
C.T.V.	Corpo Truppe Volontarie	Volunteer Troops Corps
CSIR	Corpo Spedizione Italiano Russia	Italian Expeditionary Corp Russia
DGCA	Direzione Generale delle Costruzioni Aeronautiche	General Directorate of Aeronautical Construction
Gr.	Gruppo	Squadron
M.M.I.S.	Missione Militare Italiana Spagna	Italian Military Mission Spain
M.O.V.M.	Medaglia d'Oro al Valor Militare	Gold Medal for Military Valor
MM	Matricola Militare	Military Serial
OA	Osservazione Aerea	Air observation
R.S.I.	Repubblica Sociale Italiana	Italian Social Republic
RA	Regia Aeronautica	Italian Royal Air Force
Sq.	Squadriglia	Flight
St.	Stormo	Wing
SRAM	Servizo Riparazione Aeromobili e Motori	Plane and engine reparation unit

Non Italian units

HUNGARIAN

Vadászrepülő Ezred	Fighter Wing
Vadászrepülő Század	Fighter Squadron
Vadászrepülő Osztály	Fighter Group

SWEDISH

Flottilj	Wing

Military Ranks

ABBREVIATION	ITALIAN	UK	USA
Gen. SA	Generale Squadra Aerea	Air Marshall	Lieutenant General
Gen. DA	Generale Divisione Aerea	Air Vice Marshall	Major General
Gen. BA	Generale Brigata Aerea	Air Commodore	Brigadier General
Col.	Colonnello	Group Captain	Colonel
Ten.Col.	Tenente Colonnello	Wing Commander	Lieutenant Colonel
Magg.	Maggiore	Squadron Leader	Major
Cap.	Capitano	Flight Lieutenant	Captain
Ten.	Tenente	Flying Officer	1st Lieutenant
S.Ten.	Sottotenente	Pilot Officer	2nd Lieutenant
M.llo	Maresciallo	Warrant Officer	Master Sergeant
Serg.Magg.	Sergente Maggiore	Flight Sergeant	Staff Sergeant
Serg.	Sergente	Sergeant	Senior Airman
AvSc.	Aviere Scelto	Leading Aircraftman	Airman 1st Class
Av.	Aviere	Aircraftman	Airman

CHAPTER ONE

A long and proud history

FIAT / Aeronautica d'Italia

The logo of FIAT/Aeronautica d'Italia. The name 'FIAT' was maintained although the real name of the factory, owned by FIAT, was Aeronautica d'Italia S.A., also known in that time as Aeritalia. (P.Monti)

FIAT's earliest activity in the field of aeronautics dates from 1908 and followed the decision to fully expand the company's range of interests from the automotive sector to embrace the aviation and marine industries. As the aeronautics sector was undergoing rapid expansion in the early 20th century and offered new business opportunities for the company, it was also considered necessary to design aero-engines targeted specifically at the optimisation and maintenance of engine performance at variable operational altitudes. The first aircraft engine, the FIAT SA 8/75, a V8 of 3000 cc of 50hp, derived from a competition car engine and was launched into series production in 1908. It was in this period that large-scale aircraft engine production was initiated with the creation of the FIAT A.10, of which, between 1914 and 1915, some 1,070 examples were produced.

The deployment of aircraft on combat operations at the beginning of the First World War provoked an enormous increase in demand for aircraft and their engines. In order to more adequately respond to the new market requirements, in 1916 FIAT founded a new subsidiary, which took on the name Società Italiana Aviazione (SIA), and which was dedicated to the production of complete aircraft including engines.

Among the first projects to be developed was the manufacture of aircraft inspired by the Farman series, known as the SP.2 and SP.3. The first model developed entirely autonomously by the company was the SIA S.7b which, although blessed with good general performance, was inflicted with severe structural problems which, despite modifications and strengthening measures, eventually resulted in the premature retirement of the aircraft from service.

The SIA 7b was designed and produced by the Società Italiana Aviazione, an aviation branch of the FIAT company in Turin. It was a modern and fast reconnaissance aeroplane, but in service it proved to be disappointing due to its poor workmanship, the results of which resulted in broken wings and a troublesome engine.

The Savoia-Pomilio SP.2 was a single-engine biplane for armed reconnaissance. The acronym 'SP' denoted Savoia-Pomilio for the names of its two designers. The aircraft was also produced at a number of Italian factories including Società Italiana Aviazione (SIA), an aircraft company that belonged to the FIAT group during the First World War.

Above: The original SP series was derived from a redesign of the Farman series achieved by increasing engine power. The SP.3 was a two-seat armed reconnaissance biplane used also for artillery guidance.

The SIA 9b was a new, more high-performance project compared to the SIA 7b and was equipped with the FIAT A.14 engine of around 700 hp. Although there was an increase in size and weight, performance was superior to that of its predecessor, but still it was an unreliable aeroplane.

The FIAT R.2 was a reconnaissance aircraft production of which started just before the end of the war. It was the first aircraft to be marketed under the FIAT brand after the failures of SIA aircraft.

In 1918 the SIA 9b fast bomber was produced, powered by the more potent 700 hp FIAT A.14 engine. This aircraft also achieved little success, and although hundreds of examples had been requested, by the end of the war just sixty-two had been manufactured.

At the end of hostilities SIA was completely absorbed by FIAT, becoming an internal branch of the Società, which changed its name to FIAT Aviazione. The original SIA 9b was reworked, thanks to the intervention of the designer *Ingegnere* Celestino Rosatelli, resulting in the FIAT R.2, a decent reconnaissance aircraft which remained in service until 1925.

In 1926 the aeronautical activities of Ansaldo were also acquired. Aircraft production was intensified under the guidance of Rosatelli as head of design, who had begun his collaboration with FIAT in 1918.

Under his signature were numerous fighter and bomber aircraft in the 'CR' and 'BR' series (acronyms respectively for the *Caccia Rosatelli* and *Bombardiere Rosatelli*) which established various world records in their categories. In the early 1920s the B.R. bomber formed the basis for the development of the BR.1, BR.2 and BR.3 models, which equipped numerous *squadriglie da bombardamento* of the Regia Aeronautica. In terms of fighters the CR. 1 was followed by the CR.20, which became the principal fighter aircraft of the Regia Aeronautica from the middle of the 1920s, with more than 400 aircraft constructed. The type remained in

A LONG AND PROUD HISTORY

The FIAT BR1 was an Italian light biplane bomber armed with a 7.7 mm machine gun and able to carry up to 600 kg of bombs. It was powered by the 700-hp FIAT A.14. The flight of the prototype took place in 1923 and about 150 examples were built.

A group photograph taken in front of a FIAT CR. 1. From left: journalist Guido Mattioli, test pilot Giovanni Battista Bottalla, ingegner Celestino Rosatelli and ingegner Mario Fossati. (R.Gentilli)

The FIAT CR.1 was a fighter biplane produced by FIAT Aviazione in the mid-1920s. An improved version of the CR, it was characterised by an inverted sesquiplane wing configuration, and was used by the Regia Aeronautica and the Latvian Air Force.

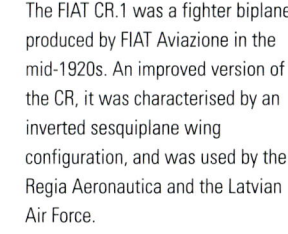

Left: A further development of the CR.1, the CR.20 was an aerodynamically more refined aeroplane, with a more powerful engine and a strengthened fuselage. It was characterised by good performance as well as good handling and manoeuvrability.

In 1918, after the failure of the SIA 7B, FIAT decided to rebrand SIA to FIAT Aviazione. Seen here is a view of the Turin plant.

The Ansaldo A.120, also known as the FIAT A.120 after the Turin company purchased Ansaldo, was a parasol-wing reconnaissance monoplane developed in Italy in the mid-1920s.

Left: In 1926 FIAT founded a new company, the Società Aeronautica d'Italia, after having taken over the Ansaldo Aeronautical factory and the adjoining airfield. The new plant was located in Corso Italia (later Corso Francia), on the edge of the city, and covered an area of approximately 31,000 square metres.

The FIAT AS.1 was a two-seat, light touring and training single-engine monoplane produced in 1929. Construction was of wood throughout, covered by plywood, fabric, and some metal. A later development, designated the TR.1, featured a metal fuselage and a shorter span wing.

FIAT B.R.G. (*Bombardiere Rosatelli Gigante*) was a three-motor heavy bomber prototype built in 1931. The only aircraft built was assigned to the 62ª *Squadriglia*, an experimental heavy bombing unit of the Regia Aeronautica.

The FIAT G-2 was a three-motor passenger aircraft of metal construction, with the exception of some fabric parts. It was the first aircraft designed by ing. Giuseppe Gabrielli to equip the Avio Linee Italiane (ALI) airline company which was owned by the FIAT group. It was later sold to the VARIG airline of Brazil.

service for more than a decade in its CR.20bis variant.

Furthermore, during the 1920s FIAT Aviazione continued with the production of a previous Ansaldo design, the high-wing A.120 reconnaissance monoplane, exporting the aircraft to Austria, and the AS.1, a high-wing, single-engine monoplane designed by Ansaldo as the Ansaldo Sport 1 (hence the A.S.1 designation), which was later produced and marketed by FIAT in the sports aviation sector.

At the beginning of the 1930s, the aeronautical element of FIAT comprised the *Ufficio Tecnico Aviazione*, comprised of two divisions directed respectively by *Ingegneri* Rosatelli and Giuseppe Gabrielli, and *Stabilimento* FIAT Aeronautica d'Italia for aircraft manufacture which, for simplicity, was known by the abbreviated denomination of 'Aeritalia'. A further section, with an associated *Ufficio Tecnico Progettativo* (design office), was the *Sezione Motori Avio*, with which there were an associated production facility and test laboratories.

In 1934 FIAT took over the activities of the Società C.M.A.S.A. (Costruzioni Meccaniche Aeronautiche S.A.), based at Marina di Pisa and which specialised in the construction of flying boats. This took the Torino company into flying boat production. The Società C.M.A.S.A. had been founded in 1921 by the German design engineer Claude Dornier in collaboration with Rinaldo Piaggio and Attilio Odero, and had achieved notable success with the production of the Dornier *Wal* flying boat. At the beginning of the 1930s FIAT Aviazione produced the B.R.G., a three-engine, high-wing monoplane bomber, but this aircraft would remain only at the prototype stage. Some years later, in 1936, FIAT also absorbed C.A.N.S.A. (Costruzioni Aeronautiche Novaresi S.A.), based at Cameri.

In the early 1930s, FIAT's two design divisions were heavily engaged in the production of new aircraft, with the office led by Rosatelli focused on a more 'classic' design and that directed by *Ingegnere* Gabrielli, who was engaged by the company in 1931, characterised principally by the study and development of new aeronautical concepts and techniques emerging during the period. This research work would come to fruition in 1932 with the production of the FIAT G.2 commercial airliner, conceived in response to a requirement for a new passenger aircraft for the Avio Linee Italiane (ALI) airline, itself part of the FIAT group. Besides being the first project designed by Gabrielli, the G.2 was also the first aircraft of modern construction produced by the manufacturer, which abandoned the mixed-construction biplane configuration in favour of an all-metal monocoque structure and a cantilever wing. Nevertheless, despite the quality of design – definitely avant-garde for the period – the aircraft failed to achieve its expected success. Successively, following increasing interest and demand from the passenger and cargo transport market, FIAT produced the G.18 and APR.2 twins, operated by the Avio Linee company.

To replace the CR.20 serving with the units of the Regia Aeronautica, the CR.30 appeared in 1932 only to be quickly replaced in the front line fighter role by the excellent CR.32.

The FIAT APR.2 was a twelve-passenger airliner built in 1935 and used by Avio Linee Italiane (ALI). At the time of its introduction, it was one of the fastest airliners in regular service in the world. Despite this, only one example was built.

The FIAT G.18 was a twin-engine, all-metal cantilever low-wing monoplane passenger transport aircraft used by the Avio Linee Italiane (ALI). In 1940 nine aircraft were militarized and used in daily connecting flights to Albania, Greece and Hungary.

This biplane fighter, a compact, robust, and highly manoeuvrable refinement of the CR.30, was held in high regard by its pilots for its excellent flying characteristics. It also gained international fame for its use in displays by Italian aerobatic teams throughout the 1930s and was also successfully employed in combat during the Spanish Civil War.

In the meantime, on 8 March 1934 the G.5bis made its first flight, a single-engine touring and training biplane constructed from a tubular steel fuselage frame, its central section clad in aluminium, and with wooden structured wings with leading edge slats. In the same year, through its CMASA subsidiary, as had occurred in the case of G.5bis production, FIAT completed sixty G.8 biplanes, the third design in the 'G' series to be produced in series and the only biplane designed by *Ingegnere* Gabrielli (the letter identifying Gabrielli's designs). The aircraft, of mixed steel and wood construction, was utilised as a basic training aircraft in the primary flying training schools of the Regia Aeronautica from the middle of the 1930s until the outbreak of the Second World War.

In 1935, in response to a requirement published by the Regia Aeronautica for a monoplane fighter powered by an air-cooled engine, FIAT submitted the G.50, the first all-metal, single-seat monoplane fighter with a retractable undercarriage and closed cockpit to be constructed in Italy. FIAT manufactured a total of 740 examples of this aircraft, in part constructed at the facilities of its CMASA subsidiary at Marina di Pisa. Although produced almost two years after the the G.50 monoplane, the CR.42 was a biplane designed by Rosatelli as a fighter. Just under 1,500 examples were constructed in the course of the Second World War making the type the most numerous constructed by the Italian aviation industry.

During 1936 deliveries commenced of the BR.20 *Cicogna*, a low-wing, twin-engine medium bomber developed by the Italian company in response to a precise requirement specified by the Regia Aeronautica. It was operated by front line units until the Armistice of September 1943. In 1940 the CR.25 entered service – a good aircraft originally designed by Celestino Rosatelli as a long-range heavy fighter which, despite the limited number of examples manufactured, became a much-appreciated asset of the Regia Aeronautica when used for reconnaissance and long-range escort.

Of particular importance was the FIAT G.12, a low-wing, tri-motor transport manufactured throughout the war. Initially designed for civilian use as an airliner, with the outbreak of hostilities it was converted to the military transport role and utilised by the Regia Aeronautica. In the post-war period many G.12 were converted back to their original configuration for civil air transport, while

A LONG AND PROUD HISTORY

The FIAT G.8 was a single-engine, two-seater touring and aerobatic training biplane built of wood and metal. The military G.8s went to the autonomous squadrons of the ZAT (Territorial Air Zones) for the training of assigned officers.

The FIAT CR.42 represented the ultimate development of the biplane fighter. After it entered in service in May 1939 it was already obsolete, but despite that, it performed well operationally in Europe and Africa in the first years of the Second World War.

Right: The G.50 was the first Italian low-wing fighter with retractable landing gear. Although it was very manoeuvrable, it was significantly slower and less well armed than British aircraft such as the Hawker Hurricane and Supermarine Spitfire. A total of 784 FIAT G.50s was produced, of which 35 were exported to Finland where they performed well during the final phase of the Winter War of 1939-1940, as well as at the beginning of the hostilities against the Soviet Union in 1941.

The BR 20 *'Cicogna'* low-wing medium bomber was developed by FIAT during the 1930s. It entered service in 1936 and featured a metal build and retractable landing gear. Modern and fast for its time, it was used during the Spanish Civil War and during the Second World War in which it equipped various bomber units of the Regia Aeronautica.

The CR.25 emanated from a FIAT proposal for a fast light bomber with advanced features which could also be used as a strategic reconnaissance aircraft thanks to its superior speed and good defensive capabilities. Only ten examples were built and were used by 173ª *Squadriglia Ricognizione Strategica Terrestre*.

Initially designed for use as a civil airliner, with the outbreak of the Second World War, the FIAT G.12 was converted to the role of a tactical transport aircraft and used by the Regia Aeronautica. At the end of the war some of the remaining aircraft returned to the role of passenger transport and were used by the newly founded national airline, Alitalia.

The FIAT-CMASA RS.14 designed by Manlio Stiavelli. The 'RS' acronym denotes Stiavelli Reconnaissance. This was an all-metal maritime reconnaissance seaplane. Very refined from an aerodynamic point of view with sleek lines, it possessed good performance.

The FIAT CANSA FC.20bis was a ground-attack aircraft of which ten examples were built equipped with one 37 mm cannon in the lower part of the nose, two 12.7 mm SAFATs on the wings and one in the dorsal turret.

a certain number were constructed as the G.212, with more powerful engines and the capacity to carry around thirty passengers. These machines were operated by the early post-war Italian air transport companies and by the newly formed flag carrier, Alitalia. In May 1941 the CMASA RS.14 flew, a twin-engine, long-range maritime reconnaissance floatplane, which was operated by the Regia Aeronautica until the Allied landings in Sicily in 1943. After the Armistice only a few aircraft remained in flying condition, but some of them found employment in southern Italy with the Regia Aeronautica, flying in Italian colours until the immediate post-war period.

Two potentially important but ultimately unfortunate pojects were the FIAT CANSA F.C. 12 and the FIAT CANSA FC.20. Developed by FIAT's Cameri (Novara) subsidiary, these two aircraft, despite the promising characteristics demonstrated by their prototypes, never entered production. The first was a monoplane intended as a dedicated trainer for ground-attack pilots, while the second, initially designed in 1940 by *Ingegnere* Giacomo Mosso as a reconnaissance aircraft, was converted into a ground-attack aircraft by the modification of its forward fuselage to accept installation of a 37 mm anti-tank cannon. The results were disappointing, principally due to the limited power of the available engines, and as a consequence any further development was quickly abandoned.

At the end of April 1942, the FIAT G.55 made its first flight, the aircraft considered to be 'the best fighter produced in Italy during the War.' The aircraft was powered by a German DB 605 engine manufactured under licence, and during the course of its brief operational service – conducted almost exclusively under the insignia of the Aeronautica Nazionale Repubblicana during 1944 – it proved to be an effective fighter and an excellent combatant.

In the difficult years of the war, at the time of its maximum expansion, the FIAT establishment at Corso Francia employed a total of more than 4,500 personnel and also housed a technical training school.

After the Second World War

After the war, following a period of uncertainty and difficulty, FIAT's aeronautical activities resumed with vigour with the production of the FIAT G.59, a reworking of the G.55 fighter as an

The FIAT G.46 was a single-engine, low-wing monoplane trainer aircraft developed by FIAT Aviazione in the late 1940s. Produced between 1948 and 1952 in both single-seat and two-seater versions, it enjoyed commercial success by serving with the air forces of Italy, Austria, Argentina and Syria.

Above: The G.82 was the first Italian-built jet trainer. Although produced in small numbers, it was used by the Aeronautica Militare Italiana (AMI) flying school and was an important test bed for the development and growth of the national aeronautical industry in the post-war period.

FIAT signed a licence production agreement with North American on 16 May 1953 under which F-86Ks would be built at FIAT's Turin-Caselle plant from US-supplied components. Similarly in the early 1960s, the Aeronautica Militare Italiana received 125 licence-built F-104G from FIAT plus twelve Lockheed-built TF-104G and 16 Fiat-built TF-104G.

advanced trainer, but powered by the British Rolls Royce Merlin engine. There were also deliveries of the G.46, a two-seat, low-wing monoplane trainer developed at the end of the 1940s.

In 1949 FIAT's aviation interests were reorganised under the new FIAT Aviazione company, which saw the design office placed under the direction of *Ingegnere* Gabrielli. With the advent of the jet engine, the Torino company began to explore collaborations of a technical nature within Europe and in the USA, resulting in 1951, in the G.80, the first Italian jet aircraft powered by a De Havilland Goblin turbojet engine. The G.80 was followed by the G.82, although this failed to achieve its much hoped for success, with production limited to only five aircraft, which were utilised for a short period by the Aeronautica Militare for pilot training.

At the beginning of the 1950s FIAT Aviazione initiated a new phase of industrial production thanks to the start of collaboration with the American aviation industry, and obtained a licence to manufacture the F-86K all-weather fighter, the only European nation to do so, reaching collaboration agreements with General Electric and Pratt & Whitney for the production of jet engine components. The experience acquired permitted the company to participate in, and win, the international competition launched in 1954 by NATO for the supply of a light tactical fighter. Thanks to this success, the G.91R, designed by *Ing*. Gabrielli, became the most important Italian aircraft of the post-war period, with more than 700 aircraft produced, being utilised in Italy and in Europe by the German and Portuguese air arms.

In 1961 FIAT Aviazione assumed the role of Italian prime contractor for the NATO F-104G aircraft and as such strengthened its collaboration agreements with Alfa Romeo Avio at Pomigliano d'Arco, near Napoli, which was controlled directly by the Italian State through the Finmeccanica company.[1]

Derived from the preceding single-engine version, the G.91Y entered service with the Aeronautica Militare, retaining the general appearance of the G.91R, but differing through the adoption of two engines which delivered a consequent increase in performance and weapon load capacity.

In the second half of the 1960s, moreover, FIAT Aviazione entered a manufacturing collaboration partnership with Douglas in America, and later with Aerfer, an aeronautics and rail transport manufacturing company founded by Finmeccanica in 1950, and with which, in 1969, it constituted the new Aeritalia company, controlled completely by Finmeccanica. As events developed, from 1972 all FIAT Aviazione's aviation activities were transferred to Aeritalia, apart from the aviation engine section. Of particular importance under the Aeritalia banner was the final design signed by *ingegner* Gabrielli, the G.222, a twin turbine tactical transport aircraft with STOL characteristics, which flew for the first time in 1970. It proved a considerable success, with more

---

[1] Now active under the name Leonardo S.p.A., this was an Italian public company active in the sectors of defence, aerospace, and security. Between 1948 and 2016 it was known as Finmeccanica S.p.A., subsequently changing its name to Leonardo-Finmeccanica S.p.A. and amalgamating under its control all the activities of the companies it previously controlled, AgustaWestland, Alenia Aermacchi, Selex ES, OTO Melara and Wass. It assumed its present name from 1 January 2017.

Designed in response to the competition for an attack and tactical support machine announced by NATO in December 1953, the FIAT G.91R conformed to the required specification. It was capable of operating from makeshift runways and unprepared terrain, had good speed and could carry offensive loads of at least 450 kg.

The FIAT/Aeritalia G.91Y was an improved twin-engined version of the G.91R. Nicknamed 'Yankee' to underline the shape of the air intake (single at the front but internally divided into two to feed the engines separately and therefore shaped like a Y), the G.91Y found service only with Aeronautica Militare Italiana as a reconnaissance and close ground-attack aircraft.

than fifty aircraft delivered to the Aeronautica Militare and numerous examples exported around the world, including around ten to the American armed forces.

Subsequently Aeritalia was involved in various multi-national programmes and initiatives, including the development and constructions the Panavia Tornado tri-national, multi-role fighter, the ATR regional airliner family, and the AMX fighter-bomber, produced in collaboration with EMBRAER of Brazil.

Aeritalia also participated in the development of the Boeing B.767 wide-body civil airliner from the beginning of the programme and played a key role in the creation of the Italian space industry. In 1990 the company was involved in another reorganisation, when together with Selenia, an Italian leader in the missile and electronics sectors, it mutated into Alenia Aeronautica.

Following the transfer of its aeronautical activities to Aeritalia, FIAT Aviazione concentrated on the development and construction of aircraft engines and transmission systems for helicopters. In 1989 the company's name was changed to FIAT Avio, and it continued to collaborate in numerous programmes involving the development of military and civilian propulsion systems. The acquisition of the major shareholding of Alfa Romeo Avio by Finmeccanica in 1997 was fundamental to the process of constituting a strategic national project aimed at reducing the excessive fragmentation of Italian business activity. This was brought to fruition in 2003 when the FIAT group, following a period of crisis in the automotive sector, decided to dispose of FIAT Avio S.p.A. to a consortium formed by an American fund and Finmeccanica S.p.A., thus bringing to an end the links between the historic company and the aviation world.

Allied bombing of the Torino industrial infrastructure

Apart from being the home of FIAT Aeritalia, Torino housed numerous other industries important to the Italian war effort such as Officine RIV, Lancia and Snia Viscosa and thus, because of its industrial importance, the city was the target for Allied bombing raids during the Second World War. It became one of the most devastated cities in northern Italy.

During the first year of the war Allied incursions struck a fairly limited number of facilities. The first bombs fell on the night of 11/12 June 1940 when, in tandem with a simultaneous attack on the city of Genova, Torino became the first Italian city in the Second World War to be subjected to an air raid that resulted in civilian victims. The attack, conducted by nine RAF bombers flying from England, saw bombs fall on the residential areas of the city, causing seventeen civilian deaths, despite the primary target being the FIAT Aeritalia factories.

The AMX (Aeritalia Macchi Experimental), designated A-11 Ghibli by the Aeronautica Militare (AM), was a single-engine, ground-attack and tactical support aircraft produced through collaboration between the then Aeritalia (46.5%), Aermacchi (23.8%) and the Brazilian Embraer (29.7%). In total, 110 single-seaters plus 26 two-seaters were delivered to AM while the Brazilian Air Force ordered 56 examples.

The FIAT Aeritalia G.222 'Panda' was a successful, twin-engine turboprop tactical transport aircraft similar, but smaller in structure and load compartment, to the American C-130. It was characterised by STOL capability.

The prototype of the Tornado MARCA was developed jointly by the United Kingdom, West Germany and Italy. It was the result of the collaboration of several European aerospace companies (Aeritalia, MBB and British Aerospace) which merged especially into the Panavia company. Three main variants were built, the IDS (Interdiction and Strike), the ECR (Electronic Combat/Reconnaissance) and the ADV (Air Defense Variant).

The FIAT infrastructure was the target of further British raids on the nights of 8/9 and 23/24 November 1940. On the night of 5/6 September it was, however, the turn of RIV in via Nizza and the FIAT Lingotto facility to be hit by British bombs. Then after weeks of relative calm, on the night of 20 November 1942, Torino suffered a particularly violent Allied attack which signalled the beginning of a long cycle of raids over the following weeks until the night of 11 December 1942. There were raids on the FIAT works at Lingotto and Mirafiori, two attacks on FIAT Ferriere, and other raids on FIAT Materiale Ferroviario, FIAT, SPA, FIAT Aeronautica, Acciaierie FIAT, Sima and the FIAT subsidiary in Corso Dante. A similar fate befell the facilities of Lancia, Fergat, INCET, SNIA Viscosa, Microtecnica, Viberti, CIMAT, Westinghouse, Nebiolo, Superga, the Arsenale Militare and other smaller companies, the overall damage being such that the entire Torino production system was almost paralysed.

Again, in 1943, significant quantities of all types of bombs fell on Torino, spreading destruction and damage to a significant number of the buildings in the city. In February the FIAT, SPA and Aeronautica facilities were the subject of repeated attacks, together with those of Lancia, Superga, RIV and others. These were precursors to more significant attacks over the following months, such as that of the night of 12/13 July – without doubt the most tragic – conducted by a force of 64 RAF bombers. Besides aiming their 760 tonnes of bombs against the industrial facilities, they struck the populated areas of the city, resulting in 729 civilian deaths.

The second half of 1943 also saw continuous and heavy bombing, in particular on 8 November and 1 December when the industrial complexes of FIAT and many other companies in the Torino industrial district were hit as well as civilian areas.

The bombing continued: on 3 January 1944 and 29 March USAAF B-17s struck FIAT and the railway yards, but the most devastating for FIAT was the raid of 25 April 1944, when 150 B-24 Liberators attacked FIAT Aeronautica, FIAT Ferriere and FIAT Fonderie and the surrounding areas, causing 37 civilian victims and 42 injuries. The bombing caused serious damage and the destruction of the production lines of the CR.42, the G.12 and partially the G.55. Numerous aircraft located around the facilities were also destroyed, including 15 G.55s, 8 G.12s, 6 CR.42s, and 6 BR.20s, while another thirty aircraft in preparation were destroyed in the assembly yards and many others damaged, including the prototype of the G.56, MM.536.

Only during June was it possible to partially resume production for the G.12 and G.55, but on 12 September all aeronautical production was suspended by order of the R.U.K. At that time, assembly details for around 100 G.55s were being prepared at Aeritalia while at least 37 were in an advanced stage of completion in the assembly yards.

The last Allied attack hit Torino on 5 April 1945, causing serious damage to the Torino-Smistamento railway station, on the southern outskirts of the city.

The extent of the bombing suffered by the city in the course of the war is confirmed by data collated at the end of the conflict. At least 54,000 homes out of a total of 217,000 were destroyed, with more than 2,000 deaths suffered by the civilian population.

The Turin factories became a major target for the Allied air forces. After an initial phase, starting from the autumn of 1942, the Allied incursions became more frequent, causing extensive damage to equipment and machinery. The plants remained under bombardment until 1945. The most devastating bombing occurred on 25 April 1944 and caused serious damage and the destruction of several production lines such as those for the CR.42, the G.12 and partially the G.55. Seen at (above right and below left) are wrecked and partially completed CR.42s and G.50s. Note the FIAT G.12 in German markings in the background in the photograph bottom right.

CHAPTER TWO

The Rosatelli biplane family

FIAT CR

IN the early 1920s, the *Commissariato di Aeronautica*[1] announced a competition for the provision of a new, nationally-built fighter aircraft to renew the fleet of the newly-constituted Regia Aeronautica, which at the time was equipped with aircraft dating from the First World War such as the Spad XIII and Hanriot-Macchi Hd.1. The winner of this competition was the FIAT CR, a biplane of mixed construction characterised by an inverted sesquiplane configuration[2] designed by *Ingegner* Celestino Rosatelli in collaboration with Manlio Stiavelli. It was powered by a Hispano Suiza HS 42 300-hp engine, of which significant quantities were available in Italian military storage facilities.

Constructed at the beginning of 1923, the CR prototypes were assigned *Matricole Militari* MM1 and MM2. The first aircraft was flown by FIAT test pilot Giovanbattista Bottalla who, in the summer of the same year, transferred the aircraft to the *Centro Sperimentale* at Montecelio. During flight-testing the aircraft achieved 264 km/h, climbing to 5,000 m altitude in sixteen minutes.

FIAT CR.1

In light of the mixed flight evaluation results displayed by the CR, which had demonstrated reasonable general performance but also some technical issues, including the development of dangerous vibrations in the engine area, in the course of 1924, *Ing*. Rosatelli reworked the design, a move that gave origin to the CR.1 of which two new prototypes were produced (MM43 and MM44). The most apparent modification to the CR.1 in comparison with the preceding CR was the replacement of the large frontal radiator that

The FIAT CR was the first fighter biplane designed by *Ing*. Rosatelli to replace the SPAD and Hd.1 in the Regia Aeronautica fighter units. Two prototypes were built, simply designated FIAT CR and registered respectively MM1 and MM2. The two prototypes differed from each other in the shape of their engine cowlings and rudders.

Test pilot Giovanbattista Bottalla (left) and designer *ingegner* Celestino Rosatelli stand in front of a FIAT CR. (R.Gentilli)

---

[1] Constituted on 24 January 1923, this had the function of controlling and managing aeronautical activity in Italy. At its head was the *Presidente del Consiglio* and Vice Commissario Aldo Finzi, to whom reported two Director Generals, one for the Regia Aeronautica and the other for civil aviation. It was transformed into the *Ministero dell'Aeronautica* on 30 August 1925.

[2] In an inverted sesquiplane the upper wings of the biplane have a smaller span than those of the lower wings.

CELESTINO ROSATELLI

Ingegner Celestino Rosatelli was one of the most famous Italian aeronautical engineers, who, working in the FIAT Project Office was the creator of numerous successful aircraft, including the CR.20, CR.32 *Freccia*, CR.42 *Falco* fighters and the BR.20 *Cicogna* bomber. (G.Apostolo)

A STAUNCH DEFENDER of the biplane design, even when that concept appeared to be technologically outdated, Ingegnere Celestino Rosatelli, the chief designer of FIAT Aeronautica d'Italia in the 1930s, was responsible for the designs of the best biplane fighter aircraft built in Italy in the decade preceding the Second World War.

Born in Belmonte Sabina (Rieti) in 1885, he attended the Scuola di Ingegneria (Engineering School) in Rome, from which he graduated in 1910. In 1915 he entered the Regio Esercito (the Italian Royal Army), and was assigned to the Direzione Tecnica Aeronautica Militare (DTAM – Military Aeronautical Technical Directorate) in Torino, working with Ingegneri Savoia and Verduzio on Ansaldo SVA's project.

Having demonstrated his aeronautical engineering skills, he was hired in 1918 by Senatore Giovanni Agnelli and posted to the FIAT Aeronautica design office, of which he quickly became director.

During his long period as an aeronautical designer, Rosatelli signed off at least fifty aircraft projects, about forty of which were subsequently produced in series including, in 1918, the BR bomber ('Rosatelli bomber') characterised by cutting edge solutions for its time and powered by a FIAT 'A.14' engine. It is no coincidence that in a BR, test pilot Francesco Brach Papa set the world speed record, reaching 270 km/h, and a height record, reaching 7,250 metres above sea level on 21 May 1919.

Undoubtedly, however, the name of Rosatelli was linked to the series of fighters identified under the 'CR' designation (Caccia Rosatelli – 'Rosatelli fighter') which saw extensive use in the ranks of the Regia Aeronautica and formed the backbone of the Regia Aeronautica fighter force until the end of the 1930s.

Despite wider technological progress, the CR.42 – the last of the family of fighter biplanes designed by Rosatelli – was the most important Regia Aeronautica fighter of the early war years, and was also utilised during the conflict as a ground-attack aircraft. It concluded its long career as late as the 1950s, having been used ultimately as a liaison and training aircraft.

Celestino Rosatelli died in Torino on 23 September 1945.

An advertisement for the CR.30 published in the aviation magazine *L'Ala d'Italia* in 1932.

crossed through the centre of the propeller hub with a new trapezoidal frontal bees nest radiator mounted above the propeller, and by a slightly flatter fuselage profile.

The inverted sesquiplane wing configuration remained unchanged, a feature of other Italian aircraft of the period such as the Caproni Ca.73 bomber. The upper wing of the CR.1 was rectangular in shape, formed by two box spars and ribs in spruce, and was connected to the lower wing by W-profile tubular steel struts, a characteristic of all biplanes designed by Rosatelli. This construction constituted a simple and rigid structure, requiring less traditional trellis structure through struts and diagonals and, because of the absence of cables and turnbuckles, offered lower drag resistance. The fuselage consisted of wooden longerons connected by steel tubes at the front and wooden crossed struts at the tail, the fuselage being clad in birch plywood which contributed in part to the robustness of the structure. The tailplanes were also wooden structures clad in fabric.

The undercarriage, made from steel tubes with a single axle, had its shock absorbers protected by

The FIAT CR.1 was an upgrade of the former CR. Around 240 aircraft were built and nine were purchased by the Latvian Naval Aviation which flew until 1936.

THE ROSATELLI BIPLANE FAMILY

An interesting study of a CR.1 of the 88ª *Squadriglia Caccia*.

The CR.1 landing gear had a fixed axle between the wheels.

CR.1s of the 77ª *Squadriglia Caccia*.

CR.1 'Asso' engines equipped the 163ª *Squadriglia* based at Rhodes and were withdrawn from service only in 1937.

an aluminium fairing, although this was often removed from aircraft in operational service, while the aircraft's tail rested on a classic wooden skid with elastic supports.

The CR.1's armament comprised two Vickers machine guns positioned inside the engine housing between the V banks of the cylinders, while the fuel tank, in a ventral position, could be jettisoned in the event of a fire thanks to a spring which in normal conditions kept it secured to its attachments.

For its time, the performance of the CR.1 was particularly favourable, the fighter demonstrating good flying characteristics and excellent manoeuvrability. Moreover, the top speed proved to be some tens of kilometres per hour faster than the aircraft of a similar class at the time. The major drawbacks encountered in its operation were caused by the precarious nature of the undercarriage in the take-off and landing phases, the aircraft having a tendency to bounce, together with the poor reliability of the engine sub-systems, in particular the connections between the various tubing elements. This was caused by problems, only partially resolved at the time, relating to structural vibrations in the fighter caused when the engine was running.

Deliveries to Italian units commenced in early 1925, and the total number of aircraft produced was around 250 examples, with manufacture shared between FIAT and another two companies, O.F.M. in Napoli which produced around forty examples, and SIAI, which completed 100 aircraft. After the attempt to offer the CR.1 with different and updated engines (which gave rise to the CR.20 and CR.5 prototypes), the adoption of the Isotta Fraschini Asso Caccia engine was particularly successful, it being twelve cylinder air-cooled and capable of delivering the impressive output of 440 hp. Identified by the designation CR.1 Asso, the adoption of the new engine prolonged the operational life of the FIAT fighter by many years, the type being used as a trainer but also operationally by the 163ª *Squadriglia* based at Rhodes Maritsa which in 1937 still had at least seven aircraft in service.

Some CR.1 – probably nine aircraft – were sold to the Latvian Air Force in 1927, remaining in service for around ten years.

CR.2/CR.5/CR.10

In 1925, with the CR.1 in production, *Ing.* Rosatelli began to consider replacing the Hispano Suiza engine with the new twelve-cylinder in-line 400 hp FIAT A.20 engine, modifying one airframe, MM1352, by installing the FIAT A.20 cooled by two radiators positioned on the undercarriage

FIAT FIGHTERS

The FIAT CR.2 was a version of the CR.1 biplane fighter powered by an Armstrong Siddeley Lynx radial engine. The aircraft was tested in 1928.

Right: The FIAT CR.5 was a version of the CR.1 biplane that was powered by a licence-built Jupiter radial engine. (P.Monti)

Below: The CR.10 retained the basic configuration of the CR.1 but was powered by the new 410-hp FIAT A.20 12-cylinder inline engine, with two Lamblin radiators located on the front legs of the fixed landing gear. A single prototype of the CR.10 was produced and tested. (P.Monti)

Above: For its time, the single-seat FIAT CR.20 fighter was produced in large numbers. Its affiliation with the FIAT family was evident in the inter-wing bracing in the form of a Warren beam and the winglets with the characteristic line of Celestino Rosatelli's designs.

Below: A line-up of CR.20s of the 79ª *Squadriglia* of 1° *Stormo Caccia* at Campoformido.

Left: The CR.20 was a classic FIAT biplane with wings of different sizes, and a carefully profiled fuselage. It was built largely of metal, with painted canvas covering. Metal panels covered the front of the fuselage. It was designed for the new FIAT A.20 engine and four prototypes were built and tested.

legs. One year later CR.1 MM1310 was modified to accept the installation of an Alfa Romeo Jupiter engine. These two prototypes were identified respectively as the CR.10 and CR.5, but saw no further development.

In 1928 a new prototype was prepared equipped with the Armstrong Siddeley Lynx 200 hp engine. Designated CR.2, this was not pursued further.

FIAT CR.20/bis/Asso

By the mid-1920s, the front line fighter force of the Regia Aeronautica was equipped principally with the FIAT CR.1, as well as Nieuport-Macchi Ni.29s, AC.2s, and SPAD XIIIs. With the availability of the FIAT A.20 410-hp V-12 engine, *Ing*. Rosatelli designed a new aircraft which was assigned the designation 'CR.20', the prototype of which, assigned serial MM61, flew for the first time from Torino Mirafiori airfield on 19 June 1926 with test pilot Giovanbattista Bottalla at the controls; after a few test flights it was transferred to Montecelio airfield for evaluation by the *Centro Sperimentale*.

The CR.20 was a single-engine, single-seat fighter biplane with an all-metal square fuselage composed of a high resistance steel tube trellis, its forward section clad in duralumin with the remainder of the fuselage and the tailplane fabric covered. The wing configuration was of the conventional sesquiplane type[3] with a rectangular shape and constant chord, the upper wing having a 9.80 m span, while the lower span was 6.82 m. The wing structure, clad in fabric, was formed by two rectangular profiled spars in duralumin with lightened sides, and ribs, these two in square aluminium tubes, the entire structure stiffened by high resistance steel tube struts and bracing wires. The ailerons and tailplanes also featured a fabric-clad aluminium structure.

As was the widespread practice on Italian aircraft of the period, to counterbalance the effects of the rotation created by the propeller, the left wings were some 10 cm longer than the right. The oval tubular steel wing struts were arrayed in a W formation, similar to the preceding CR.1, and the fuel tank, with a 280-litre capacity, was installed forward of the pilot's cockpit. The undercarriage which, as in the CR.1, represented one of the weak points of the aircraft, was single axle with shock absorbers formed from bundles of elastic cords, while under the tail was a shock-absorbing skid.

The armament comprised two Vickers 7.7 mm machine guns mounted on the nose of the aircraft and synchronised to fire through the propeller, with 500-round magazines for each gun, while a photographic camera could be installed behind the cockpit.

The engine in the CR.20, 20bis, 20B and Idro versions was the Fiat A 20, a water-cooled V-12 (60° cylinder bank), with 19-litre cylinders and a notional power of 460 hp (effectively 10 hp at 2,060 rpm). The CR.20AQ (*Alta Quota* – high altitude) version featured the same engine with the same power, but with an augmented compression ratio and consumed fuel of a different mixture (55% aviation benzine, 23% alcohol, and 22% petrol), which afforded improved performance at altitude and an additional 1,000 metres of

---

[3] In this case the upper wing has greater dimensions in comparison with the lower wing.

A view of Campoformido airfield with the fleet of two *Squadriglie* of 1° *Stormo Caccia*. On the right are the CR.1s of 80ª *Squadriglia* while on the left, the first CR.20s delivered to the 79ª and 81ª *Squadriglie*. (Via R. Bassi)

The final production version of the CR.20 was the CR.20 Asso, a CR 20bis airframe coupled to a 450-hp Fraschini Asso Caccia air-cooled engine, housed in an elegant and distinctive cowling.

CR.20 Asso of the 80ª *Squadriglia*, 1° *Stormo Caccia* at Campoformido. (Asso4Stormo).

Left: A total of 204 examples of the CR Asso (as it was also commonly known) was built between 1931 and 1932, 104 of them by Macchi, and the other 100 by CMASA.

operational ceiling. With the exception of the CR.20A, all the other versions of the fighter were externally characterised by the cumbersome frontal radiator mounted above the hub of the two bladed wooden propeller.

Operationally speaking, the CR.20 could be defined as a controversial aircraft. Because of its metal structure, it was almost 150 kg heavier than the CR.1, and despite its more powerful engine, better handling and general robustness, its flight performance was almost identical to its predecessor. The installation of the large radiator on the nose of the aircraft with the consequent slight shift forward of the centre of gravity created not a few handling problems, introducing significant instability and an increased potential to lose control of the aircraft at low speed, particularly in the turn. Accidents and swings

The CR.20 equipped the Regia Aeronautica's famous aerobatic unit and took part in the final stages of the Italian conquest of Libya, as well as in the campaign against Emperor Haile Selassie in Abyssinia as a ground-attack aircraft.

The CR.20bis therefore appeared in 1930, solving the main problem of the CR.20 through incorporation of a new undercarriage with separate legs and hydro-pneumatic shock absorbers and wheel brakes.

CR.20bis of 106ª *Squadriglia* at Massawa. The unit was deployed to Ethiopia a few weeks after it was formed late in January 1935 with 8 FIAT C.R.20s.

during take-off and landing further added to the problems associated with the early type of undercarriage, and these were frequent on Italian airfields. Despite this criticism, the CR.20 continued to serve as the basis of the Italian fighter force between 1927 and the first half of the 1930s, serving with all the principal *stormi* of the Regia Aeronautica and associating its name solidly with aerial exhibitions performed by the fighters of the *1° Stormo* commanded by *tenente colonnello* Rino Corso Fougier who was at the forefront of early mass aerobatics in Italy.

In 1930 the new CR.20bis variant entered service, with which the undercarriage problems were resolved. Generally similar in structure to the CR.20, the 'bis', featured the installation of a new undercarriage which, the anachronistic system of elastic shock absorption having been abandoned, had independent wheels equipped with oleo-pneumatic shock absorbers. These allowed a braking system to be mounted. The tail skid, supported by a steel tripod, was also equipped with a rubber pad shock absorber.

These aircraft were quickly distributed to air units in Italy and Italian East Africa. From January 1935 some aircraft were assigned to the 106ª *Squadriglia* at Asmara, and in the following month to the 107ª *Squadriglia* at Mogadishu in Somalia where they were utilised in operations against rebels for around a year, frequently making machine gun attacks, before being replaced by the Ro.1. Another unit operational in the African theatre was the 111ª *Squadriglia* in Eritrea which, in the absence of any real opposition in the air, was mainly used on missions in support of land forces or for visual reconnaissance.

In 1931 the two-seat dual control CR.20B was constructed to satisfy training requirements. The transformation was achieved by the lengthening of the fuselage by around 24 centimetres, and this modification was subsequently extended to some aircraft of the seaplane variant. During the 1930s the CR.20B served with various *Scuole di Volo* (flying schools) of the Regia Aeronautica, including those at Castiglione del Lago, Grottaglie, Aviano, Cameri, Foggia, Malpensa and Pescara. Some two-seaters were also assigned to operational units and, used

The different versions of the CR.20 ended their days as trainers assigned to various *Scuola Volo Caccia* until the eve of the war.

A seaplane version was introduced in 1928. Known as the FIAT CR.20 Idro at least 46 examples were built in equal numbers by Macchi and CMASA.

Left: The seaplane variant produced by Macchi and CMASA equipped some *'Squadriglie da Caccia Marittima'* (maritime fighter squadrons). The photograph shows the CR.20 Idro of the 162ª *Squadriglia* which operated from the station at Vigna di Valle, on Lake Bracciano.

The CR.20 Asso also flew as an aerobatic aircraft and was used by the Regia Aeronautica aerobatic teams in the mid-1930s.

as trainers alongside the single-seats, enjoyed a long operational life, at least until 1940.

Another variant developed was the CR.20 Idro, created through the installation of a pair of wooden or metal floats on inverted V mounting struts attached to the undercarriage points. The CR.20 Idro served with the 161ª and 162ª *Squadriglie* of the 80° *Gr. Aut. C.M. (Gruppo Autonomo Caccia Marittima)* based at Orbetello, subsequently transferring in 1931, with the disbandment of the unit, to the fleet of the 88° *Gr. Aut. C.M.* at Vigna di Valle. On 2 September of the same year the 161ª *Squadriglia* was relocated to Leros in Rhodes, coming under control of the *Stormo Misto Egeo,* and the CR.20 Idro flew with the unit until 1938, when they were replaced by the IMAM Ro.44.

In 1931 the final evolution of the CR.20 appeared, better known by the designation CR.20A or more simply as the CR Asso[4], which in the early 1930s equipped all the fighter units, becoming the principal participant in air displays of the period, both in Italy and in Europe. This version was powered by a 450-hp air-cooled Isotta Fraschini Asso engine. The forward part of the aircraft was redesigned with the adoption of a more aerodynamic engine cowling, thanks to the profiling of the smaller radiator air intake and the introduction of a new propeller with a spinner. The new and more streamlined layout of the new engine resolved some of the stability problems that affected the preceding version and delivered an associated increase in performance. The top speed, however, proved to be slightly inferior, a result of the higher overall weight of the aircraft. Some

aircraft, furthermore, were modified with the installation of Handley-Page slats on the leading edge of the upper wing, a modification which was subsequently applied to numerous aircraft from the preceding series.

The progressive retirement of the type from front line units commenced in 1934 following entry into service of the first CR.30 with liquid-cooled in-line engines.

Service outside Italy

With the CR.20, FIAT managed to achieve some export success. Four fighters were acquired by Poland in 1929, fifteen by Lithuania, while in the

Above left, above and below: The aircraft also enjoyed good export success, equipping the air forces of Austria, Poland and Lithuania, as shown in these photographs. Other aircraft were sold to Hungary and Paraguay and after the Anschluss of Austria, several aircraft received Luftwaffe markings and were used as trainers in German flying schools.

---

[4] Contrary to what the designation might seem to indicate, the CR.200A was the final variant of the fighter to be constructed, and the A identified the installation of the I.F. Asso engine.

FIAT FIGHTERS

This rare photograph of an aircraft in the markings of the 362ª *Squadriglia* is one of the CR.30 prototypes as seen from the 'MM164' painted under the tail. It was customary for the Regia Aeronautica to reserve three-number MMs to designated prototypes. (M.Amatiello)

same year Hungary acquired CR.20s and a two-seat CR.20B, which were followed by a further twelve CR.20bis, these being used in front line service until 1936, subsequently serving as advanced trainers.

In 1933 Paraguay acquired six CR.20bis which were operated by the 2° *Escuadron de Caza 'Los Indios'* at Isla Poi and flown in action against the Bolivian forces during the Gran Chaco War; the surviving aircraft remained in service until at least 1935.

The Austrian Bundesheer would become an important client, with the first CR.20bis acquired in 1933. Further acquisitions brought the total number of aircraft delivered to 34, of which some thirty were single-seaters and at least four were CR.20B two-seaters. Some fighters, still operational at the time of the *Anschluss* of 13 March 1938, were incorporated into the Luftwaffe and used as training aircraft. It also seems that two aircraft were passed to the Soviet Union for evaluation. At the time it left front line service, at least 650 CR.20 in various versions had been manufactured – a considerable total for the period. Of these it is believed that production included 200 CR.20, 36 CR.20Idro, of which at least sixteen were constructed by AerMacchi and twenty by CMASA, 211 CR.20, and more than 200 CR.20A Asso, with construction of the latter shared between AerMacchi and CMASA.

FIAT CR.30

The popularity of the CR.32 overshadowed its direct predecessor, the CR.30 which, unjustifiably forgotten, became the head of a series of second generation biplanes designed by *Ing.* Celestino Rosatelli. This, ultimately, resulted in the first flight of the CR.42 in 1938.

The origins of the CR.30 were linked to the excellent Fiat A.30 RA engine. This enabled the design of an aircraft that combined the good flying characteristics of the CR.20 with the power and reliability of the new engine. The A.30 RA was derived from the AS.5 as designed by *Ing.* Zerbi of FIAT for the Italian seaplane racers which participated in the Schneider Cup. It could produce around 600 hp at 3,000 m and almost 700 hp at take-off. Due to its good power/weight ratio, its relatively low specific consumption, and a limited frontal profile, Rosatelli was able to design a fighter with slim and aerodynamic lines, a robust structure, and good performance in terms of speed and manoeuvrability.

Design work on the aircraft commenced in 1930 and on 5 March 1932 the first prototype, MM164, was flown for the first time by Brach Papa, the chief pilot of FIAT Aeritalia. After a few weeks, on 13 and 20 May respectively, another two prototypes were flown, MM165 and MM166, and after a few flights to perfect the aircraft, in the month of July prototypes MM164 and MM166 participated in the *Meeting Aeronautico di Zurich*, demonstrating the validity of the new fighter. On 30 July 1932 they took first and second places in the *Coppa Dal Molin*, achieved respectively by *maggiore* Cassinelli and *tenente* Pietro Scapinelli, who at the end of the speed trials reached average speeds of 343 km/h and 336 km/h over a circuit 195 km in length.

The CR.30 was a sesquiplane with a welded duralumin tube structure and with the forward section, as far back as the cockpit, clad in the same material, from where the cladding changed to fabric. The tailplanes were also constructed from duralumin with fabric covering. The wing structure comprised two spars and ribs in duralumin, covered by fabric cladding. Ailerons were only present on the upper wing. The completely faired-in undercarriage was fixed, and featured oleo-elastic shock absorbers with compressed-air brakes, while the tailwheel was steerable.

Power was provided by the FIAT A.30RA V-12 liquid-cooled engine providing around 700 hp take-off power and driving a two-blade metal FIAT propeller with the pitch variable on the ground.

Armament comprised two Breda Safat 12.7 mm machine guns with 1,000 rounds, interchangeable with 7.7 mm guns, with the added option of a cine gun camera installation. It was also possible to attach supplementary fuel tanks or photo-mapping 13 x 18 AP 10 or AGR 61 cameras.

Production and service

Series production of the CR.30 commenced in 1933 and lasted for around two years until 1935, with a total of 116 aircraft completed in three production series. The *Matricole Militari* assigned were MM2412 to 2455, MM2457 to MM2492, and MM2553 to MM2588. Deliveries to the units began in 1934, with the first examples issued to the 1° *Stormo* at Campoformido and the 2° *Stormo* at Mirafiori. In the following year the latter unit relocated to Libya, initially in the form of its 8° *Gruppo*, followed in 1936 by the 13° *Gruppo* and the *Comando di Stormo*.

In 1934 twelve aircraft, led by the *Commandant* of the 1° *Stormo CT*, *colonnello* Da Barberino, conducted a 2,400-kilometre European tour, departing from Campoformido and calling at Stuttgart, Brussels, Paris, Tours, and Lyon. The tour concluded at Torino having completed numerous impressive aerobatic displays.

Another event which brought the aircraft to the attention of the aviation world was its victory in the *Coppa Bibesco*, conquered by *capitano* Osvaldo Baldi and *tenente* Buffa, who flew the 1,140-kilometre distance between Roma and Bucharest on 26 September 1934 at an average speed of 356 km/h. This record flight was conducted in the first two-seat CR.30B to be constructed, a version first flown by Brach Papa in

THE ROSATELLI BIPLANE FAMILY

Above, above right and below: In June 1934 the 77ª and 82ª *Squadriglia*, 2° *Stormo Caccia* received the FIAT CR.30. On 24 May 1936, the *Stormo* left Italy for Libya to operate with the CR.30 from Benina until 1938 when the fighter was replaced by the Breda Ba.65 assault aircraft.

Left: Gorizia airport: the Duca d'Aosta's aircraft photographed in front of the 97ª *Squadriglia* hangar. He was the commander of the *Divisione Aquila* and his personal CR.30 had the emblem of the 1° *Stormo Caccia* painted on the right side and on the left side that of the 4° *Stormo Caccia*. (Asso4Stormo)

CR.30, personal aircraft of the Duca d'Aosta, commander of 1° *Stormo* CT, Gorizia, 1934

April 1933 and developed for pilot training. The first example had been obtained by the transformation of the third CR.30 prototype, MM166 c/n 3, from single-seat to two-seat dual control configuration and the lightening of the aircraft through the removal of armament, radio systems, and oxygen equipment. In the course of 1934, the Regia Aeronautica requested the construction of four CR 30B, which were delivered in the following year, while in subsequent years further two-seaters were obtained via the conversion of single-seat CR.30s.

Some specialised variants of the CR.30 were also completed, including one example modified as a night fighter featuring lengthened flame-dampening exhausts, while in 1934 two aircraft were converted into the CR.30Idro seaplane version with the attachment of two pairs of floats in place of the wheels, the operation conducted by FIAT's CMASA subsidiary.

The CR.30 achieved limited export success. Six aircraft, three single-seats and three two-seaters, were acquired by the Austrian Air Force and were subsequently incorporated into the German Luftwaffe after the *Anschluss*. Other sales included two aircraft delivered to Nationalist China in 1934 and another two single-seaters transferred to Paraguay in 1937, while Venezuela acquired one aircraft at the beginning of 1938. In 1936 Hungary obtained at least fifteen CR.30, including both single- and two-seaters, as well as some former Austrian aircraft passed on from the Luftwaffe.

Right: The idea of making a two-seater version of the CR.30 came about at the end of 1932 following the success of this aircraft in the *'Coppa Dal Molin'* at Zurich. The intended use was the *'Coppa Bibescu'*, a competition held along the Rome-Bucharest route and reserved for Italian and Romanian military crews. The aim of the race was to improve the average attainable speed with fast connection aircraft. In fact, the prototype of the CR.30B was not a new aircraft, as it evolved from the transformation of the CR.30 nc3 (MM 166) from a single-seater into a two-seater, twin-engined aircraft by reworking the arrangement of the central part of the fuselage. A new profile was adopted for the wing which allowed a fair increase in top speed. The prototype was used by capitano Baldi and tenente Buffa, for the race that ran on 26 September 1933. The CR.30B managed to cover the distance of 1,140 km between Rome and Bucharest at an average speed of 356 km/h, thus winning the race.

Only 201 CR.30s were produced for the Regia Aeronautica as it was destined to be quickly replaced by the improved FIAT CR.32. Some of the CR.30s were converted as night fighters with extended engine exhausts to avoid glare for pilots.

Similar to the development of the CR.20 in 1933, the Ministry of Aeronautics asked FIAT to make a seaplane fighter variant of the CR.30, but only a handful of such aircraft were actually built.

At least three examples of the CR.30 and three of the CR.30B were purchased by the Austrian Air Force. After the *Anschluss* the aircraft were used by the Luftwaffe with *Luftwaffenkommando Österreich*.

CHAPTER THREE

Fiat CR.32

The CR.32 prototype MM201 photographed at Guidonia Montecelio during evaluation flight testing. (R.Gentilli)

AWARE of the success of the CR.30, but at the same time noting the rapid evolution of aeronautical technology, *Ingegnere* Celestino Rosatelli revisited his design to develop a new modified and improved version which would offer greater speed and enhanced manoeuvrability. The outcome of his work was the CR.32, a biplane of similar general appearance to the CR.30 but which, in reality, was actually a remake of it, albeit in smaller dimensions. Compared to its immediate predecessor, the new fighter had a wing that was one metre shorter, a fuselage about 40 cm shorter in length and, above all, a different weight distribution due to the repositioning of the fuel tanks. These adjustments gave the CR.32 considerably higher speed and handling than the CR.30 despite using the same FIAT A.30 engine, enabling it to reach a maximum speed of almost 380 km/h.

The first prototype was completed in the spring of 1933, taking off for the first time from the FIAT-Aeritalia airfield near Torino on 28 April 1933 and flown by test pilot Francesco Brach Papa. In its initial flights, the CR.32 demonstrated excellent flying characteristics and following the subsequent positive evaluation of the prototype (n/c 1, MM201) by pilots from the *Centro Studi e Collaudi* at Guidonia in the autumn of 1932, the type was the subject of an important order from the Regia Aeronautica, intended to quickly replace the CR.30 in the operational units of the Regia Aeronautica. In March 1935 the first examples were delivered to the units, firstly to the 4° *Stormo Caccia* at Gorizia and later to the 1° *Stormo Caccia* at Campoformido. Exceptionally manoeuvrable, simple to maintain, with good armament for the period, the CR.32 rapidly found favour with its pilots and maintenance crews. Indeed, such was its performance that in each unit there would invariably be a pilot who strove to become a virtuoso in the aerobatic field, for the new aircraft represented the best that could be hoped for in both a fighter and an aerobatic aircraft. Deliveries continued, and by July 1936 the CR.32 equipped all the front line fighter *Stormi* of the Regia Aeronautica.

Promotional postcard published in Italy. (P. Monti)

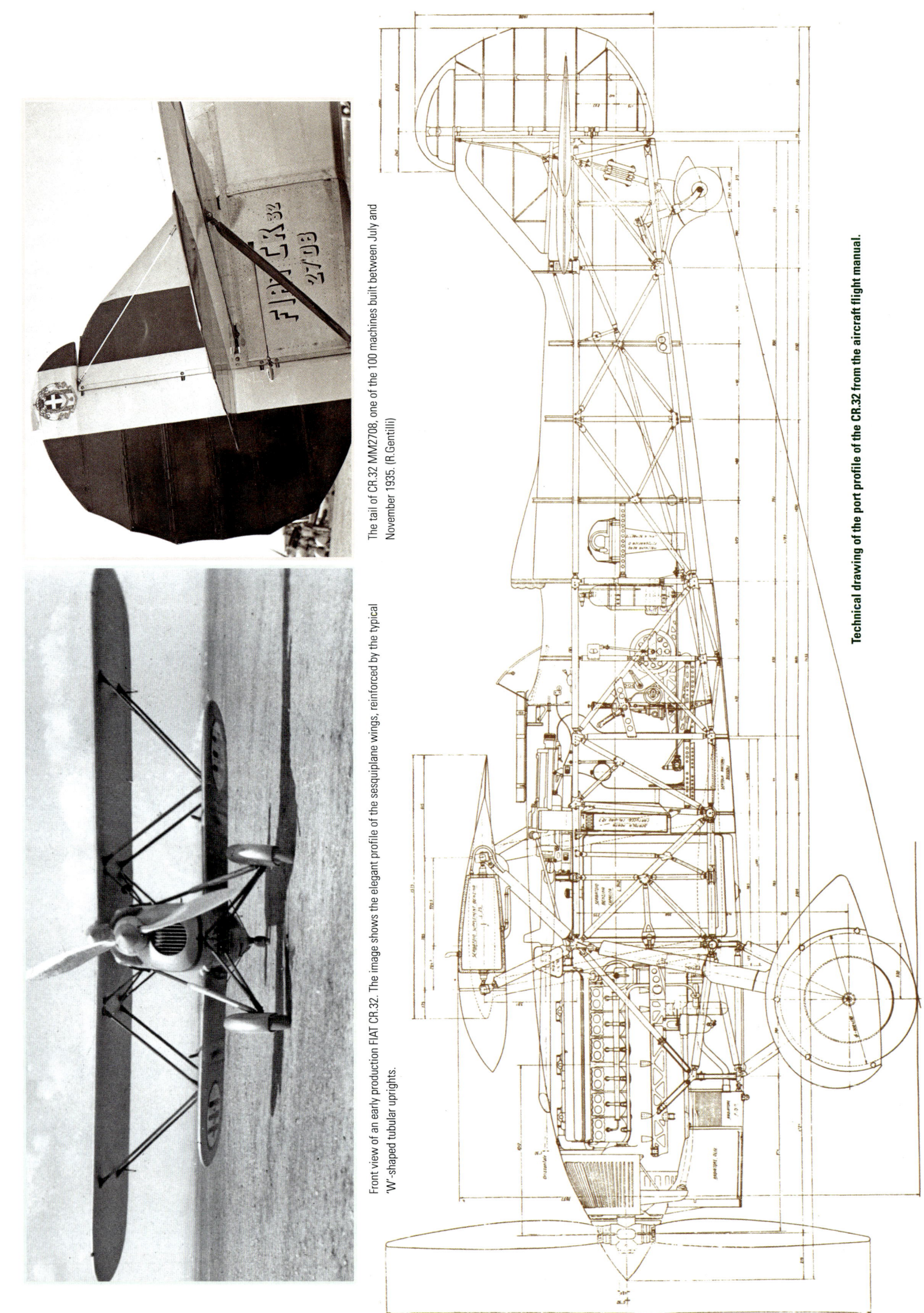

The tail of CR.32 MM2708, one of the 100 machines built between July and November 1935. (R.Gentilli)

Front view of an early production FIAT CR.32. The image shows the elegant profile of the sesquiplane wings, reinforced by the typical 'W'-shaped tubular uprights.

Technical drawing of the port profile of the CR.32 from the aircraft flight manual.

Technical data

The CR.32 was a conventional sesquiplane biplane single-seat fighter of mixed cladding, sheet metal and fabric. The fuselage was formed from aluminium and steel tubing, with false ribs in aluminium and cladding in duralumin from the nose back to the cockpit, on the dorsal surface and the surfaces under the tail, with the lateral sides and fuselage under surfaces clad in fabric.

The wings were of mixed construction, with spars and ribs in duralumin and clad in fabric. Rigid Warren-format tubular struts and steel cables provided the bracing while the ailerons, only present on the upper wing, were metal in structure and fabric clad. The tailplanes, formed from aluminium tubes and clad in fabric, were strengthened by struts and bracing wires which connected the fixed part of the horizontal tail to the fuselage and fin. The incidence of the stabiliser was variable in flight.

The main undercarriage, which was fixed, supported two independent wheels protected by aerodynamic fairings to reduce drag, and the legs were fitted with oleo-pneumatic shock absorbers. The tailwheel, which was steerable, was fixed and faired-in. The principal fuel tank was housed in the fuselage, while an auxiliary gravity feed fuel tank was aerodynamically incorporated into the centre section of the upper wing.

The engine was the FIAT A.30 RA, liquid-cooled, 60° degree V-12 (see below right and photograph following page), capable of delivering a maximum power of 600 hp at low altitude at 2,600 rpm; the engine drove a twin-blade metal propeller, the pitch of which could be varied on the ground.

The original armament for the CR.32 was two Breda SAFAT 7.7 mm or 12.7 mm machine guns, with a magazine of 350 rounds each, mounted on the engine cowling. The guns fired through the propeller disc thanks to a synchronisation mechanism.

The pilot was housed in an open cockpit protected by a windscreen, and the panel contained the standard instruments for the era. For air-to-air gunnery, the CR.32 had a special telescope gunsight placed directly in front of the pilot together with a standard free-sighting gunsight. In the final phases of its operations the aircraft was, in some cases, fitted with a reflector gunsight.

Upon the outbreak of the war, some CR.32 were also modified for ground-attack missions with the installation of hard points for the carriage of small- or medium-weight bombs (15, 20 or 50 kg) and attachments for bomblet dispensers capable of dispersing munitions of up to 2 kg each.

Three-quarter front view of the CR.32 showing the fixed undercarriage with hydraulic shock absorbers. The wheels were housed in aerodynamic fairings called spats, designed to reduce drag. Braking was pneumatically activated. (R.Gentilli)

	CR.32	CR.32Bis	CR.32Ter	CR.32Quater[1]
Engine	FIAT A.30	FIAT A.30 Bis	FIAT A.30 Bis	FIAT A.30 Bis
Wingspan metres	9.50	9.50	9.50	9.50
Length metres	7.45	7.45	7.45	7.45
Height metres	2.63	2.63	2.63	2.63
Wing area m2	22.10	22.10	22.10	22.10
Weight kg	1,325	1,400	1,390	1,386
Max Weight kg	1,850	1,970	1,915	1,905
Max speed at 0 mt/km/h	340	330	329	338
Max speed at 1000 metres	337	328	337	/
Max speed at 3000 metres	375	350	351	356
Max speed at 5000 metres	352	329	343	340
Min speed km/h	115	115	105	108
Climb to 1000 metres	1'20"	1'28"	1'35"	1'30"
Climb to 3000 metres	5'10"	5'30"	5'25"	5'10"
Climb to 5000 metres	10'	11'26"	10'20"	10'
Service Ceiling metres	8,800	8,000	7,670	7,550
Endurance hours	2	2.30	2.30	2.30
Weapons	2x12.7mm	2x12.7mm	2x12.7mm	2x12.7mm
	/	2x7.7mm	/	/

The FIAT A.30 RA V-12 aero engine

The zenith of Fiat V-12 engine development was the A-30 experimental model, quickly followed by its A-30 RA (Regia Aeronautica) and A-30 RA Bis variants. The A-30 RA Bis, designed by *Ingegnere* Tranquillo Zerbi, differed from its predecessors by means of detail modifications, including three new carburettors capable of feeding four cylinders each and the use of bearings and materials better able to withstand the thermal expansion that occurred in the cylinders, thus significantly improving the reliability of the engine.

In total around 2,500 A.30 engines were built. It has been argued that the engine's potential was limited by the fuel it used, a mixture formed of 55% petrol, 22% benzene, and 23% alcohol.

---

[1] This version of the CR.32 was assigned Latin numeral variant indicators: *Bis* means 'the second'; *Ter* means 'the third' and *Quater* means 'the fourth'.

The FIAT A.30 engine mounting. Designed in 1930, the A.30 was an inline engine, with 12 cylinders in a 60° V, with a maximum power of 600 hp at low altitude and at 2,600 rpm. It powered a two-bladed variable-pitch metal propeller (adjustable only on the ground). The engine did not use normal aviation fuel, but rather 94 octane petrol which was obtained by mixing 55% petrol, 22% benzene and 23% alcohol. (R.Gentilli)

Below: The installation of the two 12.7 mm Breda SAFAT machine guns in their forward position is visible in this photograph. (R.Gentilli)

The pilot's seat was in an open cockpit with a windscreen. This photograph also shows the San Giorgio telescopic sight (replaceable in the later series with a reflector sight).

Production versions

In the course of its career the CR.32 was manufactured in four versions. Even while the production of the first series of CR.32 was under way, the FIAT Aeritalia factory was finalising the CR.32 Bis variant, powered by the A.30Bis version of the engine, which would become the standard engine fit for all the subsequent versions of the fighter. Furthermore, to contain the weight, the RA 80-1 radio system was discarded as its presence had been ignored by many pilots on account of its poor reliability.

The most important modification, however, was the installation of the two 7.7 mm Breda SAFAT machine guns in the lower wing, increasing fire power. However, this alteration was not particularly appreciated by pilots who complained about the impact that the additional weapons had on performance, particularly during aerobatics, and the weapons were frequently stripped out of the aircraft.

After the first CR.32 had been flown by test pilot Valentino Cus, series production of this new variant commenced in the spring of 1936, but continued for little more than one year, as production switched in the summer of 1937 to the CR.32Ter. In this version the wing armament was discarded, and the airframe was further strengthened to provide the aircraft with better safety when operating from rough strips or in violent manoeuvring in flight. However, as a result of these modifications the empty weight of the aircraft remained practically unaltered, and consequently the CR.32Ter would only offer a marginal improvement in performance in comparison with the CR.32Bis.

In production for just a few months, and after the completion of around 150 examples, at the end of 1937 the CR.32Ter was replaced by the CR.32Quater, effectively identical to its predecessor but incorporating some minor aerodynamic changes that delivered a slight improvement in performance especially during flight at low altitude. Those fighters were intended for operations in Africa and were fitted with a small supplementary radiator to prevent overheating of the engine water. The majority of them were also modified with hard points for the carriage of bombs weighing between 24 and 100 kg.

Summing up, and mindful of the precarious certainty of some of the available data, it is estimated that FIAT produced a total of 1,212 aircraft. In detail, the first CR.32 production series, including the prototypes, probably numbers 383, with 282 delivered to the Regia Aeronautica and the remainder to Hungary and China. There were 328 CR.32Bis, amongst which were 283 for the Regia Aeronautica and 45 supplied to Austria. Some 103 CR.32Ter were completed, while there were 298 CR.32Quater, of which 337 were delivered to the Regia Aeronautica.

Regia Aeronautica FIAT CR.32 serials

Matricola Militare	Version	Number	Period
MM210	Prototype		
MM2589-2638	CR.32	50	March-August 1934
MM2639-2662	CR.32	24	November 1934-July 1935
MM2663-2762	CR.32	100	July-November 1935
MM2763-2870	CR.32	108	November 1935-February 1936
MM2957-3011	CR.32Bis	55	April-June 1936
MM3012-3071	CR.32Bis	60	July-October 1936
MM3072-3091	CR.32Bis	20	January-February 1937
MM3092-3169	CR.32Bis	78	February-May 1937
MM3170-3239	CR.32Bis	70	May-July 1937
MM3420-3519	CR.32Ter	100	July-November 1937
MM3520-3569	CR.32Ter	50	November-December 1937
MM3892-3961	CR.32Quater	70	January-March 1938
MM4043-4192	CR.32Quater	150	March-September 1938
MM4209-4245	CR.32Quater	37	September-December 1938
MM4465-4494	CR.32Quater	30	November-December 1938
MM4618-4667	CR.32Quater	50	September 1938-May 1939

An early FIAT CR.32bis of the 23° *Gruppo* of the 3° *Stormo Caccia*. Clearly visible in the new biplane is a Breda SAFAT 7.7 mm machine gun in each of the lower wings. These two wing-mounted weapons were found to be penalising during operations in Spain and were removed from all aircraft in the course of 1937. All subsequent production was centred on the CR.32ters with two fuselage-mounted 12.7 mm guns. (F.Bortolotti).

The CR.32ter, in production from 1937, incorporated some improvements in equipment and also the fitment of only two 12.7 mm nose guns.

A close formation flight of CR.32s led by *colonnello* D'Aurelio, commanding officer of the 6° *Stormo Caccia* in 1935.

The CR.32, MM2610, of the Duca d'Aosta with the insignia of a *generale Squadra Aerea* and also the *Brigata Aerea* (1° and 4° *Stormo Caccia*) at Campoformido.

CR.32 s of the 75ª *Squadriglia* of 18° *Gruppo*, 3° *Stormo Caccia* in flight over the Alps.

The first CR.32 were delivered to the Regia Aeronautica in the spring of 1935, joining the 4° *Stormo Caccia Terrestre* based at Gorizia, commanded by *colonnello* Augusto Bonola. The celebrated '*Cavallino Rampante*' unit was formed by the 9° and 10° *Gruppo*, each in turn controlling three *Squadriglie*, the 73ª, 96ª, and 97ª and the 84ª, 90 and 91ª, equipped until that point with CR.20A and CR.30. The next unit to convert to the CR.32 was the 1° *Stormo Caccia Terrestre*, commanded by *colonnello* Vincenzo Velardi based at Campoformido airfield in Friuli. This *Stormo* was also formed by two *Gruppi*, the 6° and 17°, respectively parenting the 79ª, 81ª, and 88ª and the 71ª, 72ª and 80ª *Squadriglie*, and until that point they had also operated the CR.20, CR.20A and, obviously, the CR.30.

Assignment of the CR.32 to the 3° *Stormo Caccia Terrestre* commenced on 18 November 1935, the unit being based at Bresso airfield on the outskirts of Milano and commanded by *tenente colonnello Pilota* Guglielmo Cassinelli. The two *gruppi* controlled by the 3° were equipped with the CR.20A, and the first CR.32 initially allocated to the *stormo* were taken on charge by the 18° *Gruppo* (83ª, 85ª and 95ª *Squadriglia*), and subsequently by the 23° *Gruppo* (70ª, 74ª and 75ª *Squadriglia*). On 1 January 1936 it was the turn of the 6° *Stormo Caccia Terrestre*, a newly formed unit under the command of *colonnello Pilota* Vincenzo Velardi, as mentioned formerly the commander of the 1° *Stormo*, who was replaced shortly after by *tenente colonnello Pilota* Plinio Locatelli. The 6° *Stormo*, whose emblem featured the famous *Diavolo Rosso* (Red Devil) insignia, received the FIAT CR.32 but retained some CR.30, a few CR.20A and some Caproni Ca.100 used for training duties. The unit comprised the 2° and 3° *Gruppo*, organised respectively by the 150ª, 151ª, and 152ª *Squadriglia* and the 153ª, 154ª, 153ª and 155ª *Squadriglia*.

Deliveries of the CR.32 to the 53° *Stormo* commenced in May 1936, at the time commanded

FIAT CR.32

A good study of a CR.32 of 154ª *Squadriglia* of 3° *Gruppo*, 6° *Stormo Caccia* taken in 1935. (P.Pesaresi)

A line-up of CR.32s of 80ª *Squadriglia*, 17° *Gruppo*, 1° *Stormo Caccia*.

CR.32s of the 357ª *Squadriglia* of the 52° *Stormo Caccia* are mirrored in a pool of rainwater at Ghedi airport.

An unusual camouflage pattern on an aircraft of 163ª *Squadriglia* flown by *tenente* Mario D'Agostini and based at Rhodes airport.

by *colonnello* Vincenzo Velardi, and composed of the 150° *Gruppo* (363ª, 364ª, and from 1 June 1936 also the 365ª *Squadriglia*) and the 151° *Gruppo* (366ª, 367ª and from 1 July 1936 also the 368ª *Squadriglia*). Three months later, another fighter unit was established: the 52° *Stormo* was assigned to *colonnello Pilota* Angelo Tessore and from 1 July 1936 located on Ghedi airfield, near Brescia in Lombardy. This new unit comprised the 22° *Gruppo* (357ª, 358ª and 359ª *Squadriglia*) and the 24° *Gruppo* (360ª, 361ª and 362ª *Squadriglia*).

On 15 January 1936 the 163ª *Squadriglia Caccia* was also constituted, assigned at the time of its activation to the 5° *Stormo da Assalto* of *colonnello* Amedeo Mecozzi. This *Squadriglia* was subsequently detached from its parent unit and transferred to the Dodecanese to operate within the structure of the *Aeronautica dell'Egeo* (Aegean Air Force).

War in Spain

On 15 July 1936, the date of the outbreak of the Spanish Civil War, the Spanish Air Force possessed a significant quantity of aircraft, but the majority of them were outdated. As a consequence, the French, British and Russians began to send supplies in support of the Republicans, while the Nationalist forces received aid from the Italians and Germans.

On 31 July 1936 the Regia Aeronautica constituted the *Aviacion del Tercio,* commanded by *colonnello* Bonomi, destined to operate within the *Tercio de Extranjeros* (Foreign Legion) of the Nationalist forces of General Francisco Franco. Shortly after the despatch of the first S.81 bombers, in early August the Regia Aeronautica gathered together a group of volunteer fighter pilots from Gorizia and Campoformido to send to Spain. Under the command of *capitano* Vincenzo Dequal twelve pilots were selected who, in accordance with the policy of masking Italian intervention, were provided with documents and passports bearing false identities. These pilots, six of whom came from the 4° *Stormo* and another six from the 1° and 6° *Stormo*, embarked on the cargo ship *Nereide* for the Iberian Peninsula on the night of 7/8 August, together with twelve CR.32. The ship docked at Melilla, in Morocco, on 14 August 1936, and the fighters, having been re-assembled on the nearby airfield at Nador were transferred, after some test flights, to Seville

Promotional postcard published in Italy. (P. Monti)

Below: Two of the first twelve CR.32s with their pilots, shortly after being unloaded from the merchant ship *Nereide* in the harbour at Melilla in Spanish Morocco. On 14 August 1936, the aircraft moved to the nearby airfield of Nador for final assembly. The aircraft were the first batch of *'Aviacion del Tercio'* machines. This first unit was also known as the *'Squadriglia Dequal'* after the name of its commanding officer. (Asso4Stormo)

A CR.32 of the Aviacion del Tercio at Caceres in September 1936. (Asso4Stormo)

Granada, Armilla, February 1937. Pilots of the *'Squadriglia Dequal'* wait for take-off. (Asso4Stormo)

Tenente Ernesto Monico, a former 4° *Stormo Caccia* pilot, was awarded the first gold medal in Spain. He had to bail out from his CR.32 and he was captured by 'militia' and executed. To remember him, his squadron mates painted on the unit's CR.32s the motto: *'Monico presente'* ('Monico is still with us'). (Asso4Stormo)

Tablada airport. From there they began to provide escort for the bombers and a quick response service, under Spanish command, to which the Aviacion del Tercio formally reported. It was not long before the CR.32 and their Italian pilots began to establish a reputation, achieving their first victory in combat on 21 August, when *tenente* Ceccherelli shot down a Nieuport 52 near Cordoba. The first Italian aviator to be killed in combat was *tenente* Monico, shot down on 31 August in the skies over Madrid by a Dewoitine. After bailing out, he landed in enemy territory, but once captured he was shot dead by the Republicans. *Sergente maggiore* Castellani, shot down in the same dogfight, was more fortunate, as he managed to fly into Nationalist-held territory before bailing out.

On 10 August another cargo ship sailed from Italy, this time with nine reinforcement CR.32s, which permitted the formation of a second *squadriglia caccia*. On 27 August, moreover, the first three CR.32s, shipped in on the merchant steamer *Morandi*, were offloaded at Palma di Majorca, these being utilised to constitute the first *gruppo di caccia* of the Italian unit in the Balearics.

FIAT CR.32

Above: The fighters based in the Balearic Islands were finished in a different colour scheme, as shown in this photograph, with two black bands on the fuselage and a large individual number.

Below: Four of the CR.32 based in Palma, Majorca in early 1937 received new emblems featuring elaborate, heraldic coats of arms, complete with crested helmets and shields. The emblem on aircraft Nr.1, flown by *sergente* Carestiato, depicted five chickens on a spit, representing five SIAI S.62s strafed on 28 August 1936 during the first two missions in the Balearics. The emblem was completed by an inscription in Venetian dialect stating, *'Soto a chi toca!'* ('Come on, who's next?').

In early September the CR.32 force of the *Aviacion del Tercio* was as follows.

— 1ª *Squadriglia Caccia* commanded by *capitano* Vincenzo Dequal with 12 CR.32s based at Caceres

— 2ª *Squadriglia Caccia* commanded by *tenente* Dante Oliviero with 9 CR.32s based at Seville Tablada

— 3ª *Squadriglia Caccia* commanded by *capitano* Giuseppe D'Agostinis, with 3 CR.32s based at Son San Juan airport in the Balearic Islands

In the same period the Italian units were reinforced by the first Spanish pilots trained to fly the Italian fighter. Amongst these were some particularly capable aviators, including *capitani* Joaquín Garcia Morato and Angel Salas Larrazabal.

In the autumn the reinforcement of the Italian contingent coincided with the arrival in Republican ranks of a similarly important delivery of combat equipment, and in particular 200 Russian aircraft, mainly Polikarpov I-15 and I-16 fighters and Tupolev SB-2 bombers. If, on one hand, the I-15 biplane did not represent a problem for the CR.32, demonstrating itself to be at the same level of performance and manoeuvrability, but inferior in terms of armament and general strength, encounters with the other two aircraft were very different. In fact, the SB-2 bombers used their speed as their most effective defensive weapon, frequently out-running the CR.32s, and forcing the Italian pilots to adopt different combat tactics that saw them organised into standing patrols, flying over the probable approach and exit routes of the Republican bombers. But what would become the real antagonist of the CR.32 was the Polikarpov I-16, known in Spain by its nickname 'Rata' (rat), a stubby, low-wing monoplane possessing a maximum speed that was faster than that of the Italian biplane. However, the *Rata* was less manoeuvrable and stable than the CR.32, and the Italian pilots quickly developed new combat tactics to confront it, trying to benefit from the longer range of their 12.7 mm SAFAT guns or

The *'La Cucaracha'* insignia

The superiority of the Italian fighters demonstrated during the first weeks of operations in Spain resulted in the creation of an unofficial emblem which was used by their pilots. This featured an insect, the *Cucaracha* (cockroach), wearing a red fez and playing seven red aircraft (like notes) on a saxophone. The most supported theory on the origins of this insignia relates that some Moroccan Legionnaires who, excited by the air combat overhead, saw the Italian fighters suddenly bursting into the sky as fast as cockroaches that had suddenly appeared in a room.

Also, on account of the chorus of a song widely known in Italy and taken from the soundtrack of the film *Pancho Villa*, as presented at the Festival del Cinema at Venezia in 1934, the nickname seemed to be so appropriate that Italian pilots decided to adopt it as the anthem of the fighters serving with the *Aviacion del Tercio*.[2]

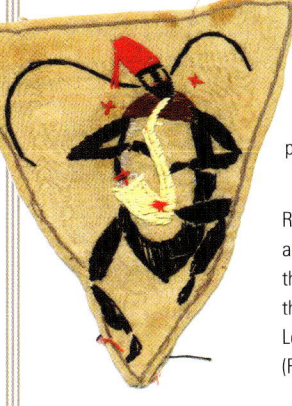

An official flying suit patch as worn by the *'Cucaracha'* pilots. (P.Monti)

Right: A humorous artwork grouping all the unit emblems of the Aviazione Legionaria. (Fibbia via F.Ballista)

[2] *'I colori dell'aviazione Legionaria'*, P. Waldis, M. de Bortoli and A. Brioschi, published by Gli Archivi Ritrovati.

Three CR.32s of the 3ª *Squadriglia* of the 1° *Gruppo Caccia* at Torrijos-Barciente in the winter of 1936/37. Note also the two Heinkel He 70 *Blitz* aircraft used by the *Legion Condor* in the reconnaissance role, undergoing maintenance with their unique, forward-hinged upper engine cowlings. (Asso4Stormo)

A flight of the newly formed 23° *Gruppo 'Asso di Bastoni'* take off from Barcience airport in the spring of 1937.

Two CR.32 of the *Aviazione Legionaria delle Baleari*. The CR.32s assigned to this unit could be recognised by the St Andrew's cross, which was different to those painted on the fighters based on the Spanish mainland, ending before the upper and lower edges of the tail rudder.

engaging Republican fighters in individual combat, where the superior agility of the Italian fighter, coupled with the better training of the Italian pilots in this form of combat, left their enemies little hope of escape.

At the end of 1936 the *Aviacion del Tercio* was disbanded and replaced by the *Aviazione Legionaria*, placed under the command of *generale* Vincenzo Velardi. Although formally placed under Nationalist command, it reported operationally to the commanders of the Italian *Corpo Truppe Volontarie*, led by *generale* Mario Roatta.

From October 1936 the two *squadriglie* operating in Spanish territory were brought together under the *Gruppo Caccia* commanded by *maggiore* Fagnani. They were equipped with 29 of the 54 CR.32s that had been sent from Italy, together with the CR.32s assigned to the 'Patrulla Azul', commanded by Spanish pilot Garcia Morato and which, since early 1937, had operated as an independent unit under the direct control of the Nationalist High Command. Another nine CR.32s were operational with the *Aviazione Legionaria della Baleari* at Son San Juan airport.

The structure of the *Aviazione Legionaria* gradually resulted in its reinforcement, including the arrival in Spain of the first CR.32Bis. By the end of January 1937 there had been a complete reorganisation of the units, with the constitution of two distinct *Gruppi da caccia* and the formation of new *squadriglie*.

The situation at the end of January 1937 was as follows:

— *1° Gruppo Caccia,* commanded by *maggiore* Tarcisio Fagnani with thirty CR.32s shared between the 1ª, 2ª and 3ª *Squadriglia* based at Torrijos-Barciente

— *2° Gruppo Caccia* commanded by *tenente colonnello* Aldo Canaveri with twenty CR.32s shared between the 4ª and 5ª *Squadriglia* based at Seville-Tablada

— *Squadriglia Mussolini* of the *Aviazione delle Baleari* with ten CR.32s commanded by *capitano* Giuseppe D'Agostinis, based at Son San Juan in the Balearic Islands[3]

In the course of the battle for the conquest of the city of Malaga, occurring on 8 February 1937, the CR.32 units were also engaged in providing support for land forces, but after mid-February, all the CR.32Bis' received with the latest reinforcements had had their wing guns removed, as their presence had caused a significant loss of agility during air combat manoeuvres.

---

[3] At the beginning of 1937 the Squadriglia delle Baleari was renamed the Squadriglia Mussolini, and a large red 'M' was painted on the rudders of its CR.32s, the initial of the Italian head of government and not, as erroneously believed by the local population, the initial of the city of Majorca.

Promotional postcard published in Italy. (P. Monti)

Towards the end of the Spanish Civil War, the aircraft of the *Gruppo delle Baleari* were painted with a new camouflage scheme and those of 101ª *Squadriglia* were adorned with the emblem of a growling mastiff. (Fibbia via F. Ballista)

The battle of Jarama, and more especially that of March 1937 at Guadalajara, demonstrated that the Republican forces had improved their effectiveness thanks to the better training of their army and the massive reinforcement of fighting equipment from the Soviets. The Italian government therefore decided to send further supplies of aircraft and combat material, amongst which were sixty CR.32s together with bombers and reconnaissance aircraft. With the influx of new aircraft and personnel, in the late spring it became necessary to undertake another of the seemingly endless reorganisations of the *Aviazione Legionaria*, with the constitution in May of the 3° *Stormo Caccia* which had three operational *gruppi* placed under its control. Consequently, in May 1937 the composition of the fighter force of the *Aviazione Legionaria*, which had also seen the renaming of the *gruppi volo*, was as follows:

3° *Stormo Caccia* – commander *tenente colonnello* Aldo Canaveri

XXIII *Gruppo* 'Asso di Bastoni' – commander *maggiore* Andrea Zotti
    18ª, 19ª and 20ª *Squadriglia* with 27 CR.32 based at Barcience

XVI *Gruppo* 'Cucaracha' – commander *maggiore* Giuseppe Casero
    24ª, 25ª and 26ª *Squadriglia* with 32 CR.32 based at Logrono

VI *Gruppo* 'Leonello'[4] – commander *maggiore* Eugenio Leotta
    31ª and 32ª *Squadriglia* with 23 CR.32 based at Tablada

---

[4] Leonello was the cover name of the commandant of the *Gruppo Eugenio Leotta*. Successively the VI *Gruppo* was identified by the name of *'Gamba di Ferro'* adopting the insignia specifically in honour of the commander of the 32° *Squadriglia*, *Capitano* Ernesto Botto, who lost a leg after being injured in an aerial duel on 12 October 1937.

Aviazione Legionaria delle Baleari – commander *generale* Vincenzo Velardi

Squadriglia 'Mussolini' – commander *capitano* Giuseppe D'Agostinis
    Eleven CR.32 based at Son San Juan

Following the failed attempt to conquer Madrid, the Nationalists decided to concentrate their attacks against the Basque region, an area of Spain which was industrialised and rich in natural resources, and then to regroup all their forces for the conquest of Madrid. By early April the two *Gruppi da Caccia* were based at Logrono and Vitoria, providing a contribution, despite the dogged Republican defence, to the fall of the city of Bilbao into Nationalist hands on 19 June 1937. The CR.32s of the two units operated from various airfields and were engaged in numerous key battles, such as those at Brunete and Santander.

In early July the *Aviazione da Caccia delle Baleari* was reinforced by the arrival from Italy of twelve CR.32s, which were used to equip two newly constituted *squadriglie*, the 101ª and 102ª. From 10 July 1937 these were assigned to the newly constituted X° *Gruppo Caccia* commanded by *capitano* Rolando Pratelli. During the second half of 1937, the Nationalist forces, despite their

The *Squadriglia Autonoma Mitragliamento Frecce* conducted its operations in the last year of the Spanish Civil War, from March 1938 to March 1939. It was a year in which the unit was heavily involved in war operations. Set up to test and execute ground-strafing and the breaking up of enemy positions, it also carried out all the other tasks assigned to the units of *Aviazione Legionaria*, from direct and indirect escort to bombers and scouts, to surveillance flights over the front lines, and from interdiction missions to the protection of airfields.

FIAT FIGHTERS

Botto, commander of the *Gruppo 'Gamba di Ferro'* photographed while attending the shooting of the movie, *Los Novios de la Muerte*.

ERNESTO BOTTO

Undoubtedly one of the most popular Italian pilots to fly in the Spanish Civil War, *Capitano* Ernesto Botto was born in Torino on 8 November 1907. A member of the '*Grifo*' course of the *Accademia Aeronautica*, he was awarded his military pilot wings in 1932 and after a period serving as an instructor was posted, in 1936, to the 57° *Gruppo* of the 1° *Stormo*. In 1937 he joined the 4° *Stormo*, assuming command of the 73ª *Squadriglia* having been promoted to the rank of *Capitano*.

On volunteering for service in Spain, he became the commandant of the 32ª *Squadriglia* of the VI° *Gruppo Caccia*. During air combat he suffered serious injuries to his right leg, which subsequently had to be amputated and replaced by a metal prosthesis, from which his nickname, '*Gamba di ferro*' (iron leg) was derived. For this action, and for his determination to return to operational service despite being partially disabled, he was awarded the *Medaglia d'Oro al Valor Militare* and in his honour the 32° *Squadriglia* received the title '*Gamba di Ferro*'. On the outbreak of the Second World War Botto returned to action in North Africa prior to returning to Gorizia to assume command of the local *Scuola Caccia* (fighter school). After the Armistice of 8 September 1943 he decided to stay loyal to his military oath of honour, contributing to the constitution of the A.N.R. and seeking to defend Italian cities from the indiscriminate Allied bombing. Not totally in tune with some of the directives issued by the leaders of the *Repubblica Sociale*, and with the Germans not appreciating his limited faith in fascism, in January 1944 he resigned from his post as commander of the A.N.R. and was replaced by *Generale* Tessari, who was more favoured by the Germans.

At the conclusion of his career as a military pilot, Ernesto Botto was attributed with five victories achieved during the Spanish Civil War and three gained in the course of the Second World War. Besides his *Medaglia d'Oro*, Botto was also awarded a *Medaglia d'Argento al Valor Militare*, the *Croce di Guerra*, and two commemorative medals from the war in Spain. He died on 9 December 1984 (aged 77) in Turin, Italy.

Botto seen just after being discharged from hospital where his right leg had been amputated, following the very serious accident suffered by him after an aerial combat. (P.Monti)

Maresciallo Fibbia proudly sits in the cockpit of a CR.32 of the *Squadriglia Autonoma Mitragliamento Frecce*. The official badge of the unit as designed by its commanding officer, *capitano* Ferruccio Vossilla, can be seen on the fuselage.

A page from the logbook of *maresciallo* Fibbia while he served with the *Squadriglia Autonoma Mitragliamento Frecce*. He ended the war with three victories. (Fibbia via F.Ballista)

efforts, never achieved a breakthrough and the capture of Madrid. A government counter-offensive, however, effectively halted Franco's troops to the point that only by mid-April were they able to capture the cities on the Mediterannean coast and isolate Catalonia.

In March 1938 the *Squadriglia Mitragliamento Frecce* was created, a unit equipped with CR.32s based at Puig Moreno airfield. It specialised in strafing, providing close air support and ground-attack, but in the following months it was frequently assigned the role of escorting bomber and reconnaissance aircraft, as well as conducting defensive patrols to protect Nationalist airfields.

By the summer of 1938 the composition of the *Aviazione Legionaria* had reached its maximum quantitative expansion thanks to further deliveries of personnel and aircraft. The organic situation of the *Aviazione Legionaria* in August 1938 was as follows:

3° *Stormo Caccia* – commander *colonnello* Venceslao D'Aurelio
XXIII *Gruppo* '*Asso di Bastoni*' –
    commander *maggiore* Aldo Remondino
    18ª, 19ª and 20ª *Squadriglia* with
    27 CR.32 based at Sarinena
XVI *Gruppo* '*Cucaracha*' – commander
    maggiore Arrigo Tessari
    24ª, 25ª and 26ª *Squadriglia* with
    32 CR.32 based at Caspe
VI *Gruppo* '*Gamba di Ferro*' – commander
    maggiore Mario Rossi
    31ª, 32ª and 33ª *Squadriglia* with
    23 CR.32 based at Puig Moreno
Squadriglia Autonoma Mitragliamento Frecce – commander *maggiore* Ferruccio Vosilla
    With 12 CR.32 based at Caspe

Aviazione Legionaria delle Baleari – commander *generale* Vincenzo Velardi
X *Gruppo Caccia* – commander *maggiore* Rolando Pratelli
    101ª and 102ª *Squadriglia* with 24 CR.32 based at Son San Juan

Commencing September 1938 Italian forces began the process of progressive disengagement from the Spanish conflict with the disbanding of the *VI Gruppo Caccia* on 27 September and the handover

FIAT CR.32

CR.32s of the 19ª *Squadriglia* of the 23° *Gruppo 'Asso di Bastoni'*. The last Nationalist offensive was in Cataluna area, after the successful battle of the Ebro.

Promotional postcard published in Italy, showing some of the unit emblems used by the *Squadriglia* in Spain. (P. Monti)

Fighters of the 29° *Gruppo 'Gamba di Ferro'* photographed while on a mission. The unit comprised the 31ª, 32ª and 33ª *Squadriglia*: the lead aircraft carried a pennant marking on the undercarriage fairing and a command marking on the rear fuselage.

The CR.32s of the 16° *Gruppo* were referred to by Moroccan soldiers as *'Cucarachas'* (cockroaches), a term that likened them to certain buzzing and annoying insects. An unknown artist with flair and brushes immortalised his interpretation of the *'Cucaracha'* on the sides of the first CR.32. The result was a cricket, with a menacing appearance, equipped with large antenna and two pincer jaws, wearing a fez with a tassel, and in the act of playing a saxophone from which an aeroplane emerges. In later versions, more than one aeroplane came out of the saxophone, certifying the *'Cucarachas'* success. (Fibbia via F. Ballista)

of its surviving CR.32s to the Nationalist Air Force. By then the situation was increasingly turning in favour of the Nationalists. After the long, bloody and eventually decisive battle of the Ebro fought between July and November 1938 in which the Republicans managed only to slow the Nationalist advance, the fall of Barcelona on 26 January 1939 and the occupation of the capital, Madrid, at the end of March 1939, the Republicans capitulated.

It is believed that at least ninety CR.32s, 112 CR.32Bis, forty CR.32Ter, and 150 CR.32Quater were utilised by the *Aviazione Legionaria* in Spain – a total of around 400 aircraft. At the conclusion of three years of war, against the loss of 156 CR.32s (76 in combat, 59 in crashes, 11 from anti-aircraft defence), the Italian pilots claimed the shooting down of 242 Polikarpov I-15s and 240 Polikarpov I-16 *Rata*s, with another 100 kills unconfirmed. Also claimed were sixty Russian-built Republican Tupolev SB-2 bombers, but only 48 of these were confirmed kills.

To CR.32s lost as a result of air operations, the *Aviazione Legionaria* lost another 80 CR.32s, destroyed on the ground by Republican air attacks or lost in flying accidents.

Promotional postcards illustrating CR.32 of Regia Aeronautica. (P. Monti)

The CR.32 during the Second World War

CR.32s were involved during the lightning war for the annexation of Albania in the spring of 1939, in the course of which the 6° *Stormo* was active, the unit being in part deployed to Brindisi airport with the role of escorting the transport aircraft engaged in transferring troops to the new theatre. It was joined for air operations over Albanian territory by the newly constituted 160° *Gruppo Autonomo* at Tirana. On 10 June 1940, the day that Italy entered the war, the Regia Aeronautica could count on a force of around 1,000 fighter aircraft, of which more than one third were CR.32, including in the overall total both serviceable and combat-ready fighters and those not combat ready, but repairable or under repair.

FIAT FIGHTERS

-Italian Fiat CR.32 aces of the *Aviazione Legionaria Italiana*

Pilot	Victories
Bruno di Montegnacco	15
Guido Presel	12
Adriano Mantelli	10
Guido Nobili	9
Andrea Zotti	9
Enrico degli Incerti	8
Giuseppe Aurili	7
Giuseppe Majone	7
Vittorino Daffara	6
Armando François	6
Giuseppe Cenni	6
Gianlino Baschirotto	6
Ernesto Botto	5
Corrado Ricci	5

Spanish aces

IN contrast to the aircraft of the *Legion Condor* which were flown exclusively by German pilots, some of the Italian CR.32s were assigned to Spanish pilots, who on many occasions achieved significant successes. The most famous of these was, undoubtedly, *Capitano* Joaquín García-Morato. Amongst other claims to fame, Morato was the highest-scoring Nationalist pilot, achieving 36 of his total of 40 aerial victories while flying the CR.32.

He was killed in a flying accident after the war when, possibly due to an engine malfunction, he crashed during a performance of aerobatic manoeuvres. The second highest scoring Spaniard was *Capitano* Julio Diaz Benjumea with a total of 26 victories (some of which were achieved while flying other aircraft types). The third-ranking ace was *Capitano* Manuel Vasquez Sagatızabal, who achieved 21 victories in the CR.32 until losing his life in combat on 23 January 1939.

Fifteen victories were recorded by *Capitano* Garcia Lopez Rengel and *Major* Angel Salas Larrazabal. After an initial victory achieved in a Nieuport-Delage 52, Larrazabal was the first Nationalist pilot to shoot down a Tupolev SB-2 bomber while flying a CR.32. After another four victories in the Fiat, he transferred to the Heinkel He 51, but would once again return to use the CR.32. His name would become particularly famous, as in the course of the same mission he managed to shoot down three SB-2 and an I-16 *Rata*.

'LOS NOVIOS DE LA MUERTE'
The Bride and Groom of Death

IN 1937 the Italian *Istituto Luce* produced a documentary film which lasted just over 30 minutes. The film documented the activities of the Italian legionnaires fighting in Spain in 1937 with particular regard to the *Aviazione Legionaria* during Nationalist operations in Aragon. It was directed by Romolo Marcellini, with a screenplay by Gian Gaspare Napolitano, assisted by operator Mario Craveri, Domenico Paolella as his assistant, and editing by Ferdinando Maria Poggioli.

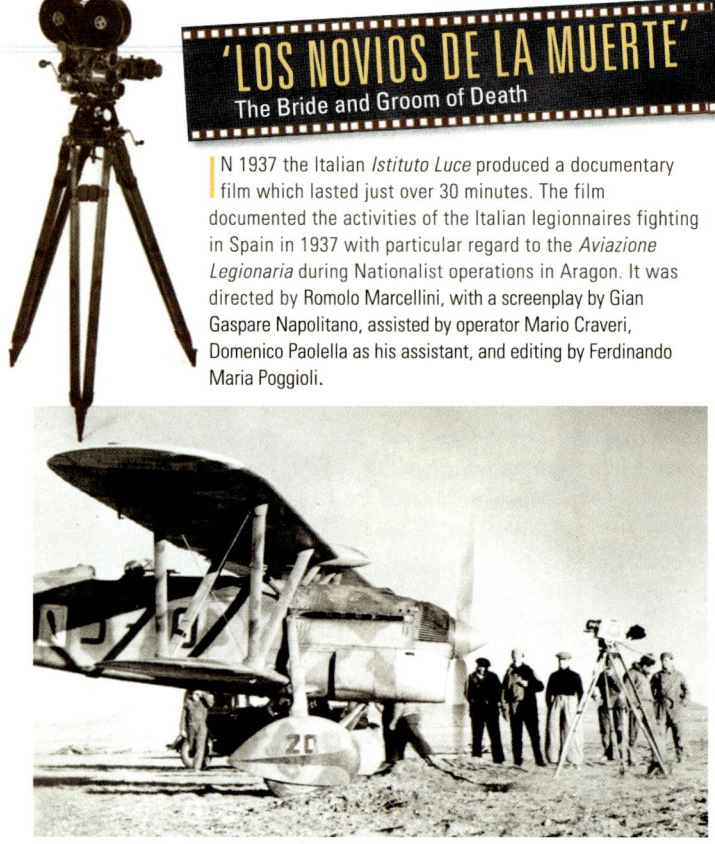

Above: The photographs were taken during the shooting of the well-known Italian motion picture/documentary, *Los Novios de la Muerte*, directed by Romolo Marcellini. Shooting took place in the summer and autumn of 1938 at different airfields including Sevilla, Lagrano, Tudela, Saragossa, Bello and finally at Teruel with aircraft of the *Asso di Bastoni*. (P.Monti)

Right: Film poster for *Los Novios de la Muerte*. (P.Monti)

A 160ª *Squadriglia* lapel badge. (P.Monti)

CR.32 of the 394ª *Squadriglia* assigned to the *Aeronautica dell'Albania* at Tirana airport in 1940.

The first CR.32s to be used on combat operations in the Second World War were the fighters deployed in Libya. From 10 June 1940 aircraft of the 2° *Stormo* began to conduct patrol flights in the skies over Tripoli and Tobruk, their first action taking place on 11 June 1940 when seven CR.32s made an unsuccessful attack on British bombers. This was followed some hours later by an attack on a formation of Bristol Blenheims by six Italian biplanes. Two British aircraft were shot down and another four were damaged with the Italians suffering no losses. The CR.32s were used subsequently on various defensive patrols in the airspace over the Libyan

FIAT CR.32

Order of Battle, 10 June 1940

FIAT CR.32-equipped units

2ª *Squadra Aerea*
HQ Palermo – commander *generale* S.A. Gennaro Tedeschini Lalli

1ª *Divisione Aerea Aquila*
HQ Palermo – commander *generale* D.A. Vincenzo Velardi

1° *Stormo* CT (26 CR.32)
  17° *Gruppo*
    71ª, 72ª *Squadriglia* – Palermo
    80ª *Squadriglia* – Trapani

3ª *Squadra Aerea*
HQ Roma – commander *generale* S.A. Aldo Pellegrini

8ª *Brigata Caccia*
HQ Ciampino Sud – commander *generale* B.A. Guglielmo Cassinelli

51° *Stormo* CT (6 CR.32) – Roma
  Sezione Allarme Caccia Notturna – Guidonia
52° *Stormo* CT (21 CR.32) – Pontedera
  22° *Gruppo*
    357ª, 358ª, 359ª *Squadriglia*
  24° *Gruppo* – Sarzana
    362ª *Squadriglia*

4ª Z.A.T. (*Zona Aerea Territoriale*)
HQ Bari – commander *generale* D.A. Augusto Bonola

2° *Gruppo* CT (34 CR.32) – Brindisi
  150ª, 151ª, 152ª *Squadriglia* – Grottaglie

Aeronautica dell'Albania
HQ Argirocastro – commander *generale* S.A. Ferruccio Ranza

160° *Gruppo Autonomo* CT (34 CR.32) – Drenowa
  394ª *Squadriglia* – Koritza

Aeronautica della Sardegna
HQ Cagliari – commander *generale* D.A. Ottorino Vespignani

6° *Stormo* CT – Monserrato (27 CR.32)
  3° *Gruppo* - Monserrato
    153ª, 154ª *Squadriglia* – Monserrato
    155ª *Squadriglia* - Alghero

Aeronautica della Libia
HQ Tripoli – commander *generale* S.A. Felice Porro

2° *Stormo* CT – Tripoli (45 CR.32)
  13° *Gruppo* – Castelbenito
    77ª, 78ª, 82ª *Squadriglia* – Castelbenito
  8° *Gruppo* – Tobruk T.2
    92ª, 93ª, 94ª *Squadriglia* – Tobruk T.2

Aeronautica dell' Egeo
HQ Rhodes – commander *generale* B.A. Umberto Cappa

163ª *Squadriglia Autonoma* (11 CR.32) – Rhodes

Aeronautica della Africa Orientale Italiana (A.O.I.)
HQ Addis Abeba – commander *generale* D.A. Pietro Pinna

410ª *Squadriglia Autonoma* (11 CR.32) – Dire Daua
411ª *Squadriglia Autonoma* (11 CR.32) – Addis Abeba

CR.32CNs belonging to a night-fighting section. Well visible are the extended exhaust pipes for night operations. The back of the photograph states that the photograph was taken in Palermo, but there is no certainty about that. (P.Monti)

A CR.32 of 410ª *Squadriglia* probably at Dire Daua airfield. (AM)

The front page of an issue of *La Domenica del Corriere* from November 1938, depicting aerial combat in Spanish skies. (P.Monti)

cities and along the Tunisian border, together with bomber escort flights and direct actions against enemy land forces. With the arrival in North Africa of the first CR.42, the tired CR.32s were reassigned to the 50° *Stormo Assalto* to be used, alongside the Breda 65, in ground-attack missions with two 100-kg bombs slung beneath their wings. The utilisation of these biplanes was brief but intense as they were flown without respite – and practically to exhaustion – in attacks against British motorised columns and even individual vehicles during the alternating fortunes of the North African front, from the Italian advance, to Sidi el Barrani, to the British counter-offensive in December, with the consequent retreat of the Italian forces and the loss of Cyrenaica at the end of 1940.

Just a few days after Italy's entry into the war, the CR.32s of the *Sezione da Allarme Notturna di Guidonia* (Guidonia Night Alarm Section) entered action to intercept presumed enemy aircraft in the sky over Roma. However, because they did not benefit from transceivers, the Italian pilots could do little more than trust in a good dose of luck to be able to enter into contact with the unidentified incursion. Confirmation of the ineffectiveness of the CR.32 for this type of mission was provided

The CR.32s of 410ª *Squadriglia* and 411ª *Squadriglia* carried the insignia of a 'red devil' wearing a tropical helmet. The FIAT biplanes represented about half of the Italian air fighting force at that time in that theatre of operations.

The 163ª *Squadriglia* operated the CR.32 from Rhodes in 1940-41, mainly in night missions.

CR.32 at Trapani Milo without insignia and wheel spats.

A CR.32 of the 160ª *Squadriglia* used in the ground-attack role in North Africa with bombs suspended from the fuselage underside. The two bombs are of the 15-kg SAP type. (R.Gentilli)

during the overflight of Roma on the night of 15/16 June 1940 by a French Farman 223-4 named *Jules Verne* which crossed the sky above the Italian capital dropping propaganda leaflets with impunity from 6,000 m. The two units equipped with the CR.32 operating in A.O.I. (*Africa Orientale Italiana* – Italian East Africa), the 410ª and 411ª *Squadriglie*, fought valiantly during a war which saw Italian and British armed forces confront each other in the Horn of Africa. The war in the A.O.I. was also the only operational theatre of the Second World War in which the Kingdom of Italy operated without the intervention of its German ally.

Despite the shortages of equipment and spares, given the impossibility of receiving reinforcements and supplies from Italy. The fighters had arrived in A.O.I. in August 1939, and were offloaded at the port at Massaua, reassembled, and delivered by air to their respective bases of Dire Daua and Addis Ababa. All the CR.32s sent to A.O.I. were drawn from the *Quater* variant batches and were adapted for desert use through the addition of a supplementary radiator and wing hard points for 100-kg bombs. During the bitter conflict the Italian pilots managed, despite the technical inferiority of their equipment, to engage British and South African aircraft, frequently clashing with more modern types such as Gladiator and Hurricane fighters and Blenheim bombers.

It would be the arrival of the Hurricanes that won the British air superiority and the few surviving CR.32s and CR.42s suffered badly. However, as mentioned, the major factor that caused the progressive reduction in the available CR.32 fleet was the impossibility of obtaining replacements and spare parts from Italy. On 10 January 1941 there were still 22 CR.32 in service, but by 31 January the fleet had reduced to fourteen, and on 5 March only eight were still in service. The last CR.32 survived until mid-April 1941. Nonetheless, although being deployed against more modern and numerically superior enemy machines, the CR.32s made an important contribution to the defence of the skies over Italian East Africa for some ten months, fighting with honour and tenacity. An example of this was given by the 410ª *Squadriglia* which, with just a handful of operational CR.32s, managed to shoot down fourteen enemy aircraft before finally running out of serviceable fighters.

Obviously, considering the age of the biplane, operational utilisation of the CR.32 on the other fronts was limited. In the Balkan theatre, prior to their replacement by the CR.42, at least fourteen CR.32s were active with the 160° *Gruppo Autonomo*, parenting the 393ª and 394ª *Squadriglia* based at Drenova in Albania. They operated together, for a brief period, with a few fighters of the 150ª *Squadriglia* of the 6° *Stormo*, flown just prior to conversion onto the G.50 and deployment to Libya. Equally limited was the use of the few CR.32s assigned to the 163ª *Squadriglia* at Gadurrà on the island of Rhodes, these being involved in the course of the operation to occupy the island of Crete. Some operational missions were also conducted by the CR.32s of the 3° *Gruppo* over Sardegna, but again in this case aircraft availability was extremely limited and was exhausted after a few weeks of operations.

From the start of 1941 the residual CR.32s were all assigned to the various *Scuole Caccia* (fighter schools), serving effectively as advanced trainers until 8 September 1943. After the Armistice only a few CR.32s remained active, and some of these saw limited service with the Aeronautica Nazionale Repubblica in northern Italy, used exclusively for training tasks.

CR.32 exported

During the 1930s the aircraft produced by the Italian aeronautical industry were considered to be amongst the best in the world and as a result of the number of records they achieved and the virtuoso displays of the CR.32-equipped aerobatic teams, a good level of export successes was achieved.

As the first CR.32s were about to be placed into service by the Regia Aeronautica, the Chinese Air Force (Chung-Hua Min-Kuo K'ung-Chün) of General Chang-Kai-Shek placed an order for 24 aeroplanes (although FIAT data indicates sixteen aircraft) similar to the prototype but equipped with Vickers 7.7 mm machine guns instead of the Breda-SAFATs, and characterised by a lack of cooling fins in the oil tank on the extreme nose. Some examples were also fitted with radio transmitters. The first fighters were delivered by sea in the spring of 1935, arriving at the port of Shanghai where they were reassembled by FIAT personnel and subsequently transferred to Nangchang airfield.

The CR.32s fought with some success during the course of the conflict with Japan and were well regarded by Chinese pilots. Nevertheless, they were subjected to a hostile campaign launched against them drawing on the strength of American industry. This accentuated the problems of the supply of spares and, above all, the difficulties in sourcing the alcohol-benzene mixture necessary to fuel the A.30 engine as well as its high cost. Despite comparative trials against the American Curtiss Hawk III and Boeing P-26 fighters which demonstrated the clear superiority of the Italian fighter, China did not order further CR.32s, and the squadron at Nanchang, which in May 1936 had just six operational CR.32s, subsequently lost all its aircraft due to accidents or air combat losses while operating against Japanese aircraft operating in the Shanghai region.

Far more important was the CR.32's service with the Magyar Királyi Honvéd Légierő (MKHL), the Hungarian Air Force which, in the mid-1930s, was still subject to the restrictions imposed after the end of the First World War. For this reason, the rearming during this period was marked by the fact that the aircraft being acquired could not carry military markings, and as such were characterised by the application of large civilian registrations applied to their fuselages. After the accords of 1938 which permitted the official reconstitution of the armed forces, on 1 January 1939 the MKHL was officially formed. A few months earlier, at the end of September 1938, all military aircraft received the new official identification markings of the MKHL – a forward-pointing arrow in the national colours of red, white and green and the civilian registrations disappeared. In reality, rearmament had been planned some years earlier and, discovering that in Italy it had found a nation agreeable to provide military equipment, in 1935 Hungary placed an initial order for twenty-six CR.32 fighters.

Delivered in the spring of 1936, the CR.32s were assigned to the *Légiforgalmi Kirendeltség 1. harci repülőezred* (Air Traffic Branch 1st Combat Aviation Wing) which was established with a 1. *vadászrepülő osztály* (1. Fighter Group). This, in turn, included three *vadászrepülő század* (fighter squadrons), the 1/1. '*Archer*', 1/2. '*Ludas Matyi*' and 1/3. '*Puma*'.

From this unit two squadrons, the 1/2. *Ludas Matyi* and the 1/3. *Puma* flew with CR.32 (the 1/1. remained equipped with the CR.20Bis), and were fitted with Hungarian 26/31M 8 mm machine guns. Civilian register codes HA-AIA to HA-AIZ were painted in small letters on the vertical tail surfaces. All aircraft had large black numbers on their fuselages.

With the arrival of the Hungarian orders in October 1936, the 1st Fighter Regiment already consisted of two groups equipped with the CR.32. The 1. *vadászrepülő ezred* (1. Fighter Wing) with the 1/1. *vadászrepülő osztály* (1/1. Fighter Group) with 1/2. and 1/3. Fighter Squadrons and the 1/II. *vadászrepülő osztály* with three squadrons (1/4. 1/5., and 1/6.). This group based at Kecskemét comprised the 1/4. *vadászrepülő század* '*Vespe*' (Wasps) (1/4. Fighter Squadron), 1/5. *vadászrepülő század* '*Camel*' and 1/6. *vadászrepülő század* '*Coeur As*' (Ace of Hearts), while the other three flights, 1/1. '*Archer*', 1/2. and 1/3. went on to constitute the 1. *vadászrepülőosztály* at Börgönd with the 1/3. detached to Veszprém.

In February 1936 the Hungarian General Staff submitted a new order for 52 CR.32s in order to equip another four squadrons with twelve aircraft each plus a number of aircraft to be assigned to a group staff flight. Deliveries of these aircraft, c/n 438 to 487, took place between the summer and autumn of 1936, and initially they also carried civilian registrations, HA-ANA to HA-AOX. In reality, it appears that only fifty CR.32s were delivered, as the consignment also included two CR.30Bs.

In the summer of 1938, on the occasion of the Munich crisis, the 1/6. was transferred to Mátyásföld airfield to defend the capital. In the same period, following the termination of restrictions and the abolishment of civil markings and identity numbers, the fighters were identified by a military serial comprising the letter V (for *vadász* = fighter) followed by a progressive number, while those aircraft destined for training wore a G-prefix serial. In this new system, the CR.32s were allocated serials from V-101 to V-176. In May 1938 another eight former Regia Aeronautica CR.32s arrived as replacements for

A CR.32, V105 of Hungarian MKHL, belonging to the *vadászrepülő század 'Vespe'* (Wasps) 1/4. (G. Punka)

These two CR.32s, of the Hungarian MKHL, belonging to the *vad.szrepülő század 'Vespe'* (Wasps) 1/4 have been involved in a ground collision. V159 has taxied into another CR.32, and if the other aircraft had been manned, with possible fatal results. (G. Punka)

Above: Early in 1936 Austria ordered forty-five C.R.32bis that were delivered in the same year and equipped *Jagdstaffeln* 4, 5 and 6 of *Fliegerregiment* Nr. 2. After the *Anschluss*, the FIATs were used for training purposes by the Luftwaffe (right and below). (R.Gentilli)

aircraft lost in accidents, these being temporarily registered HA-ATA to HA-ATH and subsequently issued military serials V-177 to V-184. Between the end of 1938 and the beginning of 1939 Germany, furthermore, delivered thirty-six CR.32 Bis' to the MKHL – former Austrian Air Force aircraft which received the serials V-060 to V-095. These aircraft were assigned to operational units, while 32 CR.32 of the first order equipped with Hungarian machine guns were progressively transferred to training duties.

The newly formed MKHL had its baptism of fire in March 1939 when Hungarian forces advanced on a region of Czechoslovakia claimed by Hungary as Kárpátalja (sub-Carpathia), part of the former Kingdom of Hungary but also claimed by the new-born Slovak state. On 24 March 1939, during a series of dogfights, the CR.32 had occasion to confront Avia BH.534 fighters, demonstrating their superiority. They were also showed good ground-attack capability by carrying eight 2-kg bombs on bomb racks. At the end of hostilities at least seven Slovak Avia B-534 fighters and Letov Š-328 light bombers were claimed as destroyed, with no losses being recorded by the Hungarians.

During the second half of 1939, the front line units were reorganised, with the 1. *vadászrepülő ezred* (1. Fighter Wing) comprising the 1/I. *vadászrepülő osztály* which controlled two squadrons of CR.32s, the 1/1. Fighter Squadron 'Richie' and the 1/2. Fighter Squadron 'Flying Dagger', both at Mátyásföld. The 1/II. *vadászrepülő osztály* with its two squadrons (1/3. and 1/4.) was stationed partially at Szolnok and Mátyásföld. The 2. *vadászrepülő ezred* (2. Fighter Wing)'s 2/I. Fighter Group was stationed with its two squadrons, 2/1. and 2/2., at Nyíregyháza, the 2/II. Fighter Group with 2/3. and 2/4. at Szolnok and Börgönd airfields.

The 2/1. was at Nyiregyháza with the newly formed 2/1. 'Teddy Bear' and 2/2 'Puma' (the former 1/3.) and 2/II. was at Börgönd with 2/3. 'Vespe' (Wasps) (formerly the 1/4.) and 2/4. 'Ludas Matyi' (formerly 1/2.) The *I Vadász Ezred*, however, possessed four flights, of which one was newly formed and was destined to replace its CR.32s with the first delivery of CR.42s.

The beginning of the Second World War saw the CR.32 still in service in Hungary, although its numbers reduced progressively due to both flying accidents and because of difficulties in obtaining a supply of spare parts. Despite this, the CR.32 took part in operations against Yugoslavia in April 1941 and at the start of the campaign against Russia, although they never saw any combat, and were progressively withdrawn from front line service being reassigned to secondary duties and training, and serving until almost the end of the conflict.

For the Spanish Ejército del Aire, in addition to the fighters left in Spain by the *Aviacion Legionaria* at the end of the Civil War, should be added the CR.32s purchased directly by Spain, comprising some sixty CR.32Ter in 1937 and a further 27 CR.32Quater in July 1938. In 1938

Spain also acquired a licence to manufacture the CR.32 and Hispano Aviacion of Seville constructed at least 100 examples from 1938, identified by the designation HA-132-L *Chirri*. Forty were converted into two-seaters and enjoyed a particularly lengthy career, being finally retired from service in the early 1950s.

Another nation that acquired a notable number of Fiat CR. 32 was Austria, ordering them for the Osterreichische Luftstreikrafte which had always demonstrated a certain interest in Italian aeronautical manufacturers, to the extent that between 1933 and 1937 it ordered more than 120 aircraft, including the Fiat Ansaldo A. 120, CR.20 Bis, CR.30, CR.32, Caproni Ca.100, Ca.101, Ca.133, Breda 28, and IMAM Ro. 37. In 1936 Austria ordered 45 CR.32 fighters in the four-gun CR.32Bis version, which were delivered in the same year and assigned to *Jagdgeschwader* 2 at Wiener Neustadt, formed by *Jagdstaffeln* 4, 5 and 6. As commonplace in Italy, the wing guns were frequently discarded, and after Austria's annexation by Germany in March 1938 the CR.32 were incorporated into the Luftwaffe and utilised for training until the end of the year, when the survivors were transferred to Hungary.

Following the successful demonstrations by the Italian aerobatic team during its 1937 tour of Latin America, in 1938 the Fuerza Aérea de Paraguay and Fuerza Aérea Venezolana, acquired five and nine CR. 32Quater respectively. Paraguay seems to have acquired at least five CR.32Quater in 1937 together with CR.30 and four Breda 25. Other Latin American sources suggest that only three were delivered, but in any case no particular details have been reported concerning their operations.

Venezuela received two CR.32Quater and a CR.30 in April 1938, and another seven between the end of 1938 and March 1939. The Venezuelan CR.32Quater were operated by the *Gruppo de Caza del Regimento de Aviaciòn* at Maracay and their pilots trained by *maggiore* Oscar Molinari of the Italian Military Mission who remained in the country until summer 1943. American reports suggest that after 1943 CR.32 never flew again, but that on 28 August 1944 there were still eight on charge, of which five were serviceable.

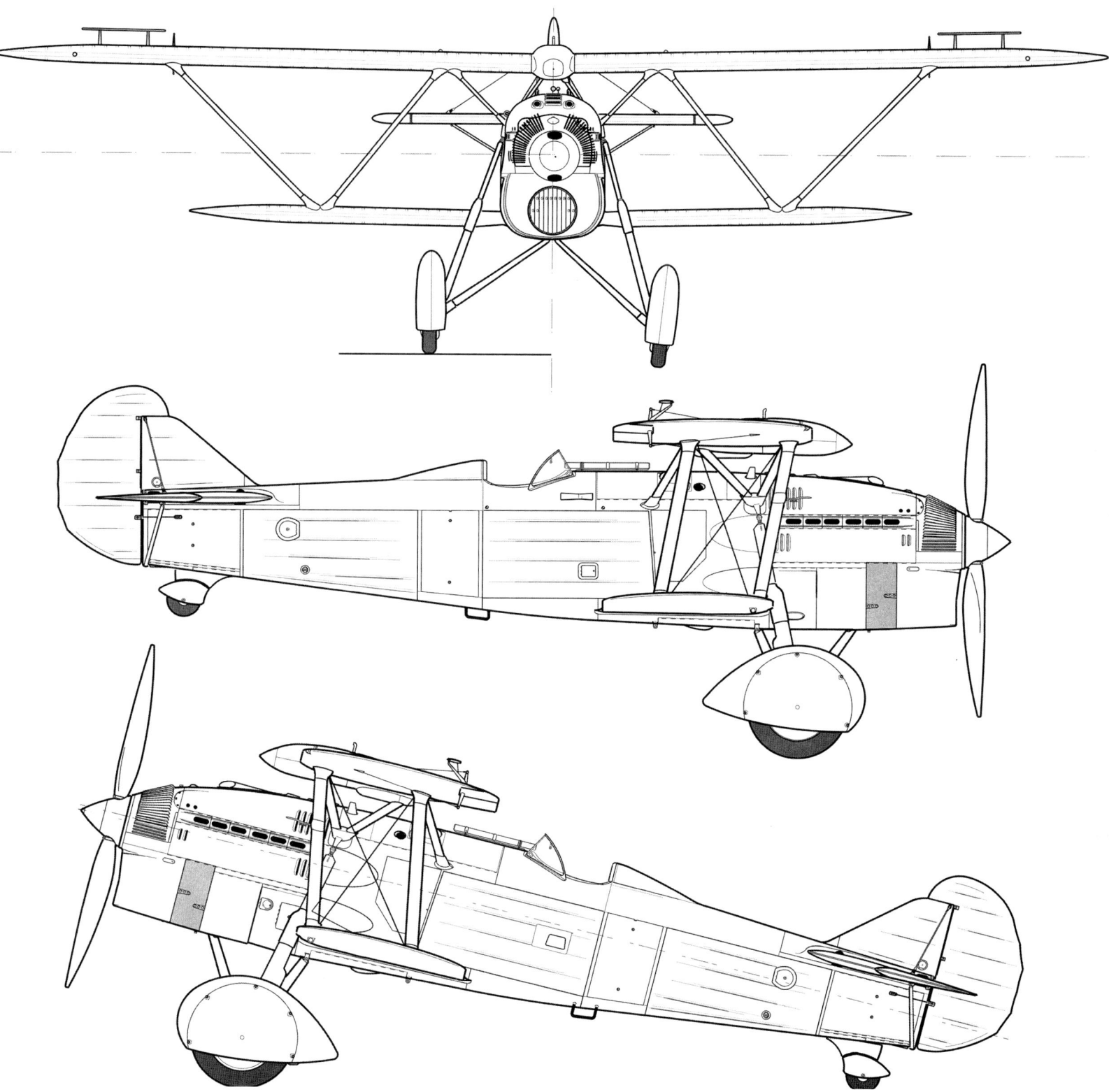

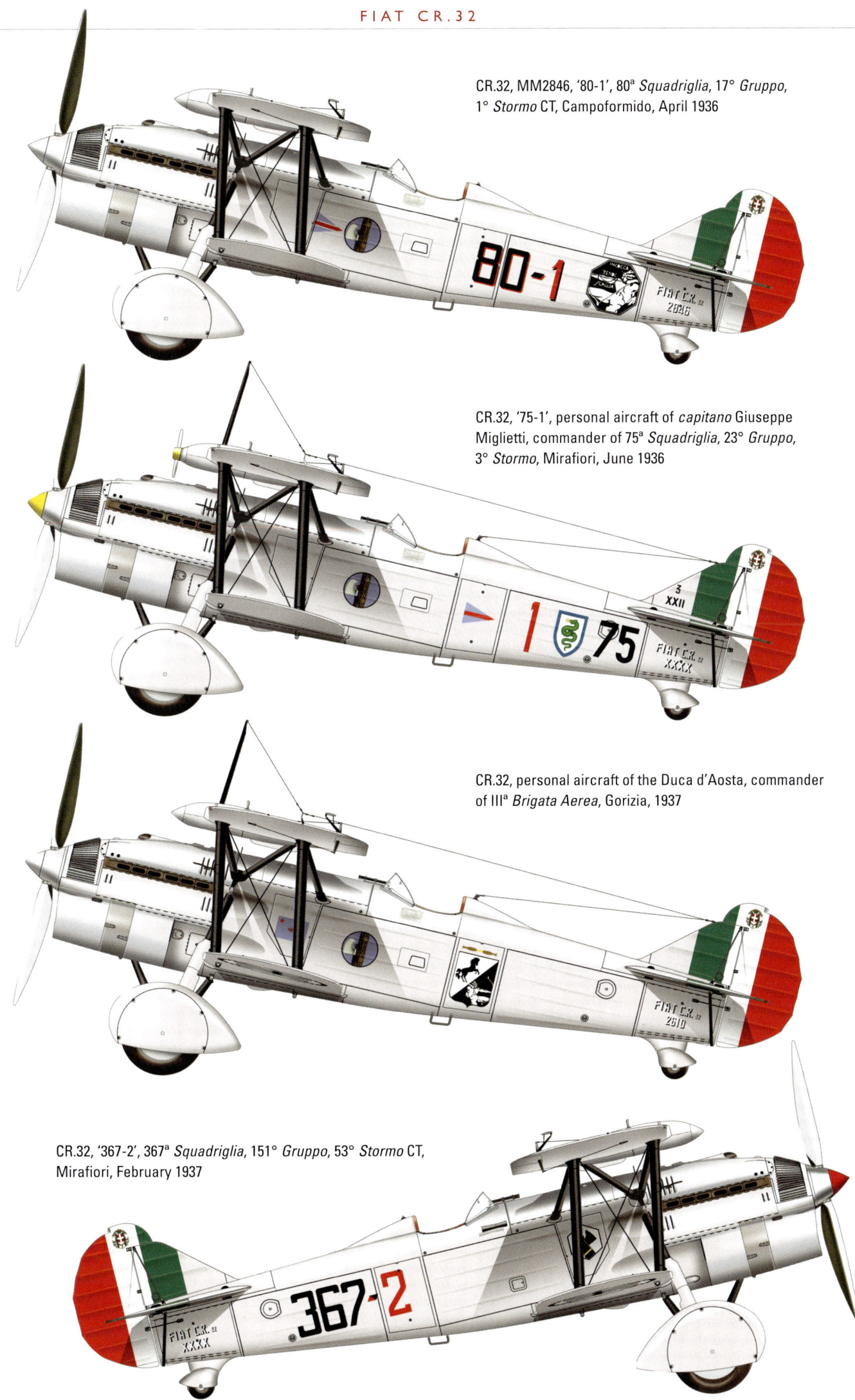

CR.32, MM2846, '80-1', 80ª *Squadriglia*, 17° *Gruppo*, 1° *Stormo* CT, Campoformido, April 1936

CR.32, '75-1', personal aircraft of *capitano* Giuseppe Miglietti, commander of 75ª *Squadriglia*, 23° *Gruppo*, 3° *Stormo*, Mirafiori, June 1936

CR.32, personal aircraft of the Duca d'Aosta, commander of IIIª *Brigata Aerea*, Gorizia, 1937

CR.32, '367-2', 367ª *Squadriglia*, 151° *Gruppo*, 53° *Stormo* CT, Mirafiori, February 1937

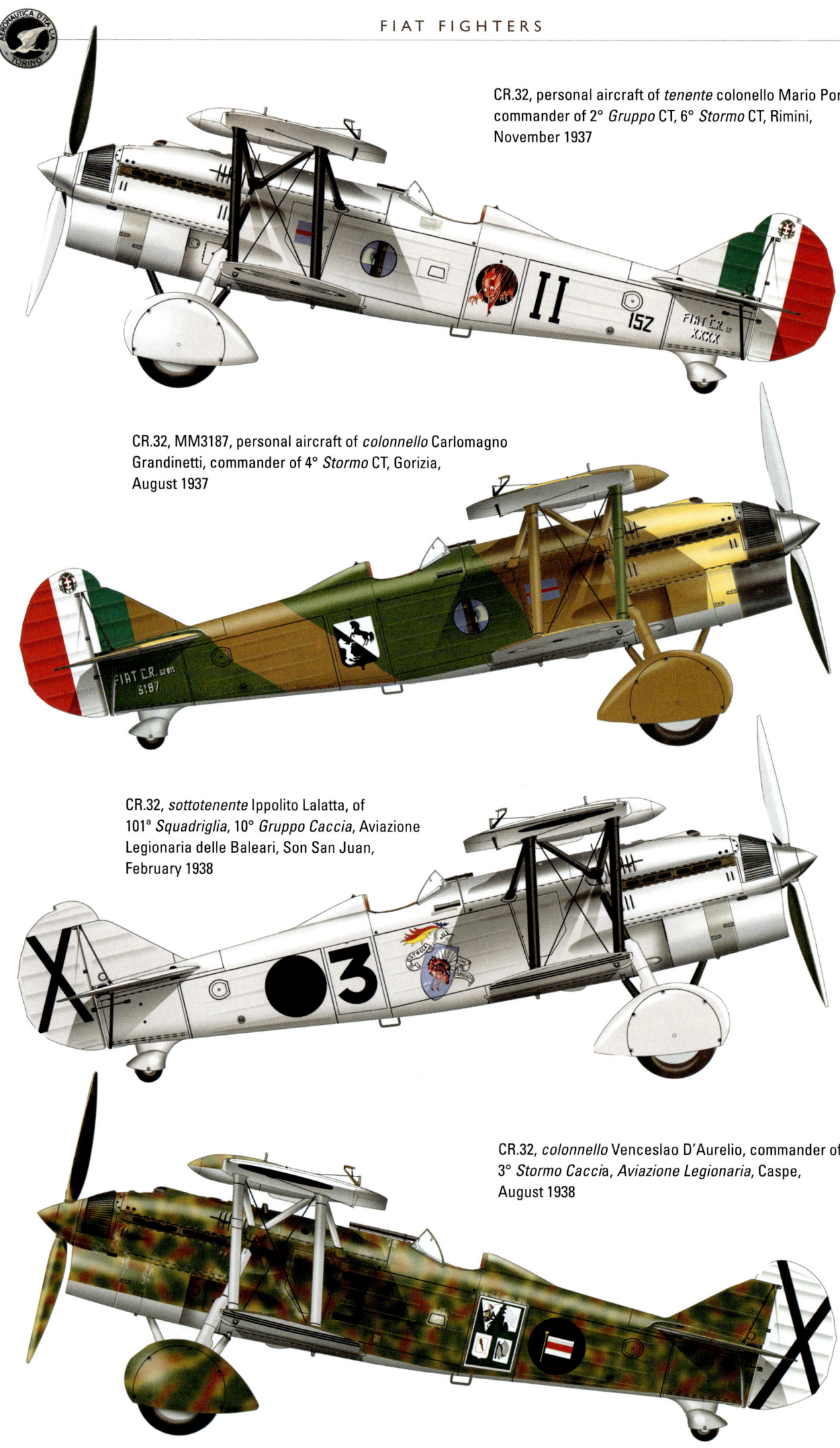

CR.32, personal aircraft of *tenente* colonello Mario Porru, commander of 2° *Gruppo* CT, 6° *Stormo* CT, Rimini, November 1937

CR.32, MM3187, personal aircraft of *colonnello* Carlomagno Grandinetti, commander of 4° *Stormo* CT, Gorizia, August 1937

CR.32, *sottotenente* Ippolito Lalatta, of 101ª *Squadriglia*, 10° *Gruppo Caccia*, Aviazione Legionaria delle Baleari, Son San Juan, February 1938

CR.32, *colonnello* Venceslao D'Aurelio, commander of 3° *Stormo Caccia*, *Aviazione Legionaria*, Caspe, August 1938

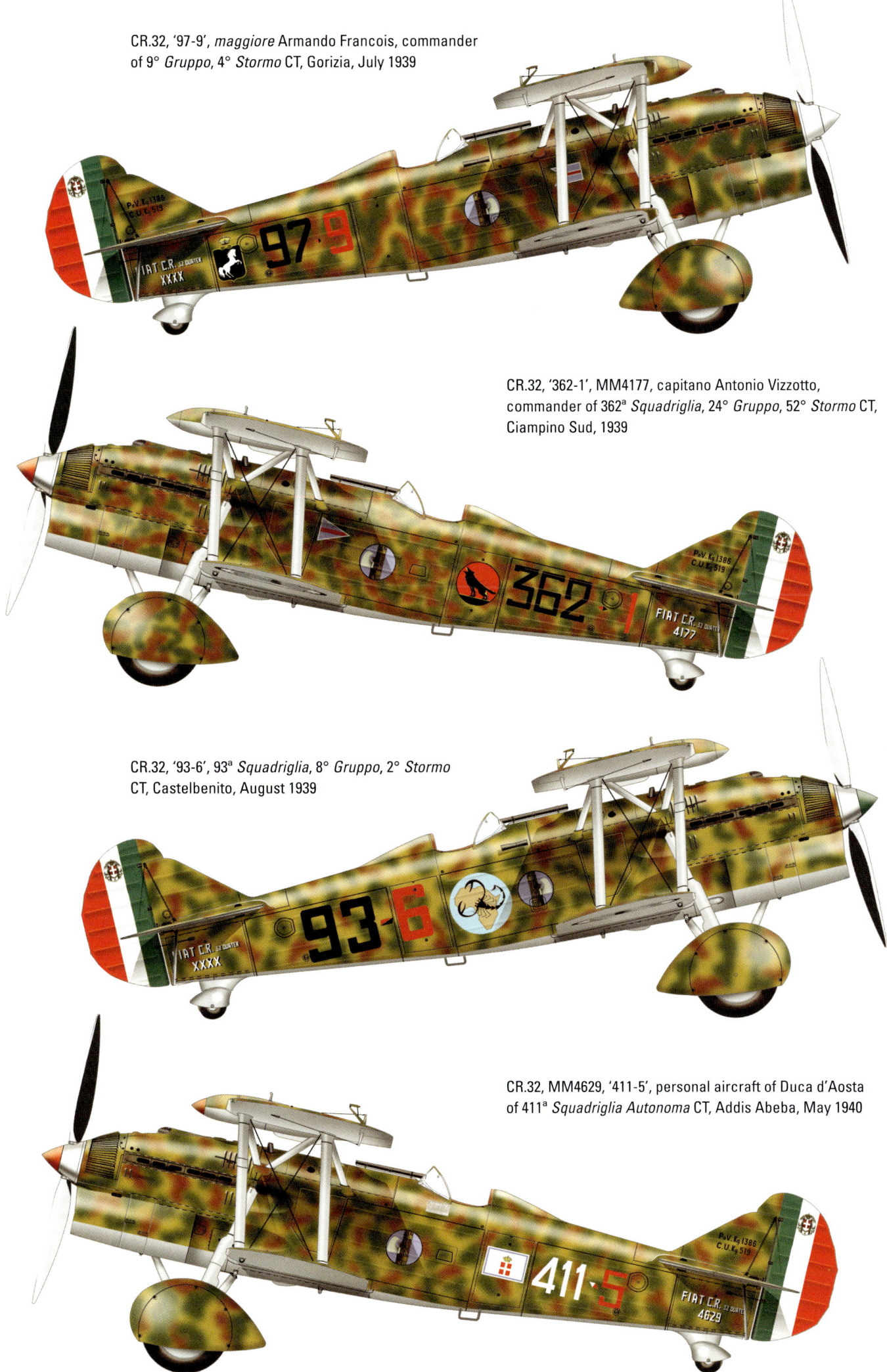

CR.32, '97-9', *maggiore* Armando Francois, commander of 9° *Gruppo*, 4° *Stormo* CT, Gorizia, July 1939

CR.32, '362-1', MM4177, capitano Antonio Vizzotto, commander of 362ª *Squadriglia*, 24° *Gruppo*, 52° *Stormo* CT, Ciampino Sud, 1939

CR.32, '93-6', 93ª *Squadriglia*, 8° *Gruppo*, 2° *Stormo* CT, Castelbenito, August 1939

CR.32, MM4629, '411-5', personal aircraft of Duca d'Aosta of 411ª *Squadriglia Autonoma* CT, Addis Abeba, May 1940

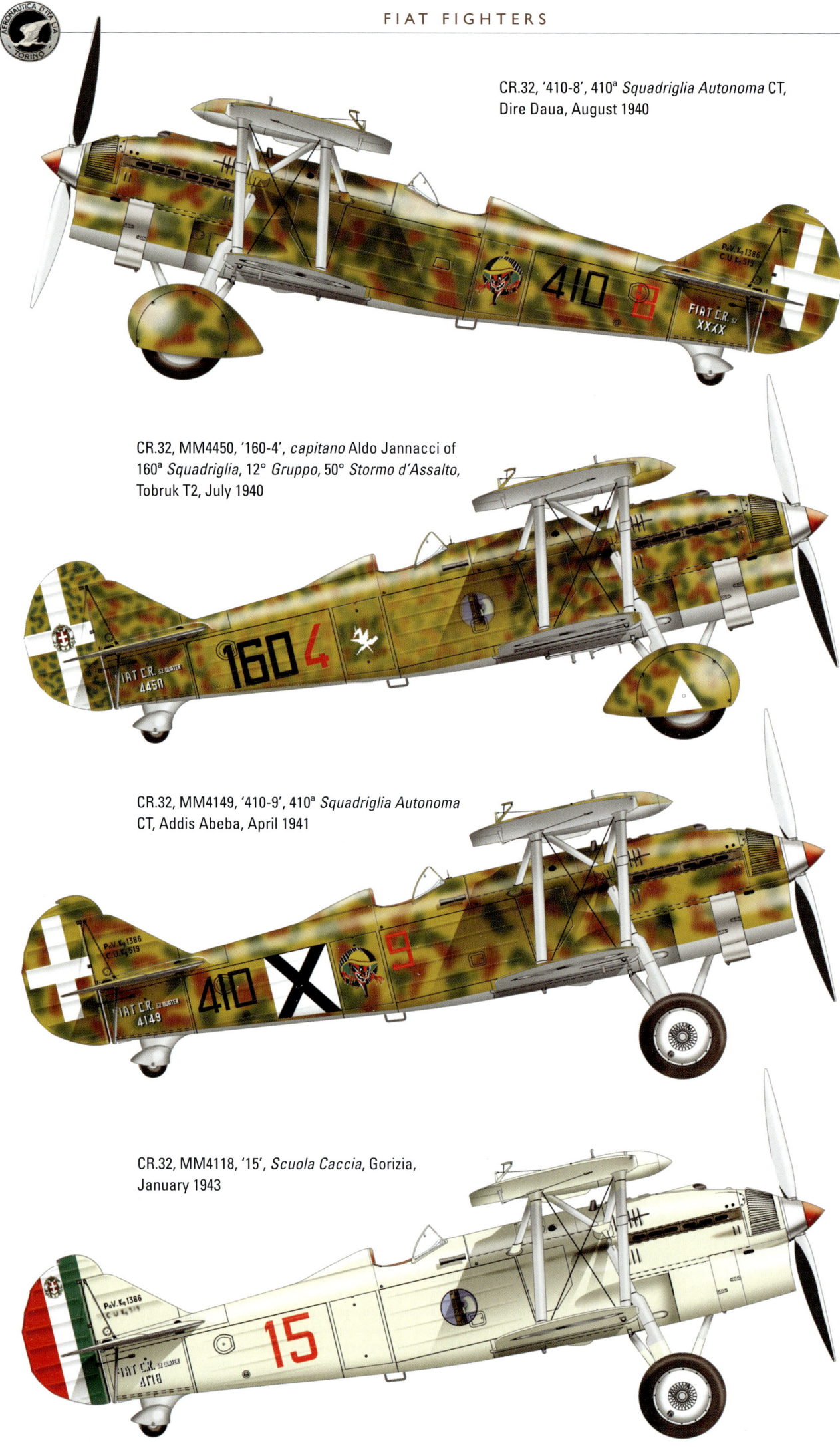

CR.32, '410-8', 410ª *Squadriglia Autonoma* CT, Dire Daua, August 1940

CR.32, MM4450, '160-4', *capitano* Aldo Jannacci of 160ª *Squadriglia*, 12° *Gruppo*, 50° *Stormo d'Assalto*, Tobruk T2, July 1940

CR.32, MM4149, '410-9', 410ª *Squadriglia Autonoma* CT, Addis Abeba, April 1941

CR.32, MM4118, '15', *Scuola Caccia*, Gorizia, January 1943

CHAPTER FOUR

The 'Volo Folle' years

The origins of formation aerobatics in Italy can be traced back to the end of the 1920s when, at Campoformido airfield near Udine, some pilots defied the directives of their commanders by conducting aerobatic manoeuvres and flights in close formation. These aerobatics were also directly linked to the aircraft designed by Ingegnere Celestino Rosatelli, since at the time all the units were equipped with biplane aircraft built by FIAT Aeritalia.

* * * *

This sharp 1930s photograph provides a glimpse of the facilities available at Campoformido airfield, a true centre of aerobatics for the Regia Aeronautica in the 1930s. Visible taking-off is a formation of CR.20s.

Commemorative postcard painted by the illustrator Ernesto Porta of the Arizona Aviatori guesthouse, where aviators gathered and met at the end of the flight display. (P. Monti)

FOLLOWING the re-equipping of the 1° *Stormo* with the CR.20, on 10 January 1930 the unit's pilots offered proof of their expertise when they performed at a display in Roma organised to celebrate the wedding of the Principe di Piemonte Umberto di Savoia and Maria Josè. By now the path to permitted aerobatics was clear, and in the following months such flying was intensified, becoming an integral part of the training of pilots. At the same time, new manoeuvres were developed, and a specific aerobatic display was devised for presentation at the Iª *Giornata dell'Ala*, a large air display, open to the public, organised for the month of June at Littorio airport near Roma, intended to replicate the style of the Hendon display of 1928. The event was divided into twelve distinct segments, with the participation of hundreds of aircraft engaged in flypasts, tactical demonstrations, competitions, and solo pilot displays, the latter involving Arturo Ferrarin and Mario de Bernardi. The most important events, however, were undoubtedly the aerobatic exhibitions by formations from the 1° and 2° *Stormo*, led by their respective commanders, *tenenti colonnelli* Fougier and Sacchi. The public was able to admire an aerobatic spectacle of the highest level, with pilots 'drawing' some classic shapes in the sky, such as 'a bow about to release an arrow', or the words '*Rex e Dux*' (King and *Duce*), 'the flight of the storks' and also an enormous letter 'V', drawn in the sky by twenty-seven aircraft of the 2° *Stormo*. The pilots

This page and opposite: Three of the geometric figures on display at Littorio as performed by the aircraft of the 1° *Stormo Caccia* during the '1ª *Giornata dell'Ala*' of 8 June 1930. The first (at right) was known as the 'chain formation'; in the second (opposite page top), the formation formed the word 'Dux' and the last (opposite page lower right) was known as the 'Arrow'. (P.Monti)

of the 1° *Stormo* performed an aerobatic programme composed of a series of breathtaking shapes and crossovers, concluding with the execution of the '*bomba*'[1], a manoeuvre which, from that day, would become the symbol of Italian formation aerobatics. In truth, however, this manoeuvre – conducted for the first time at Littorio by five CR.20 of the 71ª *Squadriglia* led by *tenente* Ariosto Neri – had been conceived as a tactical attack manoeuvre against ground targets, while the subsequent crossover was intended to be a final strafing pass. However, the manoeuvre attracted so much admiration and amazement that it became the visiting card for all acrobatic teams that followed.

The task of representing Italy at the Bucharest air display of 14 September 1930, known as the *Crociera dell'Europa Orientale* (Cruise of Eastern

---

[1] The '*bomba*' involves a formation rolling off the top of a loop, and during the descent, splitting apart – the individual aircraft then flying away from the display reference point in different directions. After a certain time, they reverse course, and head back to the reference point, with the team aircraft crossing over the reference point simultaneously at varying heights.

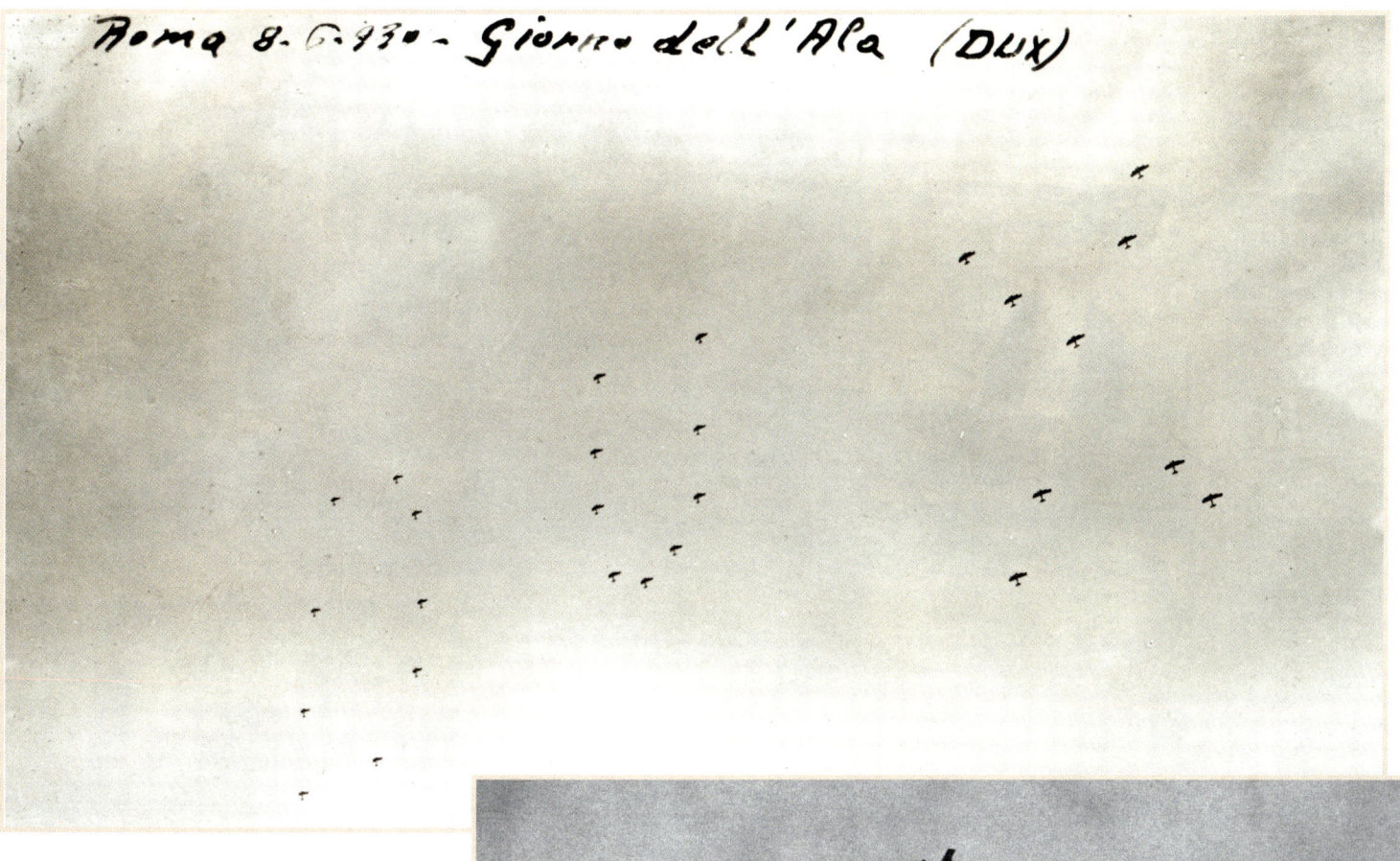

Europe), was naturally entrusted to the 1° *Stormo*. After receiving the new CR.20bis, nine aircraft departed from Campoformido on 5 September for an initial stopover in Hungary, where on 9 September, Fougier's pilots displayed over the airfield at Mátyásföld in front of military authorities and members of the royal family. Other legs saw the 1° *Stormo* formation perform at Belgrade and Sofia prior to Bucharest where, over the Romanian airfield of Baneasa, the Italian pilots delivered an impressive aerobatic exhibition in front of King Carol and senior civilian and military authorities.

At Littorio airport on 27 May 1932 the Regia Aeronautica organised the '*II^a Giornata dell'Ala*', which proved, without doubt, to be one of the greatest European air shows of the year, with carousels of hundreds of aircraft admired by a public estimated to number more than 50,000 and graced by the presence of the Italian royal family and the civil and military dignitaries. All the units of the Regia Aeronautica participated in the gathering, and in particular the aircraft of the 1° *Stormo* from Campoformido once again stunned the spectators, presenting a display of three nine-aircraft formations with the internal formation members' aircraft linked by elastic cords! After performing some formation aerobatic manoeuvres in the Roman skies, the cords were detached, and the twenty-seven CR.20, performed the '*gran ruota*' (big wheel) formation in line astern and a further series of daring aerobatics, closing their display with the much-anticipated '*bomba*' manoeuvre. Following the CR.20 of the 1° *Stormo*, the '*Squadriglia di Alta Acrobazia*' of the 71^a *Squadriglia*, from the same *Stormo* but equipped with the Breda 19, performed a new display, baptised the '*volo folle*' (crazy flight), which involved a formation flying line abreast, overflying the runway, all at differing angles of bank. From this moment, this manoeuvre and terminology would mark out displays by subsequent Italian formation teams. In the same year, at Torino, on 17 July an air display was staged in which teams participated from the 2° *Stormo* and 1° *Stormo* from Campoformido, which was in the course of a deployment to Zurich in Switzerland to take part in the *Meeting Internazionale*, which was held between 22 and 31 July.

In 1934, following a pause for conversion onto the CR.30, the aerobatic team of the 1° *Stormo* resumed its activities. Amongst the most important events in which the team participated was the *Crociera dell'Europa Occidentale* (Cruise to Western Europe), which saw the pilots from Campoformido participating in displays at Brussels-Evere on 3 June and Paris Le Bourget on the 7th. On its return to Italy, the 1° *Stormo* team took part in the *III^a Giornata dell'Aria*, held at Furbara airfield on 20 June 1934, an event which proved to be of a lower profile than the preceding editions.

From 1935 the CR.32 began to replace the CR.20 and CR.20 Asso in the units of the Regia Aeronautica. However, if the CR.32 became a key participant in aerial combat in Spain, that fighter also became extremely popular thanks to

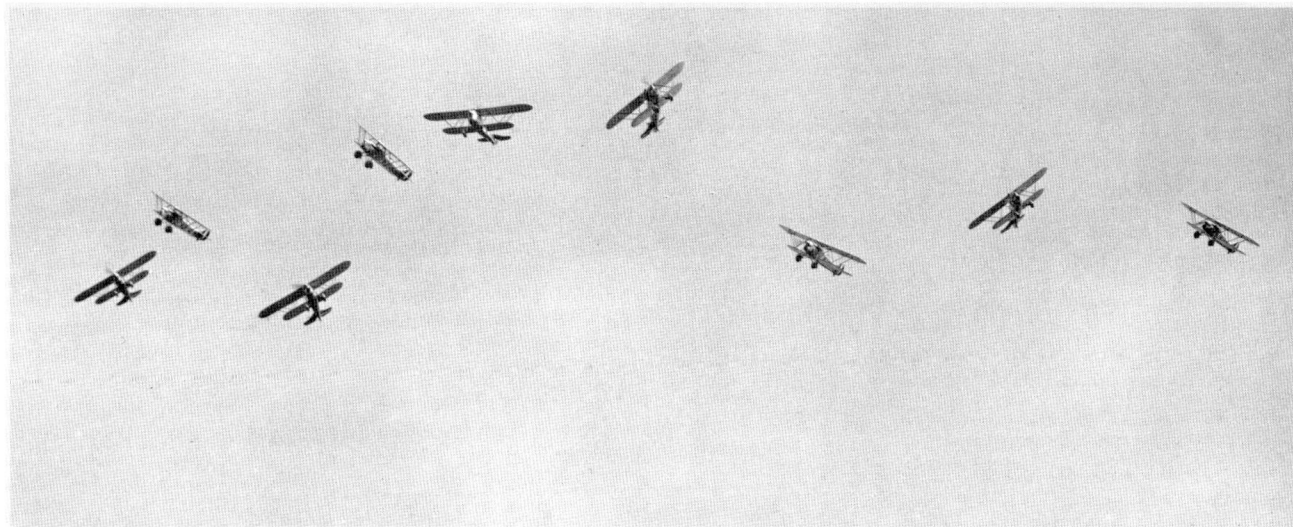

This page: Some of the acrobatic manoeuvres performed by the CR.32 formations, including the famous 'Volo Folle'.

the numerous air demonstrations that took place almost everywhere in Italy and Europe in the same period.

After a year of limited aerobatic activity by the front line units, resulting from their transition onto new aircraft and the demands imposed by the war in Ethiopia, 1936 saw the constitution of the first aerobatic team equipped with the CR.32, created from the 53° *Stormo* at Torino Mirafiori. The beginning of the year, furthermore, saw the establishment of the 6° *Stormo* at Campoformido on 15 January 1936, with some personnel being drawn from the ranks of the 1° and 4° *Stormo*.

On 28 March 1936, the IV^a *Giornata dell'Ala* was staged at Littorio airport in Roma, and the 4° *Stormo* presented a new aerobatic team, commanded by *capitano* Antonio Moscatelli, composed of ten CR.32 divided into two formations. The same team was sent to represent Italy at the air display of 14 June 1936 organised at Mátyásföld airfield in Hungary in the presence of Archduke Joseph of Austro-Hungary, the Regent Horthy, along with military and civilian authorities.

On 4 April 1937 it was again the turn of the 4° *Stormo* to display over Roma for the celebration of the foundation of the Regia Aeronautica and at Furbara on 3 June at the conclusion of a series of military manoeuvres in the presence of the German War Minister, *Generalfeldmarschall* Werner von Blomberg. At Budapest on 20 June, however, there was a joint display by teams from the 4° and 6° *Stormo*, offering the public a performance of extraordinary interest and demonstrating exceptional formation flying skills.

The second half of 1937, moreover, saw the important transfer of two formations of a total of twelve CR.32 of the 1° and 53° *Stormo*, commanded by *capitani* Molinari and Viola, to South America, where they participated in the 1° *Congresso Panamericano dell'Aviazione* at Lima in Peru. The event was organised to commemorate Geo Chavez, the Peruvian aviator, who was the first to overfly the Alps in 1910, dying when his Bleriot crashed on arrival at Domodossola.

The aircraft and pilots arrived in Peru by sea on 15 September, participating in their first air display at Lima on the 23rd, on the occasion of the inauguration of a monument to Chavez. Subsequently, the Italian formation performed a series of minor demonstrations before displaying on 28 October at Los Cerrillos airfield near Santiago del Chile. In the following weeks, having flown in formation over the Andes, the Italian pilots were involved in widely acclaimed displays on 14 and 20 November at Buenos Aires, on 28 November at Montevideo, on 26 December at Rio de Janeiro, and at the end of the year at Sao Paulo. Having been on tour for four months, flown ten public exhibitions, and having established the record of making the first formation crossing of the Andes, the delegation returned to Italy.

In the course of the same year, the *Meeting Internazionale* at Budapest-Budaors, arranged for the occasion of the inauguration of the Hungarian capital's new airport, resulted in another success for Italian aerobatics, with formations from the 4° and 6° *Stormo* presenting a full acrobatic programme. The display comprised an initial element, the execution of a series of figures and formation changes by ten aircraft from the two units, and by a second element, which saw the separation of the two teams in order to execute their own aerobatic programmes prior to a final re-join to perform the '*volo folle*', the '*bomba*' and finally, a formation landing.

For the *Campionati Mondiali di Acrobazia Aerea* (World Aerobatic Championships), scheduled for the weekend of 24 and 25 July 1937 at Zurich-Dübendorf airport in Switzerland, all the principal European aerobatic teams were gathered together, including French, Czechoslovak, Jugoslav, Austrian, Romanian, Polish and British participants. The Regia Aeronautica sent a mixed team from the 4° and 6° *Stormo*, commanded respectively by *capitani* Aldo Remondino and Giovanni Borzoni. The Italian pilots had prepared scrupulously for this important appointment, and

The CR.32s parked at San Paolo, Brazil, at the end of 1937. (AM)

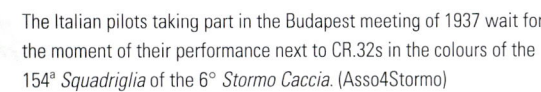
The Italian formation flying over the monument dedicated to Geo Chavez on 23 September 1937. (AM)

The Italian CR.32s taking off from Las Palmas airport in Lima during the first part of the Cruise of Latin America. (AM)

The Italian pilots taking part in the Budapest meeting of 1937 wait for the moment of their performance next to CR.32s in the colours of the 154ª *Squadriglia* of the 6° *Stormo Caccia*. (Asso4Stormo)

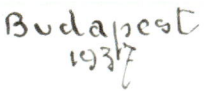

The *'Volo Folle'* performed over Pão de Açúcar at Rio de Janeiro. (AM)

A panoramic view of Budapest airfield with some of the participating aircraft. Visible from the left, Messerschmitt Bf 109 Bs of the Luftwaffe, FIAT CR.32s of the Austrian Air Force, CR.32s of the Italian team and three Ju 52/3ms of the Hungarian Air Force. (P.Monti)

The members of the Italian team that performed at Zurich in 1937. In the centre with gray cap is *maggiore* Raverdino, mission leader. Also seen are *capitano* Remondino, *tenente* Pezze', *sergente maggiore* Montanari, *sergenti* Renzi, Romandini and Tonello, *capitano* Borzoni, *tenente* Borgogno and *sergenti* Castelletti, Agonigi, Zorn and Stabile. (Asso4Stormo)

The Italian CR.32 formation of ten aircraft pass overhead during one of the aerobatic performances in Zurich.

Below: Some of the acrobatic manoeuvres performed by the CR.32 formations, including the famous '*Volo Folle*'.

presented an excellent and perfectly conducted aerobatic programme, with the execution of more than twenty geometric figures and formation changes. Surprisingly, however, the highest award was given to the Czechoslovak team, with the Italian formation placed second, only half a point behind.

In May 1938, CR.32s were protagonists in the huge air show organised at the conclusion of '*Operazione H*', military exercises conducted in concomitance with the state visit of the Chancellor of the Third Reich, Adolf Hitler. The newly promoted *maggiore* Remondino was assigned the role of leading a 'formation' of twenty-eight CR.32s belonging to the aerobatic teams of the 1°, 3°, 4° and 6° *Stormo* in a memorable exhibition. They performed a series of aerobatic figures in a practically perfect formation, amongst which, worthy of note, was the execution of two simultaneous loops by formations of twenty-one and seven aircraft and the '*Volo Folle*' with all twenty-eight aircraft. Later in the year the teams from the 3°, 6° and 53° *Stormo* were engaged in presentations at various air displays, including those at Ancona, Rimini, Firenze, Forlì, Ravenna, Venezia, Roma, Treviso, Bresso, Caselle, Cerveteri and Milano, while on 4 June the teams from the 1° and 4° *Stormo* were deployed to Belgrade, participating in the *Esposizione Aeronautica Internazionale*.

By now winds of war were beginning to blow through Italy, but despite reduced aerobatic activity, in 1939 the 4° *Stormo* organised a new formation team commanded by *capitano* Ernesto Botto, who was known as '*Gamba di Ferro*' (Iron Leg – see also Chapter Three). The formation took part in two celebrated exhibitions in Germany, the first on 21 June in Berlin in the presence of the Commander in Chief of the Luftwaffe, *Generalfeldmarschall* Hermann Göring, and the other on the following day at Staaken airfield, on the outskirts of the capital, as part of a large air display in honour of the *Legion Condor* and in the presence of the State Secretary in the Reich Air Ministry, *Generaloberst* Erhard Milch.

The epilogue to this aerobatic pinnacle achieved by the Regia Aeronautica and Rosatelli's fighters can be considered to be the performance flown on 6 July 1939 when, on the occasion of the change of command of the 1ª *Divisione 'Aquila'*, a grand display was organised, but restricted to military spectators. This event saw the participation of the majority of aircraft from the 1°, 4° and 6° *Stormi* in a subsequent cycle of aerobatic flights.

The very last aerobatic formation formed before the war, was the team formed with five CR.42 by 367ª *Squadriglia* of 53° *Stormo* CT commanded by *capitano* Simeone Marsan. The formation performed briefly, but made an acclaimed demonstration on 15 May 1939 during a visit of Mussolini to Turin. It was the final official event involving Italian formation aerobatics, a practice which would be resumed only some years later, with unchanged vigour and success, following the tragic interruption of war.

With the delivery of the first CR.42 to 53° *Stormo* CT, the 367ª *Squadriglia* pilot's organised an aerobatic formation with five biplanes led by *capitano* Marsan. The formation performed an acclaimed demonstration on 15 May 1939 during a visit by Mussolini to Turin. However, the time for acrobatics was coming to an end and, sadly, the winds of war were beginning to blow. (E.Leproni)

CHAPTER FIVE

Fiat CR.42 *FALCO*
The Last Biplane

Genesis and Production

The CR.40 was the ancestor of a generation of radial-engined fighters; it was fitted with a Bristol Mercury IV radial developing 525 hp.

WHEN, in July 1935, the *Ministero dell'Aeronautica* issued the basic technical design specification requirements for new monoplane fighters, it seemed that the biplane was passing into history. However, in the same period, *Ingegner* Rosatelli, mindful of the potential of the new FIAT A.74 radial engine, believed that there was still some margin for improvement in the biplane concept. He initiated design studies for a new fighter that would exploit the successful technical aspects of the CR.32, but wedded to the new engine. His view was that this would offer a performance that, if not similar, would be only marginally inferior to the earlier monoplane fighters, retaining the superb handling agility of the CR.32. This concept was also in accordance with a ministerial decision to favour radial engines, supporting power derived from air-cooled engines. This conviction had solid foundations in the fact that it was believed, not incorrectly, that air-cooled radial engines were less vulnerable than liquid-cooled ones, offering greater reliability and operational safety. Only later, with experience, would it be clear that there was a serious aerodynamic penalty in stellar engines that was not repaid by the (albeit questionable) greater operational safety.

The prototype of the CR.41, created by installing the Gnome-Rhône 14Ksf Mistral Major in a CR.40 airframe developing 900 hp.

The forerunners of the CR.42

To achieve what became the CR.42, in a rapid and somewhat unproductive process, *Ingegner* Rosatelli designed a series of aircraft which, although remaining at prototype stage, were characterised by technical innovations and powered by radial engines, elements that would be vital in the creation of the new fighter.

Following development of the A.33 RC 710-hp engine in 1934, which was derived directly from the A.30 and fitted with a compressor, in 1935 *Ingegner* Rosatelli conceived the CR.33. Despite closely resembling the CR.32 it was, in reality, a new design. The prototype, MM296, made its first flight in September 1935 flown by test pilot Rolandi. The aircraft's flight trials lasted several months, and were dedicated, principally, to the fine tuning of the engine. Nevertheless, following the decision to prioritise radial engines over in-line engines, FIAT decided to abandon development of the A.33, and as a consequence the CR.33 was also suspended, despite the construction of another two prototypes, which were assigned serials MM297 and MM298.

In 1933, the FIAT *Ufficio Tecnico* commenced work on the design of a version of the CR.30/CR.32 fitted with a Bristol Mercury IV A engine, developing 525 hp at 4,500 m. The prototype, completed in 1933, was designated the CR.40 and was the first fighter designed by Rosatelli to feature a radial engine. Characterising the prototype, MM202, was the adoption of a gull wing to offer the pilot better visibility in view of the bulk of the radial engine. Brach Papa flew the aircraft in March 1934 and test-flying continued for several months, but the results did not meet design expectations. The CR.40, in effect, proved to be only slightly faster than the CR.32, achieving 380 km/h, but its rate of climb and handling were decidedly inferior, and the aircraft was also less stable. When the prototype was destroyed during a transfer flight in 1935, FIAT prepared a second aircraft to continue experiments with the radial engine and this was designated the CR.40bis.

Identical to its predecessor and slightly lighter, the 'bis' differed by use of the FIAT A.59 E engine which was some 200 hp more powerful than the Mercury. This engine constituted one of the first steps taken by FIAT to respond to the trends of the period, which favoured air-cooled engines, and was nothing more than a reproduction, under licence, of the American Pratt & Whitney Hornet SDG.

The prototype was flown for the first time by test pilot Valentino Cus in 1935, but the performance of this aircraft, despite the increase in power offered by the engine, did not come up to expectations, and after being utilised for some experimental engine trials, development of the model was abandoned.

Developed with the CR.40bis, the CR.41 represented another step in the experimental 'CR.' series. The engine adopted was derived from the Gnome-Rhône 14 Ksf Mistral Major, capable of producing 900 hp at 4,500 m. It was amongst the best in its category, and negotiations progressed for its licence production by FIAT as the A.58.

On 30 March 1935, a few days after the first flight of the CR.40bis, the CR.41 also commenced flying. The tests were protracted, lasting several months, so as to ensure the aircraft was fine-tuned, including trials with two-bladed and three-bladed propellers, and these obtained impressive speed results, reaching 400 km/h. Despite this, in 1936, in view of the importance of the CR.32 and the fact that with the availability of the new FIAT A.74 engine the CR.42 was taking shape, the CR.41 project was abandoned.

Selection of the CR.42

Despite not resulting in any subsequent production, the construction of a variety of prototypes with radial engines was significant, as it enabled FIAT to understand how it would be possible to improve the already proven CR.32 through the installation of an air-cooled radial engine. As early as the conclusion of comparison trials conducted at Guidonia between a CR.32bis and the CR.41 fitted with Mistral engines, the margins of improvement were perfectly evident. In particular was the maximum speed, with that of the CR.41 being more than 50 km/h greater; this was coupled with a ceiling that exceeded 10,000 m. A report produced at the end of the trials suggested that with the installation of the new FIAT A.74 840-hp radial engine into a fuselage similar to that of the CR.41, the attaining and possible exceeding of a speed in the order of 400 km/h could be envisaged.

Rosatelli's work progressed with the preliminary design of the CR.42 which was presented to the Regia Aeronautica towards the end of 1937. This quickly resulted in authorisation for the construction of a prototype. Rosatelli did not waste time and despite the work overload at the FIAT factories, which were fully committed to production of the CR.32, B.R.20 and their variants, the engineering process was relatively simple. The prototype CR.42 was completed in the spring of 1938.

The first CR.42 took to the sky from Torino Aeritalia on 23 May 1938 flown by test pilot Valentino Cus. It is likely that none of those present could have foreseen that this elegant but somewhat anachronistic biplane – placed into production at the same time as the first two Italian monoplane fighters that had won the 1938 competition – would eventually become the Italian fighter manufactured in the largest numbers during the Second World War. Some 1,782 aircraft rolled off the assembly lines, which worked almost uninterruptedly between 1939 and 1944. The aircraft would conclude its military career in 1949 in the midst of the jet age.

The trials, conducted and overseen by FIAT test pilot Valentino Cus, assumed a particularly intense rhythm, with prototype NC 1 often flying three or four test missions a day, passing constantly from the hands of the test pilots to those of the engineers, who introduced new modifications and improvements. It would be during these test flights that problems arose with the functioning of the FIAT/Hamilton propellers, and after a series of tests with other propellers had been conducted, the issues were resolved with the adoption of a different gearing of the propeller torque reduction. This modification subsequently gave rise to a specific variant of the engine, identified with the designation A.74 R1C/38, but which unfortunately precluded the possibility to make it interchangeable with those fitted to the other aircraft that used the model, such as the G.50 and C.200.

In mid-June 1938 the prototype was transferred to Guidonia to undergo a test cycle with the 1° *Centro Sperimentale* and at the end of July the test pilots proffered assessments that were particularly favourable in respect of the aircraft. The lengthy technical report produced by the commander of the 1° *Centro Sperimentale*, *tenente colonnello* Pier Luigi Torre and published on 8 September 1938, concluded

> '...on the basis of the characteristics and reports submitted by the pilots who have evaluated the aircraft, it seems that the CR.42 is a very well-developed fighter which adds to the well-known qualities of handling and agility of the CR.32 those of outstanding performance.'

After undergoing further evaluation by the pilots and engineers of the 3° *Centro Armamenti Aerei* at Furbara, the CR.42 was again considered to be technically and operationally ready for service, and ready for large-scale production. The latter was possible because FIAT – confident in the probable selection of the fighter by the Regia Aeronautica – had already pre-arranged the supply of material and components for production. It also planned to utilise a large part of the infrastructure used to manufacture the CR.32. At the same time, however, this resulted in the creation of a paradoxical situation, as the biplane had become an 'outsider' in terms of the selection process for a new *monoplane* interceptor fighter, in which FIAT was participating with the G.50, AerMacchi with the C.200, and IMAM with the Ro.51. Nevertheless, despite not responding to the basic requisites of the competition, the CR.42 proved to be the only example of the new designs that was free of constructional or development problems, demonstrating good behaviour in flight, excellent aerobatic qualities, and was demonstrably stable, safe, and relatively easy to fly, even for a fairly inexperienced pilot.

Consequently, the CR.42 manifested itself as a real 'transition fighter', ideal for minimising the qualitative leap required by young pilots to fly the new monoplanes. At the same time, it also represented an element of safety for the Regia Aeronautica in the case of a possible failure of one of the new monoplane fighter designs. This also thereby avoided the risk scenario that the front line fighter force would be short of modern aircraft and still equipped with the obsolete CR.32. The ability to commence production in a short time, combined with a high level of output, were sufficiently important factors to influence the Regia Aeronautica to proceed with large-scale production. Indeed, at the end of 1938, FIAT

The CR.42 prototype at the FIAT/Aeritalia Torino Mirafiori plant. The first flight was performed on 23 May 1938 with Valentino Cus at the controls.

Left: The NACA cowling of the A.74 engine that turned a 2.8-metre, three-bladed Fiat Hamilton variable pitch, constant speed propeller.

The Principe Amedeo di Duca d'Aosta, was a skilled pilot and the photograph shows him climbing into the cockpit of the CR.42 prototype at Guidonia for a test flight. (P.Monti)

received a significant order from the DGCA for an initial batch of 200 examples, with encouragement to accelerate assembly of the new machine as quickly as possible.

In February 1939, following a series of representations and requests from Caproni, whose Ca.165 design had previously been rejected by the DGCA, the *Stato Maggiore* of the Regia Aeronautica decided to conduct a direct comparison between the CR.42 and the Caproni Ca.165. This latter biplane had made its first flight on 16 February 1938 and had good handling characteristics. However, within the DGCA doubts were growing about the Ca.165, in particular over the poor reliability of the 900-hp Isotta Fraschini Asso L.121 RC40 V-12 in-line, liquid-cooled engine which was not yet fully developed. Another initial peculiarity of the Ca.165 was the adoption of a retractable radiator in the forward fuselage, although after the first flights this was removed and replaced with a fixed and faired-in version. Prior to delivery to Guidonia, the prototype had also undergone modifications to the fuselage behind the cockpit to improve the pilot's rearward visibility. The flight evaluations conducted by the test pilots of the 1° *C.S.A.*, despite demonstrating

The Caproni Ca.165 prototype at Guidonia. In a direct comparison, general performance was in favour of the C.R.42 alongside the higher production cost of the Ca.165 – almost double that of the FIAT. This guaranteed the FIAT fighter supremacy over its adversary.

Right: A view of the CR.42 prototype photographed during evaluation tests at Guidonia in 1938. (R.Gentilli)

A FIAT CR.42 advertisement featuring artwork by the famous painter Mario Sironi. He was also a sculptor, architect, illustrator, set designer and graphic designer. (P.Monti)

Left: The FIAT CR.33, MM298, one of the three examples built of this improved version of the CR.32 fitted with a 700-hp A.33 RC33 12-cylinder, water-cooled engine.

the slight superiority of the Caproni's performance in comparison with that of the CR.42, also identified serious problems with engine cooling and a general inferiority in flight compared to that of the FIAT biplane which, amongst other key factors, also had an acquisition cost that was lower than that of the biplane offered by Gianni Caproni.

In concluding the flight trials, the final part of the resulting technical comparison report was clear:

'...in mock combat the Ca.165 proved to be superior. It is necessary, however, to keep in mind that the two aircraft are not at the same point as regards to configuration and development. To be specific, the CR.42 can be considered to be completely equipped and ready to enter into service, while the same cannot be said for the Ca.165.'

Moreover, the Regia Aeronautica had already formalised its first orders with FIAT for the CR.42 and the 'family continuity' of the new biplane with the CR.32, meant that senior officers in the Regia Aeronautica much preferred the CR.42. The initial order assigned to Caproni for a pre-series of twelve aeroplanes was cancelled simultaneously.

The strong performance capability of the biplane was further confirmed at the end of a series of trials organised at Guidonia in March 1940, when it was set against the three fighters selected to re-equip the front line units of the Regia Aeronautica. Incredibly, at the conclusion of the nine demanding tests, the CR.42 emerged as the best fighter in comparison with the G.50 and C.200, winning eight of the nine comparative trials, and being penalised only in the element of horizontal speed.

CR.42 Production and Versions

SERIES PRODUCTION of the CR.42 commenced at the FIAT Aeritalia factory in Torino in February 1939, quickly reaching a monthly output of more than 40 aircraft and also involving the other satellite agencies of the FIAT Aeritalia company. CR.42 production, subdivided into fourteen production series, and continuing until 1944, saw the completion of 1,782 aeroplanes, of which 157 were exported, making it the Italian fighter aircraft manufactured in the greatest numbers. This was remarkable when considering the type's relative inadequacy in comparison with contemporary British and American aircraft which offered far more advanced capabilities. Unfortunately, because of industrial/political reasons, as illustrated in the companion volume to this work describing the AerMacchi fighters, at the end of the 1930s FIAT held the monopoly on fighter construction for the Regia Aeronautica. Undoubtedly, therefore, the company was able to lobby heavily to maintain its business and employment levels, to the point that, as will be understood, it was capable of rejecting opportunities to produce aircraft for other manufacturers.

In the course of its operational life, the CR.42 was not characterised by the development of particular versions, but only by the production of variants that involved modifications to the basic design/build, either to meet the requirements of a theatre of operations, or to adapt the aircraft for specific missions, such as night fighter or ground-attack operations. An example of this sub-variant 'culture' is exemplified by the aircraft destined to operate in the Eastern Mediterranean known as **CR.42 *Egeo*** (Aegean). With just a few tens of examples produced, this variant featured the installation of a radio transceiver and an extra 80-litre tank which increased endurance, as fighters operating in the area were frequently engaged in long flights over water.

Those aircraft utilised by the C.A.I. were often identified by the designation **CR.42CAI**. They received specific modifications such as an armoured seat (a feature already adopted as standard in the course of production series I), an 80-litre auxiliary fuel tank in the fuselage, and the replacement of one 12.77 mm gun with a 7.77 mm weapon as a weight-saving measure. There was also an improved oxygen system and new instrumentation. Some aircraft were fitted with the SAFAR AR C.1 radio receiver, although it was decidedly unreliable.

Another variant prepared for a specific use was known as the **CR.42AS**, developed with

Below: The FIAT CR.42 production line at the FIAT/Aeritalia plant in Turin. The aircraft at the rear are in a later stage of completion, while those nearest the camera are having cowlings and spinners fitted.

Fuselage assembly and panelling shop with pneumatic riveting of the fuselage panels. Note the strong lattice construction of the fuselage, tailplanes, and fuselage end. The uncovered areas will have inlaid cladding.

A view of the FIAT/Aeritalia factory. It appears to show an aircraft finishing or repair department, with a range of different types, while the CR.42 airframes appear to be at different stages of disassembly.

The CR.42AS was a 'tropicalized' version intended for operations in North Africa. It was equipped with a sand filter on the carburettor air intake, extended radiator, and a larger propeller spinner. The sub-variant CR.42AS/BA (*Africa Settentrionale/Bombe Alari*) introduced bomb racks able to carry loads up to a weight of 100 kg, located beneath the strong point where wing struts connected to the lower wing.

particular emphasis for operations in North Africa and equipped with a sand filter on the carburettor air intake, and a larger propeller spinner. In 1942, by which time the biplane had shown its general inferiority in fighter-vs.-fighter air combat, the **CR.42ba** (*bombe alari*) sub-variant appeared. Two CR.42s, MM4443 and MM5691, were modified with the installation of Angeloni hardpoints under the wings, in a position corresponding with the attachment points of the wing struts, and these could support 50-kg bombs.

The **CR.42CN** (*Caccia Notturna*) was a specialised night fighter version. It possessed exclusive and specialised equipment adapted for night flying, the installation of an artificial horizon, and, in most of aircraft, a radio transceiver. It was this shortcoming that often impeded the essential coordination between an aircraft and its ground control station. The aircraft was additionally equipped with lengthened flame-damping exhausts under the fuselage and powerful spotlights under the wings, the energy for which was generated by a small windmill generator positioned at the junction of the upper wings. Special launchers to mount illuminating flares could also be fitted under the wings. To compensate for the increase in weight, one or both of the 12.7 mm guns could be replaced by 7.7 mm guns, and, at least initially, the CR.42CN was finished in an overall matt black colour scheme. The description regarding the use of the fighter was paradoxical, suggesting that it should be utilised 'on luminous nights'.

At the end of 1944 there was a requirement for a pre-operational, dual-control aircraft to operate alongside the G.50B with the *scuole di pilotaggio di 2° period* (second-stage flying schools), the *Gruppi Complementari* (Complementary Gruppi) and the *Scuole Caccia* (fighter schools). The need was for an aircraft to offer handling and speed characteristics similar, if not identical, to operational aircraft and the Regia Aeronautica was convinced it had to develop a trainer with a very different performance from the usual touring aircraft it had converted for the role in the past. FIAT consequently proceeded with a revision of the CR.42 design, also incorporating the studies completed for a two-seat version of the CR.42DB, and the result was the **CR.42B** (*biposto* – two-seater). This proposal was motivated by the fact that after entry into service of the C.202 and RE 2001, a good number of aircraft were available

The CR.42CN 'night fighter' was the result of a joint effort between FIAT and the Regia Aeronautica to equip itself with a nationally produced aircraft suitable for night combat. The main modifications consisted of two long flame-suppressors on the engine exhausts, one or two powerful lamps hanging from the underwing struts, the installation of a lighting system for the dashboard and a propeller-driven electric energy generator installed on the upper wing.

for conversion, coupled with the fact that the biplane was still in service with numerous operational units.

The new trainer variant was created by installing a second cockpit, achieved by the lengthening of the engine housing to equalise the principal centre of gravity. The second cockpit, identical to the front one, was fitted with identical controls, while to improve visibility from the rear seat, the front headrest was reduced in size. With these modifications the length of the aircraft increased by 68 cm to 8.94 m, while the total weight rose to around 2,300 kg. Maximum speed was 430 km/h at 5,300 m and during hostilities the two machine guns were often retained. Conversions into the trainer version were interrupted by the events of the Armistice, this work having been contracted at the beginning of 1943 to Agusta and Caproni at Trento. Before the events of 8 September 1943, the two companies

One CR.42 was tested with underwing smoke generators to spread a smokescreen to protect sensitive targets.

had delivered at least seven aircraft each, while another twelve single-seaters, awaiting conversion, were demolished after the Armistice. It also seems, furthermore, that some aircraft were modified into two-seater configuration at unit level.

Post-war production

Incredibly, in the immediate post-war period, the FIAT biplane was offered a new lease of life, despite the fact that ten years after its first flight and the advances in aviation technology, the aircraft appeared outdated. The CR.42 would play its part in the history of the reconstructed Aeronautica Militare, demonstrating that it could still contribute to the role of pilot training for the nascent air force in the immediate post-war period. Eleven uncompleted CR.42LW airframes were discovered in the workshops of Caproni at Gardolo (Trento), originally intended to satisfy a Luftwaffe order, and in 1946 the Aeronautica Militare decided to order their completion in dual control configuration for assignment to the *Scuola di Volo* at Lecce. The conversion work involved MM8485 / 6282 / 8996 / 7020 / 8972 / 4325 / 9245 /5608 / 9853 / 7030 / 7469. Subsequently another four CR.42Bs were prepared, MM8956 / 6986 / 9134 / 7502, which were also delivered to the 2° *Gruppo Scuole di Volo* at Lecce. In 1948, the Aeronautica Militare advanced a further request for twenty aircraft, comprising fifteen single-seaters and five two-seaters, but in view of the onerous costs involved in reactivating the production lines and the availability of new and more modern aircraft such as the G.55/B and T-6, the request was withdrawn.

Some fighters were also modified for photographic reconnaissance with the installation of an RB.50 camera.

Some CR.42s were also modified as glider tugs, with a rapid hook-up and release system installed under the fighter's tail. The objective was to utilise the aircraft to tow and release assault gliders being designed for the Regia Aeronautica. Photographic evidence has also revealed that during the war trials were conducted with a CR.42 featuring two smoke generators mounted under the wings, which were intended to mask valuable targets from Allied bombers.

The last real operational variant to be constructed was the **CR.42LW,** a night ground-attack version developed in 1944 for the Luftwaffe, fitted with flame-damping exhausts, new radio apparatus, wing hardpoints for four 50-kg bombs, and the removal of the undercarriage fairings to facilitate operations off the muddy ground of semi-prepared airstrips.

Versions that remained at prototype stage

CR.42Idro

Towards the end of 1939 FIAT was assigned the task of constructing a seaplane fighter prototype developed from the CR.42, although by that time the idea appeared obsolete in comparison to carrier-borne or catapult-launched fighters. The order, potentially, was for forty examples, with the intention of using them to replace the IMAM Ro.44 fighters in service following the failure of the IMAM RO-51. FIAT, which was already overrun with orders, entrusted its associate company, CMASA at Marina di Pisa, the task of constructing a prototype. This was to be achieved by the installation of two floats on the airframe of a standard fighter through the modification of the floats used on the FIAT RS.14 seaplane.

Further modifications were made to the engine housing, the lower wing was moved slightly further forward, and the lower part of the aircraft was strengthened and given enhanced protection. CR.42 MM4967 was selected for conversion into seaplane configuration, and at the end of 1939 the aircraft made its first flight. Following floating trials on Lake Massaciuccoli, near Viareggio, conducted by test pilot Trojano, the modified fighter was transferred to Vigna di Valle for a cycle of tests which confirmed its good overall performance with a maximum speed achieved of 423 km/h, a range of around 950 km, and a ceiling of 9,000 m. Nevertheless, despite the planned initial order for forty machines intended to re-equip the 88° *Gruppo Caccia Marittima* at Vigna di Valle, a subsequent re-evaluation of the outdated biplane formula resulted in the decision to stop further work on the project. Given the ease and rapidity of the re-conversion process, the planned forty aircraft ordered were converted into landplane fighters.

A seaplane version was under study at FIAT since 1938, and the company entrusted its construction to CMASA of Marina di Pisa. The only prototype was built in 1940. At the beginning of 1941 testing began in Vigna di Valle on Lake Bracciano. As it was not preferred over the IMAM Ro.43 and IMAM Ro.44, it did not enter production. (GC.Polidori)

CR.42DB

As has already been mentioned, in 1939 the Italian engine situation was extremely precarious, as the range of available types – essentially comprising air-cooled radials offering power output of less than 1,000-hp – had been overtaken in terms of the international 'state of the art'.

At the end of that year the *Ministero della Regia Aeronautica* decided to acquire a licence to construct the German Daimler Benz DB 601 engine, an inverted V-12 1,175-hp motor, production of which was entrusted to FIAT.

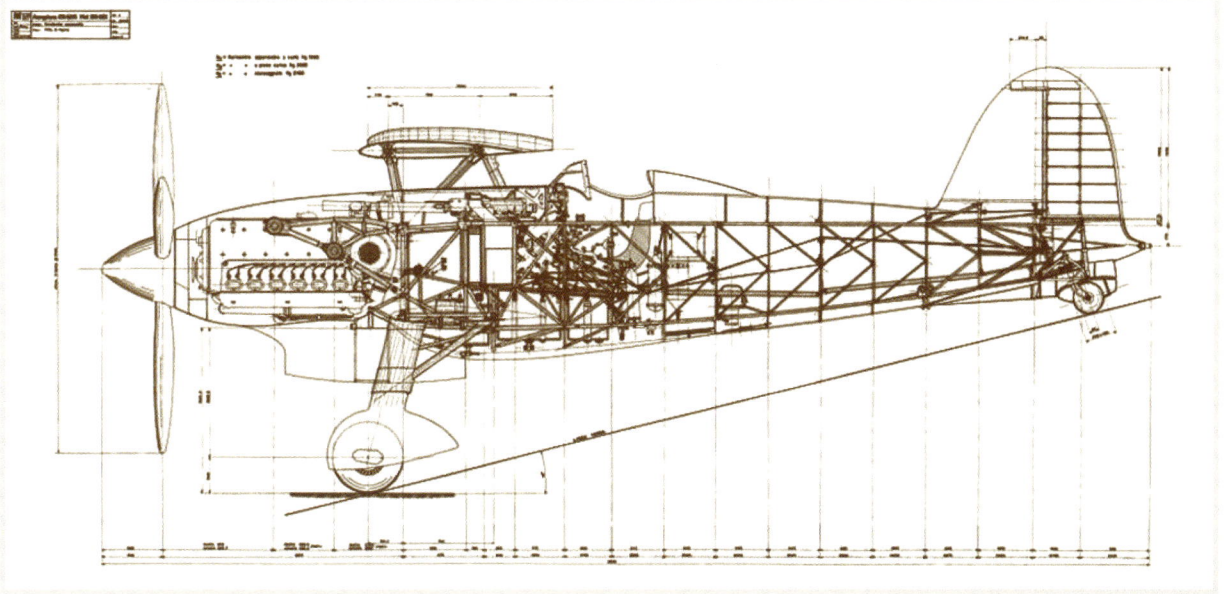

A technical drawing of the profile of the CR.42DB. The intention to increase performance was fully realised and the CR.42DB was able to reach 520 km/h, compared to 430 km/h for the normal version. (G.Valdonio)

For the CR.42DB the transition from the radial-engined FIAT A74 RC8 to the 1,175-hp DB 601 A occurred without the need for extensive remodelling of the fuselage, although arrangement of the engine systems and the cooling circuit was no small problem.

The CR.42DB, which had the MM 469, was built quickly and first flew in March 1941. The flight tests were entrusted to test pilot Commander Valentino Cus who had flown the prototype of the CR.42. (E.Leproni)

The Torino company had already initiated development of two different designs for liquid-cooled engines. The first was a V-12 1,000-hp engine, while the second had sixteen cylinders and was intended to develop 1,250-1,400 hp. Nevertheless, although a great deal of faith had been placed in these engines, development problems resulted in the projects being abandoned, and licence manufacture of the German engine became the preferred option.

On the basis of a proposal from the DGCA and with the availability of the DB 601, FIAT decided to utilise the German engine to develop what would have been, without doubt, the fastest biplane ever constructed. In a short time the CR.42DB was prepared by modifying MM469, a series production aircraft, through installation of a DB 601 which provided 1,175-hp at take-off. To install the in-line engine it was necessary to prepare a new engine housing with spars and to make some structural modifications to the forward fuselage section of the CR.42. Because the German engine was a fuel injection model, it was also essential to modify the fuel supply system, while further changes were made to the engine cooling and lubrication systems through installation of a new and bulky radiator for cooling liquids. The fitment of the DB 601 also required the redesign of the fighter's front end, with a new aerodynamic cowling and the adoption of an Alfa Romeo variable pitch propeller. The prototype was rapidly prepared, enabling test pilot Valentino Cus to make its first flight in March 1941. In the course of its early test flights the fighter demonstrated good speed performance, achieving a maximum of around 520 km/h. Transferred to Guidonia for the 1° *Centro Sperimentale*, the fighter confirmed its performance level, and the acquisition of at least 150 examples was proposed. However, at the same time it was clearly evident that it would be a pointless operation to utilise the excellent German motors with a biplane formula whose time had passed. As a consequence, having pondered over the version's use as a two-seat fast reconnaissance aircraft, the project was abandoned. Some sources report that the CR.42DB was converted back to a standard version with the serial MM90750.

Technical Data and Description

The Fiat CR.42 was a single-seat biplane fighter with an all-metal fuselage structure formed from a welded chrome-molybdenum steel tube lattice skeleton, the front section extending as far as the cockpit, with the top of the fuselage, and the area around the tailwheel all clad in duralumin. The remainder of the fuselage was covered in cotton fabric.

The wings, the upper of which had a greater span (9.7 metres) compared to the lower (6.5 metres), were constructed from two long duralumin spars, with an aluminium leading edge and the remainder covered in painted canvas. The lower wings were of similar construction and were fixed to the fuselage by four robust bolts. The two wing sets were connected by tubular steel struts in the Warren profile typical of many FIAT biplanes. Ailerons were only present on the upper wing, while the rudder and stabilisers had the same structure as the wings.

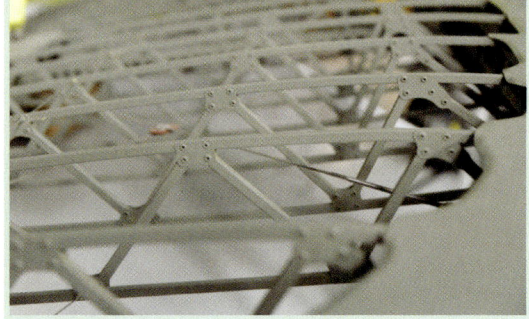
Two photographs of The Fighter Collection's CR.42 at Duxford, England, taken during its restoration showing the intricate construction of the wing.

The tailplanes were entirely constructed from duralumin with the exception of the attachment points, which were made from high resistance steel. The fixed elements of the tailplanes were also clad in aluminium, while the mobile parts were covered in cotton fabric. The rudder controls were push rods, while the other mobile control surfaces were connected by cables. The aircraft

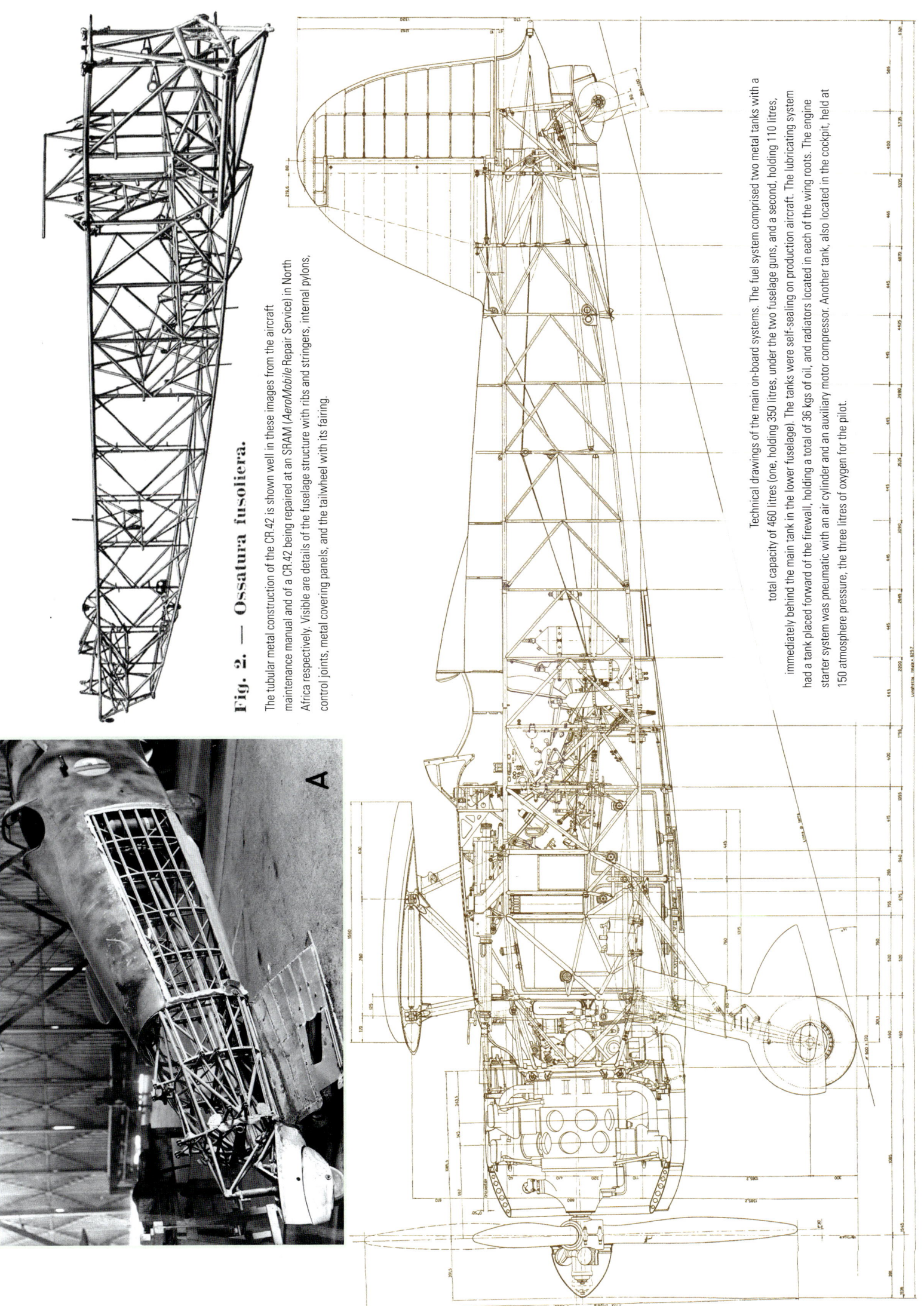

Fig. 2. — Ossatura fusoliera.

The tubular metal construction of the CR.42 is shown well in these images from the aircraft maintenance manual and of a CR.42 being repaired at an SRAM (*AeroMobile* Repair Service) in North Africa respectively. Visible are details of the fuselage structure with ribs and stringers, internal pylons, control joints, metal covering panels, and the tailwheel with its fairing.

Technical drawings of the main on-board systems. The fuel system comprised two metal tanks with a total capacity of 460 litres (one, holding 350 litres, under the two fuselage guns, and a second, holding 110 litres, immediately behind the main tank in the lower fuselage). The tanks were self-sealing on production aircraft. The lubricating system had a tank placed forward of the firewall, holding a total of 36 kgs of oil, and radiators located in each of the wing roots. The engine starter system was pneumatic with an air cylinder and an auxiliary motor compressor. Another tank, also located in the cockpit, held at 150 atmosphere pressure, the three litres of oxygen for the pilot.

Fig. 74. — Sezione longitudinale dell'apparecchio.

Detail views of the main and tail landing gear with fixing struts and brackets, for the latter taken from the maintenance manual. The photograph shows the main landing gear fairing in detail.

Tailwheel fairing with shock absorber.

featured a fixed faired undercarriage, with FAST oleo-pneumatic shock absorbers and 600 mm diameter wheels; it was fitted with a compressed air braking system, with the air contained in an 8-litre tank positioned on the right-hand side of the fuselage behind the pilot. This air reserve was also used when starting the engine. The tailwheel, retractable on the prototype, was changed to fixed on production examples, and was partially protected by a fairing.

The open cockpit was located in the forward part of the fuselage structure and contained an adjustable seat and the oxygen system, with a 3-litre bottle pressurised at 150 atmospheres, providing an oxygen supply that matched the endurance of the aircraft. The fighter did not carry a radio.

The fuel system comprised two metal self-sealing tanks, the first mounted below the machine guns just forward of the firewall and containing 350 litres, the second 110-litre tank in a lower position just ahead of the cockpit, resulting in a total of 460 litres available which, at 5,500 m altitude and at a speed of 380 km/h, assured a range of around 850 km. The oil system, the two radiators for which were installed in the wing root, where the lower wings joined the fuselage, utilised a 34 kg tank mounted on the lower part of the firewall, while another emergency tank held around 2 litres, giving an effective total of 36 kg.

The control column with, on top, the brake button and the trigger lever for the two synchronized 12.7 mm SAFAT machine guns.

Above right: The control transmissions were rigid for the elevators and flexible for all other moving surfaces. A peculiarity of Italian aircraft was that the throttle travel functioned in a reverse manner compared to British, German and aircraft of today. To accelerate, the pilot had to pull the throttle backwards, while to decelerate it had to be pushed forward.

FIAT CR.42 FALCO

Above: Detail views of the instrument panel and the San Giorgio Tipo B gunsight of the restored CR.42 at The Fighter Collection at Duxford.

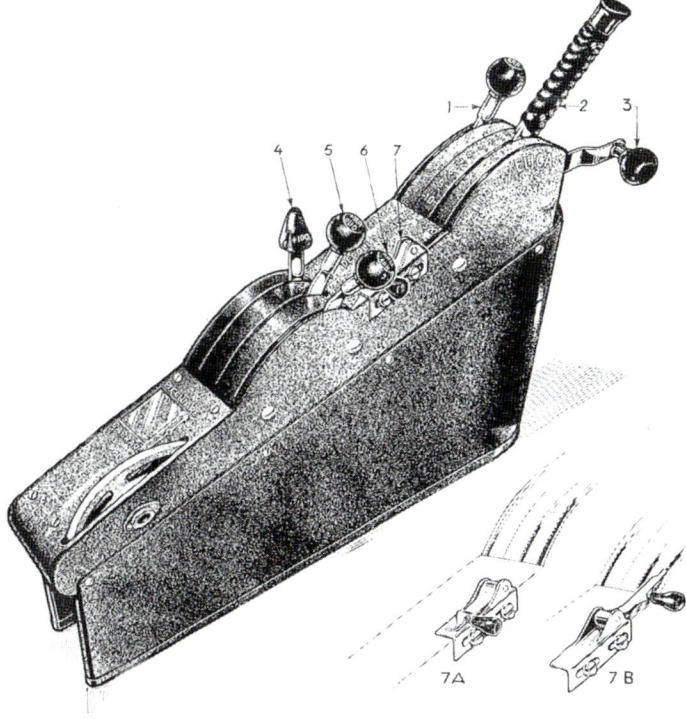

Fig. 55. — Disposizione delle leve di comando motore.

1. Leva di comando dell'arricchitore per il decollo e la salita. — 2. Leva del gas. — 3. Leva comando regolatore dell'elica a giri costanti. — 4. Leva comando soprapressione per il decollo. — 5. Leva comando parzializzatore del radiatore olio. — 6. Leva comando presa aria calda del carburatore. — 7. Piastrina d'arresto della leva 3 in posizione di 2400 giri. — 7 A. Piastrina in posizione di riposo: permette la corsa totale della leva 3 cioè fino al passo minimo (2520 giri). — 7 B. Piastrina ribaltata in avanti: arresta la leva 3 in posizione di 2400 giri.

Engine control console from the aircraft maintenance manual:
1) mixture; **2)** throttle; **3)** propeller; **4)** +100 (rpm); **5)** oil radiator control; **6)** carburettor air control; **7)** propeller lever stop; **7A)** off: 2,520 rpm allowed; **7B)** on: maximum 2,400 rpm.

Fig. 37. — Schema del cruscotto laterale destro.

LEGGENDA
1 - Indicatore di livello.
2 - Orologio.
3 - Telepirometro.
4 - Commutatore per telepirometro.
5 - Bottone sincronizzazione arma sul motore.
6 - Bottone idem.
7 - Inalatore ossigeno.
8 - Magnetino d'avviam.
9 - Pulsante iniettore pneumatico.
10 - Rubinetto avviamento motore.
11 - Reostato per collimatore.
12 - Rubinetto per riarmo pneumatico.

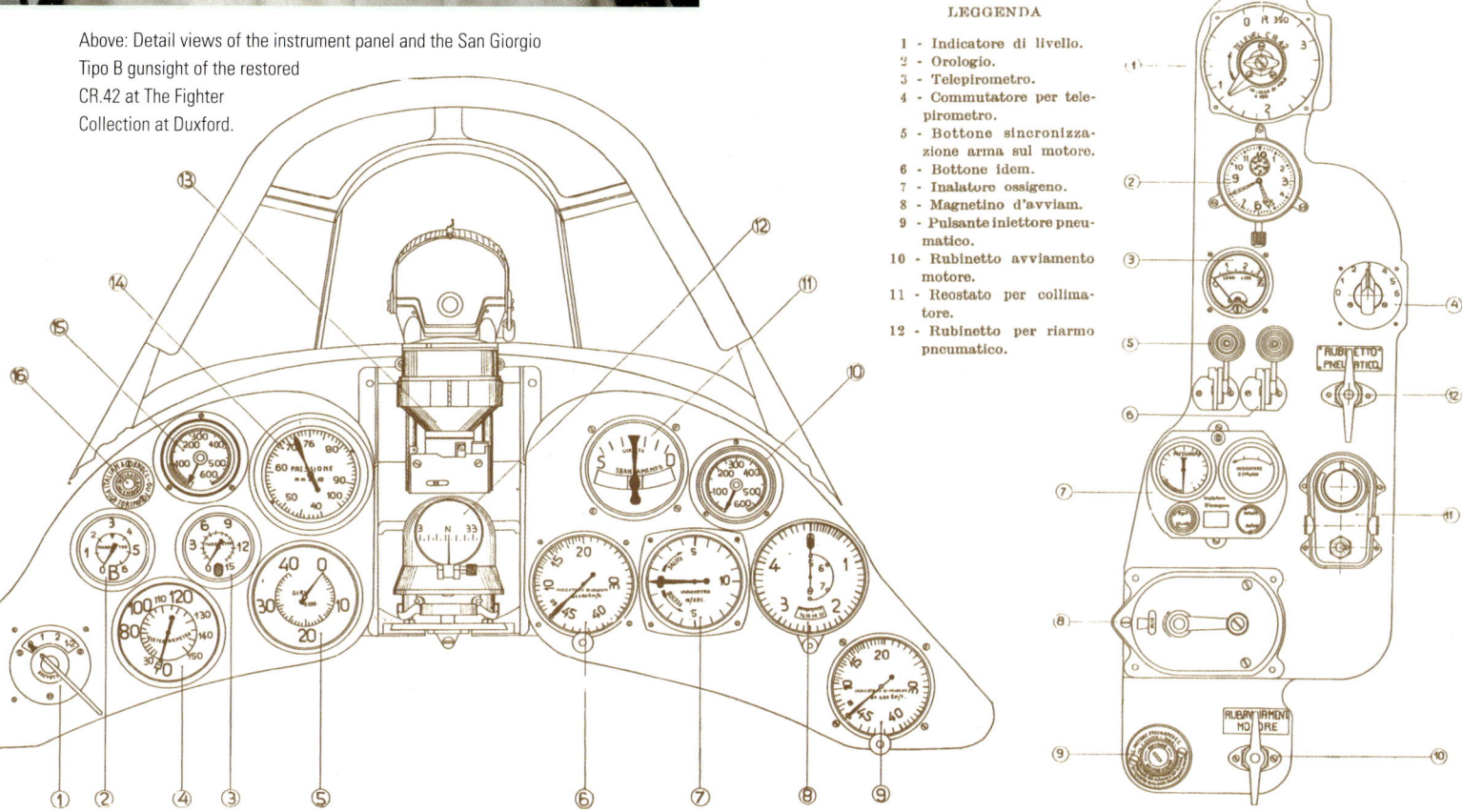

LEGGENDA
1 - Commutatore d'accensione.
2 - Manometro benzina.
3 -   »   olio.
4 - Teletermometro.
5 - Contagiri.
6 - Indicatore di velocità.
7 - Indicatore di salita e discesa.
8 - Altimetro.
9 - Indicatore di velocità.
10 - Contacolpi arma destra.
11 - Indicatore di virata.
12 - Bussola.
13 - Traguardo di puntamento.
14 - Indicatore di pressione.
15 - Contacolpi arma sinistra.
16 - Avvisatore d'incendio.

Fig. 33. — Schema del cruscotto centrale.

Left and above: Main instrument panel and sub-panel from the aircraft maintenance manual.

Far left and above: The CR.42 engine was faired in an elegant NACA cowling and drove a 2.8-metre, three-bladed FIAT Hamilton variable pitch, constant speed propeller. The cowling joined the upper fuselage with a slight bulge under which were accommodated the aircraft's two machine guns.

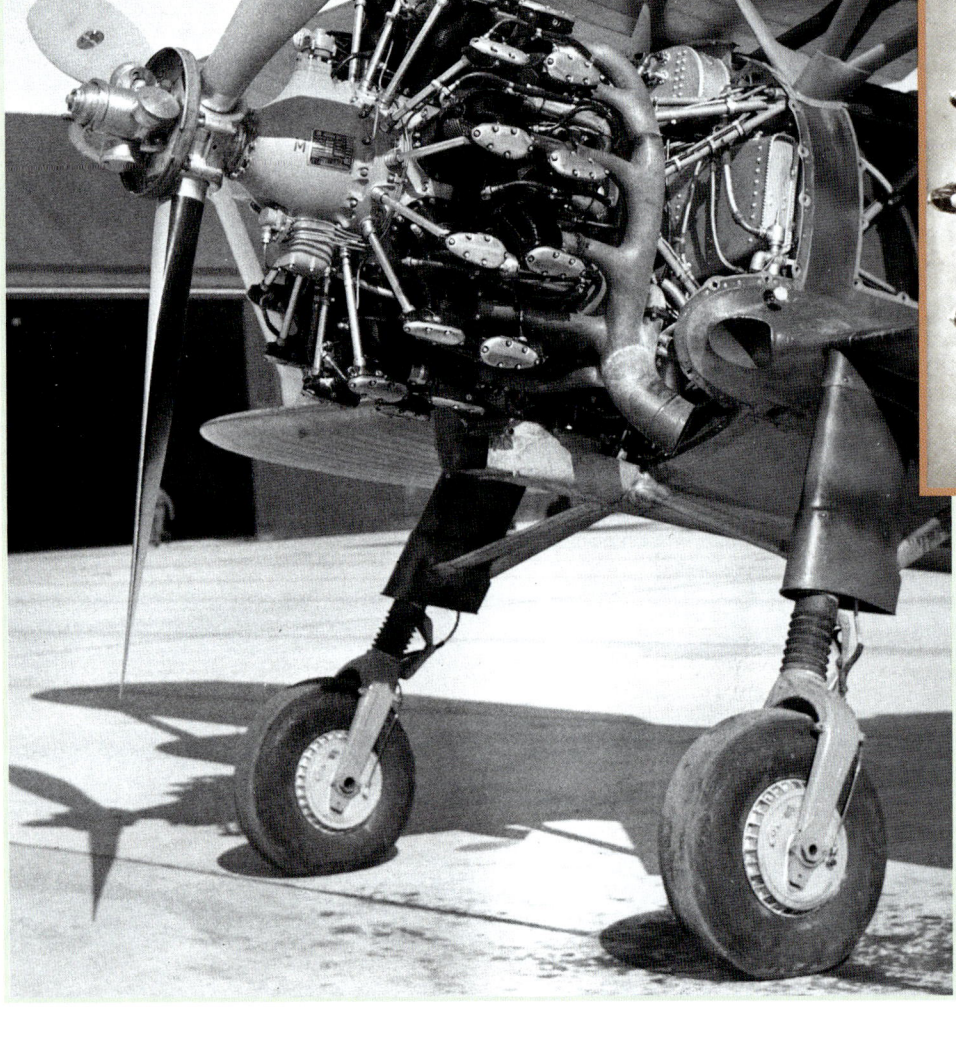

Left and above: The FIAT A.74 RC38 engine, equipped with reduction gear and supercharger, was rated for a maximum output of 840 hp at 2,400 rpm, with a 790-mm manifold pressure at 3,800 m altitude.

Installed within a Magni-NACA cowling was the FIAT A.74 R1C.38 14 cylinder, twin-row engine, air-cooled, and fitted with a compressor and reducer, delivering maximum power of 840 hp at 2,400 rpm at 3,800 m and 740 hp take-off power. The three-bladed variable pitch FIAT propeller rotated to the right and had an overall diameter of 2.8 m.

A negative aspect of this engine in the CR.42 was the fact that the R1C.38 designation identified it as a special version of the A.74 engine, with a reduced engine/propeller reduction ratio intended to avoid over-revving problems during the dive. Together with other details, such as the elimination of the hydraulic pump starter, the overall result was that the A.74 mounted on the CR.42 was very different from the version installed in other aircraft of the period, creating understandable maintenance, spares support, and logistical problems.

The principal armament comprised two Breda SAFAT 7.7 mm calibre machine guns with 500 rounds per gun, synchronised to fire through the propeller disk and fired by the pilot by pressing a switch on the control column. Below the weapons, behind the ammunition magazine box, was a box that collected the spent cartridges and used ammunition belts. One of the two guns could be substituted by a Breda SAFAT Mod 1928 7.7 mm calibre machine gun to save weight. Furthermore, during the war CR.42s were modified with the installation of underwing racks to support the use of 100-kg bombs, and at least six aircraft were afforded the possibility for a Rb50 camera to be installed. For gun aiming the pilot utilised a San Giorgio *tipo* B reflector gunsight.

Technical Data*

Length	8.257 m
Height	3.585 m
Wingspan upper	9.7 m
Wingspan lower	6.5 m
Wing area	22.40 m2
Empty weight	1,730 kg
Max T/O weight	2,295 kg
Powerplant	Fiat A.74 R1c38
Power at 3,800 m	840 hp
Max speed at 5,300 m	428 km/h
Max speed at sea level	342 km/h
Cruising speed	380 km/h
Minimum speed	128 km/h
Climb to 1,000 m	1'25"
Climb to 3,000 m	4'15"
Climb to 6,000 m	9'10"
Ceiling	10,050 m
Normal range	775 km
Take-off run	210 m
Landing roll	340 m
Armament	2 x 12.7mm machine guns; up to 100 kg bombs

* Data extracted from *Manuale Istruzione e Norme di Montaggio, Regolazione e Impiego del velivolo CR.42*, 1940.

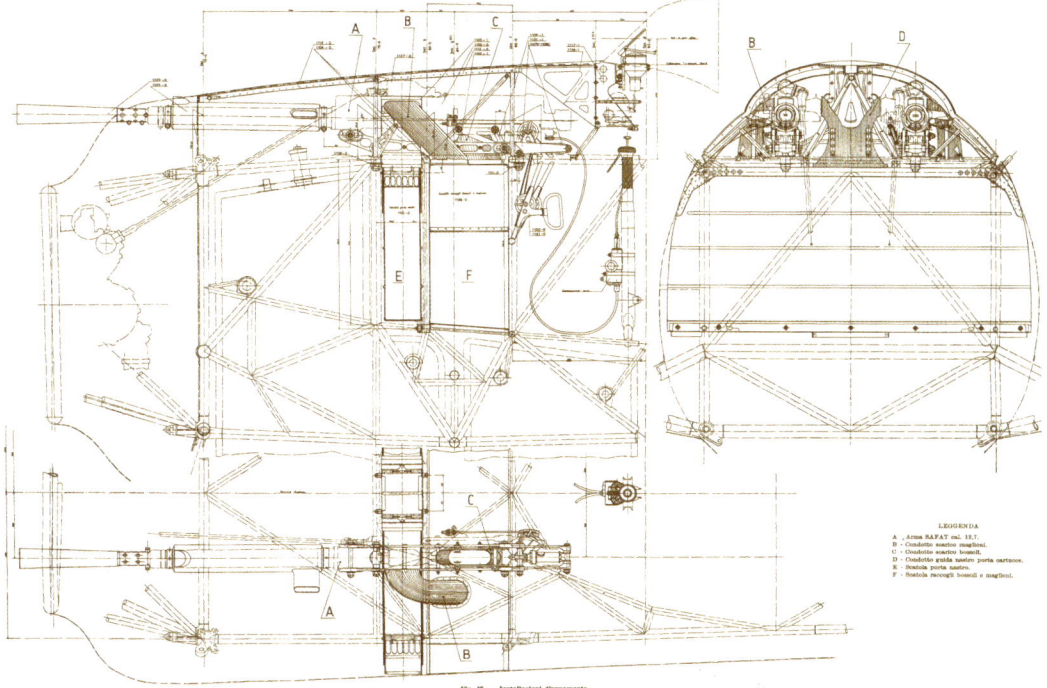

Drawing of the twin machine gun installation taken from the aircraft maintenance manual: **A**) SAFAT 50 machine gun; **B**) link discharge duct; **C**) spent cartridge discharge duct; **D**) ammunition feed chute; **E**) ammunition magazine; **F**) link and spent cartridge collector.

Detail photograph of The Fighter Collection's CR.42 showing **E**, the ammunition magazine and **F**, the link and spent cartridge collector, as in the drawing above.

Some CR.42s were modified internally in the fuselage, similar to the CR.32 in the photograph at right, in order to accommodate AC.81 type cameras.

Above: In early 1941, the urgent need for a ground-attack aircraft gave rise to the CR.42/ba ('wing bombs') equipped with Angeloni type bomb pylons capable of supporting weights of up to 100 kg per wing or bombs of different weights and numbers until the set weight was reached.

Above and below: An interesting sequence of photographs showing the fitting of 50-kg bombs as used normally on the CR.42AS. This variant equipped three *Stormi* and *altre Squadriglie autonome* until the Armistice.

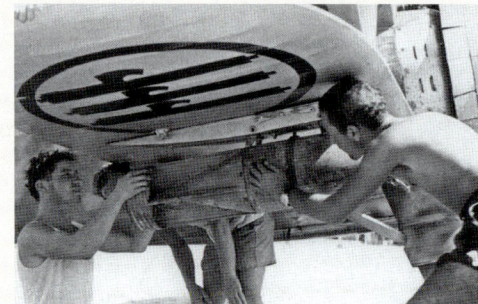

The FIAT CR.42 in service

The situation on 10 June 1940

A CR.42 from the 369ª *Squadriglia* of the 152° *Gruppo* of the 54° *Stormo* CT at Treviso which operated biplanes received from the 4° *Stormo* for a while in 1939. Paradoxically, a few months later, the two *Stormi* exchanged aircraft again with the 54° *Stormo*, which was re-equipped with AerMacchi C.200s. (F.Ballista)

ON the outbreak of war in Europe in September 1939, the CR.42 equipped three units of the Regia Aeronautica, while another five were equipped with the CR.32 and one each operated the G.50 and C.200.

On 10 June 1940, the date on which Italy initiated hostilities, the CR.42 'Falco' with more than 300 aircraft in service, 200 of which were combat ready, represented 40% of the entire fighter force. The units equipped with the biplane were, on that date, drawn up in the ranks of the 1ª *Squadra Aerea*, and comprised the 53° *Stormo* which had received its first aircraft in May 1939, composed of the 150° *Gruppo* at Torino Caselle with the 363ª, 364ª and 365ª *Squadriglie*, and the 151° *Gruppo* at Casabianca (Torino). Another unit completely equipped with the *Falco* was the 3° *Stormo*, with bases at Novi Ligure (Alessandria) and Albenga (Savona) airfields, being composed of the 83ª, 85ª and 95ª *Squadriglie* of the 18° *Gruppo*, and the 23° *Gruppo* based at Cervere (Cuneo).

A unit with a mixed fleet of CR.32s and CR.42s was the 1° *Stormo*, parented by the 2ª *Squadra Aerea*, which had recently moved to Palermo housing the 17° *Gruppo* and at Trapani,

Unidentified CR.42s operating from an airfield in Italy during the early weeks of war for Italy.

Above: An Italian promotional postcard depicting FIAT CR.42s published in 1939 when the first biplane fighters began operations with the Regia Aeronautica. (P.Monti)

CR.42s of the 85ª *Squadriglia*, 18° *Gruppo*, 3° *Stormo* CT at Torino Mirafiori taken a few days before the attack on France. The pilot on the bicycle is *sergente* Bortolotti. (F. Bortolotti)

FIAT FIGHTERS

At the end of 1939 the 18° *Gruppo* of 3° *Stormo* CT operated from Mondovì airport, in the Piemonte region.

Below: The commander of 18° *Gruppo*, *maggiore* Ferruccio Vossilla, stands next to one of his unit's CR.42s at Albenga, where it operated during the short war with France.

which was the home of the 157° *Gruppo*. The final unit based in Italy with the *Falco* was the 9° *Gruppo* of the 4° *Stormo* CT, controlling the 73ª, 96ª and 97ª *Squadriglie*. At the beginning of the conflict, the CR.42 equipped numerous units outside Italy, such as the 13° *Gruppo* of the 2° *Stormo* at Castelbenito and the 10° *Gruppo* of the 4° *Stormo* at Tobruk, with the 84ª, 90ª and 91ª, *Squadriglie*. These two units also had a mixed fleet, as they were in the process of replacing their old CR.32s with the new biplane. In *Africa Orientale Italiana* (Italian East Africa), the *Falco* equipped the 412ª *Squadriglia* at Massaua and Gura and the 413ª *Squadriglia* at Assab.

Order of Battle

Fiat CR.42 units, 10 June 1940

1a *Squadra Aerea*, Milano
2a *Divisione Aerea* 'Borea', Caselle Torinese

3° *Stormo* CT based Novi Ligure
18° *Gruppo* CT – based Novi Ligure
83ª *Squadriglia* based Novi Ligure
85ª *Squadriglia* based Albenga
95ª *Squadriglia* based Novi Ligure
23° *Gruppo* CT based Cervere
70ª *Squadriglia*
74ª *Squadriglia*
75ª *Squadriglia*

53° *Stormo* CT based Caselle Torinese
150° *Gruppo* CT based Caselle Torinese
363ª *Squadriglia*
364ª *Squadriglia*
365ª *Squadriglia*
151° Gruppo CT based Casabianca
366ª *Squadriglia*
367ª *Squadriglia*
368ª *Squadriglia*

4° STORMO CT based at Gorizia
9° Gruppo CT
73ª *Squadriglia*
96ª *Squadriglia*
97ª *Squadriglia*

2a *Squadra Aerea*, Milano
1a *Divisione Aerea* 'Aquila', Palermo

1° *Stormo* CT based Palermo Boccadifalco
17° *Gruppo* based Palermo Boccadifalco
(still equipped with CR.32)
71ª *Squadriglia*
72ª *Squadriglia*
80ª *Squadriglia*
157° *Gruppo* CT
384ª *Squadriglia*
385ª *Squadriglia*
386ª *Squadriglia*

***Aeronautica Della Libia*, Tripoli**

2° *Stormo* CT based Castelbenito
13° *Gruppo* CT based Castelbenito
(converting from CR.32 to CR.42)
77ª *Squadriglia*
78ª *Squadriglia*
82ª *Squadriglia*
8° *Gruppo* CT based Tobruk T2
92ª *Squadriglia*
93ª *Squadriglia*
94ª *Squadriglia*

4° *Stormo* CT based Tobruk T2
10° *Gruppo* CT based Tobruk T2
84ª *Squadriglia*
90ª *Squadriglia*
91ª *Squadriglia*

***Comando Aeronautico Africa Orientale Italiana*, Addis Ababa**

412ª *Squadriglia* CT based Massaua and Gura
413ª *Squadriglia* CT based Assab

The French Campaign – June 1940

On 10 June 1940, the date of Italy's entry into the war, the operational units of the Regia Aeronautica had been on a war footing for several days. Amongst these units was the 3° *Stormo*, which was the first fighter unit to be called into action on 13 June, although throughout the previous days some of its CR.42s had been tasked with responding to reports of aircraft over Genova and conducting patrols along the French border. The principal duties assigned to the pilots of the 3° *Stormo* were the provision of bomber escort and the strafing of French airfields in Provence. Consequently, in the early morning of 13 June, when operations commenced against the French, the 23° *Gruppo Caccia* sent 23 CR 42s into action, tasked with machine-gunning the airfields at Fayence where no claims were made while 151° and 150° *Gruppo* strafed Hyéres, where some 20 French aircraft were claimed hit on the ground and a Chance Vought V-156 Vindicator of AB3 was shot down. During this first mission, the Italian fighters encountered no opposition from French fighters, despite the fact that in the south of France there were units equipped with aircraft superior to the Italian biplanes, such as the excellent Dewoitine D 520 and the Bloch 152. On the following 15 June, 67 CR.42s drawn from the 18° and 23° *Gruppo* of the 3° *Stormo* and the 150° *Gruppo* of the 53° *Stormo* conducted strafing attacks in the morning on Cuers and Cannet des Maures airfields, destroying or badly damaging around 15 French aircraft on the ground (D520 and MS406 of GC III/6, V-156 of AB3 and a British Douglas civil aircraft). This attack was, however, opposed by French fighters, and the fighters of the 18° *Gruppo*, in particular, engaged in multiple clashes with the Bloch 151s of Aeronavale fighter squadron AC 3, and with the Dewoitine D.520s of GC III/6 'Roussillon'. Despite the French fighters being decidedly more modern than the Italian aircraft, and flown by pilots of the highest level, such as Cap Assolant and *Adj* Le Gloan, the Italian fighter pilots managed to destroy in combat at least four French Bloch 151 fighters, and heavily damaging two more despite claiming ten as destroyed. Five CR.42s were lost, one of which made an emergency landing for technical reasons with the capture of its pilot, and a BR.20 bomber was lost. Over the following days, complicated by poor weather, the Italian fighters were essentially utilised for patrol missions along the Ligurian coastline and to protect the city of Genova. On 21 June the 23° *Gruppo* was relocated to Villanova d'Albenga airfield as the runway at Cervere had become unusable because of the abundant rain. On the same day, and for several to follow, the Italians launched an operation to push across the Alpine border with France in order to capture territory which could subsequently be claimed around the peace table.

For this operation, the Italian fighters were used to protect BR.20 bombers and also to attack French positions immediately behind the front line. Despite intense operational activity, the results were in part impeded by the weather conditions, with cloud which frequently prevented the identification of targets. The weather also highlighted the difficulties encountered by pilots in operations at very high altitudes.

On 22 June CR.42s were engaged in what was probably the last operational sortie for the FIAT fighter during the brief conflict with France when the escorted S.79s engaged in bombing the French port of Biserta. Two weeks after the start of combat operations, on 24 June 1940, an armistice was signed with France, and the 23° *Gruppo* moved to Torino Mirafiori while the 18° *Gruppo* remained at Villanova d'Albenga.

During the brief campaign against France, CR.42 operations had totalled more than 1,750 flying hours. Ten French aircraft had been shot down, and around fifty damaged or destroyed on the ground by eleven strafing attacks. For its actions during the French campaign the 3° *Stormo* CT was decorated with the *Medaglia d'Argento al Valor Militare*. A few days after the end of hostilities with France, however, on 9 July 1940 the *Comando* of the 3° *Stormo* CT was informed that its two *gruppi* would be reassigned to other units and the *Stormo*, without operational *gruppi*, was placed at 'quadro' status in the following month of September.

A CR.42 of the 367ª *Squadriglia* of 151° *Gruppo* of 53° *Stormo* CT. At the time the aircraft of the Regia Aeronautica still had the Italian tricolour painted on their rudders, but this was later changed to the Savoy Cross so as not avoid confusion with the aircraft of the French Armée de l'Air. (F.Ballista)

A FIAT CR.42 of the 150° *Gruppo* of 53° *Stormo* CT flying over the peaks of the Western Alps while on armed reconnaissance duties over the French-Italian frontier. (F.Ballista)

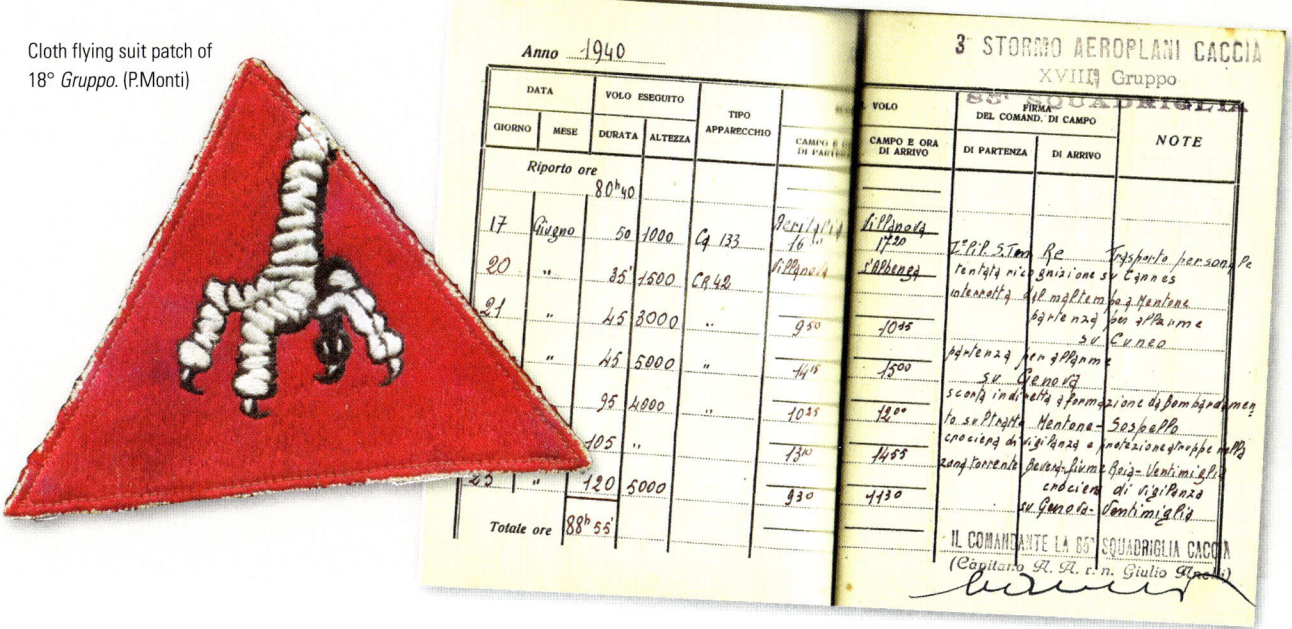

Cloth flying suit patch of 18° *Gruppo*. (P.Monti)

A page from the logbook of *sergente* Guido Fibbia of 85ª *Squadriglia* of 18° *Gruppo* of 3° *Stormo* CT showing operational combat patrols over Genoa and the Ligurian coast. (F.Ballista)

Fiat CR.42s of the 85ª *Squadriglia* based at Albenga in early June 1940 on a patrol flight over Genoa. (R.Gentilli)

Operations in Italian East Africa

(Africa Orientale Italiana – A.O.I.)

Capitano Santoro with a CR.42 of the 413ª *Squadriglia Autonoma* is greeted by ground personnel on 20 August 1940 after returning from a mission having shot down the Blenheim Mk.I, L8474, of 39 Squadron, RAF. (F.Sanetti)

WHEN Italy entered the war on 10 June 1940, the CR.42 was assigned to two autonomous operational *squadriglie*, the 412ª and 413ª which possessed a combined strength of 36 aircraft. The two *squadriglie* were assigned to the northern operational sector, the 412ª *Squadriglia* being based at Massaua and Gura, commanded by *capitano* Antonio Raffi, and the 413ª *Squadriglia* at Assab, commanded by *capitano* Corrado Santoro. A third *squadriglia,* the 414ª, was constituted immediately after the beginning of the war, although it had only limited strength.

On 12 June the CR.42s in the AOI theatre had their baptism of fire when fighters of the 412ª *Squadriglia* intercepted a formation of Vickers Wellesleys over Asmara. One of the British bombers was severely damaged and was eventually destroyed in an attempted forced landing. Two days later, *tenente* Mario Visintini, also of the 412ª *Squadriglia*, recorded the first of seventeen victories credited to him in East Africa

A CR.42 of 413ª *Squadriglia Autonoma* takes off from Dire Daua. (F.Sanetti)

A CR.42 of 413ª *Squadriglia Autonoma* in flight over Somaliland in August 1940. (Asso4Stormo)

A CR.42 of the 413ª *Squadriglia Autonoma*. (R.Gentilli)

Insignia in cloth of the 410ª *Squadriglia Autonoma*. (P.Monti)

Insignia badge of 412ª *Squadriglia Autonoma*. (P.Monti))

when he shot down Vickers Wellesley K7743 of 14 Squadron flown by P/O Reginald Patrick Blenner Plunkett, which together with Wellesley L2652, was en route to bomb Massaua.

On 6 November 1940 CR.42s of the 412ª *Squadriglia*, led by *capitano* Antonio Raffi, clashed with Gladiators of 1 Squadron SAAF and at the conclusion of the dogfight they had shot down five of the British aircraft. Also on 6 November, another flight of Gladiators, preparing to attack a formation of Caproni Ca.133 bombers, was intercepted by CR.42s. A sixth Gladiator was hit and claimed as destroyed by the Italian pilots, who returned to their own base unscathed.

Asmara, 12 December 1940. During a strafing run over Ghez Regheb airfield, *capitano* Antonio Raffi along with his fellow pilots, destroyed four Hawker Hardys. Raffi's aircraft was hit in its oil tank however, and on his return flight he was forced to land in British occupied territory. *Tenente* Visintini (in the white helmet) landed next to him and, taking Raffi on board, as shown in this doctored photograph (to recreate the event), brought him back to their base. (L.Slongo)

A.O.I. were often deployed on ground-attack and in the strafing of enemy troops and airfields. Such intense activity, however, resulted in a significant number of losses, and with the difficulties in delivering replacement aircraft to this region by ship, it was decided to organise an air bridge, utilising the capacious holds of SM.82 transports which, with only minor internal adjustments, could accommodate a complete CR.42. For ferry flights the CR.42 was partially dismantled, the fuselage being positioned longitudinally in through the wide ventral bay doors, and the wings and propeller placed along the internal sides of the transport. Between 23 August 1940 and 28 March 1941, fifty-one of these delivery flights were completed, reinforcing, albeit not in sufficient quantity, the by then exhausted units.

In the initial phases of the war, the *Falcos* coped well against the RAF and SAAF in the

Below and right: Since it was not possible to supply fighter reinforcements to the A.O.I. by air, they could only arrive by means of SM.82s, the only transport aircraft with the capacity to carry a dismantled FIAT CR.42 plus a spare engine and wings. Between 23 August 1940 and 28 March 1941, fifty-one of these delivery flights had been completed.

Worthy of mention is a mission flown on 12 December 1940, when five CR.42s of the 412ª *Squadriglia*, guided by an S.79, were tasked with attacking the airfield at Ghez Regeb, in eastern Sudan, the base of an element of the RAF's 237 Rhodesian Squadron. While two CR.42s remained at altitude to provide top cover, three more launched an attack, strafing the parked Hawker Hardys, destroying four aircraft and causing significant damage to equipment and infrastructure on repeated strafing passes. During its last pass, the CR.42 of *capitano* Antonio Raffi, the 412ª *Squadriglia* commander, was hit, the pilot being forced to make an emergency landing in British occupied territory. Without hesitation, *tenente* Visintini landed alongside. After setting the damaged CR.42 alight and having discarded his parachute, Raffi climbed into Visintini's CR.42 and the pair flew safely back to their base at Asmara.

The vast extent of the front, the different operational sectors which ranged from Sudan to Kenya, from Somaliland to Aden, from French Somalia to the Red Sea, the scarcity of supplies, the modest existing infrastructure, the environmental, orographic, logistical difficulties, and the insecurity of certain areas which were not pacified, created technical, logistical and, not least, physical and morale challenges for Italian personnel required to function in a torrid climate amidst desert and mountainous terrain. The environmental and material difficulties were accompanied by opposition from well-armed and aggressive British forces which possessed human and technical resources that the Italians could only dream of, this enabling them to conduct combat operations against Italian forces with a continuity and confidence across all the operational sectors.

Besides operating in the usual fighter and bomber escort roles, the CR.42s operating in the

Gondar, October 1941. The last airworthy CR.42 in the A.O.I., MM7117 of *tenente* Ildebrando Malavolta (MOVM) prepares to take off to carry out one of the last missions of the Regia Aeronautica in East Africa.

Left: *Tenente* Malavolta probably photographed before his last mission. On 24 October 1941 he volunteered to carry out a visual reconnaissance over a small bridge at Kulkaber despite the adverse views of his commander because of the known presence in the area of a large number of enemy forces, particularly aircraft of No.3 Squadron SAAF. Malavolta took off for the mission, but his comrades waited for his return in vain. Malavolta's fate was known the following day when a 3 Squadron SAAF Gladiator dropped a message over the Italian positions at Ambazzo: 'Tributes to the pilot of the FIAT. He was a brave man. South African Air Force.'

Below: One of the last CR.42s still in Italian East Africa was captured by the British. Most likely an inoperable aircraft, it had no unit markings but on the fuselage it retained the St. Andrew's Cross as used during the last period of fighting. (R.Gentilli)

African theatre engaging mainly Gloster Gladiators, Fairey Battles, Vickers Wellesleys and Hawker Harts. However, this would change radically with the arrival in theatre of the Hawker Hurricane, and in the spring of 1941, with the arrival of British reinforcements, the Italians gradually began to lose their strongholds. By October 1941 only the garrison at Gondar was still resisting, and there were just two CR.42s in flying condition. It was in one of these two remaining serviceable aircraft that *sottotenente* Ildebrando Malavolta met his death, the last Italian pilot to be involved in an aerial battle in the theatre, when, during an armed reconnaissance mission, he was attacked by some South African Gladiators. After an uneven dogfight, they managed to shoot down the courageous Italian pilot. The following day, a British fighter dropped a message on the airfield at Gondar honouring the courage of the pilot in his isolated action against the Gladiators.

The dramatic situation and the state of mind of the men in the A.O.I. is well evidenced in the following letter sent by *sergente maggiore* Antonio Giardinà to his commander, *capitano* Corrado Ricci, who had been repatriated some weeks earlier for health reasons:

Gondar, 23 July 1941
Signor capitano Ricci,

Within a few days an aircraft should arrive from Italia, and in the hope of offering you a little pleasure, I am taking this occasion to let you have some African news and some about the survivors of the glorious 410ª. Puliti was taken prisoner at Amba Alagi. Sottotenente Folcherio and Volpe, with sottotenente Lusardi, tenente Caputo and others left here in

a Ca 148 and stopped at Jeddah. Here there are just three pilots remaining with two CR.42 aircraft: *sottotenente* Malavolta, *maresciallo* Mottet and myself. From Alomatà I was transferred to Sciasciamanna and then on to Gimma. In the latter area I shot down a Junkers and a Hurricane. I have been decorated with the Medaglia di Bronzo in the field for some important reconnaissance and escort flights, and within days I will be awarded the Medaglia d'Argento. Here at Gondar, I shot down a Wellesley in collaboration with *maresciallo* Mottet, and one morning, during two scrambles lasting together around an hour, I shot down a Blenheim in the first and a Wellesley in the second, and I hit another two. So, these five will be added to the other victories of the 410a. For the action over Giggiga we have been proposed by His Royal Highness, the Duca d'Aosta for a Medaglia d'Argento, which will be awarded at the end of the war.

I am very calm, and I don't, in fact, believe that I will become a prisoner; however, sometimes I ask myself if mine isn't an illusion, when I expect to see a powerful fighter squadron arrive, naturally commanded by you, and with which we can do the same damage to our friends in the Hurricanes as they have done to us, and that they have been doing in recent days. I would like to remain in Africa for several more years to see if this dream of mine comes true. Despite everything, I hope so, and I will not give up, even if the enemy were to occupy Gondar. The base is commanded by colonnello Busoni, a good commander, well-liked by all of us. The entire air force of our empire is present here with our two fighters and a Ca 133, badly hit in recent days, but already nearly serviceable... The end of the glorious CR.32 occurred at Gimma; for ours, I hope it never happens, or is very late, when we no longer need it. Everyone, especially me, is waiting for your promise to be fulfilled: 'I will return with a squadriglia of RE 2000s...' I hope so, and I wish it to come true for you, because you have many things to avenge here. A few days ago, needing a spare part for an engine, I went to recover the remains of poor Omiccioli's aircraft. I also placed a wreath of flowers on his grave in the name of all the members of the 410a. All of us hope to resist until your arrival ...

On 22 November the last serviceable CR.42 present in Italian East Africa, flown by *maresciallo* Mottet, conducted the final mission for its type over this difficult and battle-weary front, attacking British artillery positions. When it returned from this last flight it was to a base without any more bombs or ammunition. The CR.42, now redundant, was burnt at Gondar on 26 November 1941 to avoid it falling into enemy hands, bringing an inglorious closure to the glorious pages of the history of the Regia Aeronautica in *Africa Orientale Italiana*.

MARIO VISINTINI

DECORATED with the *Medaglia d'Oro al Valor Militare*, Visintini was first among the aces of the Regia Aeronautica and the pilot with the highest number of aerial victories of all the belligerent air forces in the A.O.I.

Flying the CR.42, he obtained seventeen confirmed victories and another seven probables, which have to be added to those he is credited with from the Spanish Civil War during operations with the *Aviazione Legionaria*.

His involvement in an action of 12 December 1940 was celebrated; Visintini saved his commander, bringing him back to base in his single-seat aircraft, a feat that resulted in a promotion to *capitano* 'per meriti di guerra' – on merit.

In the course of fifty air combats he shot down at least five British Blenheims, and an even greater number of Wellesleys, as well as three Hurricanes. To these should be added those destroyed on the ground at Gadaref and Agordat airfields, which according to British sources cost the RAF tens of aircraft. On 11 February 1941, by then promoted to *capitano*, Visintini took off from Asmara for his last flight, which, ironically, was not a combat sortie intended against British fighters, but rather a rescue mission, searching for two pilots who had been forced to land in the desert due to bad weather. Unfortunately, Visintini flew into a thick bank of fog over Nefasit and with the total lack of visibility, crashed into one of the slopes of Mount Bizen.

Sottotenente Mario Visintini in front of a CR.32 of the 25ª *Squadriglia* 'Cucaracha', August 1938.

Tenente Mario Visintini stands by his personal CR.42 with Ebro, a canine mascot. (L.Slongo)

Operations in the central Mediterranean

One of the FIAT CR.42s of the 385ª *Squadriglia* of 157° *Gruppo*, 1° *Stormo* CT photographed at Trapani 'Milo' field. (E.Leproni)

OPERATING in Sicilia with a mixed fleet of CR.42s and CR.32s at the outbreak of hostilities was the 157° *Gruppo* of the 1° *Stormo* CT, (384ª, 385ª and 386ª *Squadriglie*), a unit which became autonomous in early July 1940. From July 1940 the FIAT biplanes of the 157° *Gruppo* were joined by 29 CR.42s of the 9° *Gruppo* of the 4° *Stormo Caccia*, commanded by *maggiore* Ernesto Botto, and detached to Comiso airfield with its 73ª, 96ª and 97ª *Squadriglie*. For a period, these biplanes provided the principal fighter escorts for the bombers engaged in countering British naval traffic in the central Mediterranean. Additionally, since the new AerMacchi C.200s of the first series, operated by the 6° *Gruppo Autonomo CT*, had been plagued by a series of technical issues that eventually resulted in the suspension of their operational activities, the biplanes also conducted attacks against the island of Malta.

On the day after their arrival in Sicilia, the CR.42s of the 9° *Gruppo* were tasked with their first operation over Malta, escorting a pair of S.79s from the 34° *Stormo BT* which conducted a photographic reconnaissance mission over Hal Far

Promotional postcards published in Italy in 1941. (P. Monti)

Left: CR.42s were the main escort aircraft for Italian bombers over both the Mediterranean and Balkan theatres in the first year of war.

airfield. The mission was completed without contact with the British fighters defending the island, at the time comprising a few Gloster Gladiators of the Hal Far Fighter Flight and the first Hurricanes which had been delivered at the start of July for operations with 261 Squadron.

A very different outcome befell the mission of 3 July 1940, when nine CR.42s escorting S.79s on a photographic reconnaissance mission clashed with some of the newly arrived Hurricanes. The intervention of the Italian fighters failed to

prevent one of the S.79s being shot down by Hurricane Mk I P2614 piloted by F/O John Lawrence Waters which was, in turn, badly damaged by the Italian fighters. It was destroyed in a subsequent emergency landing at its base, the pilot escaping uninjured. The following day, 4 July 1940, twenty-four CR.42s, once again led by *maggiore* Botto, took off from Comiso for a strafing attack on Hal Far airfield, a mission which resulted in only damage to some Swordfish of 830 Squadron, while some CR.42s returned to Comiso with damage caused by the British base's anti-aircraft defences.

The biplanes of the 9° *Gruppo* were again tasked to protect S.79s engaged in photographing the military installations on the island, but they could achieve little against the much faster Hurricanes, which easily managed to penetrate the escorting defensive shield, and on 9 and 10 July three S.79s were shot down. On 11 July the 9° *Gruppo* received orders to relocate to North Africa, replaced at Comiso airfield by 29 CR.42s of the 23° *Gruppo Caccia Autonomo*, commanded by *maggiore* Tito Falconi, and comprising the 70ª, 74ª, and 75ª *Squadriglie*. In mid-July therefore, besides the CR.42s of the 23° *Gruppo*, the fighter fleet in Sicilia comprised the biplanes of the 17° *Gruppo* operating with the 71ª *Squadriglia Caccia* and 72ª *Squadriglia Caccia* at Palermo and the 80ª *Squadriglia Caccia* based at Trapani Milo flying a mixture of CR.42s and C.200s.

Early victories, and first losses

On 16 July 1940 the second victory by an Italian fighter over the island of Malta was recorded, but also the first loss of a fighter of the Regia Aeronautica. On that day the CR.42s of the 23° *Gruppo* had been sent to Malta on an offensive armed reconnaissance mission. To oppose them, the island defences scrambled F/Lt Peter Gardner Keeble in Hurricane Mk. I P2623 and F/Lt George Burges in Gladiator N5524 who engaged the Italian fighters. While attempting to attack a CR.42, Keeble was, in turn, attacked and hit by a pair of biplanes flown by *tenente* Maria Pinna and *sottotenente* Oscar Abello. The British aircraft crashed out of control near Fort Rinella. Just a few minutes later, the CR.42 MM4368, piloted by *tenente* Mario Benedetti of the 74ª *Squadriglia* crashed close to the wreckage of the British Hurricane. The British pilot was killed. The Italian pilot, Benedetti, survived the initial impact, but died soon afterwards at the civilian hospital, having succumbed to his injuries. In precedence, on 13 July, there had been another dogfight involving the CR.42s of the 23° *Gruppo*, but despite claims of victories reported by some Italian pilots, the British aircraft were heavily damaged.

Combat patrols and escort duties for bomber and reconnaissance protection continued over the following days, and on 21 July 1940 a Swordfish, which had descended to machine-gun some survivors of a ditched S.79, was shot down by a CR.42 of the 72ª *Squadriglia*, 17° *Gruppo*.

On 31 July 1940, eight CR.42s of the 75ª *Squadriglia*, escorting an S.79 on a photo-reconnaissance mission over the Mediterranean island were attacked by a Hurricane Mk. I and three Sea Gladiators, airborne from Kalafrana. At the end of the encounter the CR.42 of *capitano* Antonio Chiodi and Gladiator N5519 flown by F/O Hartley failed to return to their respective bases, the latter, however, managing to parachute to safety from his fighter despite the severe burns inflicted as his aircraft caught fire.

In the meantime, the defences of Malta had been significantly reinforced, with the delivery of further Hurricanes in early August, transported to the theatre by the carrier HMS *Argus*. With the arrival of these aircraft, on 2 August 1940, 261 Squadron was constituted, amalgamating under its control the remaining Gloster Gladiator and all the Hawker Hurricanes. On the morning of 24 August 1940, nineteen CR.42s of the 23° *Gruppo Autonomo*, led by *maggiore* Falconi, departed to provide direct and indirect escort to six S.79s sent to bomb Hal Far airfield. The British defences were quick to scramble four Hurricane Mk.Is of 261 Squadron, and the inevitable dogfight developed. The rounds fired by *tenente* Mario Rigatti of the 75ª *Squadriglia* damaged Hurricane Mk.I N2730 piloted by F/Lt. George Burges, forcing him to make a ruinous emergency landing. However, the Hurricane piloted by F/Lt Taylor hit, in turn, the CR. 42 of *sergente maggiore* Renzo Bocconi of the 74ª *Squadriglia*, who was forced to

Above and above right: CR.42s of 18° *Gruppo* photographed at Pantelleria's 'cave' hangar during the transfer of the unit to *Africa Settentrionale*. (R.Gentilli)

Sergente Bortolotti stands in front of a CR.42 of 23° *Gruppo* before the transfer of the unit to *Africa Settentrionale*. (F.Bortolotti)

This combat damaged CR.42 of the 75ª *Squadriglia*, 23° *Gruppo* returned home after operations in the skies over Malta.

A CR.42 of 74ª *Squadriglia* on patrol over the Sicilian coast.

CR.42s escorting Savoia-Marchetti S.79 bombers.

bail out over the sea and was captured by the British. During the dogfight, the CR.42 flown by *tenente* Rigatti was struck in numerous locations but Rigatti, who was injured, managed with difficulty to return to Comiso, clinging on to life due to the abundant loss of blood from his injuries. Having resumed his service, for his action over Malta *tenente* Rigatti was decorated with the *Medaglia d'Oro al Valor Militare*, the medal being attached to his chest by Benito Mussolini in person during a visit to the unit. From September 1940 the CR.42s of the 23° *Gruppo* also began to escort Italian Stukas engaged in attacking targets on Malta, while in the same month the *Gruppo* received the residual CR.42s left in Sicilia by the 157° *Gruppo* of the 1° *Stormo* CT, which had returned to Torino to transition onto new aircraft.

In the meantime, the island fortress of Malta had been further reinforced, although in mid-November, a further despatch of Hurricanes airborne from HMS *Argus* was not successful: the majority of the fighters were launched too early and only four managed to land on Malta, while another ten failed to reach the island after running out of fuel.

On 23 November 1940 a violent dogfight took place involving eighteen CR.42s of the 23° *Gruppo Aut.* CT and eight Hurricane Mk.Is from 261 Squadron. Despite numerous claims, only one Hurricane was destroyed, and this following an emergency landing, while the CR.42s returned safely to Comiso. On the following evening six CR.42s strafed Luqa airfield, and on their return, having been hit by anti-aircraft fire, *tenente* Ezio Monti was forced to bail out from his damaged fighter. The anti-aircraft defences on the island proved to be dangerously effective and on 26 July *tenente* Giuseppe Beccaria of 23° *Gruppo* was probably shot down by Hurricane N2701 of Sgt. Kenneth Dennis Ashton. The British pilot was killed after this combat when he was shot down by the CR.42 piloted by *capitano* Guido Bobba. On the 28th, *sergente maggiore* Arnaldo Sala, failed to return to base, having probably been shot down or damaged by anti-aircraft fire. He was lost without trace.

With the situation in North Africa becoming increasingly difficult following the British counter-offensive and the loss of Cyrenaica, on 16 December 1940 the 23° *Gruppo* was ordered to relocate to Castelbenito, leaving just a few operational aircraft at Comiso. From 20 January 1941, and following the delivery of other aircraft, they went on to constitute the fleet of the newly created 156° *Gruppo Caccia* CT, organised around the 379ª and 380ª *Squadriglie*.

The unit was equipped with eighteen CR.42s. Meanwhile, in late January 1941 the units in Sicilia equipped with the FIAT biplane were the

A CR.42 of the 156° *Gruppo Autonomo* CT. Under the command of *capitano* Luigi Filippi, the unit was established from the 379ª and 380ª *Squadriglia* from the three 'bis' units of the 23° *Gruppo* CT remaining in Sicily. The white band around the fuselage, also known as the optical band, became necessary for quick recognition by German aircraft, and was first adopted on the Greek-Albanian front where serious incidents had occurred.

Below: A CR.42 of the 70ª *Squadriglia*, 23° *Gruppo Caccia* in Libya during the evacuation of Cyrenaica.

17° *Gruppo* of the 1° *Stormo* at Trapani, with the 71ª, 72ª and 80ª *Squadriglie* equipped with CR.42s and, incredibly, a few CR.32s, alongside the new 156° *Gruppo Autonomo* CT at Comiso airfield. The latter unit, however, would have a short existence, as in April 1941 it was re-absorbed into the 23° *Gruppo Autonomo* CT when it returned to Comiso from North Africa.

As the Malta theatre had become a stalemate, and with problematic situations on the Albanian and North African fronts, Italian forces were obliged to accept assistance from Germany, which came to fruition at the beginning of 1941 with the arrival in the North African and Mediterranean theatres of the troops of what would become known as the *Deutsches Afrika Korps* under *Generalleutnant* Rommel. Also arriving in Sicilia from Norway and France were elements of the X. *Fliegerkorps*, a command formation particularly trained for maritime combat operations and tasked with cooperating with the Regia Aeronautica to counter the movements of the British fleets in the central Mediterranean and to neutralise the island of Malta. As a consequence, the operations of the CR.42s in the skies above Malta became of less importance, albeit that such operations had become particularly dangerous for the fragile biplanes when confronting an ever-increasing number of Hurricanes. Indeed, in the late spring of 1941 the RAF could draw upon three squadrons to defend Malta: 185, 261 and 249 Squadrons. Nevertheless, despite their demonstrably technical inferiority, the CR.42s continued to fly over the central Mediterranean, although their missions – such as convoy escort, submarine-spotting patrol flights, and sporadic armed reconnaissance missions over Malta – were selected to avoid potential engagement with the faster and better armed British fighters. To provide escort for the shipping engaged in delivering supplies from Italy to North Africa and because of the endurance of the CR.42, the latter frequently operated from the islands of Pantelleria and Lampedusa, south of Sicilia. Moreover, during the spring of 1941, the CR.42s carried out attack missions against enemy shipping, carrying under their wings 50-kg bombs. The CR.42s carried out the escort missions because they had a longer range than the G.50s and C.200s of the time – which were still used operationally – and in daylight they were quite as effective as Blenheim and Beaufort interceptors. They participated, albeit without achieving appreciable results, in the air operations surrounding Operation 'Harpoon', when eight CR.42s were sent to attack a British convoy from Gibraltar consisting of five freighters and an oil tanker, escorted by an AA cruiser, nine destroyers, and three minesweepers, with a covering force of a battleship, two carriers, three destroyers and eight other ships. Operating in conjunction with torpedo attack and bomber aircraft, Italian efforts were apparently without any appreciable results.

With the movement of the 17° *Gruppo* of the 1° *Stormo* CT to Campoformido in order to undergo conversion to the C.202 *Folgore*, on 21 June 1941 the 23° *Gruppo Autonomo* CT was transferred from Comiso to Trapani Milo, together with some CR.42s still in service with the 54° *Stormo* CT on convoy escort duties. Continuing with this important but relatively peripheral mission, in July 1941 the 24° *Gruppo Autonomo* CT was deployed to Sardegna with twenty CR.42s. Here, in virtue of their longer endurance, they were used to reinforce and in part replace some of the FIAT G.50s previously operated by the unit. On 1 October 1941 the 171° *Gruppo Autonomo* CT was posted to Gela airfield with its 301ª and 302ª *Squadriglie* equipped with CR.42CNs, specialised for the night fighter role. However, after a brief period of existence the unit was disbanded and its CR.42CNs distributed, in part, to various night fighter sections based on the island, while others were sent to partner the AerMacchi C.200s of the 377ª *Squadriglia Autonoma* CN.

By late 1941, following the conversion of the 23° *Gruppo Autonomo* CT onto the C.202, the only operational CR.42s present in Sicilia were the handful of aircraft operated by the night fighter sections.

At the end of 1942, it is estimated that there were at least fifteen CR.42s present on Sicilian airfields, both normal and CN versions, but little more than ten on the eve of the Allied landing of 9 July 1943.

Above: CR.42s of an unknown unit (possibly the 377ª *Squadriglia)* fly close to the Sicilian coastline.

The 377ª *Squadriglia Autonoma* was engaged in the defence of Sicily, operating from various airfields on the island. The unit fielded aircraft optimised for night-fighting as well as CR.42s with standard day camouflage schemes for the defence of the island's military facilities.

Italian pilots photographed before an escort flight over the Mediterranean. Note the *MARUS* flight suit, *M.I.T.A.* 'sausage' lifejackets, *Giusti* flight helmets, one in brown leather and one in Havana canvas, as well as protective flight goggles. (P.Monti)

North Africa and Italy

A CR.42 of the 77ª *Squadriglia*, 13° *Gruppo* of 2° *Stormo* CT, probably at Tobruk in June 1940. Note the insignia painted unusually on the undercarriage fairings.

ON Italy's entry into the war on 10 June 1940, two units of CR.42s were operating in Libya, the 10° *Gruppo* of the 4° *Stormo* CT and the 2° *Stormo* CT with its two *gruppi*, the 13° and 8° *Gruppo*. The 13° *Gruppo* was based at Castelbenito near Tripoli, controlling the 77ª, 78ª and 82ª *Squadriglie* with a mixed fleet of CR.32s and CR.42s, while the 8° *Gruppo*, formed of the 92ª, 93ª and 94ª *Squadriglie*, which on the outbreak of hostilities had been entirely equipped with the CR.32, would only begin to receive its first CR.42s on 20 June.

In total some fifty CR.42s were present in North Africa, intensely involved in combat operations as well as struggling against the insidious ambient conditions. Indeed, aside from wear as a result of combat operations, during this period the biplanes also suffered from a high level of technical problems due to the sand and the variations in temperature between day and night. Furthermore, in addition to technical and logistics problems was a scarcity of spares. The most prominent shortage, which on first sight seems incredible considering the operational environment, was the initial unavailability of sand filters for the engine air intakes and protective measures against sand infiltration into weapons which caused frequent jamming. Only after the summer did sand filters become available, resulting in an improvement in efficiency.

The first clash with British fighters took place on 14 June 1940, when a formation of CR.42s on a patrol mission attacked a Gladiator, claiming its destruction, although this was not confirmed by the British. Over the following days further encounters took place involving Gladiators and Blenheims which resulted in claims, but that which could be considered the first Italian air combat victory in North Africa was obtained by *sergente* Giuseppe Scaglioni who, on 19 June 1940, shot down a Gladiator. During the same dogfight, which saw the participation of the first Hawker Hurricane Mk.Is to arrive in Africa, the first Italian loss was also recorded, when the CR.42 piloted by *sergente* Ugo Corsi was shot down by a British monoplane, the pilot losing his life. The *Gruppo* commander, *tenente colonnello* Armando Piragino, was also shot down and taken POW. On 21 June a Sunderland, tasked with a reconnaissance mission over Tobruk, was heavily damaged by some CR.42s from the 8° *Gruppo* and 10° *Gruppo*.

In the meantime, the requirement to reinforce the North African front saw, on 13 July 1940, the deployment of another element of the 4° *Stormo Caccia* CT, the 9° *Gruppo*, which took its thirty CR.42s from Comiso airfield in Sicilia to El-Adem T-3. At the end of August, the 5ª *Squadra Aerea*, the command headquarters for the sector, received further CR.42 reinforcements to integrate into the units in place, but also to finally replace the CR.32s. This increased the presence in theatre by the end of the first summer of war to a total of 190 CR.42s in Libya. Towards the end of September, 151° *Gruppo Caccia* CT also arrived in North Africa, bringing its 366ª, 367ª and 368ª *Squadriglia* and deploying to the Bengasi/K.2, Tmimi and Derna airfields, allowing a pause in operations for the fighter pilots of the 10° *Gruppo Caccia*. This enabled the SRAM (*Servizo Riiparazione Aeromobili e Motori*) to conduct a deep maintenance programme of the majority of its fighters.

In the same month of September, a further reinforcement of biplanes arrived, and by the end of the month the *Falcos* sent to North Africa between April and September 1940 totalled around

A FIAT CR.42 of the 2° *Stormo* CT taxiing on a desert airstrip in the summer of 1940. Both the white wing tips and the black St. Andrew's cross on the lower wing undersurfaces were tactical markings used in North Africa in the first months of war for aircraft deployed in the theatre until the adoption of white fuselage bands.

A formation of the 73ª and 96ª *Squadriglia* of 9° *Gruppo*, 4° *Stormo* CT on patrol over the desert in North Africa. The CR.42s have no sand filters, but have optical identification markings on their wing tips.

FIAT CR.42s of the 91ª *Squadriglia*, 10° *Gruppo*, 4° *Stormo* CT at El Adem T3 in September 1940. They are finished in a standard three-tone scheme of green and brown over a sand background, with grey undersides and white upper wing tips. The emblems are a black prancing horse on white shield, with the squadron insignia on wheel spats (a black griffon) and white spinner.

A pilot of the 3° *Gruppo* of 6° *Stormo* CT proudly observes the unit's 'Red Devil' symbol.

Left and below: Ground-attack CR.42s of the 388ª *Squadriglia* of 158° *Gruppo*, 50° *Stormo d'Assalto* at Abu Nimeir, Egypt in August 1942. The unit's emblem, a diving duck on a white cloud in a light blue sky, was applied to vertical tail surfaces, being the same used on Italian-flown Ju 87s.

A rare colour photograph of CR.42s of the 387ª *Squadriglia*, 158° *Gruppo Autonomo* CT.

CR.42s of 18° *Gruppo* of 3° *Stormo* CT probably at Castelbenito in the summer of 1940.

240. The availability of the aircraft permitted the organisation of increasing numbers of offensive missions and bomber escorts. These included that mounted on 22 September, which saw forty SM.79s escorted by 42 CR.42s. Another mission on 31 October involved thirty SM.79s escorted by 37 CR.42s, targeting military installations at Marsa Matruh. In this period the CR.42s also began to be utilised for night offensive missions, strafing enemy airfields in Egypt.

The British counter-offensive of December 1940, which resulted in the retreat of Italian forces, saw the pilots of the Regia Aeronautica pushed to the limits of their physical capabilities and their aircraft to their mechanical capabilities; they fought not only the enemy, but also a thousand difficulties, aggravated by the continual movement of the front line and the consequent abandoning of airfields. Aircraft availability reduced significantly, many aircraft were grounded for technical reasons, including lack of essential maintenance and then lost to advancing British troops. The consequences of the British offensive and the threat looming over Tripolitania, with the presence of the British on the threshold of Sirte, were worrying. This made it necessary to further reinforce the CR.42 fleet in North Africa to replace the losses suffered by the 5ª *Squadra Aerea* and to compensate for the repatriation at the end of the year of the exhausted personnel of the 2° *Stormo* and 9° *Gruppo* who were worn out by five months of a war of attrition. On a practical level, at the end of the year, little more than thirty CR.42s were combat ready. For this reason, on 16 December, Castelbenito saw the arrival of the 23° *Gruppo Autonomo* CT, commanded by *maggiore* Tito Falconi, with the 70ª, 74ª and 75ª *Squadriglie* and 32 CR.42s. The *Gruppo* was quickly relocated to Cyrenaica in an attempt to stall the British advance, being heavily involved, together with the *Falcos* of the 151° *Gruppo* and 10° *Gruppo*, in ground-attack strafing missions against British armoured columns.

Air combat with British fighters occurred on almost a daily basis; after a dogfight with Gladiators on 26 December, the commander of the 74ª *Squadriglia*, *capitano* Guido Bobba, failed to return, while on 4 January 1941 *capitano* Pietro Calistri, the commander of the 75ª *Squadriglia*, managed to shoot down two Hurricane. On the following day, however, the 23° *Gruppo* suffered a heavy defeat, losing five aircraft, with four pilots killed and another escaping. The Hurricanes suffered no losses. Continuous clashes occurred during the withdrawal towards Sirte, and numerous pilots fell in action until February 1941, when the 23° *Gruppo Autonomo* CT, in its continuous westward retreat, was temporarily relocated to the airfield at Sorman in Tripolitania, from where it was repatriated to Italy for reorganisation of its technical and personnel assets.

At the end of January, a replacement unit arrived with the transfer to North Africa of the 18° *Gruppo Autonomo* CT, commanded by *maggiore* Vosilla, which had only recently returned to Italy after its unfortunate interlude with the C.A.I. on the English Channel front. At Tripoli airfield it underwent a brief period of technical preparation, receiving further overhauled CR.42s, some of them intended initially for the 83ª *Squadriglia*. These machines were modified with underwing racks capable of carrying 50-kg bombs for the fighter-bomber role. With this modification the aged biplane demonstrated unexpected and incredible versatility thanks to the robustness of its construction and the reliability of its engine. It proved capable of mounting effective operations in the Tobruk area, as long as it was escorted by C.200s or C.202s, and it worked in tandem with the G.50s of the 2° *Gruppo Caccia*, this unit also having arrived in North Africa between December and January, as well as with Italian and German Stuka units. This variant of the CR.42, known as the CR.42ba (*bombe alari* – wing bombs), revealed unexpected effectiveness when used against armoured vehicles, tanks and troop concentrations, and had the ability to perform surprise attacks on British airfields and infrastructure by both day and by the light of the moon.

FIAT FIGHTERS

A CR.42 of the *Sezione Autonoma Aviazione Sahariana* is seen here wrecked after cartwheeling on landing, while based at Sebha. (R.Gentilli)

In February 1941 the CR.42 force amounted to around seventy biplanes, with the aircraft of the 18° *Gruppo* participating actively in the recapture of Cyrenaica and the siege of Tobruk. In May, the 376ª *Squadriglia Autonoma Assalto* also became operational in the theatre, the first unit to be entirely equipped with the CR.42ba. This *squadriglia* operated from Berka airfield together with a few CR.42s modified with bomb racks in the field by the 18° *Gruppo Autonomo* CT and was involved in some successful attacks against British fixed and mobile targets, such as depots, motor transport and armour. Frequently, the CR.42s, having dropped their bombs, returned to a target to strafe it with machine gun fire. It could be stated, paradoxically, that this was the beginning of a second career for the FIAT biplane, and throughout the summer, new units equipped with the CR.42ba arrived in Libya, amongst which the 3° *Gruppo Autonomo* CT with its 153ª, 154ª and 155ª *Squadriglie* arrived from Albania, and the 160° *Gruppo Autonomo* CT with the 375ª, 393ª and 394ª *Squadriglie*, while the 18° *Gruppo* returned to Italy to be re-equipped with the C.202 *Folgore*.

On 18 November British forces, recovered after the reversals suffered in the spring, commenced a new offensive operation and managed, after strong attacks by armoured elements, to push back the Italo-German front line into Cyrenaica. Very active in this new battle were the CR.42bas and of the eighty CR.42s present in North Africa in the autumn, more than fifty were ground-attack versions. At the start of 1942, however, the total CR.42 fleet had reduced to little more than fifty aircraft, operating with the 3° and 160° *Gruppo Autonomo CT*, and the 236ª *Squadriglia Autonoma*, while ten *Falcos* were serving with the *Aviazione Sahariana*.

With the British offensive stalled, on 18 January 1942 Italian and German forces began a new counter-offensive, managing to push back the Eighth Army, reconquering Cyrenaica, isolating and capturing Tobruk, and breaking through the Egyptian border in an advance that extended as far as El Alamein. In this phase of the war in North Africa, once again the CR.42ba units distinguished themselves, obtaining notable results against enemy motorised columns and armoured vehicles, destroying hundreds of vehicles in day and night actions that were conducted with great determination and effectiveness.

Meanwhile, at the end of May the 50° *Stormo Assalto* was re-formed under the command of *tenente colonnello* Ferruccio Vosilla and was entirely equipped with the CR.42ba. The new *Stormo* was quickly transferred from Aviano airfield to Castelbenito, and then relocated to Derna with its two assigned units, the 158° *Gruppo* with the 236ª, 387ª and 388ª *Squadriglie* and the 159° *Gruppo* with the 389ª, 390ª and 391ª *Squadriglie*, operating 76 CR.42ba which were split between the airfields at Martuba 5 and Derna. Also based at Martuba 5 was the 3° *Gruppo d'Assalto*, which had recently converted from the fighter role to that of ground-attack. Operations against the garrison at Tobruk commenced on 30 May involving the increasingly important participation of all the ground-attack units. They continued to perform such a role until the conquest of the important British fortress and the ensuing capture of more than 33,000 Allied prisoners together with enormous quantities of

Detail view of a 50-kg bomb attached on the starboard wing bomb pylon of a FIAT CR.42.

As the aircraft's engine runs, armourers prepare to attach a 50-kg bomb to the wing pylons of a CR.42ba.

military equipment. Operations continued over the Egyptian border, with deployments to the airfields at Sidi el Barrani, Abu Haggag, and Abu Nimeir, although these were subjected to night attacks conducted by teams of British commandos.

Following the arrival of the 101° *Gruppo d'Assalto* in Libya in mid-July (previously equipped with the German Ju 87 R), between late August and early September, the 15° *Stormo Assalto* also arrived in Africa with its 46° *Gruppo* (20ª and 21ª *Squadriglie*) and the 47° *Gruppo* (53ª and 54ª *Squadriglie*). The unit possessed forty-eight CR.42ba aircraft and was tasked with operating in the Tobruk and El Alamein areas at a particularly critical moment in the conflict for the Axis forces. This was characterised by intensive ground-attack operations, but also by significant losses, as the FIATs had to confront the latest cannon-equipped versions of the Hurricane and Spitfire. The units moved constantly between bases, following the progress of combat operations, their continuous assault missions vainly supporting the Axis counter-offensive launched by the *Afrika Korps* under *Generalfeldmarschall* Rommel. On the eve of the final battle of El Alamein, almost all the CR.42ba assault units of the Regia Aeronautica were concentrated in North Africa, with an overall strength of 100 *Falcos*, of which were just some twenty residual aircraft of the classic fighter version.

Describing the countless actions carried out by the pilots of the assault units is a difficult task due to the enormous number of missions and events in which the *gruppi* were involved. Not only that, but they did their work in extremely difficult conditions and were short of aircraft, spare parts and fuel. Despite this, the CR.42 units operating in Libya and Egypt continued their activities, following the retreat of the Axis troops across North Africa after the beginning of the British counter-offensive in early November, resulting in the epilogue of their entrenchment in Tunisia prior to the withdrawal from North Africa in May 1943. From December some units began to return to Italy, including the 101° and 158° *Gruppo*, handing over their remaining aircraft to other units remaining in Libya and still involved in the attempts to halt the Allied counter-offensive while beginning their retreat into Tunisia. The CR.42s of the *Aviazione Sahariana* were also prominent with around ten examples which operated alongside various other aircraft engaged in armed reconnaissance, being particularly active between the end of December and early January 1943 against advancing British mechanised columns.

However, the fate of the Axis war effort in North Africa was now sealed, and in January the units equipped with the residual CR.42s – little more than eighty aircraft – returned to Italy, thus concluding the unfortunate, but courageous African saga of Rosatelli's fighter.

A FIAT CR 42 of the 50° *Stormo Assalto* probably from the 46° *Gruppo Assalto* at Castelbenito in June 1941.

The two forms of insignia that decorated the tails of CR.42s of 368ª *Squadriglia*. The first one was the 151° *Gruppo Autonomo* CT insignia, the second was the humorous *Squadriglia* insignia of the cat in boots (right).

A CR.42 of the 54ª *Squadriglia* of 47° *Gruppo Autonomo* CT photographed during the transfer flight from Italy to North Africa. This former bomber unit converted to the FIAT biplane when it became a ground-attack unit in May 1942.

CR.42s of the 388ª *Squadriglia*, 158° *Gruppo Autonomo* CT ready to take off for a bombing mission.

A fine study of a CR.42 of an unknown unit, but probably 50° *Stormo Assalto* in North Africa.

Sergente Fantazzini pictured with his aircraft, a CR.42 of the 151° *Gruppo Autonomo* CT at Sorman. The unit was in Africa from 8 September 1940 and was immediately engaged in operations preceding the Italian offensive on Sidi el Barrani.

A CR.42 with wing bombs bombs, with the markings of 20ª *Squadriglia* of 15° *Stormo Assalto* in North Africa in the autumn of 1942.

Metal jacket badge with the insignia of the 151° *Gruppo* during the period in which it was autonomous from the Wing to which it belonged, the 53° CT. It was inspired by a battle during the first weeks of the war in which a pilot of the unit, *sergente* Cicognani, suffered the loss of an arm.

The 15° *Stormo d'Assalto* insignia of a flying duck, complete with underwing bombs, adorned the tail of the CR.42-equipped unit.

Official FIAT advertisement published in *L'Ala d'Italia* magazine in 1941.

A bleak 'monument' of the war over the African desert. The remains of a FIAT CR.42 of the 4° *Stormo* CT from which fuselage codes and group insignia were 'souvenired' by Australian soldiers, photographed in the Libyan desert.

Below: A flight of CR.42s make a low-level pass over a column of Italian armoured vehicles.

The Balkans

ON 28 October 1940 Italy declared war on Greece, which had a British political alignment. Initial Italian flying operations included the FIAT fighters of the 160° *Gruppo Autonomo* based in Albania which were joined a few days later by the aircraft of the 24° and 150° *Gruppo Autonomo* CT and the newly constituted 154° *Gruppo Autonomo* CT. Underlying operations was the fact that the conditions on local airfields were somewhat deficient, with minimal infrastructure and significant logistics and supply issues, as well as telegraph and telephone communications that were extremely sub-standard. The choice to commence operations at the end of Autumn was, to say the least, somewhat unfortunate, as up until early November the meteorological conditions were so bad as to preclude any type of flying activity.

In this new operational theatre the CR.42s were initially opposed by aircraft of an equivalent level, such as Greek Gladiators, a few PZL 24s. The Italian offensive ran into several difficulties caused by Greek resistance which was supported by assistance from British aircraft and by the weather conditions which forced the Italian units to move their aircraft closer to the front line, often operating from makeshift airfields. Of the more than 150 days which comprised the campaign in Greece, just 64 offered weather conditions that were acceptable for flying.

The inclement weather created not a few problems for the CR.42s which were forced to operate from runways which quickly turned to mud. This forced the units to remove the wheel spats from their aircraft so as to be able to taxi them with even a minimum margin of safety.

However, in the few flight-clear days CR.42s were engaged in combats with Greek aircraft, and the first victory scored by the type was credited to a CR.42 of the 393ª *Squadriglia* which, on the first day of the war, intercepted and shot down a Greek Hs 126 reconnaissance aircraft of the 3 *Mira*. Further victories were achieved by the Italian fighters, which had little to be concerned about when facing the Ἑλληνικὴ Βασιλικὴ Ἀεροπορία (Royal Hellenic Air Force), although the Greek airmen did continue to fight courageously. The first Regia Aeronautica casualty was *sergente* Ardesio of the 393ª *Squadriglia* who, during an attack on Koritza airfield by some Greek Blenheims, was killed when his CR.42 was caught by a bomb exploding while on his take-off run to intercept the bombers. On 7 November CR.42s of the 150° *Gruppo* with two G.50s of the 154° *Gruppo Autonomo* CT managed to effectively deter a raid by RAF Wellingtons intent on bombing the port of Valona. Two bombers were shot down.

The following day, *sottotenente* Pietro Jannello of the 363ª *Squadriglia* was shot down by anti-aircraft fire during a strafing attack against Greek Army positions. With an improvement in the weather, the pilots of the small Greek Air Force provided a clear demonstration of their courage, frequently engaging in bitter clashes with Italian fighters. The inferiority of the Greek PZLs was compensated by the resoluteness of their pilots, and despite their successes the Italian fighter pilots also suffered some losses. On 15 November, CR.42s of the 393a *Squadriglia* again managed to shoot down a Blenheim, while *S.Ten* Di Robilant, single-handedly, shot down two. Three PZL fighters were also shot down on 18 November following a ferocious dogfight with some CR.42s of the 160° *Gruppo Autonomo* CT near the Greek/Albanian border.

For the Italian fighter pilots, however, the situation would change radically with the appearance of the British fighters of the RAF which intervened in support of the Royal Hellenic Air Force. The first direct encounter between the fighters of the Regia Aeronautica and the RAF was recorded on 19 November, when ten Gladiators of 80 Squadron RAF, accompanying some Greek PZLs on a patrol mission, surprised a formation of five CR.42s of the 160° *Gruppo Autonomo* CT. At the conclusion of the dogfight the British pilots claimed three CR.42s as shot down, together with a G.50 of the 355ª *Squadriglia* which had intervened to assist the Italian biplanes, while another CR.42 returned to base damaged with an injured pilot, while only one Gladiator was heavily damaged in return and its pilot wounded.

The arrival of the RAF in Greece came as a bitter surprise for the Italian fighter pilots. This was evidenced by the tragic encounter fought on 27 November, when twelve Gladiators conducting an offensive reconnaissance mission entered into contact with CR.42s of the 150° *Gruppo Autonomo* CT which were escorting a formation of S.79 bombers. In the ensuing dogfight the CR.42 of *capitano* Nicola Magaldi, commander of the 364ª *Squadriglia*, was shot down. On the following day, *capitano* Giorgio Graffer, commander of the 365ª *Squadriglia*, was also shot down in flames. In the course of the same action a CR.42 collided with a Gladiator, and the two aircraft fell to the ground, the RAF pilot losing his life, while *sergente* Pacini was forced to parachute to safety. Four Gladiators were damaged in return and Flt. Lt. Jones wounded.

To offset these losses, on 3 December a formation of eighteen CR.42s of the 160° *Gruppo Autonomo* CT initiated an unequal dogfight with six PZLs of the 23 *Mira*, claiming one of the Greek fighters shot down. On the following day RAF Gladiators clashed with twelve CR.42s of the 150° *Gruppo Autonomo* CT and the Fiat G.50bis of the 154° *Gruppo Autonomo* CT. The British claimed the destruction of nine Italian aircraft, but in reality the Regia Aeronautica lost only the CR.42s of *tenente* Alberto Triolo and *sottotenente* Paolo Penna. The British commander, Sqn. Ldr. Hickey was shot down and crash-landed unhurt. Small revenge was achieved on 7 December 1940, when three Blenheim bombers were shot down over Valona by fighters from the 150° *Gruppo Autonomo* CT.

Throughout the month, air combat between the RAF and Regia Aeronautica fighters continued at a furious level. On 21 December fifteen CR.42s of the 150° *Gruppo Autonomo* CT, alongside other fighters from the 160° *Gruppo Autonomo* CT, were involved in an extended dogfight with twenty Gladiators. At the end of the encounter, three CR.42 pilots were shot down, with two pilots *tenente* Mario Gaetano Carancini and *tenente* Mario Frascadore losing their lives, while *maggiore* Molinari was wounded. They were all of the 160° *Gruppo Autonomo* CT. Two Gladiators were destroyed with the loss of both pilots including the commander, Hickey. The combative British presence resulted in the reinforcement of the Italian units with the assignment to the Balkan theatre of other fighter units equipped with the C.200, although they were deployed to Bari and Brindisi airfields.

The beginning of 1941 saw, on 12 January, the shooting down by ground fire of the CR.42 flown by *tenente* Gatti of the 365ª *Squadriglia*, who was engaged in an attack against enemy lines. On 9 February another encounter between Gladiators and CR.42s occurred. The Italians lost two fighters and two damaged, while 80 Sqn lost one and had another force landed. In mid-February the first RAF Hurricanes began to arrive in Greece, which shifted the progress in the air war decidedly in favour of the British. On 27 February one of the first aerial clashes between these monoplanes and the Italian biplanes took place at the end of which two CR.42s had been shot down with one pilot managing to survive. The Hurricanes had been unable to protect their bombers, two of which were shot down by the CR.42s. On the following day there was a series of encounters between the British fighters and formations of Italian bombers escorted by CR.42s and G.50s: despite the elevated British claims, at the end of the day just two fighters had

A CR.42 of the 364ª *Squadriglia* of the 150° *Gruppo Autonomo* CT takes off from Valona airfield in Albania, winter 1940. (E.Leproni)

Escort flight by three CR.42 to cover an S.79 bomber over the Balkans.

CR.42s of the 394ª *Squadriglia* of 160° *Gruppo Autonomo* CT that operated in Albania until summer 1941 when deployed in North Africa.

CR.42s of the 394ª *Squadriglia*, 160° *Gruppo Autonomo* CT. The location may be Tirana.

been lost, while the Italian fighter pilots claimed six victories.

In March Italian forces attempted to launch a massive counter-offensive to force the Greeks out of Albania but it ended in a bloody failure. The war then passed into a stalled situation until April 1941 when Germany intervened in force in the Balkan region. In a lightning action German forces invaded Yugoslavia and Greece, forcing the latter to capitulate after a short campaign. In this period the CR.42s began to be used for ground-attack missions, and from February a large part of the biplanes of the 160° *Gruppo Autonomo* CT were fitted with shackles for the attachment of munitions dispensers which could be used to spread 2-kg bomblets over concentrations of enemy troops and vehicles in a similar manner to what had been practised in the Aegean and North Africa.

By April some thirty CR.42s were still serving on the Balkan front, all on charge of the 160° *Gruppo Autonomo* CT and these aircraft also participated in the brief conflict with Yugoslavia. The attack on the Balkan nation was a consequence of the German intervention in support of the failing Italian campaign in Greece. Hostilities commenced on 6 April, with Italian and German forces invading Yugoslavia in an extremely rapid campaign; in just ten days it was concluded with the conquest of the country by Axis forces, consequently permitting an easier intervention by the Germans against Greece.

The 160° *Gruppo Autonomo* CT was the only unit operating the CR.42 in support of air operations, undertaking visual reconnaissance, protective patrols, and ground attacks without suffering losses.

After the occupation of Greece and Yugoslavia, Axis forces were faced with confronting an active guerrilla movement and it became essential to reorganise their units to provide adequate support to the occupying troops. The irrepressible CR.42s were once again protagonists and at the end of 1942 a section was

CR.42s of the 394ª *Squadriglia*, 160° *Gruppo Autonomo* CT probably at Devoli, Albania.

Left: By the time of the armistice at least twenty CR.42s from 383ª *Squadriglia* were still in service in the Slovenia-Dalmatia area. (F. Sanetti)

Below: A CR.42 of the 164ª *Squadriglia* at Rhodes Gadurrà. The unit was the third *Squadriglia* of the 161° *Gruppo Autonomo* CT formed in the summer of 1941 with CR.42s equipped with bomb-carrying wing pylons.

Ground crew assist a pilot of the 163ª *Squadriglia* of 161° *Gruppo Autonomo* CT based at Gadurrà with his parachute and starting his aircraft shortly before he climbs into a CR.42 in the summer of 1942.

Below: Bomb arming for a CR.42 of the 164ª *Squadriglia* of 161° *Gruppo Autonomo* CT. Note the wheel spats have been removed to ease operations on rough and muddy terrain.

A good colour photograph of a CR.42 of the 162ª *Squadriglia* of 161° *Gruppo Autonomo* CT photographed at Maritza airport on Rhodes. The unit insignia shows an aggressive cat with the inscription, in the language of the Veneto region, 'Varda che te sbrego' ('Watch it, or I'll slash you')..

organised at Zara airfield to operate the biplanes in their CR.42ba (*bombe alari* – wing bomb) variant, tasked with combatting partisan activity. The good results obtained resulted in the constitution on 17 January 1943 of the 383ª *Squadriglia Autonoma Assalto* which was assigned a fleet of more than fifteen CR.42ba. These machines continued to operate effectively until the armistice, conducting more than 600 missions while losing two aircraft in combat. In the same period in Albania, Tirana airport became the operational base of the 392ª *Squadriglia Autonoma* which was equipped with a variety of aircraft, among them CR.42s, C.200s, G.50s and Ro.41s.

The FIAT CR.42 in the Dodecanese

The first CR.42s to arrive in the Dodecanese area in early July 1940 were the nine fighters sent to support and to gradually replace the CR.32s of the 163ª *Squadriglia Autonoma* based at Gadurrà airfield on the island of Rhodes. These aircraft were subsequently followed by the CR.42s assigned to the 162ª *Squadriglia Autonoma* based at Maritza and Scarpanto. The two *squadriglie* were placed under the control of the *Comando dell'Aeronautica dell Egeo*, led by *generale* n. B.A. Umberto Cappa.

Recorded on 4 September 1940 was what could be considered one of the most positive and important missions flown by the fighters in the Aegean, when CR.32s and CR.42s of the 163ª *Squadriglia* confronted an attack against Maritza airfield by Fairey Swordfish aircraft of the Fleet Air Arm, operating off carriers sailing near Rhodes. The day concluded in triumph for the Italian fighter pilots who managed to bring down five British biplanes, including two which were seized and subsequently returned to flying condition by Italian engineers.

Under the command of *generale* Ulisse Longo, who had replaced *generale* Cappa at the head of the *Aeronautica dell'Egeo*, in early January 1941 the Order of Battle on Rhodes was as follows:

— 162ª *Squadriglia Autonoma* CT commanded by *tenente* Mario D'Agostini based at Rhodes Maritza airfield with a detachment at Scarpanto and operating fourteen CR.42s, of which twelve were serviceable

— 163ª *Squadriglia Autonoma* CT, commanded by *tenente* Mario Rovere based at Rhodes Maritza airfield with a mixed force of CR.32s and 42s

FLEET AIR ARM ATTACKS AIRFIELD ON RHODES

On 4 September 1940 twenty-one Fairey Swordfish from the carriers HMS *Illustrious* and HMS *Eagle*, at sea off the island of Rhodes, were launched for a morning attack on Italian airfields on the island of Rhodes.

At 0315 HMS *Eagle* catapulted twelve Swordfish with the base at Maritza as their target, while at 0345 eight Swordfish of 813 Squadron departed HMS *Illustrious* to attack the airfields at Gadurrà and Callato. Another four Swordfish on HMS *Illustrious* were prevented from taking off following an accident on the flight deck.

From the Italian perspective, the official report on the event provided by the commander of the 163ª *Squadriglia* includes the following:

'At 0505 the airport sirens announced an imminent air attack. At 0508 the first three CR.32s on standby took-off. Meanwhile most of the pilots, using a variety of methods, went to the dispersal area where the CR.42s were parked, and where the technical personnel also were. While the pilots were preparing for departure, a first formation of enemy aircraft appeared in the sky, arriving from the south-east. Once over the airfield, they released their first bombs from a height of approximately 3,000 metres. Once they had dropped their bombs, they machine-gunned the fighter aircraft and the adjacent personnel. Despite this, the take-off signal was still given, and while this would have to take place during the bombing and machine-gunning, it was considered more opportune to take-off individually. During this operation a CR.42 aircraft, just airborne, was caught up in the splinters of an exploding bomb, which resulted in the seizure of its engine. The other machines managed to take off and to quickly enter into combat despite the anti-aircraft batteries and machine gunners firing intensely. On the appearance of the first fighter aircraft the enemy interrupted their bombing, trying, in a disorganised way, to find refuge over the sea at low level, flying in the direction of Anatolia. Pursued individually, they were caught up by some fighters, which, having manoeuvred into a favourable position for an attack, opened fire, shooting down some of them, of which four were confirmed. The remaining enemy aircraft, despite being repeatedly machine-gunned and hit, and taking advantage of the favourable light conditions, probably managed to escape.

Five CR.42s and three CR.32s participated in the action. The enemy aircraft put up a fierce defence with their movable weapons. Total flying hours 6.55'.

Rhodes, 5 September 1940

The few bombs released over Maritza airfield caused minor damage to some hangars and some injuries amongst the base personnel. At Gadurrà however, the Swordfish from HMS *Illustrious* struck the base with hardly any meaningful response from the Italians, and two S.79 bombers of the 39° *Stormo* BT were destroyed on the ground with three others damaged, while further damage was caused to two Cant Z.1007bis, an S.81 and an SM.82 transport. The bombs caused four major and twenty minor injuries amongst the personnel, and damage to a hangar and the fuel storage. The attack on Callato resulted in just one injury and some damage to the electric grid.

Swordfish shot down during the operation of 4 September 1940

K8403 E4-M 813 NAS
Forced into an emergency landing at Scarpanto. The crew were captured, and the Swordfish was recovered and flown to Guidonia, where it was evaluated, being supported operationally by the stripping of Swordfish K8422 for spares.

K8422 E4-H 813 NAS
Force-landed on Kasos island, the crew captured. K8422 was repaired and utilised by the Regia Aeronautica for communications flights until the end of 1941, when it was grounded to provide spares for Swordfish K8403.

K8414 E4-K 813 NAS
Forced to ditch after the attack on Maritza. The pilot was killed and the other two crew members captured.

K8398 E4-C 813 NAS
The biplane was shot down by Italian fighters, crashing into the sea with the loss of its entire crew.

????? E4-? 813 NAS
This aircraft was forced to descend into the sea after an attack by Italian fighters. The crew were rescued by an Italian submarine, becoming prisoners of war.

Left and above: One of the five Swordfish of 813 Naval Air Squadron, Fleet Air Arm, K8422 E4-H, which took off from HMS Eagle and was shot down by FIAT biplanes of 163ª *Squadriglia* over the night of 3/4 September 1940 during an attack by Fleet Air Arm biplanes on the airfield at Maritza. The Swordfish was recovered, almost intact, off the coast of Rhodes. (F. Ballista)

The Swordfish K8403 E4-M of 813 Naval Air Squadron, Fleet Air Arm was forced into an emergency landing at Scarpanto. It was recovered and flown to *Centro Sperimentale* at Guidonia for evaluation. Note the crews' three-man inflated life raft. (F. Ballista)

On 10 January the 162ª *Squadriglia* suffered its first loss with the death of *sergente* Bellini in a take-off accident while departing on a reconnaissance mission targeting Crete and the airfield at Heraklion. In the early afternoon of 20 January the Cretan airfield was attacked by two CR.42s of the 162ª *Squadriglia* led by *tenente* Mario D'Agostini and three CR.32s of the 163ª led by *tenente* Mario Rovere, airborne from Scarpanto. While the CR.42s attacked the anti-aircraft positions, the CR.32s concentrated on strafing the airfield infrastructure and dropping 48 2-kg sub-munitions. Two days later a pair of CR.42s of the 162ª *Squadriglia* airborne over Crete attacked a Walrus seaplane, but it managed to avoid the

Italian fighters. At the beginning of spring 1941, the CR.42s of the two *squadriglie* conducted numerous missions over Crete, including machine gun attacks on airfields, during which at least two CR.42s were lost, shot down by anti-aircraft fire. On 11 February three fighters of the 162ª *Squadriglia* conducted a low-level attack on Heraklion airfield, hitting a Bristol Bombay transport aircraft. The operation was repeated in the afternoon by another five aircraft of the *squadriglia* which attacked the base infrastructure.

From 25 February the fighters of the 161° *Gruppo* were engaged in combatting the British landing at Kastelorizo (the so-called Operation 'Abstention'), performing numerous attack and strafing missions against British shipping and troops, and providing air cover when the Italian forces recaptured the island.

The month of March saw the Italian fighters engaged in patrol and bomber escort over the Aegean, with some sporadic encounters with British fighters that achieved no results. On 22 March CR.42s of the 162ª *squadriglia* again attacked Heraklion airfield, badly damaging a reconnaissance aircraft. Two of the fighters were hit by anti-aircraft fire, and on returning to Scarpanto one of them was damaged on landing. Heraklion was revisited on 25 March by the 162ª *Squadriglia*, the raid destroying a Bristol Blenheim on the ground.

On 4 April, during one of the continual attacks on Heraklion, the CR.42 of *sergente* Domenico Chiappa was hit by anti-aircraft fire and caught fire, causing the pilot to bail out and become a prisoner of war. Some days later, on 15 April, it was the turn of *tenente* Luciano Orsini to jump from his fighter after suffering the same fate over Heraklion airfield. During these operations, the Italian fighters encountered British Hurricanes and Fulmars embarked on carriers. In the meantime, the 163ª *Squadriglia* began to receive the CR.42 as replacements for their worn out CR.32s, which were relegated to training duties.

Activity in the month of May 1941 was far more intense, especially during *Untermehmen Merkur*, the Axis operation for the occupation of the island of Crete, with the Italians providing direct escort mainly for the Ju 87 B dive-bombers engaged in repeated attacks against the military installations on the island and in particular against Heraklion airfield. In the course of numerous patrol and strafing missions, on 25 May, possibly due to a technical problem, the CR.42 of *sergente maggiore* Guglielmo Mari was lost, although he managed to escape and return to his unit a few days later.

On 5 June 1941, the 161° *Gruppo Autonomo* CT was created which incorporated the 162ª and 163ª *Squadriglie* to which, in July 1941, the pilots and aircraft that had been involved with the 155ª *Squadriglia* in *Esigenza Irak*[1] were added. After having returned from Iraq, they were redesignated the 164ª *Squadriglia* on 7 July 1941, being placed under the command of *capitano* Sforza: this brought the fleet of CR.42s based on Rhodes to 42 aeroplanes. From the end of August, the 161° *Gruppo Autonomo* CT, command of which had been assumed by *capitano* Sforza, received a pair of G.50s, but continued to fly the FIAT biplanes on continuous patrol missions, unsuccessful scrambles and extended maritime patrol missions, performing an anti-submarine function by arming the biplanes with 100-kg wing bombs. The majority of the CR.42s of the 161° *Gruppo Autonomo* CT were the '*Egeo*' variant, characterised by the adoption of an additional internal fuel tank which increased the endurance of the fighter to around four flying hours. Some of these machines were utilised by a variety of alarm sections deployed on islands around the archipelago, and also to organise two night fighter sections at Maritza and Gadurrà airfields, the latter under the command of *tenente* Piero Ghiacci. These units were informally nicknamed '*le Falene*' (the moths).

Of particular interest is the description of the activities of this small section given personally by *generale* Ghiacci to fellow historian, Nicola Malizia, who has kindly authorised a partial reproduction of his testament:

'For this mission type the aircraft was painted matt black, utilising large doses of carbon black mixed with normal emailite[2]*. The exhaust pipe had been lengthened by little more than a metre and the armament modified, with the substitution of one machine gun with a 7.7 mm gun and the adoption of a flame shield over the muzzles. Special ammunition belts were prepared with the 12.7 mm gun firing 12.7 mm armour-piercing, explosive and incendiary shells, while the 7.7 had a tracer round after every seventh cartridge. We were not able to introduce substantial modifications to the cockpit instrumentation, and initially any radio communications was lacking. The eventual recognition of friendly aircraft at night was done visually, utilising the daily substitution of the three position lights, which were changed every evening into different colours following a pre-established agreement. It should be stated, however, that these lights were only turned on if necessary. The area in which the night fighters could freely roam was coordinated with the Comando della Difesa Contraerea dell'Egeo (Aegean Anti-aircraft Command) to prevent the aircraft becoming the target of our own artillery.*

'Normally four pilots were assigned to the alarm shift, and the operational criteria required that each would fly at a different altitude so as to afford each of them a 1,000-metre altitude band for free fighter operations. Usually the patrols were flown at mid-point in the altitude band, permitting a visual check 500 metres above and 500 metres below the cruising altitude. In this case any aircraft encountered would have to be considered as hostile... In the event that one of our aircraft engaged in the mission had for any reason to intrude the designated operational area of another, it had to immediately turn on its position lights in the colour layout agreed for that day. For this same reason, the anti-aircraft artillery was informed of the means of recognition.'

Over the summer CR.42s of the 161° *Gruppo Autonomo* CT continued their usual patrol missions over the sea and attempted, always unsuccessfully, to intercept British reconnaissance aircraft. During 1941, following the closure of the Greek front and the conquest of Crete, the importance of combat operations in the Dodecanese was reduced, but not, however, the routine activities of the fighters of the 161° *Gruppo Autonomo* CT.

In mid-January, the aircraft assigned to the *Gruppo*, commanded by *maggiore* Enrico Meille, still comprised an astonishing mixture of seven CR.32s, 27 CR.42 and nine G.50s, divided between the three *squadriglie* operating from Maritza and Gadurrà airfields and with a detachment at Kos, while four CR.42s were assigned to the night fighter *sezione* led by *tenente* Piero Ghiacci.

With the repatriation of the 161° *Gruppo Autonomo* CT and its replacement by the 154° *Gruppo Autonomo* CT with its eighteen G.50s, the career of the CR.42 in the Aegean skies was not concluded, as the new *gruppo* took on charge at least 28 of the remaining biplanes. Flying operations, despite the obsolescence of the aircraft, were continuous, albeit in certain aspects monotonous and frustrating, especially for the night fighters, which never managed to make contact with any British aircraft, and in December they suffered the loss of two pilots in flying accidents. At the beginning of 1943 the 154° *Gruppo Autonomo* CT still had 23 CR.42s and eight G.50s on charge, although not all of them were serviceable. With the arrival in February of the first AerMacchi C.202s, the worn out CR.42s and G.50s were relegated to patrol and convoy escort missions, operating until the Armistice of 8 September 1943, at which time the 154° *Gruppo Autonomo* CT still had a fleet of fourteen CR.42s, four of which were night fighters, nine G.50s and six C.202s.

During their operations in the Aegean, the Italian fighter pilots claimed the destruction of twelve British aircraft, against the loss of four of their own aircraft shot down, nine destroyed on the ground in RAF attacks, and at least another six fighters lost in flying accidents.

---

[1] *Esigenza Irak* was the name commonly adopted to identify the operation intended to support Iraq.
[2] The aircraft dope lacquer that is applied to fabric-covered aircraft used in Italy.

'Mission IQ':
The *Squadriglia Speciale Iraq*

A rare photograph of a CR.42 of the '*Squadriglia Speciale Irak*' probably taken at Gadurra on Rhodes during its transfer to Iraq. To be noted are the application of Iraqi markings and the underwing bomb pylons. (R.Gentilli)

HAVING become an independent kingdom after the First World War, until 1932 Iraq remained under a British colonial mandate, but developed its own armed forces, including an air arm, which was equipped with Italian aircraft such as the Breda 65 and S.79B. Yet despite its formal independence, Iraq always remained under British 'influence'. But on 1 April 1941, profiting from the war being fought between the European nations, the Iraqi nationalist leader, Rashid Ali al-Gaylani, who was sympathetic to the Axis cause, launched a coup d'état to overturn the government of the Regent, Prince Abd al-Ilah, and simultaneously to eject British forces from the country. The revolt was quickly suffocated by the British through the despatch of troops and equipment, and ended with the Iraqi coup leader fleeing to Iran.

The two Axis powers, being unable to intervene directly with ground forces, sent some fighter, bomber and transport units to Mesopotamia. Italy, lagging slightly behind the Germans, sent munitions and weapons as well as a *gruppo* of twelve CR.42 fighters. On 12 May 1941 *Superaereo* ordered the 155ª *Squadriglia* of the 3° *Gruppo*, 6° *Stormo* CT to begin preparations for a somewhat vague expedition to the Middle East codenamed '*Missione IQ*'. A group of twelve pilots was selected for the mission, and the redesignated 155ª *Squadriglia Speciale Irak*, commanded by *capitano* Francesco Sforza, was established at Ciampino Sud airport where the pilots received colonial uniforms and were saluted by the *Capo di Stato Maggiore* of the Regia Aeronautica, *generale* Francesco Pricolo. While at the Roma airfield the *Squadriglia* received twelve newly constructed CR.42s in the *Egeo* version which offered increased endurance and armour for the pilot. The biplanes were painted in the usual FIAT camouflage scheme with green and brown blotches on a sandy background and the standard visual recognition markings for the period, including a white fuselage band and a yellow engine cowling. All the aircraft were given Iraqi national insignia on their fuselage and wings, while their rudders were painted in the national colours of Iraq – green, white, red and black. The serial numbers of the aircraft assigned were MM7463, 7464, 7467, 7470, 7472, 7474, 7475, 7476, 7477, 7478, 7501 and 7511.

The Italian fighter formation departed from Ciampino Sud for the long transfer flight to Iraq at 1240 on 22 May, accompanied by an S.79 trimotor. The first planned stop was Valona airfield in Albania where CR.42 MM7511, piloted by *tenente* Bruno Contaldi, ran off the runway on landing and collided with a parked aircraft, Contaldi suffering injuries and his aircraft being destroyed. The remaining eleven aircraft left on the following day for Rhodes-Gadurrà, but the poor weather conditions would only permit them to take off from the Greek island for the final staging post of Aleppo in Syria on 27 May 1941. On the following day, 28 May, the eleven fighters arrived at Mosul divided into two groups, joining their Luftwaffe colleagues on the Iraqi airfield, the latter having already been in action in the Middle Eastern skies for some days.

Despite their late arrival, the Italian pilots did not waste time, and on the morning of the same day conducted their first combat mission, two CR.42s being scrambled to counter an attempted attack by two Bristol Blenheims. That afternoon, the Italian contingent was relocated to Kirkuk airfield. On the following morning three CR.42s took off on an offensive reconnaissance mission to Habbaniya airfield where the British units were based equipped with Gloster Gladiators, Hawker Audaxes, and Bristol Blenheim bombers. The Italian pilots were intercepted by a pair of Gladiators and three Audaxes of 94 Squadron which engaged them in combat. At the end of the encounter, the Italian pilots claimed two Gladiators and one Audax destroyed. On their part, the RAF pilots shot down CR.42 MM7476, piloted by *tenente* Lucio Valentini who, after bailing out, was taken prisoner. Another two CR.42s returned to Irkuk with minor damage.

On the same day three CR.42s blocked a raid by Blenheims on Irkuk airfield, while on 30 May seven CR.42s were scrambled to intercept a British attempt to bomb the Baghdad area. On their return from the mission two CR.42s, MM7463 and 7477, were seriously damaged on landing, the accidents caused by the irregular surface of the runway. In the afternoon four CR.42s conducted the last combat mission in Iraq, attacking columns of British troops and armour at the gates of the capital.

The military and operational situations had, in fact, turned firmly in favour of the British, and as the coup d'état had effectively failed, Rashid Ali and his supporters left Iraq, and as a consequence the Italo-German forces were forced into an inevitable withdrawal. At dawn on 31 May 1941 seven CR.42s departed for Aleppo in Syria, with three damaged and unrepairable CR.42s (MM7477, 7473 and 7470) abandoned at Kirkuk airfield. The balance of the brief and unfortunate expedition saw the execution of a total of 155 flying hours in Iraqi skies, with 3,800 machine gun rounds fired and two Gladiators claimed as shot down, against the loss of a CR.42 in combat and another four in a variety of incidents. On 1 June the CR.42s took off from Aleppo for the airfield at Rhodes, where the 155ª *Squadriglia Special Irak* was formally disbanded. Assuming a new identity as the 164° *Squadriglia* CT, it was reassigned to the control of the local 161° *Gruppo Autonomo* CT.

The CR.42CN night fighter

A CR.32Quater modified as a night fighter with an extended exhaust pipe. However, the total lack of adequate specialist equipment both on the ground and on board the fighter resulted in several accidents. (P.Monti)

TOWARDS the end of the 1930s the *Centro Sperimentale* at Furbara conducted some initial experiments with night fighters, modifying the FIAT CR.30, and successively the CR.32, with the installation of lengthened engine exhausts intended to prevent the pilot being dazzled. Given the total lack of radios and navigation equipment in the aircraft, however, the results achieved were somewhat disappointing. On the outbreak of the war, the night fighter as a stand-alone speciality was practically non-existent in Italy, as there were no dedicated or modified aircraft capable of performing that role. The first night air raids provided stark evidence of the total ineffectiveness and inefficiency of DICAT (*Difesa Contraerea Territoriale*), the Italian national air defence system, which lacked an effective reporting network and revealed almost complete confusion amongst the various authorities established to discharge the role.

The Regia Aeronautica attempted to redress this shortcoming, and in the course of the first summer of the war, constituted various *Caccia Notturna* (CN – Night Fighter) *Sezioni* CN, generally formed by three aircraft from the fighter units based near the principal Italian cities. Accordingly, these *Sezioni* were tasked with the defence of the industrial and military installations in their respective areas. The 53° *Stormo* CT activated a *Sezione* CN at Torino Mirafiori, the 54° *Stormo* CT at Lonate Pozzolo, the 4° *Stormo* CT at Treviso, the 6° *Stormo* at Brescia, the 3° *Stormo* at Novi Ligure, the 51° *Stormo* CT at Roma Ciampino, the 52° *Stormo* at La Spezia Sarzana, the 2° *Gruppo* CT at Taranto, the 13° *Gruppo* at Tripoli, the 10° *Gruppo* at Bengasi, the 1° *Stormo* CT at Palermo and the 9° *Gruppo* CT at Cagliari-Elmas.

Autonomous Sezioni CN were also activated in Albania, the Aegean, and in Italian East Africa. The aircraft types assigned to this duty were somewhat ad-hoc – a few CR.32s and the more 'modern' CR.42, both modified with elongated exhausts and flame shrouds applied close to their gun barrels. Specific role training was practically non-existent, while the operational conditions proved to be extremely precarious as the pilots had to fly literally blind, without any radio communications, hoping that a stroke of luck would see an enemy aircraft come into sight thanks to the light of the moon. Confirmation of this handicap is provided by the experience of *capitano* Corrado Ricci of the 410ª *Squadriglia* CT based at Dire Daua airfield in Ethiopia. On 17 September 1940, during a night interception mission in his CR.32, he opened fire with his machine guns at two Bristol Blenheims and consequently suffered problems with his vision caused by the flashes of the un-screened machine guns, the effects forcing Ricci into a long period of inactivity before his sight recovered and he was able to resume operations.

A CR.42CN of the 167° *Gruppo Autonomo* at Grottaglie during summer 1943. The *Gruppo's* biplanes were assigned to the night fighter role. Unusually this aircraft is also equipped with bomb racks under the fuselage. (Garello via F.Ballista)

Below: A biplane of the 303ª *Squadriglia*. It is probably a standard CR.42 of the unit and not a CR.42CN as it has no extended exhaust pipe and the lower part of undercarriage spats have been removed.

CR.42s of the night fighter section based at Genoa. (R.Gentilli)

Despite the precarious technical state of affairs, in the months following Italy's entry into the war other night fighter *nuclei autonomi* and *Squadriglie* were formed, and by mid-1941 at least twenty *Sezioni da Caccia Notturna* were operational. In general, however, the results obtained were fairly minimal, given the insufficiency of the aircraft and the minimal ground organisation. Nevertheless, in this early stage of night fighter defence operations, the Italian pilots did manage to achieve some results, and what could be considered as the first nocturnal air victory was attributed to *capitano* Giorgio Graffer, the commander of the 365ª *Squadriglia*, 150º *Gruppo*, 53º *Stormo CT* who, on the night of 13/14 August 1940, at the end of a protracted intercept, managed to make contact with a Whitley Mk.V bomber, P4965 ZA-H, of 10 Squadron RAF, flying from RAF Abingdon to bomb the Fiat engine factory in Torino. On trying to open fire with the SAFAT machine guns of his CR.42, they jammed (other sources suggest that he had run out of ammunition), and Graffer decided that the best solution would be to ram his fighter into the British bomber and parachute to safety. This he did, and despite the damaged suffered, the bomber managed to struggle back as far as the English Channel, where it eventually crashed with the loss of its two pilots.

Superaereo quickly began to appreciate the importance of the night fighter mission and the associated inadequacy of the available equipment, yet it had no other technically sufficient alternative than to introduce modifications to the CR.42 fleet, the only aircraft available in any quantity, and the modifications to which could be completed directly by their operating units. This included the installation of elongated exhaust pipes to prevent the pilot becoming dazzled by exhaust flames and to impede any enemy aircraft from potentially spotting the fighter in flight, anti-flash sleeves for the weapons, and instruments with illumination. With the introduction of the CR.42CN version, special illuminating rocket launchers were added, together with two high-intensity searchlights mounted in faired pods beneath the wings, together with an essential windmill electrical generator located on the wing. To complete the 'nocturnal' modifications, an overall black or dark smoke grey colour scheme was adopted. Furthermore, on some occasions, in order to save weight, one of the two 12.7 mm SAFAT guns was replaced by a 7.7 mm alternative.

It was only during 1941 that the Regia Aeronautica began to explore the possibility of obtaining aircraft specialised for the mission, but all the Italian designs examined were proposed conversions of aircraft designed for other roles, offering no concrete solutions. This left the CR.42CN as the only aircraft available to conduct the mission. Besides the existing limitations of the aircraft, it was also particularly penalised by the lack of radio telephony transmitters and receivers, which for a long time left the night fighter pilots 'deaf' and 'dumb' with grave repercussions for operational potential and impeding the pilots in their ability to operate with a certain level of effectiveness. Again, only towards mid-1941 was the installation of the ARC.4 radio receiver and the Allocchio Bacchini B.30 radio receiver and transmitter explored, and it would be from 1942 that the Allocchio Bacchini transceivers were routinely fitted, offering the pilots air-ground contact. New instructions for coordination with the DICAT were issued in 1941 under which it was established that up to 3,000 m altitude, air defence was delegated to the anti-aircraft artillery, while fighters would operate at higher altitudes, supported by searchlights. Nevertheless, the limitations of the available aircraft and the overwhelming difficulty of coordinating the air defences – still, despite the efforts of the personnel involved – hampered any significant results.

Driven by the need for a solution to the dilemma and lacking in alternative technology, in the course of the second half of 1941 *Superaereo* once again reorganised the air defence section with the creation of the *Comandi Intercettori* within

A CR.42 of the 1° N.A.I. *(Nucleo Addestramento Intercettori)* based at Treviso. (P.Monti)

The crash of the *Serie* XII CR.42CN, MM.9129, '1+5' of the 1° N.A.I based at Treviso.

Metal jacket insignia of the 377ª *Squadriglia Autonomo* CT. (P.Monti)

A CR.42CN, of the 377ª *Squadriglia Autonoma* CT. Note the style of the exhaust compared to the example below. (Garello via F.Ballista and Gentilli)

Below left and below: Two photographs of CR.42CN, 'Red 6' of the 377ª *Squadriglia Autonoma* CT which operated some FIAT biplanes converted for night fighter operations from Palermo Boccadifalco and from other Sicilian airfields. (Garello via F.Ballista and Gentilli)

The inscription on the engine cowling of this CR.42CN was painted by the assigned ground crew. It reads '*Io la notte non posso più dormire*' ('I could no longer sleep in the night.' (AM)

individual units. It was established that all fighter units based on the Italian mainland should, alongside their normal operational activity, participate in the defence of Italian national airspace by ensuring that at least one third of the aircraft present on each base would be available for the night alert service. The highest-ranking officer amongst the commanders of the fighter units would assume, for air defence purposes only, the role of *Comandante degli Intercettori*. If at an airfield there was already provision for a night fighter service through the presence of a dedicated *Sezione*, the *Comandante degli Intercettori* would become responsible for the deployment of all the assigned aircraft and their associated personnel. As a consequence, some thirty *comandi intercettori* were activated, often in practice in tandem with a similar number of *sezioni* CN present on the bases. This solution soon proved to be less than optimal, but it was necessary to wait until 1 October 1941 for the Regia Aeronautica to be able to deploy the first unit specifically dedicated to night fighting in the shape of the 171° *Gruppo Autonomo* CN, operating from Gela airfield in Sicilia. Formed by the 301ª *Squadriglia*, the second 302ª *Squadriglia*, although planned to be constituted, never became operational. The unit was placed under the command of *maggiore* Giovanni Buffa and was equipped with some fifteen CR.42s, although only part of the fleet was in CN configuration. Over the course of its brief operational life (the unit was disbanded in the December of the same year), the results obtained were fairly disappointing, although the *Squadriglia* did manage to record one aerial victory on 28 October 1941, when a CR.42 managed to intercept and shoot down a Fairey Albacore of the Fleet Air Arm's 828 Naval Air Squadron near Capo Scaramia.

With the disbanding of the 171° *Gruppo*, the CR.42CNs of the 301ª *squadriglia* remained in Sicilia and were distributed amongst the various *sezioni* CN based at the principal airfields on the island.

A victory was also obtained by the *sezione notturna* operating in Albania when, on the night of 16 March 1941, *sergenti maggiore* Desideri and Penna of the 160° *Gruppo* managed to shoot down a Wellington which had attacked their base at Tirana. In the course of the same mission, another two British twins were attacked and damaged.

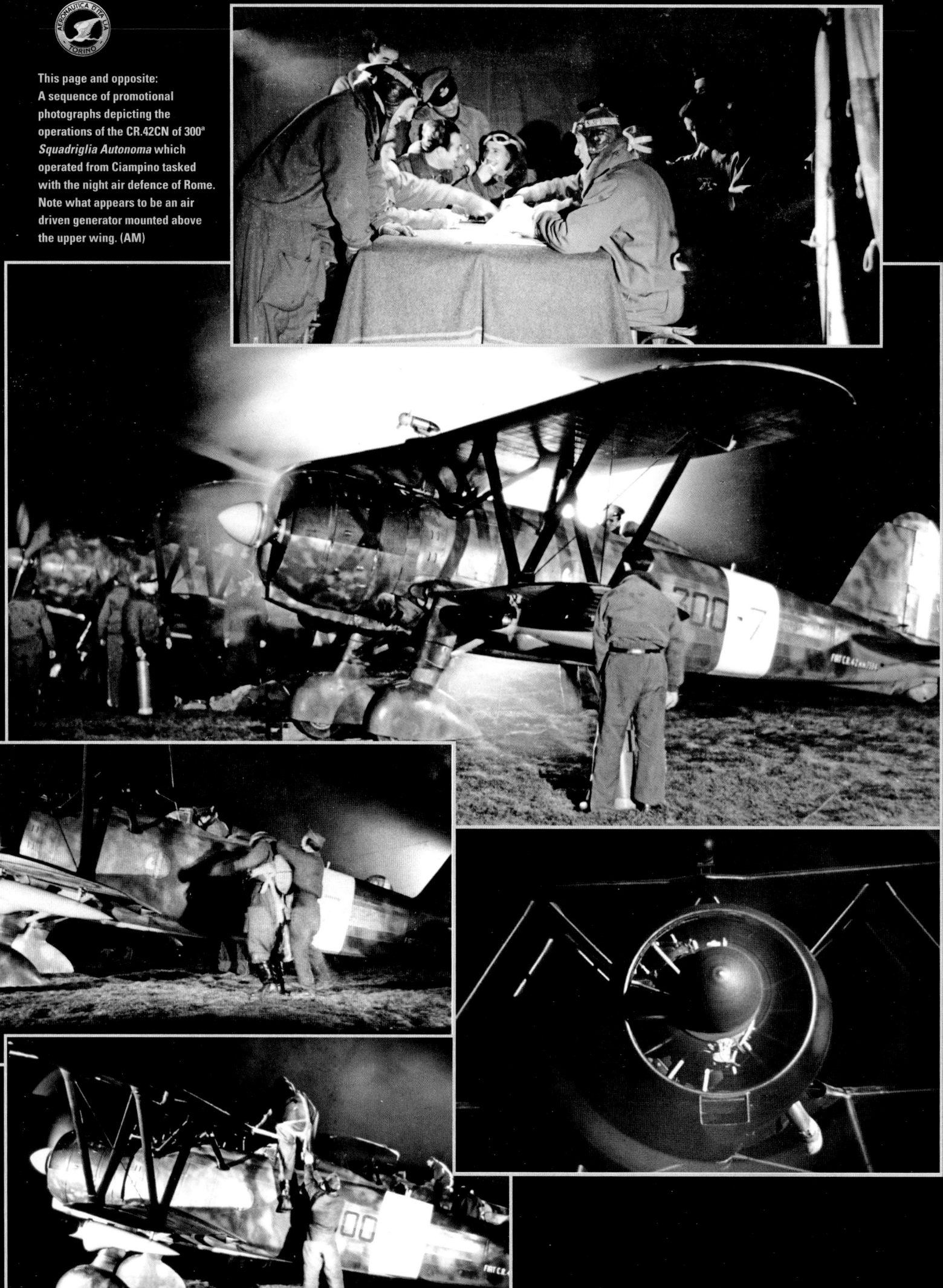

This page and opposite: A sequence of promotional photographs depicting the operations of the CR.42CN of 300ª *Squadriglia Autonoma* which operated from Ciampino tasked with the night air defence of Rome. Note what appears to be an air driven generator mounted above the upper wing. (AM)

On 12 July 1941 another Wellington was shot down near Bengasi by a CR.42 piloted by *sergente maggiore* Felice Squassoni of the 18° *Gruppo*, while on 28 October 1941, *sottotenenti* Parmeggiani and Calafiore of the 376ª *Squadriglia*, engaged in a mission in defence of the city of Napoli, claimed the destruction of a Wellington bomber of 104 Squadron which crashed near Paterno S. Arcangelo (Salerno). Some weeks later, on the night of 6 December 1941, *maresciallo* Vincenzo Patriarca of the 356° *Squadriglia*, 21° *Gruppo*, 51° *Stormo* managed to shoot down Wellington R1066 of 40 Squadron over the Gulf of Napoli.

At the beginning of 1942 the night fighter force of the Regia Aeronautica was reorganised completely, with the sections deployed around the various Italian airfields being joined by the first specialised units, such as the 167° *Gruppo Autonomo C.N./Intercettori* led by *maggiore* Corrado Ricci, which was tasked with the defence of Lazio and in particular the Italian capital. The *Gruppo* was composed of two *Squadriglie*, the 300ª and 303ª, deployed to various airfields around Roma and equipped with a particularly diverse fleet of aircraft including, besides the ever-present CR.42CN, the Reggiane RE.2001CN, Fabrizi F.5, and AerMacchi C.200.

Of particular importance, however, was the establishment in February 1942 of the *Comando Intercettori Leone*. This command was intended for the defence of the industrial cities of northern Italy and it was assigned a single operational unit, the 41° *Stormo Intercettori*, which comprised the 59° and 60° *Gruppo*. While still operating CR.42CNs, which represented the backbone of the operational fleet, it also numbered Re.2001CNs from the airfields at Venegono and Lonate Pozzolo. Also placed under the control of the *Comando Intercettori Leone* were two training units, the 1° N.A.I. (interceptor training section) at Treviso and the SVSV (*Scuola Volo Senza Visibilità* – Instrument Flying School) at Linate,

these units operating a diverse mix of aircraft. Towards the end of 1942 two night fighter *gruppi*, the 59° and 60°, were operational in the defence of northern Italy, together with a few *sezioni da caccia notturna* organised by the other operational units, the total available force amounting to around fifty CR.42CNs. For the defence of central Italy the 167° *Gruppo* possessed ten CR.42CNs, while another twenty biplanes were in service with a few autonomous *sezioni da caccia notturna* based in Sicilia and Sardegna.

On the night of 23 October 1942 an attack on Genova by RAF bombers terminated with a victory gained by *tenente* Catania of the 13° *Gruppo*, who managed to intercept and shoot down Lancaster R5566 coded OL-B, the wreckage of which was discovered two weeks later near Sori. In the course of the same night *tenente* Calvani, operating with the *Sezione CN Autonoma* (autonomous night fighter section) at Albenga, also claimed the destruction of a British four-engine bomber. The first victory recorded by the *Comando Intercettori* Leone, however, was attributed to *capitano* Giovanni Scagliarini, the commander of the 233ª *Squadriglia* of the 59° *Gruppo*, who, having scrambled from Caselle (Torino) in a CR.42CN on 21 November 1942,

managed to reach and shoot down Halifax DT 571 coded MP-M of 76 Squadron, which crashed near Bardonecchia (Torino). These victories were, in reality, achieved by the courage and efforts of the pilots, rather than their equipment, and it would only be from the spring of 1943 that the Italians began to operate more capable and specialised German-supplied aircraft, such as the Do 217 J equipped with airborne radar systems, and which worked in cooperation with ground-based radar stations, these also provided by the Germans.

In any case, even despite another of the continual reorganisations of the Regia Aeronautica's night fighter force in 1943, caused by the introduction of the first aircraft specialising in the role and the introduction of radar detection systems provided by the Germans, the CR.42CNs continued to be used as night fighters, working alongside more capable aircraft supplied by Germany. The importance of Rosatelli's biplane in this role lies in the fact that of the nine night victories confirmed by the Regia Aeronautica, some eight were obtained by pilots flying the FIAT CR.42, and only one victory, obtained on 17 July 1943 by *capitano* Ammannato, was achieved by an aircraft, the Do.217J, that had been expressly configured for the role.

Victories achieved by the FIAT CR.42CN

Date	Pilot	*Gruppo*	Type	Serial
16.08.40	*Cap.* G. Graffer	150° *Gruppo*	Whitley Mk V	N1497
28.10.40	unknown	171° *Gruppo*	Albacore	
16.03.41	*Serg. M.* Desideri/Penna	160° *Gruppo*	Wellington	R1837
28.10.41	*S. Ten.* Parmeggiani/Calafiore	376ª Sq. Aut.	Wellington	
05.12.41	*Serg. M.* Patriarca	21° *Gruppo*	Wellington	R1066
23.10.42	*Ten.* Catania	13° *Gruppo*	Lancaster I	R5566
23.10.42	*Ten.* Calvani	13° *Gruppo*	Bomber (?)	
21.11.42	*Cap.* G. Scagliarini	59° *Gruppo*	Halifax	DT571

After the Italian Armistice

VARIOUS sources report that on 8 September 1943, the date of the Armistice, the units of the Regia Aeronautica that were spread around the various theatres of the war had around 100 CR.42s on strength, of which little more than half were combat ready.

The announcement of the Armistice took Italian units by surprise, and lacking in orders and direction from senior officers, they entered a period of profound chaos with dismembered units and personnel who, in part, moved to the north and, in part, to the south, where they were incorporated into the Regia Aeronautica del Sud. In the post-armistice confusion there were even cases in which pilots preferred to defect to nearby Switzerland rather than remain and to collaborate with, or worse, be captured by, the Germans. For example, on 10 September 1943, *capitano* Mario Anselmi of the 234ª *Squadriglia*, 60° *Gruppo Autonomo Caccia Intercettori*, took off from the airfield at Venegono in his CR.42CN

At the time of the Armistice of 8 September 1943, Italian servicemen made their choice: some went to the south, some to the north, and some moved to a neutral nation, as did this CR.42CN of the 234ª *Squadriglia* of 60° *Gruppo* C.I. which went from Venegono to land at Magadino in nearby Switzerland. (R.Gentilli)

MM9128 and landed at the Swiss airfield of Magadino where pilot and aircraft were interned. Returned to Italy after the end of the war, the CR.42 was placed into service with the *Scuola di Volo e Addestramento Caccia* (Flying and Fighter Training School) at Brindisi in 1947. On a previous occasion, on 21 September 1942, a G.50 had also been interned when a navigation error caused by bad weather forced G.50bis MM6158, flown by *maresciallo pilota* Alfredo Porta, to land at Emmen airfield.

It is estimated that just under ten CR.42s were in service with the Regia Aeronautica del Sud.

Order of Battle
CR.42 units as at 8 September 1943

1 Squadra Aerea Milano
2° *Gruppo Autonomo Caccia Intercettori* (152ª and 358ª *Squadriglia*) = 12 CR.42
60° *Gruppo Autonomo Caccia Intercettori* (234ª and 235ª *Squadriglia*) = 5 CR.42

3 Squadra Aerea Lazio
15° Stormo Assalto
46° *Gruppo* (20ª and 21ª *Squadriglia*) = 15 CR.42
47° *Gruppo* (52ª and 53ª *Squadriglia*) = 13 CR.42

167° *Gruppo Autonomo Caccia Intercettori* (302ª and 303ª *Squadriglia*) = 6 CR.42

Comando Forze Aeree Corsica
160° *Gruppo Autonomo* CT = 2 CR.42

Aeronautica Dell'Egeo
154° *Gruppo Autonomo* CT (395ª and 396ª *Squadriglia*) = 8 CR.42

Sezione Autonoma Caccia Intercettori = 5 CR.42

Aeronautica Dell'Albania
392ª *Squadriglia Autonoma* CT = 11 CR.42

Aeronautica Della Grecia
Nucleo Autonomo Caccia Intercettori = 4 CR.42

Aeronautica in Yugoslavia
383ª *Squadriglia Autonoma Assalto* = 22 CR.42
1ª *Squadriglia Forze Navali* = 2 CR.42

Note: Quantities of aircraft assigned are speculative

A CR.42 of the Regia Aeronautica del Sud. The biplanes which served with what is known commonly as the 'Aeronautica Cobelligerante' were mostly aircraft flown by pilots wishing to leave northern Italy or the Balkan possessions to join the 'cobelligerent' forces based in the Puglia region. (E. Leproni)

FIAT CR.42 FALCO

A Luftwaffe CR.42/Lw photographed in the FIAT-Aeritalia yards and badly damaged by American bombing on 25 April 1944. (ASF)

Left: Groundcrew of 1./NSGr 9. From left: Grampe, Günther Helbig, *Fw.* Engelmaier, Heinisch (above) and Gruber. The CR.42 behind them shows to advantage its flame-dampers and white spinner. This aircraft lacks even the cut-down wheel fairings typical of NSG 9's Fiats. (Nick Beale)

The majority of these had belonged to the 8° *Gruppo Autonomo Caccia Terrestre*. After a brief period with the *Scuola Caccia* in Sardegna they were concentrated at Lecce Galatina airfield, being relegated to weather reconnaissance and liaison duties, operated by the *Squadriglia Autonoma del Comando Unità Aerea* (*Comando Unità Aerea* liaison flight) or as advanced trainers by the 3ª *Squadriglia* of the 2° *Gruppo Scuola Volo Caccia* based at Lecce-Leverano, where they were still active in late spring 1945.

Initially, at least twenty CR.42s were recovered by the A.N.R. on airfields in northern Italy. Over the weeks following the Armistice these were joined by a few more, being utilised for training and communications duties, but only a few managed to survive until the end of hostilities.

The Luftwaffe
With thanks to Nick Beale

It is calculated that on 8 September 1943 and in the days that followed, the FIAT CR.42s requisitioned in Italian territory by the Germans, including those which were unserviceable, amounted to around 150 examples, to which can be added a further fifty aircraft recovered in the Balkans and Aegean. Many of the CR.42s were transferred to Austria to be used as trainers at Graz, Bad Voslan and Vat airfields. The aircraft ferry flights were conducted by Italian pilots from the G.T.V. (*Gruppo Trasporto Velivoli* – aircraft transport squadron), which carried several transfer missions. The captured aircraft in best condition were placed into service by the Luftwaffe together with further new-build aircraft. In fact, following the seizing of the armament manufacturing infrastructure in northern Italy by the R.U.K., the German authorities issued an order for the construction of 200 biplanes identified by the specific CR.42/Lw designation, indicating a version optimised for night ground-attack. The Allied bombing in the early months of 1944 which destroyed the FIAT facilities in Torino prevented the completion of the order, although not before some 112 of these aircraft had entered service with the Luftwaffe.

The CR.42/Lw was substantially modified compared to the versions flown by the *Regia Aeronautica*. The most important changes were the inversion of the throttle control[1], modified cockpit instrumentation, the installation of an efficient German-built FuG 17 radio and FuG 16[2] guidance system. Extended exhaust pipes with flame

---
[1] In Italian fighters, in contrast to German and Allied aircraft, pushing forward on the throttle did not initiate an increase in power, but rather its reduction.
[2] This system comprised a receiver for the signals from the radar guidance system, in practice a passive signal tracker which could intercept and track signals emitted by other radio localising equipment.

The CR.42/Lw were biplanes requisitioned at various Italian airfields, in the Balkans or delivered by FIAT. German pilots used the aircraft for advanced training and to carry out night attacks on the bumpy roads of the central Apennines, hunting down slow-moving Allied columns heading for the front lines.

Posing by this CR.42 which has the red spinner of 2./NSGr 9 are, from left: *Gefr.* Franz Spörr, *Fw.* Horst Rau, *Uffz.* Schmeiduch, *Fw.* Horst Greßler and (on his shoulders), *Gefr.* Ewald Kapahnke. (Nick Beale)

suppressors were fitted, underwing ETC 50 racks permitted the carriage of four 50-kg bombs and the lower undercarriage fairings were removed to permit operations from unprepared terrain. The Luftwaffe proposed using the biplane for night-attack missions behind enemy lines against limited targets, such as artillery positions, logistical concentrations, or vehicle columns, exploiting the darkness and agility of the fighter to compensate for its limited performance.

The first unit constituted in Italy to be equipped with the CR.42/Lw was 1./*Nachtschlachtgruppe* 9 (NSG₁. 9), formally established on 30 November 1943 at Caselle airfield, initially with the Caproni Ca. 314, which proved unsatisfactory; establishment of a second *Staffel* was ordered on 28 January 1944. By the end of February, 1. and 2./NSGr. 9 had five and 14 CR.42s respectively. Caselle was where all new production CR.42/Lw aircraft were delivered and was close to the *Scuola Addestramento Caccia* at Venaria Reale where German pilots underwent type conversion.

The first modified CR.42/Lws were camouflaged for night operations by adding 'clouds' of brown and either pale blue or pale grey on the upper surfaces and dark green on the undersides over the original Italian paint. 1./NSGr. 9's aircraft carried the unit codes E8+_H in black, while the individual aircraft letter was outlined in white, a colour repeated on the spinner; the 2. *Staffel's* aircraft had a red individual letter outlined in white and a red spinner.

Six or seven CR.42s of 1./NSGr. 9 deployed to Viterbo on about 10 March 1944, five of them going into action against artillery positions in the Anzio-Nettuno beachhead on the night of the 11/12th. On this occasion, however, bad weather hindered the mission, and prevented the complete execution of the attack and the identification of any results. Lacking blind-flying aids these missions were, in the main, limited to periods of clear moonlight. 1./NSGr. 9 had re-equipped with the Ju 87 D by the end of March and began operations over the front in April. The 2. *Staffel* lost its first and only CR.42 to an RAF Beaufighter on 2 June, converting to the Ju 87 in the second half of the month. In their three months of operations over the front, the CR.42s had proved a difficult target for the night fighters, their slow speed forcing pilots to drop their flaps and lower their landing gear to avoid overtaking the slow-flying biplanes and get into a firing position.

Probably the majority of the CR.42s recovered after the Italian Armistice and adapted for the specific mission operated in Croatia, beginning in February 1944, with the *Stab* and three *Staffeln* of *Nachtschlachtgruppe* 7, engaged in attack missions against Marshal Tito's partisans, striking depots, logistics hubs, headquarters and shipping among the Adriatic islands by both day and night. In April 1944 *Fliegerführer Croatia* was advised that, unlike the Heinkel He 46, the 'CR.42 with super-heavy machine guns is preeminently suited for attacking wooden ships'. Nine of NSGr. 7's CR.42s were destroyed and five damaged when Velika Gorica was strafed on 2 February 1945. Although 1./NSGr. 7 was withdrawn to Graz in Austria and the whole *Gruppe* was ordered disbanded in early April, orders were given that the remaining elements should still be employed as long as there was fuel available. The unit's fuselage code was 4X and *Staffel* letters were H, K and L. Camouflage varied, some aircraft having an Italian scheme of hazelnut brown dappled over dark green and pale grey undersides, while others had cloudy patches reminiscent of NSGr. 9.

The CR.42 in foreign service

IN the period immediately preceding the war, many air arms recognised the need to modernise their front line forces, and on many occasions they turned to the Italian aircraft industry. As mentioned earlier, the good reputation earned by the FIAT biplanes during the Spanish Civil War influenced the selection by some air forces of the new FIAT fighter, which achieved good export successes.

Magyar Királyi Honvéd Légierő – Hungary

The Magyar Királyi Honvéd Légierő of Hungary was the first European air arm outside Italy to equip itself with the CR.42. The first aircraft of the initial batch of eighteen aircraft ordered was delivered to the airport at Szombathely on 17 June 1939. Subsequently an order was placed for another fifty aircraft, together with forty spare engines. The CR.42s, which were delivered

The CR.42, coded V-250, of the 1/4 *'Szent György'* (Saint George) fighter squadron

The CR.42, coded V-228, of the 1/4 *'Szent György'* (Saint George) fighter squadron with the earlier style identification markings and Italian style camouflage. (G. Punka)

This CR 42, coded V.204, belonged to the 2/4 *'Kőr Ász'* (Ace of Hearts) squadron, during 1941. (G. Punka)

A Hungarian Air Force CR.42 in flight with the new national markings adopted after 1942.

without camouflage, received the Hungarian designation V.2, and military serials V.201 to V.270. Only subsequently were they camouflaged using the four typical 'Krayer'[1] colours of grey, brown, dark green and blue. In total, the type equipped four fighter units of the 1. *vadász ezred* and 2. *vadász ezred*; the 1/3 *osztály* (previously 1/6 *osztály*) *'Kőr Ász'* (Ace of Hearts), the 1/4 *osztály 'Szent György'* (Saint George), the 2/3 *osztály 'Ricsi'* (Ritchie – a dog's name) and the 2/4 *osztály*, *'Tőr'* (Dagger).

The FIAT fighters quickly found employment during the brief campaign of April 1941 against Yugoslavia, and were then called into action against the Soviet Union from late June 1941. Only three of the four CR.42 units took part in hostilities there, initially 2/3 *osztály* and subsequently 2/4 *osztály*. This latter unit was, however, quickly recalled home because of the limited activity and high number of flying accidents, leaving the 2/3 *osztály* to operate alone until it was relieved by 1/3 *osztály* in mid-July. On its return to Hungary, on 13 July, after seventeen days of operations 2/3 *osztály* had recorded five confirmed aerial victories. For its part, 1/3 *osztály* fought doggedly until the end of the campaign, only returning to Hungary on 26 November 1941 having completed 144 combat missions totalling 447 sorties and 800 flying hours. During the period the unit was accredited with seventeen aerial victories and one probable, but suffered the loss of two pilots in combat.

During the months of operations on the Russian front, the CR.42s were involved in some particularly significant missions. Among these was that of 7 August 1941 when, at the conclusion of a hard-fought dogfight, despite the loss of just a single aircraft, the *Falcos* of 1/3 *osztály* destroyed seven enemy fighters above the bridgehead in the Zaporozne area. Another particularly important operation was that conducted on 12 August 1941, when twelve CR.42s, together with six Reggiane 2000s, escorted three Caproni CA 135s on a bombing raid against the bridge at Nikolayev on the River Bug. On that occasion, the Hungarian fighters shot down some seven Russian I-16s against the loss of just one Reggiane.

Subsequently, all the remaining CR.42s were progressively utilised as trainers, and it is known that they continued in this role until at least 1944, after which they were withdrawn from service. Worthy of mention is CR.42, V209, which, in April 1941, was experimentally modified with a Weiss Manfred WM14A 910-hp engine, (a licence-built version of the Gnome-Rhône 14K). The engine proved to be unsuitable for use with the fighter, however, and the concept was not followed up.

Aéronautique Militaire – Belgium

As part of a process to satisfy an urgent requirement for modern combat aircraft, just prior to the outbreak of the Second World War in September 1939, the Belgian Air Force sent an official mission to FIAT in Torino to negotiate the acquisition of forty CR.42s to re-equip the II *Group de Chasse*, which was formed of two flights still equipped with an obsolete British-built aircraft, the Fairey Firefly. Despite an elevated purchase price, a contract was signed in December of the same year, based on the assurance that FIAT would be able to deliver the fighters within three months of the date of signing.

The first aircraft were delivered on 6 March 1940 to the *Etablissements de l'Aéronautique* at Evere for assembly, and after their test flights, they were divided between 3/II/2 *'Cocotte Rouge'* and 4/II/2 *'Cocotte Blanc'*, based at Nivelles airfield. At the time of the German invasion of Belgium on 10 May 1940, thirty aircraft had been delivered, identified by the individual serials running from R-1 to R-30, although there were fewer operational fighters, as one aircraft (R-10) had been destroyed during its delivery flight, and another in an

---

[1] Krayer was the largest paint manufacturer in Hungary.

FIAT FIGHTERS

CR.42, coded R-1, of 3/II/2Aé 'Cocotte Rouge'. It was destroyed at Brustem airport on 10 May 1940. (D. Brack)

CR.42, coded R-14, of 3/II/2Aé 'Cocotte Rouge', damaged and abandoned during the attack on Nivelles airfield on 10 May 1940 (D. Brack)

CR.42, coded R-17, of 3/II/2Aé 'Cocotte Rouge', destroyed at Brustem airport on 10 May 1940. (D. Brack)

accident during training, while a further two aircraft (R-2 and R-21) were grounded for maintenance.

In the morning of 10 May, the CR.42s were transferred to Brustem St. Truiden airfield, in the process losing an aircraft (R-30) in a landing accident. Shortly after arriving at the new base, the Italian fighters were involved in combat when, during the morning, they attacked a formation of Ju 52s of 17./KGzbV 5 in the Tongres area, forcing one of the tri-motor transports to make an emergency landing near Maastricht, while the CR.42 of Sgt Roger Dellanay was shot down in the course of a dogfight with a Bf 109 E of Luftwaffe I./JG 1. Following the overflight of the airfield by a Luftwaffe reconnaissance aircraft in the early afternoon, just after 1400, Major Lamarche, the commander of the II *Group de Chasse* ordered his fighters dispersed amongst the trees of the adjacent forest, but there was not sufficient time to hide them all. Half an hour later came the first machine gun attack on the airfield by some Bf 109Es, which was followed by a heavy raid by the Stuka dive-bombers of I./St.G 2. By the end of this attack some fourteen aircraft had been destroyed on the ground, despite the strenuous defence mounted by some CR.42s which managed to take-off while the raid was in progress. On return, their pilots claimed the destruction of three German aircraft. Just prior to the attack Lt Werner de Mérode of 3/II/2, returning from a patrol mission, intercepted a Do 17, possibly the reconnaissance aircraft that had flown over Brustem airfield. He attacked it, and it came down in flames near Waremme.

On the following day, 11 May 1940, the surviving CR.42s were incorporated into the fleet of 4/II/2 '*Cocotte Blanc*', which was moved to the airfield at Nieuwkerke-Waas in northern Belgium. Over the next few days the Belgian pilots were involved in other actions, suffering further losses, such as the two aircraft lost on 14 May in a duel between five CR.42s and fifteen Bf 109s, while another was shot down by a Do 17. On 16 May the remaining fighters, at least six aircraft, were moved to Chartres airfield in France, where, however, they would once again be the target of a raid by Do 17 bombers on 19 May, in which CR.42 R-26 was completely destroyed. After four days of operations the operational balance registered twenty aircraft lost, of which four in combat, and claims of six German aircraft shot down.

On 1 June another three aircraft of the order arrived by train (R-31, R-32 and R-33) while a fourth (R-34) was stuck on a road due to a problem with the truck on which it had been loaded. Following the loss of another two CR.42s (R-23 and R-28) during a German attack on 3 June, the Belgian fighters were moved again, firstly to Bordeaux-Mérignac and then on to Montpellier, where the last remaining aircraft (R-24, R-29, R-31, R-32 and R-33) were subsequently captured by the Germans. The final fate of the captured CR.42s is uncertain, but they were probably placed into use by the Luftwaffe as trainers for use with *Jagdgeschwader* 107 at Toul.

A J 11 of F 9 wing is rolled out of the 'cave' hangar at Save. (P. Lindquist)

Two fine studies of J 11 Nr 11 of the F 9 wing on patrol duty. (P. Lindquist)

Despite its inferiority in comparison with German fighters, the Belgian CR.42s performed very well in combat and on the date of the armistice, 28 June 1940, the Italian-supplied fighters had flown 35 operational missions, claiming five aerial victories and six probables, against the loss of just two fighters in combat.

Flygvapnet – Sweden
With thanks to Mikael Olrog

Sweden had made some efforts to strengthen its fighter force before the war, placing orders for the Gloster Gladiator and the Seversky EP-1. However, after the outbreak of war it was realised that more was needed, especially after Sweden sent 12 out of 55 Gladiators to Finland with the Swedish volunteer unit F 19. By the end of 1939 Sweden was trying to place orders for the Bf 109 in Germany, and Hawker Hurricanes as well as additional Gladiators in England, but neither attempt met with success. The FIAT CR.42 was evaluated and available for delivery, but it was deemed to be obsolete at the time. Rather, an offer for 144 Vultee 48C Vanguards from the USA was accepted.

Swedish support for Finland was very strong and several different initiatives were put in place to generate funds with which to purchase and then gift urgently needed equipment. Some of these initiatives were focused on sourcing additional fighter aircraft – a result of the systematic and

J 11s of F 9 wing undergoing maintenance on a snow-covered airfield, probably Kiruna in Lappland, during the spring of 1942. The aircraft (far left) appears to be in the process of being converted from its wheeled undercarriage to skis. Note the wheels and an undercarriage spat lying on the snow.

A sequence showing the fitment of skis intended for operating on snowy terrain. (P.Lindquist)

The skis when fitted used the axle of the wheeled undercarriage strut as the mounting and pivot point. (P.Lindquist)

A rear tail skid replaced the tailwheel for winter operations. (P.Lindquist)

ruthless Russian bombings of Finnish cities and civilians that was covered in detail in the Swedish press. Since the FIAT CR.42 was available for delivery, it became the focus of efforts and the Finns agreed to accept a gift of 12 such aircraft despite the fact that they regarded it as obsolete. There was one advantage with the CR.42: its fixed landing gear could be fitted with skis. It was, however, urgent that the order was placed since both Belgium and Norway were also keen on the aircraft.

The plan was to have the 12 CR.42s with F 19 wing by the beginning of April 1940. A first contract of five aircraft was signed on 15 February, with a second contract of seven signed on the 24th. The purchase of the aircraft was financed by a mix of private individuals and various organisations, and each aircraft had an assigned donor. The first CR.42s were in transit on a ship from Italy when the Winter War ended on 13 March which changed the situation. Finland no longer had interest in the obsolete CR.42 and instead wanted the funds to help finance the purchase of the Brewster B-239 Buffalo that had been ordered in the USA. The Swedish government agreed to take over the 12 CR.42s with the intention of using them in the reconnaissance role with F 3 wing at Linköping which was operating the even more obsolete Fokker CV (S 6).

The first five aircraft arrived in Göteborg in April. They were assembled and test flown by an Italian pilot before being transferred on 27 April to F 3 wing. At the time of delivery, the aircraft were painted in Italian camouflage, but had Swedish national markings in the M/37 style, and serial numbers in black, while the unit code and individual aircraft number was to be applied at the Wing. In Swedish service the aircraft received the designation J 11. A challenge for the Swedish pilots was the handling of the throttle control which was operated in the opposite direction to other Swedish aircraft. In quick succession, two out of the five aircraft were lost. The first crash occurred on 30 May after engine failure, and the second on 4 June, when a soldier positioned himself prone on the airfield in front of a CR.42 as it took off in order take a photograph. He was hit by the landing gear and killed. The landing gear sustained heavy damage and the pilot had to leave the aircraft by parachute since landing was deemed impossible. The second batch of seven CR.42 arrived in the Finnish harbour of Petsamo in early June 1940, only to be transported overland to Göteborg for assembly. The harbour of that city could not be used due to the invasion of Norway and Denmark.

A third order for 60 CR.42s was signed by Sweden on 7 October 1940 to compensate for the US cancellation of Swedish orders for the last 60 Seversky EP-1s and the 144 Vultee 48C Vanguards. Payment for these aircraft was made partially in raw material such as different types of steel, zinc, tin, copper, mica and crude rubber. This time delivery of the aircraft to Sweden was made by rail through Germany between December 1940 and June 1941. It had been decided to raise two new fighter wings, F 9 (Göteborg) and F 10 (Malmö) with the former being equipped with the CR.42.

The CR.42 would mainly be used to guard Swedish neutrality, escort damaged foreign aircraft to an airfield and sometimes to shoot down drifting barrage balloons during its service with F 9 Wing. In February 1944, three CR.42 were loaned to the newly raised F 13 Wing in Norrköping, later supplemented by 18 more when F 9 Wing began to convert to the Swedish designed FFVS J 22 fighter. By March 1945, the last CR.42 had been struck off charge from the Air Force.

A total of 31 aircraft had been written off due to accidents. Some aircraft were gifted to vocational schools while 13 airworthy CR.42s were sold as target tugs to Svensk Flygtjänst AB based at Bromma airport in Stockholm, with an additional six used as a source for spare parts. Two aircraft were lost while on target tug duties. But, already by 1946, the CR.42 was replaced by the more appropriate Miles Martinet with just two CR.42s being retained for spares and flown occasionally until 1949 while the remainder were scrapped.

The Swedish CR.42s received RSwAF serials 2501 to 2572 painted in small black digits in front of the tailplane. RSwAF National insignias applied included the M/37 or M/40 styles, combined with the Wing number '3' or '9', together with an individual aircraft number painted on the fin and the nose in large digits. Civilian registrations used on Svensk Flygtjänst AB's aircraft were SE-AOH, -AOI, -AOK to -AOP, -AOR, -AOS, -AOU, -AOW and -AOX.[1]

---

[1] Forslund M, *J 11 Fiat* CR.42, Mikael Forslund Produktion, Falun, 2011

Two good views of Save airfield near Gothenburg, the home of the F 9 wing. The field had a large hangar in a 'cave', dug into the adjacent hillside. (P.Lindquist)

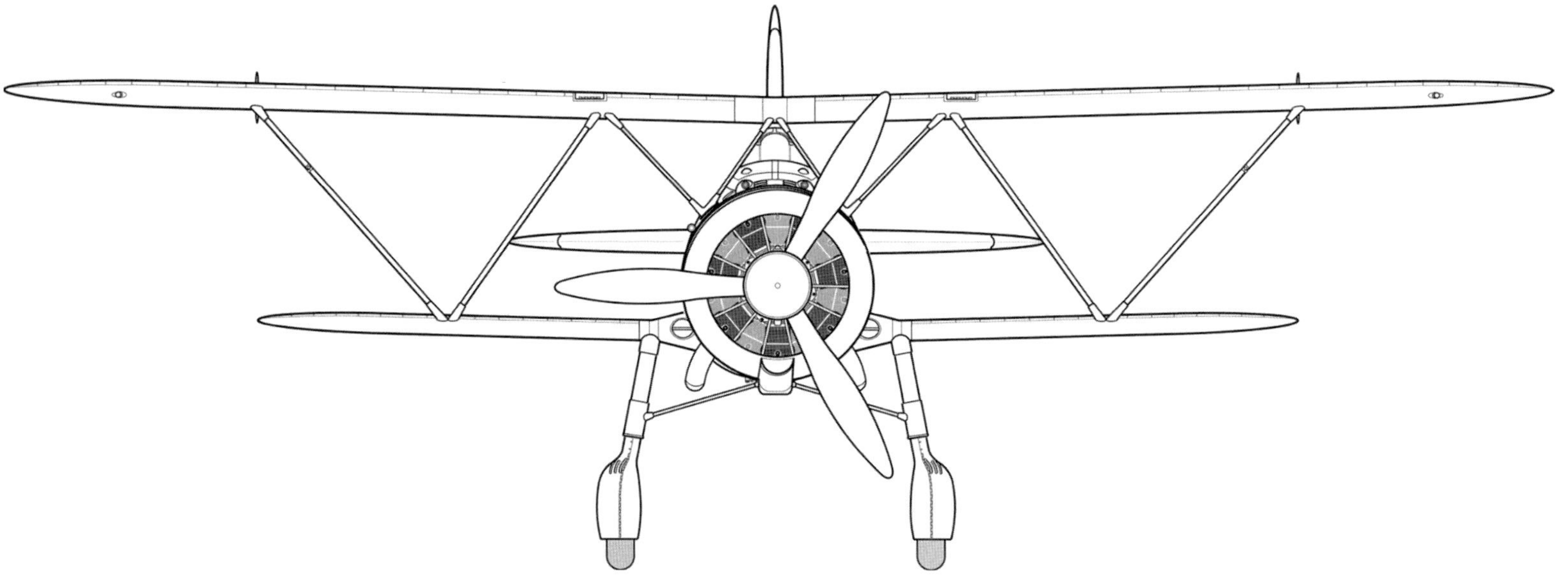

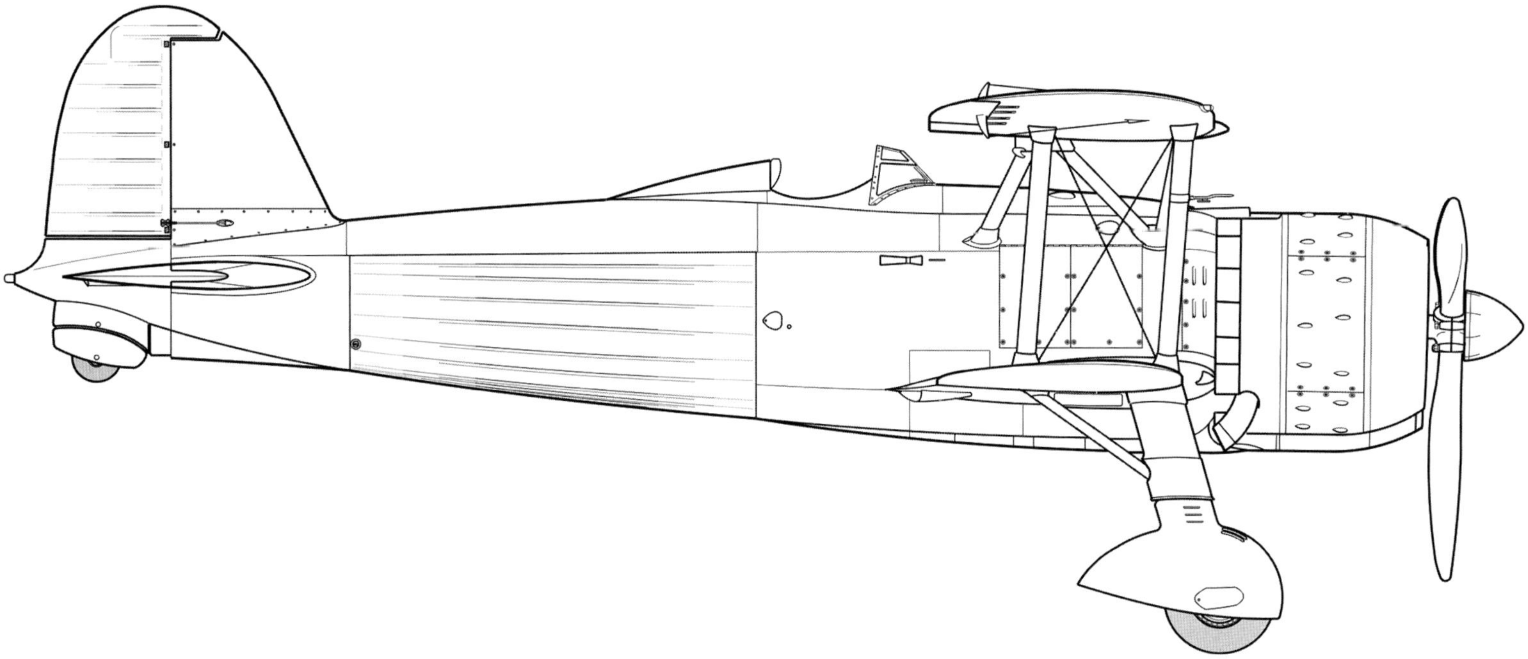

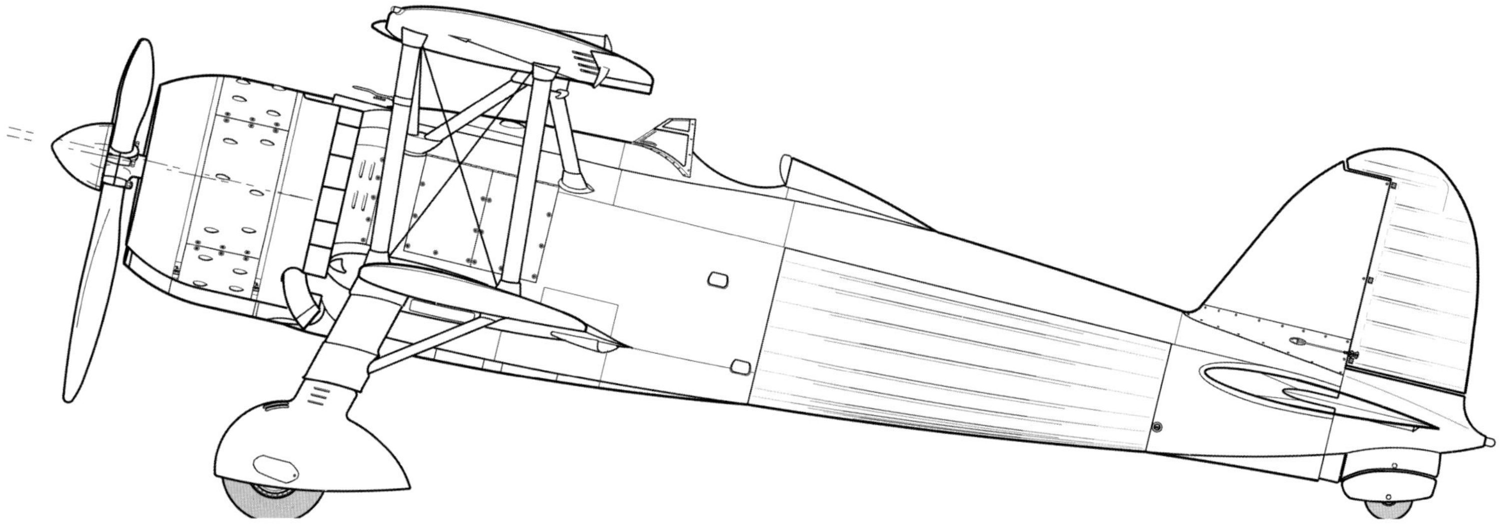

FIAT FIGHTERS

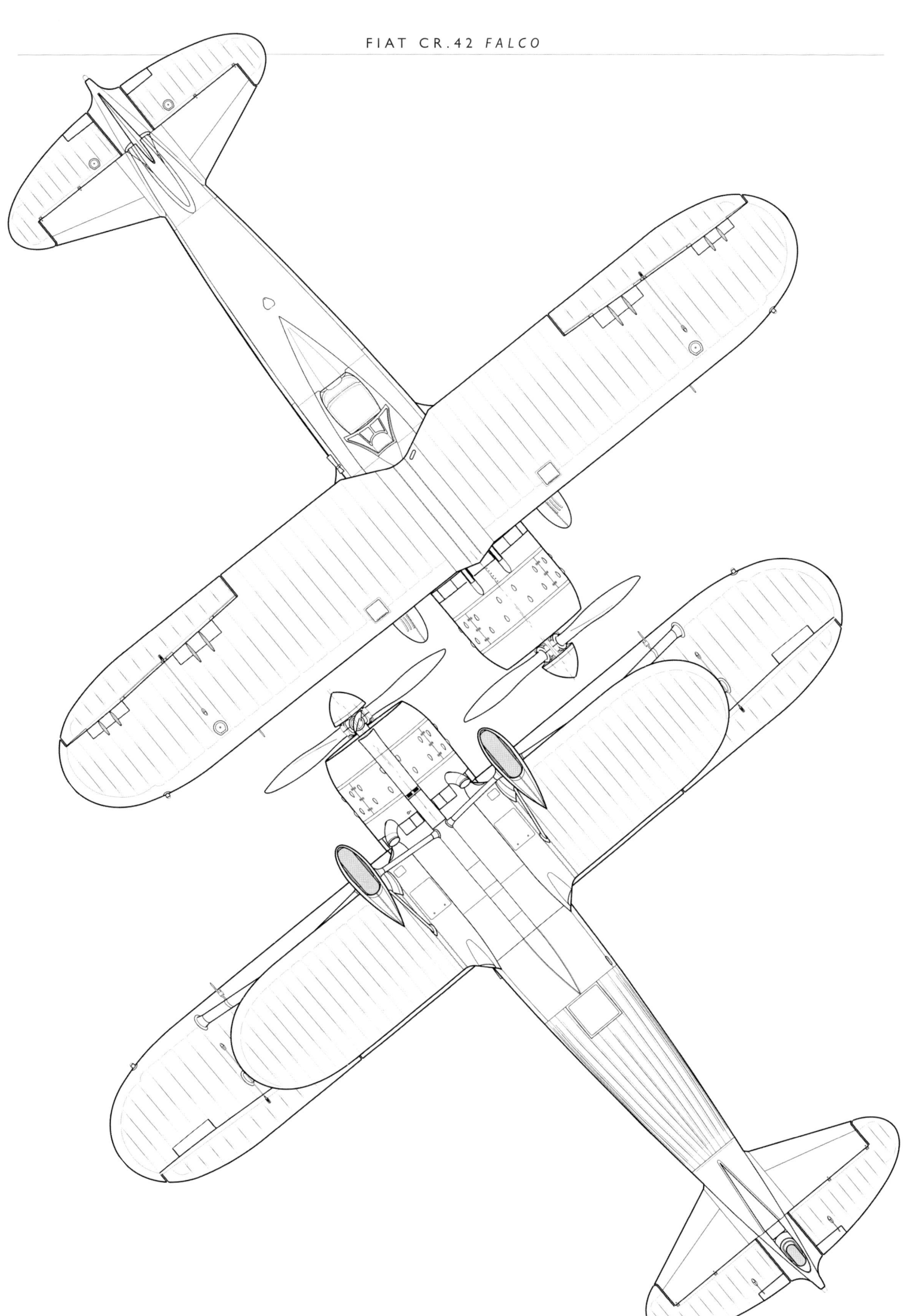

CR.42 prototype (no *Matricola Militare* assigned), Guidonia, June 1938

CR.42, 367ª *Squadriglia*, 151° *Gruppo*, 53° *Stormo* CT, Torino Caselle, May 1939

CR.42, MM5567, '91-10', 91ª *Squadriglia*, 10° *Gruppo*, 4° *Stormo* CT, El Adem, September 1940

CR.42, '74-10', 74ª *Squadriglia*, 23° *Gruppo Autonomo* CT, Comiso, October 1940

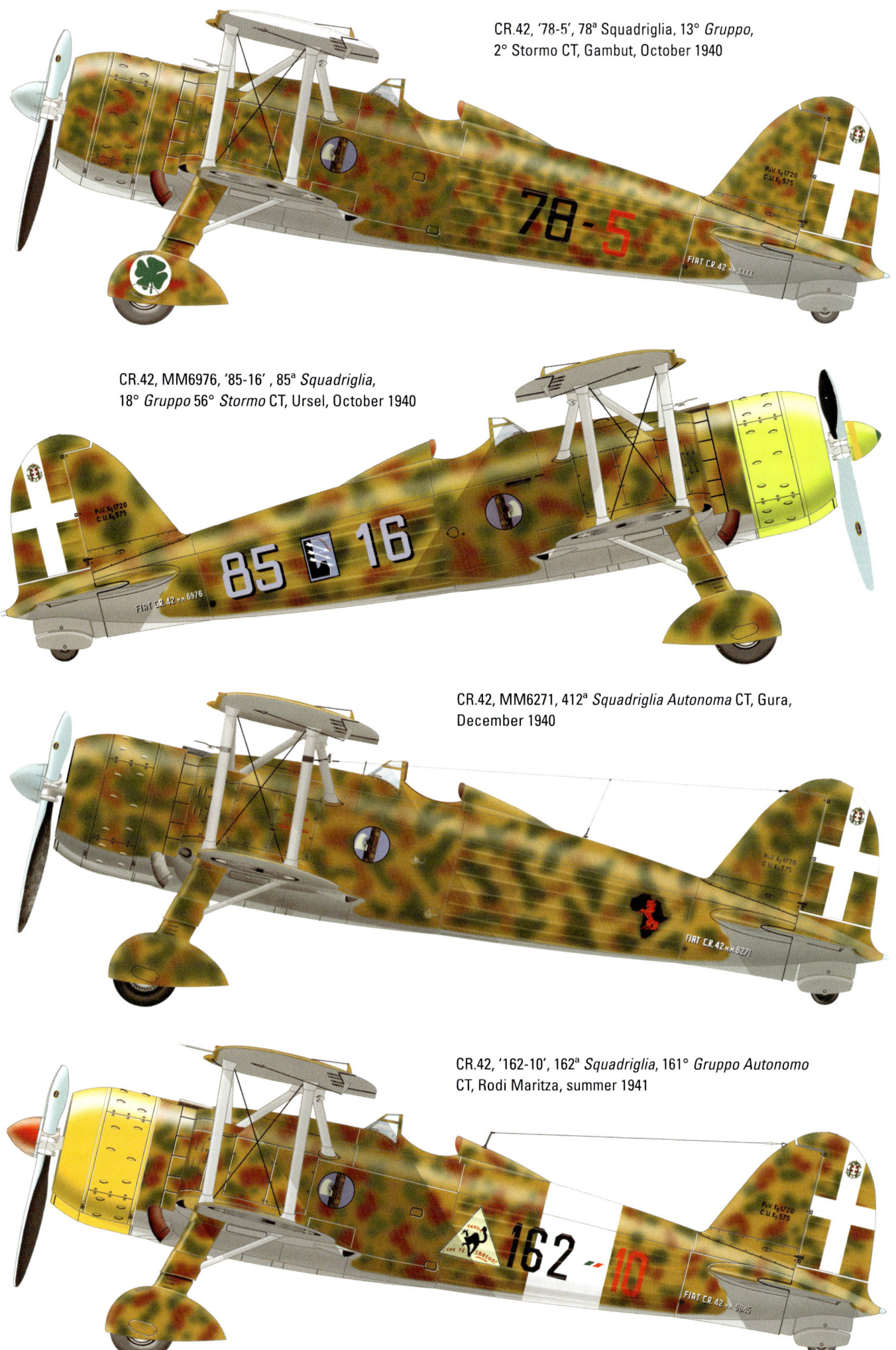

CR.42, '78-5', 78ª Squadriglia, 13° Gruppo, 2° Stormo CT, Gambut, October 1940

CR.42, MM6976, '85-16', 85ª *Squadriglia*, 18° *Gruppo* 56° *Stormo* CT, Ursel, October 1940

CR.42, MM6271, 412ª *Squadriglia Autonoma* CT, Gura, December 1940

CR.42, '162-10', 162ª *Squadriglia*, 161° *Gruppo Autonomo* CT, Rodi Maritza, summer 1941

CR.42, personal aircraft of *maggiore* Tito Falconi, commander of 23° *Gruppo Autonomo* CT, Trapani, July 1941

CR.42, 413ª *Squadriglia Autonoma* CT, Gondar, October 1941

CR.42CN, '377-4', 377ª *Squadriglia Autonoma* CT, Palermo Boccadifalco, May 1942

CR.42ba, 387ª *Squadriglia*, 158° *Gruppo*, 50° *Stormo d'Assalto*, Abu Nimeir, August 1942

FIAT CR.42 FALCO

CR.42, MM7584, '300-7', personal aircraft of capitano Corrado Ricci, commander of 300ª *Squadriglia*, 167° *Gruppo Autonomo* Caccia, Notturna, Ciampino, September 1942

CR.42b.a., personal aircraft of *colonnello* Raffaello Colacicchi, commander of 15° *Stormo d'Assalto*, Barce, October 1942

CR.42CN, MM9128, *capitano* Mario Anselmi, 234ª *Squadriglia*, 60° *Gruppo Autonomo Intercettori Notturni*, Venegono, September 1943

CR.42, 'E8+GK', 2./*Nachtschlachtgruppe* 9, Torino Aeritalia, April 1944

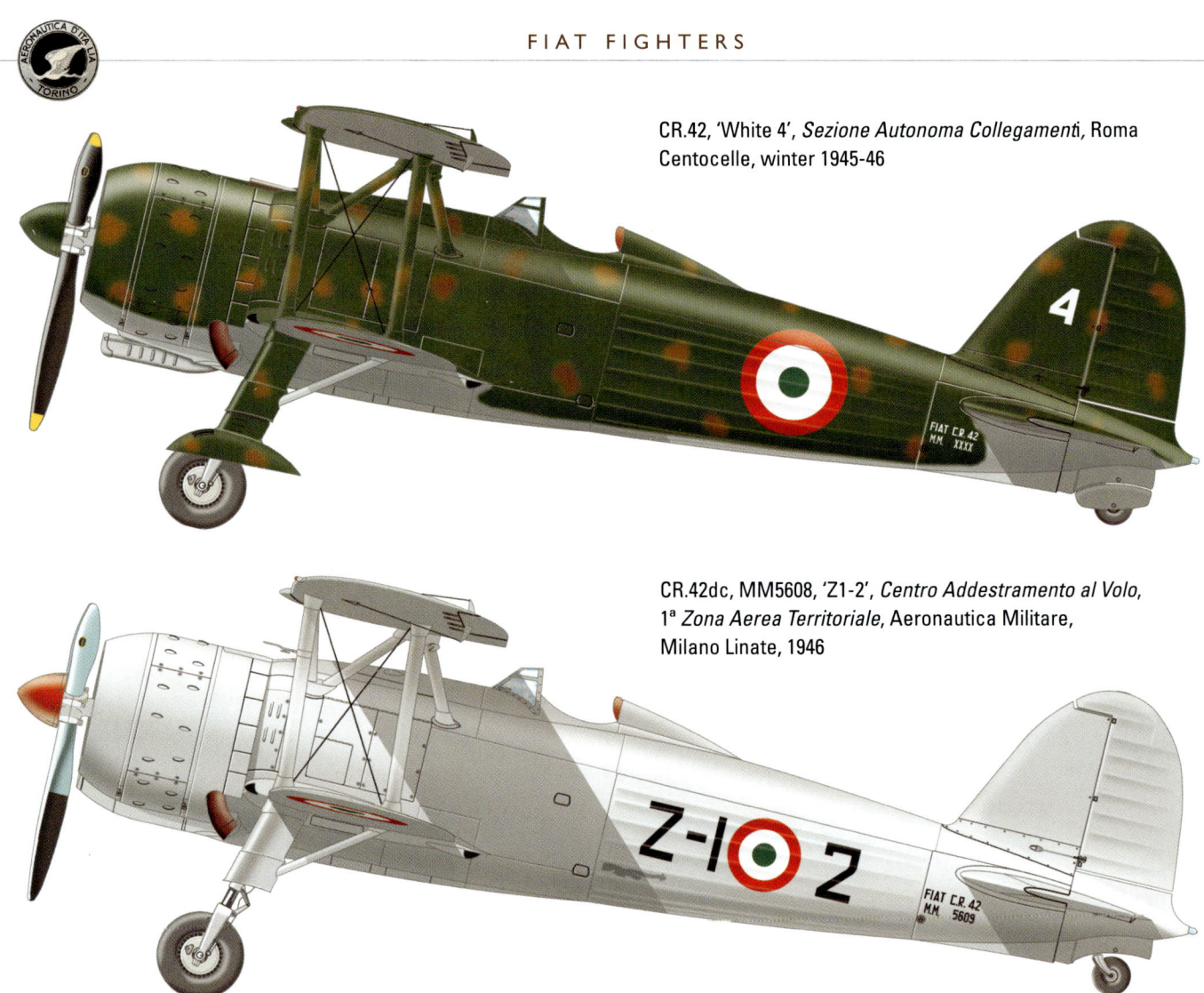

CR.42, 'White 4', *Sezione Autonoma Collegamenti*, Roma Centocelle, winter 1945-46

CR.42dc, MM5608, 'Z1-2', *Centro Addestramento al Volo*, 1ª *Zona Aerea Territoriale*, Aeronautica Militare, Milano Linate, 1946

CHAPTER SIX

Fiat G.50 *FRECCIA*
First Monoplane Fighter

The first prototype of the FIAT G.50 *Freccia*, MM334, still without armament, in its original colour scheme. A similar scheme was used many years later by other FIAT prototypes, such as those of the G.91 and G.91T light fighter. (ASF)

Development

DESPITE the fact that, for the Regia Aeronautica, it represented a transition from biplane fighters with fixed landing gear to a new generation of monoplanes with retractable landing gear, Italian pilots have never 'loved' the Fiat G.50.

Maresciallo Federico Tassinari flew the CR.32 in Spain with the 19ª *Squadriglia* of the 23° *Gruppo* '*Asso di bastoni*' from 6 August 1937 to April 1938 and then the G.50, and finally, during the Second World War, as a test pilot with SAI Ambrosini, recalled:

'*The G.50 only "theoretically" had a maximum speed close to 500 km/h, but when it arrived with the units, with its open canopy and the armour protecting the pilot, it barely reached 430 km/h. Every aeroplane is good if it is not expected to do what it cannot do: the G.50 could not be asked to be a good fighter.*'

The life of the Fiat G.50 was troubled from the start, chiefly due to the inexperience of the designers and the workshops in tackling the construction of a newly developed form of aeroplane, but also because of the continually changing specification requirements on the part of the leaders of the Regia Aeronautica.

The laborious development continued for almost two years. During this period the firm worked also to improve the speed performances of the new aircraft, which had been significantly below what had been requested by the Air Force. However such lengthy manufacturing periods were common to most of the early monoplanes in all nations; for example, the first production order for the Spitfire, issued in 1936, needed more than three years to complete.

These factors delayed the sending of the G.50 to Spain and confounded the Regia Aeronautica's plans.

The origins of the G.50 date back to 1935 when the Italian *Ministero dell'Aeronautica*

A 1941 advertisement published in *L'Ala d'Italia* magazine. (P. Monti)

GIUSEPPE GABRIELLI

GIUSEPPE GABRIELLI was born at Caltanissetta on 26 February 1903, but at a young age relocated with his family to Torino, graduating on 31 July 1925 from the *Politecnico di Torino in Ingegneria Industriale Meccanica* (Industrial Mechanical Engineering). He later refined his studies at Aachen in Germany having received a study scholarship. In this period, he was a student of the celebrated aeronautical engineer, Theodore von Kármán, with whom he enjoyed a relationship which proved to be fundamental for his career, and which was based on a profound friendship. On gaining his Doctorate in aeronautical engineering, Gabrielli returned to Italy in 1927 and became part of the Piaggio design team at Finale Ligure, managed by *Ing.* Giovanni Pegna, while also beginning a brilliant university lecturer career at the *Politecnico di Torino*.

Ing. Giuseppe Gabrielli, first right, with FIAT test pilots in front of a FIAT G.91 jet fighter.

In 1929 Gabrielli was tasked with the redesign of the metal version of the famous wooden-built Savoia Marchetti S.55 flying boat and in doing so, came to the attention of the founder of FIAT, Giovanni Agnelli. Agnelli recognised his potential and recruited him in 1931, into the company's aircraft design unit. The first design work assigned to Gabrielli was that for the FIAT G.2, a six-passenger monoplane tri-motor, characterised by a low cantilever wing and all-metal construction, which flew in 1932. The G.2 was also the first aircraft with a modern configuration produced by the company which had abandoned the biplane formula. Although the type achieved no success, it signified a turning point in the FIAT company's aeronautical production. This aircraft was followed by other designs, amongst which was the G.18 passenger transport and more importantly, the G.50 of 1937, the first all-metal monoplane fighter. In 1942 Gabrielli designed what could be considered as the best fighter produced in Italy during the Second World War, the G.55. His activities continued into the post-war period, and after being elected as a member of the *Consiglio Direttivo* of FIAT and a director of the technical design division, he became without doubt one of the major protagonists in the resumption and relaunch of Italian aeronautical activity.

In these later years Gabrielli designed the first Italian produced jets, the FIAT G.80 and G.82, and signed off the G.91 design, the winner of a NATO competition of 1957 for a lightweight fighter-bomber. Over 800 examples of the G.91 were manufactured, being used by the Aeronautica Militare in Italy, by the Luftwaffe, and by Portugal. At the beginning of the 1960s, Gabrielli was particularly active in the field of VTOL aircraft, while in 1970 he created the G.222 short take-off and landing tactical transport aircraft. Nominated as President of Fiat Avio in 1982, he never abandoned his academic activities at the *Politecnico di Torino* as holder of the chair of Aeronautical Construction and Design and Scientific Research. He signed off more than 200 publications and became a member of numerous associations and scientific and technical research groups around the world.

Giuseppe Gabrielli passed away in Torino on 29 November 1987 at the age of 84, having signed, during the course of his extraordinary and brilliant career, as designer for the drawings of 142 aeroplanes.

---

approached the principal national aeronautical manufacturers with a request for the design for a prototype of a modern fighter. The *Ministero* sought the hypothetical creation of two specific categories of aircraft: firstly, an interceptor and secondly, a combat fighter capable of undertaking both air defence and attack missions. At the time of the ministerial request, FIAT Aviazione had two design offices, the most historic of which was led by *Ingegner* Celestino Rosatelli, the father of a long series of biplane fighters, and another, created in 1931, entrusted to twenty-nine-year-old *Ingegner* Giuseppe Gabrielli, who specialised in the design of all-metal commercial monoplanes, the last of which, the G.18 twin, was an aircraft in the same class as the American Douglas DC 2.

In consideration of his experience in the subject, FIAT Aviazione charged the designer with the task of creating the first entirely metal monoplane fighter for the Regia Aeronautica, to be built around an 800-hp radial engine that FIAT Motori Avio was developing at the time. It should be remembered that this type of engine had been selected by the Regia Aeronautica for a specification of the previous year which called for a monoplane fighter equipped with an air-cooled radial engine.

For FIAT, this was a double technical challenge, as until that point the company had produced biplane fighters equipped with in-line engines of their own manufacture. Nevertheless, having only recently acquired a licence from Pratt & Whitney to manufacture the 700-hp Hornet SDG and 800-hp Twin Wasp R-1535, *ingegneri* Tranquillo Zerbi and Antonio Fessia had developed, from the Twin Wasp, the FIAT A.74 RC38 design. This engine produced 840 hp at 3,800 m and became the base engine for the Italian fighters that participated in the subsequent ministerial competition of 1936. It was this engine that would equip not only the future G.50 from Gabrielli, but also the other competitors in the ministerial competition for a new fighter announced in 1936.[1] Nevertheless, as Gabrielli would later write:

> 'The design for the new fighter was not followed with total conviction in either Regia Aeronautica circles or those within FIAT itself. There remained a certain scepticism about the monoplane formula, together with the selection of an air-cooled engine, while the British, Germans, and French were orientated towards liquid-cooled engines, which demonstrated a certain discordance on the path to be followed. The Italian authorities preferred air-cooled engines, as they considered them to be less vulnerable than those cooled by liquid.'

Despite the capability of the designer, the G.50 was born under an unlucky star, as from amongst the three alternatives proposed for the ministerial requirement of 1935, FIAT had selected the specification for a fighter capable of undertaking both defence and attack missions. Armament was specified as two 12.7 mm machine guns and a 20 mm cannon, together with a small bomb bay for the dropping of sub-munitions, all coupled with a maximum speed of 460 km/h at 3,500 m. Once the project had been defined towards the end of 1935, preliminary design was developed by the FIAT design office for a final draft. However, at the beginning of 1936, the competition announced by the Ministry was revised, probably in the light of the technical progress of new bomber aircraft in other nations.

The need, therefore, was to find a successor to the existing fleet of biplane fighters as a priority, and Italian companies were invited to present a project for an exclusively air defence fighter, still powered preferably by a radial air-cooled engine but with lighter armament. Only one 12.7 mm machine gun was initially required, and the requirement to drop sub-munitions was abandoned.[2] At a later stage the specifications were further amended, to require a fighter armed with two machine guns, a speed of at least 500 km/h, the ability to climb to 6,000 m in around 5 minutes, with at least two hours' endurance.

---

[1] The FIAT A.80 RC41 (1,000 hp), also developed on the basis of the American engine and installed in bombers and transport aircraft, did not achieve a similar success, as it never managed to deliver sufficient power and reliability.

[2] Further details of the development of monoplane fighters for the Regia Aeronautica can be found in *Aeronautica Macchi Fighters – C.200 Saetta, C.202 Folgore, C.205 Veltro*, Luigino Caliaro, Crecy Publishing, 2024.

The G.50 prototype, MM334, photographed at Guidonia. With its ivory colouring and light red trim, its graceful, modern lines and its technical features, the G.50 aircraft could well be described as a 'fast touring monoplane'. (ASF)

Above and below: The prototype, MM334, begins to take on the appearance of a fighter aircraft with the two synchronised SAFAT cowl-mounted guns. It received a colour scheme with transversal bands that appear more decorative than anything intended for camouflage purposes. (R.Gentilli)

Another photograph of the now armed and camouflaged prototype MM334.

A promotional postcard from 1941 published by *edizioni d'arte V. Boeri*. (P. Monti)

In the meantime, in the summer of 1936 at CMASA of Marina di Pisa, the associated company of FIAT Aeritalia to which manufacture of the aircraft had been entrusted, the construction of the first prototype of the G.50 had begun. As mentioned, this was designed as a multi-purpose aircraft, the original design having been subjected to radical changes in order to adapt it to the new specifications. *Ingegnere* Gabrielli was forced to completely redesign the aircraft, thereby losing precious months of work. He therefore preferred to adapt the existing project by accepting compromises and penalties in terms of weight and aerodynamics, since the presence of the originally planned bulky bomb compartment had influenced the design of the fuselage in terms of shape and aerodynamics. Furthermore, the work of remaking the G.50 to adapt it to the new requests did not prove at all simple since it would hardly have been able to completely satisfy the parameters of the competition; its speed was around 460 km/h while in the climb, performance saw it struggle to 5,000 m in 6 mins 30 secs.

Due to delays and problems, caused partly by the inexperience of the CMASA workforce, the prototype was only completed in January 1937. It was subsequently transferred by road to Torino and to the airfield of FIAT Aeritalia. Having been assigned *Matricola Militare* MM334, the aircraft flew for the first time from Torino on 26 February 1937, flown by test pilot Giovanni De Briganti and remaining airborne for around 15 minutes. Following a series of flights in the summer of 1937, the aircraft was taken to Pisa San Giusto, which CMASA utilised as its airfield, and was moved subsequently to Guidonia to be subjected to an extensive programme of evaluation at the *Centro Sperimentale*.

In the meantime, and following pressure from FIAT company management, the *Ministero dell'Aeronautica* issued an order for fifty aeroplanes, five of which were to be in two-seat configuration. But the *Ministero* reserved the right to delay the possible launch of series production until the results of comparative trials with the AerMacchi C.200, then still under construction, had been assessed. From the first flights of the prototype, it appeared evident that the G.50 would have a long path to follow before it was perfected, appearing far from realising the leap in quality expected by the Regia Aeronautica. The flight trials and entry into service were further hampered by the tragic incident which involved the second prototype, MM335, on 8 November 1937.

On that day, during the course of a demonstration in the presence of various civilian and military authorities, the prototype crashed into the ground while recovering from a high-speed dive, killing test pilot De Briganti. After a long investigation, the disaster was attributed to the phenomenon of aileron flutter, although it is very probable that the principal cause was spin, in Italy known as '*autorotazione*', an aerodynamic phenomenon that characterised the life of the G.50 in common with that of the C.200, although in the FIAT fighter it was less pronounced and less ominous. This phenomenon was caused, as would be discovered later, by the constant profile of the wings which, at certain speeds and flying conditions, resulted in a loss of control of the aircraft, allowing no margin of recovery if occurring at low altitude.

In the spring of 1938, following a series of opportune modifications, the G.50 prototype was the subject of a comparison trial with the other two new fighters in preparation – the AerMacchi C.200 and the IMAM Ro.51. The latter was quickly eliminated from the evaluation, while the comparison between the C.200 and G.50 revealed

The second prototype of the Fiat G.50 with the initials 'MP', denoting the plant of the FIAT subsidiary manufacturer CMASA at Marina di Pisa. The aircraft, MM335, was destroyed during a test at Pisa S. Giusto airfield resulting in the death of test pilot De Briganti. (R. Gentilli)

that the AerMacchi offered better performance, probably thanks to its refined aerodynamics and lower empty and loaded weights, exceeding by more than 40 km/h the speed of the G.50 and climbing to 6,000 m in 6 mins 25 secs, as opposed to the 7 mins 30 secs taken by the FIAT fighter. Despite this result, the *Ministero dell'Aeronautica* still decided to sanction production of the G.50, considering a variety of factors and peculiarities. In fact, although the C.200 was mostly superior in terms of flight performance, the G.50 offered some positive characteristics, such as a greater simplicity in performing checks, inspections and repairs, as well as an ability to manoeuvre on a par with its rival in combat. At the end of the trials, the principal modifications requested for FIAT's aircraft were limited to the adoption of an open cockpit, a mechanical device for locking the undercarriage, an automatic engine starting system, and the incorporation of an oxygen system of the type used by the *Reparto Alta Quota* (High Altitude Unit, a Guidonia-based trials unit).

Another no less important aspect which influenced the decision of the *Ministero dell'Aeronautica* to pursue series production of the G.50 was the necessity to maintain stable employment for the workforce of the Marina di Pisa factory. For this reason, in January 1939 a further 36 aircraft were ordered, with the intention of supplying, together with the 45 single-seaters of the first order, the unit establishment of a *Stormo*.

The bizarre results of this controversial competition were the fact that there were two winners (the G.50 and C.200), not just one, and that the *Ministero dell'Aeronautica* never managed to consolidate the fighter force onto just one type. What emerged as the right and proper winner was the outsider, the FIAT CR.42, which, not being a monoplane with a fixed undercarriage, did not match the requirements of the competition, but nevertheless represented an aircraft with fewer 'unknowns' than the monoplanes.

The G.50 prototype, MM334, was exhibited in the Italian section of the 1937 *Salone Internazionale Aeronautica* at the Milan Trade Fair.

Complaints from pilots about the closed cockpit of the G.50, C.200, Ro.51 and F.5 types found consensus in the DGCA which proposed various solutions: this example, MM3574, shows an example of a semi-open cockpit with folding side panels and extended engine hood. (R.Gentilli)

The G.50 in Production

AS stated previously, even before the G.50 prototype had flown, an order had been placed for 81 aircraft. Subsequently, this order was cancelled in 1937 after the initial flight evaluation of the G.50 and in anticipation of the result of the comparative trials with the C.200, the first flight of which was at the end of the year. The outcome would influence the choice of an aircraft to produce in series. Nevertheless, bearing in mind that CMASA had already established a production line and had commenced the assembly of the first G.50s, the *Ministero*, demonstrating not a little uncertainty about how to proceed, authorised the production of a pre-series of 50 aircraft, five of which were two-seaters.

These first aircraft featured a closed cockpit, lacked self-sealing fuel tanks, undercarriage doors and other minor details. They were assigned to a specially formed *Reparto Sperimentale Caccia* (Experimental Fighter Unit) at Ciampino, commanded by *maggiore* Mario Bonzano and tasked with developing the aircraft, as well as deploying a group of twelve aircraft to Spain in March of the same year to conduct an operational evaluation. The findings of this experimental squadron were particularly important in identifying some of the principal defects in the aircraft, the most prominent of which was the tendency of the machine to enter a spin in determined attitudes and speeds, the requirement to modify the canopy, which deteriorated quickly and was difficult to open in flight, and the lack of a lock on the retracted undercarriage.

A somewhat worrying opinion on the G.50 of the first series was expressed by Commander Cap. Tullio de Prato, who flew to Spain and later was commander of the 150ª *Squadriglia* of 2° *Gruppo Caccia* in Africa, equipped with the G.50bis.

The G.50, MM5439, was one of the last 100 aircraft from the IV *Serie* produced by CMASA. The photograph shows the aircraft just before delivery to the Regia Aeronautica.

With the production of MM3570, the first G.50 production aircraft, the FIAT fighter took on a more military appearance, exemplified by the 'field/continental' camouflage. The photograph was taken during test and evaluation at Guidonia in June 1938.

He wrote in a memoir:

> 'You couldn't let go of the control stick for even a moment without serious consequences. One of my wingmen, S.Ten. Mancini, fell into a spin while sailing in horizontal flight and in formation. The G.50 auto rotated upon landing, and not because it was heavy or had advanced landing gear, but because it had an impossible wing. The descriptions spread by the press are blasphemy: evidently they were derived, optimistically, from the naked prototype. Not to mention the weapons which couldn't fire, the air intake at ground level that sucked in more sand than oxygen; the constant sensation of walking on ice that unnerved the more experienced pilot and made him regret not flying the manoeuvrable, quiet CR.42, only slightly slower when fully loaded. The engine, after two days in Libya, consumed more oil than petrol and required endless taxiing before, with anguish for the pilot, the wheels lifted from the ground…'[1]

This first group of I Series aircraft was later assigned to the 51° *Stormo* at Ciampino, but they were quickly replaced by the G.50s of the II Series.

Delays to the start of series production of the AerMacchi C.200, which resulted in a programme slippage of at least nine months, together with the understandable concerns over the introduction into service of the new monoplanes, favoured the production of the CR.42 biplane. Output of the CR.42 did not stop at the 200 examples initially planned, but would continue until the end of the war, the aircraft becoming the most produced Italian fighter. For this reason, despite the marked preference expressed for the C.200, and probably following understandable pressure from the FIAT company, the Regia Aeronautica decided that it would be inadvisable to interrupt the production of the unexceptional G.50. It was also felt that it would require at least nine months to establish a production line at Torino for the C.200 and to obtain the revenue from 100 aircraft. The *Stato Maggiore* of the Regia Aeronautica meanwhile decided to afford maximum priority to initiating production of the C.200, although including in this decision further orders for the G.50 but allowing for possible technical or production problems with the Macchi fighters. This procrastination resulted in a failure to standardise the Italian fighter force

The G.50 production line at the CMASA factory at Marina di Pisa.

---

[1] Tullio de Prato, un pilota contadino, STEM MUCCHI 2019.
Author note: In fairness, this severe personal judgement by Tullio De Prato does not coincide with the opinions expressed by other authoritative pilots who flew the aircraft and which are not so negative.

The year 1940 saw the emergence of the G.50Bis version with modified fuselage and cowling with small bulges, an improved protective spinner for the propeller, rear tail gear without fairing and fuel tanks of 419 litres capacity. The photograph shows the G.50bis, MM5944, which served with the 363ª *Squadriglia* of 150° *Gruppo* CT flying from Martuba in 1942.

on a single aircraft type. The evaluations, coupled with the political machinations on the part of the companies involved, who sought to promote their own products, would lead to the Regia Aeronautica experiencing a long and difficult war with a heterogeneous fighter fleet comprised of aircraft types of very different performance and operational potential.

Construction of the II Series, deliveries of which commenced in September 1939, saw the aircraft undergo some substantial modifications, including the removal of the sliding canopy that had proved to be so problematical; the installation of lateral transparent deflectors above the cockpit sides (which were, however, frequently removed in the field); and a redesigned headrest to improve visibility to the rear. Furthermore, undercarriage doors were installed together with the addition of a compressor offering self-starting. The principal alteration, however, was a redesign of the rear of the aircraft, with a new fin featuring a rebalancing of the rudder intended to eliminate the annoying flutter problems. However, the aircraft of the II Series had only a limited combat capability, as they lacked armour for the pilot, and with no modifications being made to their fuel tanks,

possessed a limited endurance of little more than one hour. Production of this batch of aircraft was entirely delegated to CMASA, as the FIAT production lines in Torino were engaged in the construction of BR.20 bombers and the CR.42, the output of which were failing to meet the requirements, not exceeding twelve aircraft manufactured per month, to the point that on the outbreak of the conflict just 118 aircraft had been delivered to the Regia Aeronautica.

Despite this less than exceptional situation, a so-called '*Programma R*' was aimed at developing the Regia Aeronautica quantitatively and qualitatively, calling initially for the placing into service of exactly 3,000 aeroplanes of which 2,000 would be of a, as then, undefined new type. A further fifty G.50s were ordered, subdivided into two series, one of thirty and another of 100 aircraft, with which the Regia Aeronautica should have been able to equip one *stormo* and a *gruppo* (see G.50 Production table below).

G.50bis

In an attempt to improve the G.50 following an evaluation of the trials at Guidonia and the early results of operations with the units, FIAT/CMASA

created an enhanced version of the fighter, designated G.50bis, the prototype of which, MM5933, was flown for the first time from Torino by test pilot Rolandi on 13 September 1940. Despite remaining very similar to the original G.50, the new aircraft incorporated some modifications intended to resolve the major problems identified by the units which had initially operated it.

One of the first enhancements involved the re-design of part of the tail, with a fin of increased area and augmented chord, reduced height, and the adoption of a pointed tail end. The fuselage also saw modification to its aerodynamic profile, making it more streamlined, as well as the adoption of an anti-sand filter and a spinner cover to protect the propeller mechanism. Other variations involved the cockpit layout, the installation of a new 24 V electrical system, and enhanced protection for the pilot with armour around his seat. Substantial modifications were also made to the undercarriage, with the replacement of the original Messiers with another made by Magnaghi, while there was an increase in endurance thanks to the installation of a new 100-litre fuel tank in the ventral bay previously used for the Nardi munitions dispenser. This extended the endurance of the fighter to almost two hours. On the G.50bis, moreover, underwing shackles were fitted capable of carrying bombs up to a maximum 160-kg payload.

These modifications, however, resulted in an increase in weight which, by impacting on the performance of the aircraft, did not seem to offer significant improvements.

With a reduction in workload on BR.20 bomber production at Torino, an assembly line for the G.50bis was organised, but despite the good industrial organisation at the company, production

G.50 Production

1-2 prototypes		MM334-335 *
Prototype G50V		MM479 (conversion of G.50 I Serie MM3581)
		MM ? (G.50ter)
I *Serie*	45	MM3570-3614
II *Serie*	36	MM4721-4756
III *Serie*	30	MM4937-4966
IV *Serie*	100	MM5361-5460

* The second prototype was destroyed in an accident on 8 November 1937. The prototype was replaced by another aircraft assigned the same *Matricola Militare*.

V *Serie*	25	MM5461-5485	CMASA
	315	MM5933-6247	FIAT/AERONAUTICA D'ITALIA
VII *Serie*	87	MM6328-6414	CMASA
VI *Serie*	10	MM6953-6962	CMASA
	35	MM8561-8595	FIAT/AERONAUTICA D'ITALIA

peaked at a maximum of 27 aeroplanes a month(!) in 1943, even when production lines were active at both Torino and CMASA at Marina di Pisa. Delays in the launch of production at Torino and fine-tuning of the modifications would enable the entry into service of the 50bis only in the spring of 1941.

From the available data, it appears that 472 G.50bis were manufactured: (see table above).

THE TWO-SEAT G.50B

The Regia Aeronautica identified a requirement for a two-seat version of the G.50 for pilot training, and CMASA was charged with creating a variant, designated G.50B (B for *biposto* – two seat). Construction of a I *Serie* of five aircraft (MM3615-3619) was quickly prepared. The two-seater was created by the complete removal of armament and

In 1938 work progressed to develop a G.50 two-seater trainer version. The first example to be built, MM3615, was based on a series production aircraft and appeared in 1940 with two seats in tandem, one closed, the other semi-open.

the installation of a second tandem cockpit, dual controls, and an intercom system. The final design suffered from notable delays, caused by the fact that the first solution proposed by CMASA, having been requested by the DGCA in 1938, saw two open cockpits similar to that of the single-seater. Formation of turbulence around the tail, already investigated in the studies for the fighter, induced *Ingegner* Gabrielli to insist on the installation of a semi-enclosed cockpit, requiring the redesign of the upper section of the fuselage. Consequently, a configuration was studied with the front cockpit fully enclosed, with the canopy blending into the instructor's rear cockpit which, by contrast, was still open, this countering the formation of dangerous and penalising turbulence around the tail.

The first flight of the G.50B took place on 30 April 1940, with test pilot Guerra at the

A FIAT G.50, probably of 21° *Gruppo* CT, airborne during late 1940.

Frontal close-up of a G.50bis fitted with a sand-proof spinner used on the final examples. Visible also is the anti-sand filter under the cowl.

FIAT G.50 FRECCIA

The majority of the G.50Bs were employed by the Regia Aeronautica's fighter schools, but some were also assigned to the headquarters of *Grandi Unità* as fast liaison aircraft. (F.Ballista)

controls, and series production commenced immediately. In total, CMASA manufactured 108 two-seat G.50Bs which served with the *Scuole Caccia* of the Regia Aeronautica. At the end of the war a single example survived, which was utilised by the *Scuola Caccia* at Lecce until 1948 as an intermediate trainer prior to conversion onto the AerMacchi C.205 and the Spitfire.

I *Serie*	5	MM3615-3619	CMASA
VII *Serie*	20	MM6308-6327	CMASA
VII *Serie*	75	MM6415-6489	CMASA

Experimental Versions

Several variants of the G.50 were designed and achieved prototype stage but did not continue into series production.

G.50ter

The reasoning that lay behind the creation of the G.50ter was the adoption of the Fiat A. 76 RC. 40S 14-cylinder, twin-row, air-cooled engine, offering a maximum power of 1,000 hp at 2,400 rpm. The prototype was created by modifying the wings, undercarriage and armament of a standard G.50. It flew for the first time on 17 July 1941, with test pilot Agostini at the controls. The early flights revealed that there were development problems with the engine. This led to the abandonment of the engine project and the consequent cancelling of the 'ter' variant.

G.50V

With the availability of the in-line 1,050-hp Daimler Benz DB 601 engine, the prototype of the

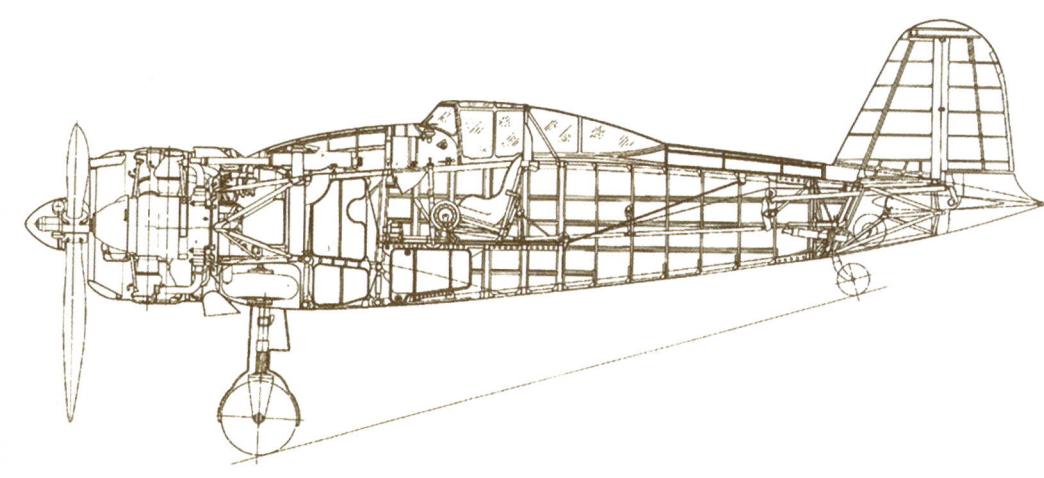

Above and below: The G 50ter was to be fitted with 1,000-hp A.76 engine. This engine was an A.74 with increased displacement, which never went into production because, plagued by problems, it did not pass the certification tests. The engine was also supposed to power the AerMacchi C.201.

An official company photograph, touched up to show the lines of the G.50/V equipped with a DB 601 engine as produced by CMASA. The aircraft, piloted by *tenente colonnello* Guerra, reached a horizontal speed of 580 km/h. It was used to prepare for the impending G.55 project.

This is probably the only photograph known to exist of the G.50V during a ground engine test at the CMASA plant. (G.Valdonio)

G.50V (V = *Veloce* – fast) first flew on 25 August 1941 with test pilot Ezio Guerra in the cockpit. It took off from the FIAT airfield at Torino. The aircraft, constructed by CMASA, was assigned serial MM479 and was almost certainly produced by converting a G.50 from the I *Serie*, MM3581. From the minimal details and drawings that emerged in the post-war period, the installation of the engine required a complete re-design of the original G.50 forward fuselage, while there was a slimmed down fuselage, a reduction in size of the 'humpback', the installation of a large radiator under the cockpit and a closed canopy. From the few photographs and drawings available, it appears that there were no substantial changes to the aircraft's wings or tailplanes. Transferred to Torino for flight-testing, the fighter demonstrated fair performance, achieving a speed of 570 km/h and climbing to 6,000 m in 5 mins 30 secs, but it seems that its handling qualities were unexceptional, and the engine cooling system was ineffective. In any case, the aircraft appeared at the same time as its potential rivals, the C.202 and RE.2001, were entering service, and as the much more modern and promising G.55 was also on *Ingegner* Gabrielli's drawing board at the time, the G.50V project was abandoned. It should be mentioned that FIAT proposed a two-seat reconnaissance version designated G.53, but this never attracted any interest from the Regia Aeronautica.

G.50Bis/A

This variant was created with the aim of bolstering the armament of the G.50 to enable it to function in the ground-attack role. The aircraft made its first flight on 3 October 1942, flown by test pilot Valentino Cus, and was utilised for a series of weapons trials at Furbara. As it proved impossible to install additional weapons without modifying the basic structure of the aircraft, the G.50bis MM8595 was modified with an increased wing area of 21 m² by inserting new wing sections between the central tranche and the outer sections, these housing a Breda SAFAT 12.7 mm machine gun with 300 rounds each, plus shackles for a 100-kg bomb. However, the empty weight of the aircraft increased by 355 kg, with a negative impact on performance, especially on the maximum speed, which fell to around 420 km/h, and the project was abandoned.

The increase in wing area was, nevertheless, subsequently re-adopted for proposals for a single-seat fighter and a two-seat reconnaissance and attack aircraft to be embarked in the aircraft carrier *Aquila*, but these were never realised.

G.50OR

To provide an embarked fighter for the future Regia Marina aircraft carriers, *Aquila* and *Sparviero*, FIAT also presented its design for a modified G.50. Nevertheless, as the Reggiane RE 2001OR had been pre-selected as the type to be procured (OR signifying *Organizzazione Roma*, the conventional code adopted for any activity related to the carriers), *Superaereo* selected the G.50 for the pilot training role in view of the entry into service of the RE.2001OR. Consequently, a batch of sixteen aircraft of this type was ordered,

The G.50/A (Assault) prototype, MM855, was built in 1942 to provide an aircraft suitable for the ground-attack role. The additional 12.7 mm SAFAT machine guns with 600 rounds each and mounting points for up to 50-kg bombs were contained in a new wing portion between the wing centre section and outer wing panels.

designated G.50OR, with the first eight intended for use in initial training for carrier-based take-offs and landings with the aid of an arrestor hook. The G.50OR had been lightened through the removal of armament, radio and other equipment that was not indispensable, while the eight aircraft planned would feature full naval equipment, and would be used to train pilots directly in the new operational techniques.

The first G. 50bis were modified in accordance with the requirements of the *Organizzazione Roma* project, with the application of reinforcements to the tail end of the fuselage, installation of an arrestor hook, and a fitting for attachment to a catapult. Other minor modifications included the installation of a new headrest for the pilot and new dorsal safety straps. The modifications were undertaken by *Officine Meccaniche S. Giorgio* at Pistoia, and the first deliveries commenced in April 1942, with the assignation of MM4963, 5988 and 6330 to the *Centro Sperimentale* at Guidonia for evaluation. At the beginning of February 1943, the modified fighters were assigned to the 160° *Gruppo* CT, the unit which had been designated to operate the embarked aircraft. Intensive training in take-offs and short and arrested landings quickly commenced, utilising an arrestor system constructed by the German company DEMAG and installed on the runway at Perugia S.Egidio airport. This featured a reproduction of the proposed flight deck complete with illumination for night landings. For take-offs the fighters were launched with a Gagnotto/Borgiacchi steam catapult. Obviously the events surrounding the Armistice of 8 September resulted in the programme relating to *Organizzazione Roma* being abandoned, along with the suspension of all associated ongoing activity and projects.

Mention should be made of a design by CMASA for the G.50 bis/A-N (*assalto-navale*), an embarked attack aircraft design which was stopped by the Armistice, as was that of a two-seat, carrier-borne reconnaissance aircraft, the G.50/ON (*Osservazione Navale*), which would have featured an enlarged wing and new radio and photographic systems.

Above and below: G.50bis MM5988 experimentally fitted with catapult-launching devices and an arrester hook for intended use from the carrier *Aquila*.

Unfulfilled studies and designs

Other variants of the G.50 were considered, but these remained on the designers' drawing boards. Of note amongst these, was the G.50I (*Idrovolante* – seaplane), the G.50bis/T (*Tuffo* – dive) intended for dive-bombing and carrying two 100-kg wing-mounted bombs and one 250 kg bomb mounted ventrally, and the G.50bis/CN (*Caccia Notturna* – night fighter). Another variant proposed, but not progressed, was the G.50B/RT (*Ricognizione Terrestre*), which was to be achieved by converting the trainer into a two-seat reconnaissance aircraft through the removal of the dual controls, the installation in the rear cockpit floor of a window for the observer, and a long focus length camera installed in the fuselage.

FIAT G.50 Technical Data and Description

THE FIAT G50 was an all-metal, low wing monoplane with a structure partly of stressed skin (monocoque) and partly of framework. This last technique was adopted only for industrial reasons, as FIAT was rich in the specialised workers and machinery needed to produce and solder frameworks of pipes. Thus the central part of the fuselage, that connected the wings, was designed as a frame to use this area which otherwise would have remained unused. The stressed skin, however, was something totally new for the workshops and presented many production problems.

Additionally, there was a shortage of suitable materials to provide perfectly finished cladding.

The fuselage was made from duralumin and was of significant section, testimony to the original concept of the aircraft being capable of conducting attack missions, with a flat underside that would support a bomb rack. It was semi-monocoque in structure, formed by seventeen ribs attached to four longerons, and in shape was a rectangular prism, clad in sheet metal with half of the rivet heads embedded and half exposed, contributing to the overall resistance.

The low cantilever wing was composed of three sections: a central tranche made from chrome-molybdenum steel tubing, integrated with the fuselage, and containing the two oil radiators with their air intakes on the leading edge, and two outer wing sections formed by two duralumin spars with duralumin ribs, covered in metal cladding. The ailerons were also duralumin metal structures, but clad in fabric, balanced both statically and aerodynamically, while the flaps were slotted and divided into four sections, two positioned on the outer wings and two on the central tranche. They were hydraulically controlled and retracted automatically when the aircraft passed a defined speed. The rear fuselage section was also a tubular steel structure together with vertical and horizontal tail surfaces: the fixed

Above and below: The G.50 was formed of a dialuminium monocoque fuselage made up of four angular longerons within the plating and connected by 17 frames.

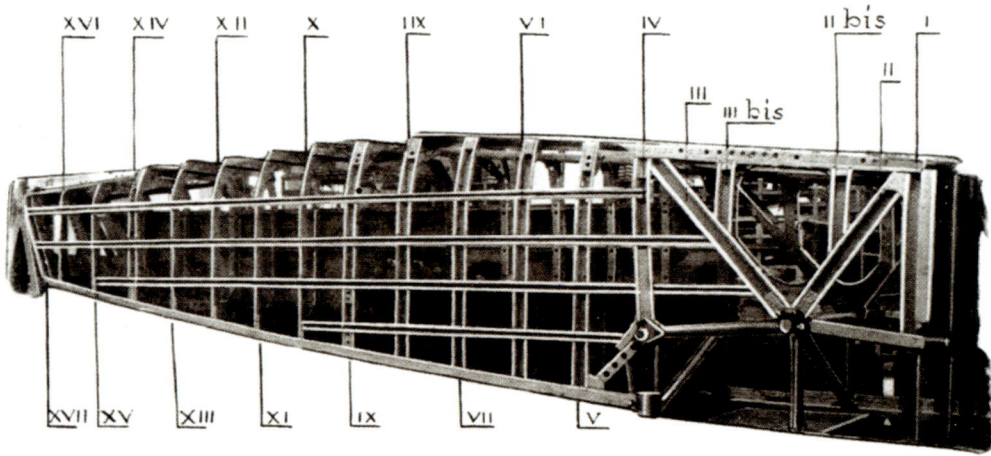

Fig. 9. — Ossatura fusoliera.

Below: The G.50 wing was an all-metal structure consisting of two spars connected by ribs.

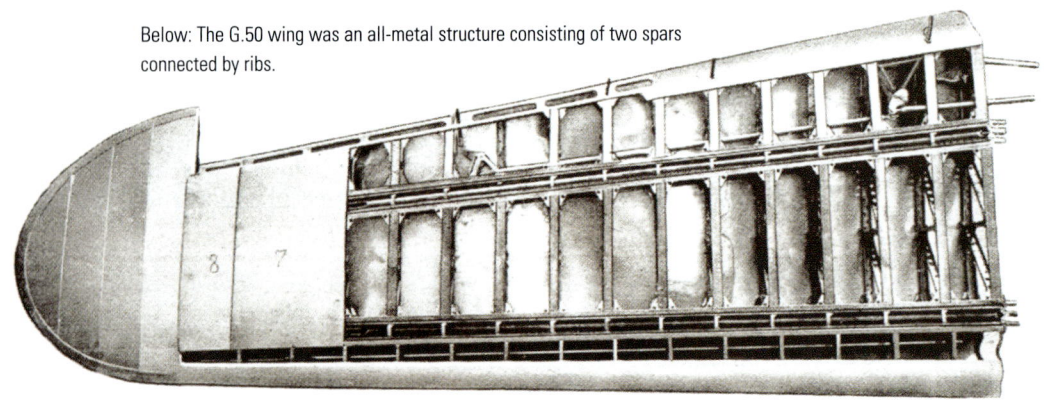

The tailwheel was non-retractable in the early production series and could be made retractable on the G.50bis. The unit had all-metal fixed parts and metal-framed and fabric-covered movable parts.

Left and right: Close-ups of the starboard undercarriage leg and the wing centre section and wheel wells.

The engine mount was made of chrome-molybdenum steel tubes, connected to the fireproof bulkhead with four bolts.

Power for the G.50 was provided by the FIAT A.74 RC38 delivering 840 hp at 3800 rpm and driving a 3-metre diameter constant speed FIAT-Hamilton metal airscrew. For emergency use the A.74 could be boosted to 950 hp, but only for a short period.

tailwheel was shock-absorbed and faired, and could rotate 45° off its main axis. The tailplanes were monocoque, of mixed steel and duralumin, and their mobile parts were clad in fabric. The Messiers main undercarriage, later replaced by a Magnaghi alternative, was housed in the central wing tranche. It retracted to complete enclosure inwardly, controlled by an oleo-pneumatic circuit for retraction and a pneumatic system for lowering, connected by optical indicators that displayed its exact status to the pilot. In case of a malfunction, the undercarriage could be lowered manually. Its telescopic legs incorporated the shock absorbers, and both wheels possessed pneumatically controlled brakes, assisted by a Garelli motor compressor, which was also available for automatically starting the engine.

The powerplant was a FIAT A.74 RC.38 14-cylinder, twin-row radial engine which developed a maximum of 960 hp at 2,400 rpm at 4,000 m. The take-off power available was 740 hp, which could be increased to a total of around 960 hp using, for a short period, the over-boost system known as *+100*.

The engine was fitted with reduction gear and a compressor for maintaining power at high altitude and supercharging, and drove a three-bladed metal FIAT 3D/41-1 variable pitch, 3-metre-diameter propeller. The engine was mounted on a structure of chrome-molybdenum steel tubes fixed to the fuselage with elastic supports enclosed inside a large cowling that could be opened in sections.

In its two external sections, the wing contained two 44-litre fuel tanks, while two other main tanks were housed in the fuselage, one with a capacity of 68 litres and another of 100 litres, as well as an emergency tank of approximately 50 litres, providing an overall total of approximately 310 litres of fuel.

The oil radiators were positioned on the leading edge of the central wing section at the junction with the fuselage, the oil tanks being housed within the engine mounting ahead of the firewall. In the forward fuselage section, just behind the engine, were two large hatches, one on each side of the fuselage, which facilitated maintenance access for the fuel tanks and armament. The latter was composed of two Breda-SAFAT 12.7 mm machine guns with a belt feed featuring disintegrating metal links positioned on the nose of the aircraft forward of the cockpit and synchronised with the propeller. They were re-armed pneumatically. The guns were mounted on shock-absorbing supports and connected to their ammunition belt box which could carry up to 600 rounds. There was a box for the recovery of the shell cases and ammunition belt remains. Under the wings, on the G.50AS version, two

Fuel tank layout. The fuel tanks had a capacity of 316 litres in the G.50 and 411 litres in the G.50bis respectively.

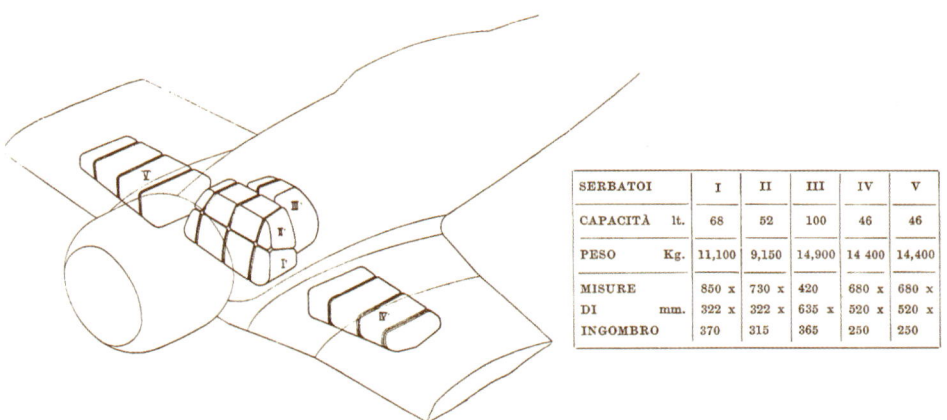

N. 8. — Schema installazione serbatoi benzina.

SERBATOI	I	II	III	IV	V
CAPACITÀ lt.	68	52	100	46	46
PESO Kg.	11,100	9,150	14,900	14 400	14,400
MISURE DI INGOMBRO mm.	850 x 322 x 370	730 x 322 x 315	420 x 635 x 365	680 x 520 x 250	680 x 520 x 250

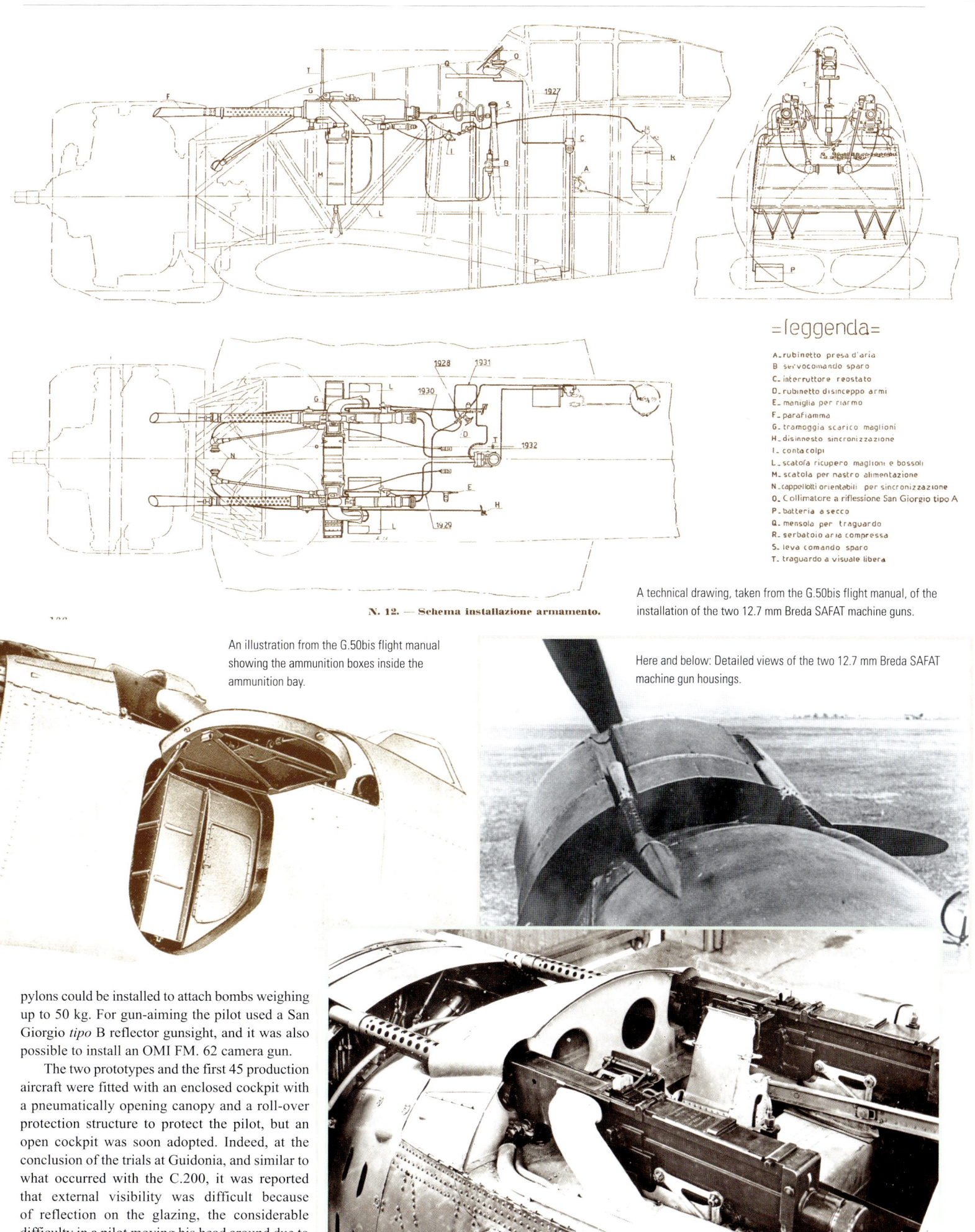

A technical drawing, taken from the G.50bis flight manual, of the installation of the two 12.7 mm Breda SAFAT machine guns.

N. 12. — Schema installazione armamento.

=leggenda=

A - rubinetto presa d'aria
B - servocomando sparo
C - interruttore reostato
D - rubinetto disinceppo armi
E - maniglia per riarmo
F - parafiamma
G - tramoggia scarico maglioni
H - disinnesto sincronizzazione
I - contacolpi
L - scatola ricupero maglioni e bossoli
M - scatola per nastro alimentazione
N - cappelletti orientabili per sincronizzazione
O - Collimatore a riflessione San Giorgio tipo A
P - batteria a secco
Q - mensola per traguardo
R - serbatoio aria compressa
S - leva comando sparo
T - traguardo a visuale libera

An illustration from the G.50bis flight manual showing the ammunition boxes inside the ammunition bay.

Here and below: Detailed views of the two 12.7 mm Breda SAFAT machine gun housings.

pylons could be installed to attach bombs weighing up to 50 kg. For gun-aiming the pilot used a San Giorgio *tipo* B reflector gunsight, and it was also possible to install an OMI FM. 62 camera gun.

The two prototypes and the first 45 production aircraft were fitted with an enclosed cockpit with a pneumatically opening canopy and a roll-over protection structure to protect the pilot, but an open cockpit was soon adopted. Indeed, at the conclusion of the trials at Guidonia, and similar to what occurred with the C.200, it was reported that external visibility was difficult because of reflection on the glazing, the considerable difficulty in a pilot moving his head around due to the extremely tight configuration of the hood and

the rapid deterioration of the canopy caused by the poor quality of the transparent material, and that it could be difficult to open the canopy in flight in the event of the need to bail out. As a consequence, various open cockpit configurations were trialled on the fifth production aircraft (MM3574). Ultimately, this settled on lateral transparent panels and an open top, with a seat headrest incorporated into a robust, roll-over protection structure.

The fighter's cockpit was easy to access and egress, even while wearing a parachute, and was fitted with a height and tilt adjustable seat with a well to accommodate the parachute. The flying controls were arranged sensibly, and there was limited play on the control column and rudder pedals: the throttle and mixture controls could be moved gradually. The flap lever, placed in front of the pilot, lowered the flaps with just one manoeuvre, but raising them required two distinct moves. The brakes could also be used gradually. The presence of a handbrake for safety and parking was praised by the test pilots, while the principal instruments were grouped in three panels facing the pilot. The radio apparatus, only installed later in the production run and not always present in operational aircraft, consisted of an A.R.C.1 medium wave receiver housed behind the pilot's seat and powered, as was the entire electrical system, by two batteries located under the cockpit floor. The antenna was strung between the wing tips and the fin, and connected to the receiver via a high-isolation cable.

The **G.50bis** variant was essentially similar to the original aircraft, but was recognisable by a slightly modified fuselage profile, tailplanes increased in area and reduced in height, improved pilot protection and an increase in endurance thanks to the installation of an additional tank in the original and redundant bomb bay. Thanks to this new fuselage tank, the fuel capacity increased to 411 litres, while a new 24-volt electrical system was installed, enabling the introduction of an R.B.30 radio receiver, although this proved only little more reliable than the old A.R.C.1. Other recognisable external variations from the initial model were the adoption of a propeller spinner and small bulges in the engine cowling.

Technical Data*

	G.50	G.50bis
Length	8.03 m	8.29 m
Height	3.28 m	3.28 m
Wingspan	10.99 m²	10.99 m²
Wing area	18.25 m²	18.25 m²
Empty weight	1,963 kg	2,015 kg
Max t/o weight	2,402 kg	2,522 kg
Powerplant	FIAT a 74 rc38	FIAT a 74 rc38
Take-off power	840 hp	840 hp
Max speed at 5,000 m	470 km/h	470 km/h
Max speed at sea level	400 km/h	400 km/h
Minimum speed	123 km/h	123 km/h
Climb to 2,000 m	1' 50"	1' 50"
Climb to 3,000 m	3' 10"	3' 27"
Climb to 4,000 m	4' 38"	5' 00"
Climb to 5,000 m	6' 03"	6' 30"
Climb to 6,000 m	7' 30"	8' 00"
Ceiling	10,700 m	10,700 m
Normal range at 5,000 m	around 640 km	around 1,000 km
Armament	2 x 12.7 mm machine gun; up to 100-kg of bombs	

*Data extracted from the *Manuale Istruzione e Norme di Montaggio, Regolazione e Impiego del velivolo G.50/G.50bis, 1939-1940.*

This page and opposite top right: Views of the G.50 cockpit showing the main and lower auxiliary instrument panels, plus cockpit controls, throttle, trim wheel, control column and S. Giorgio gunsight.

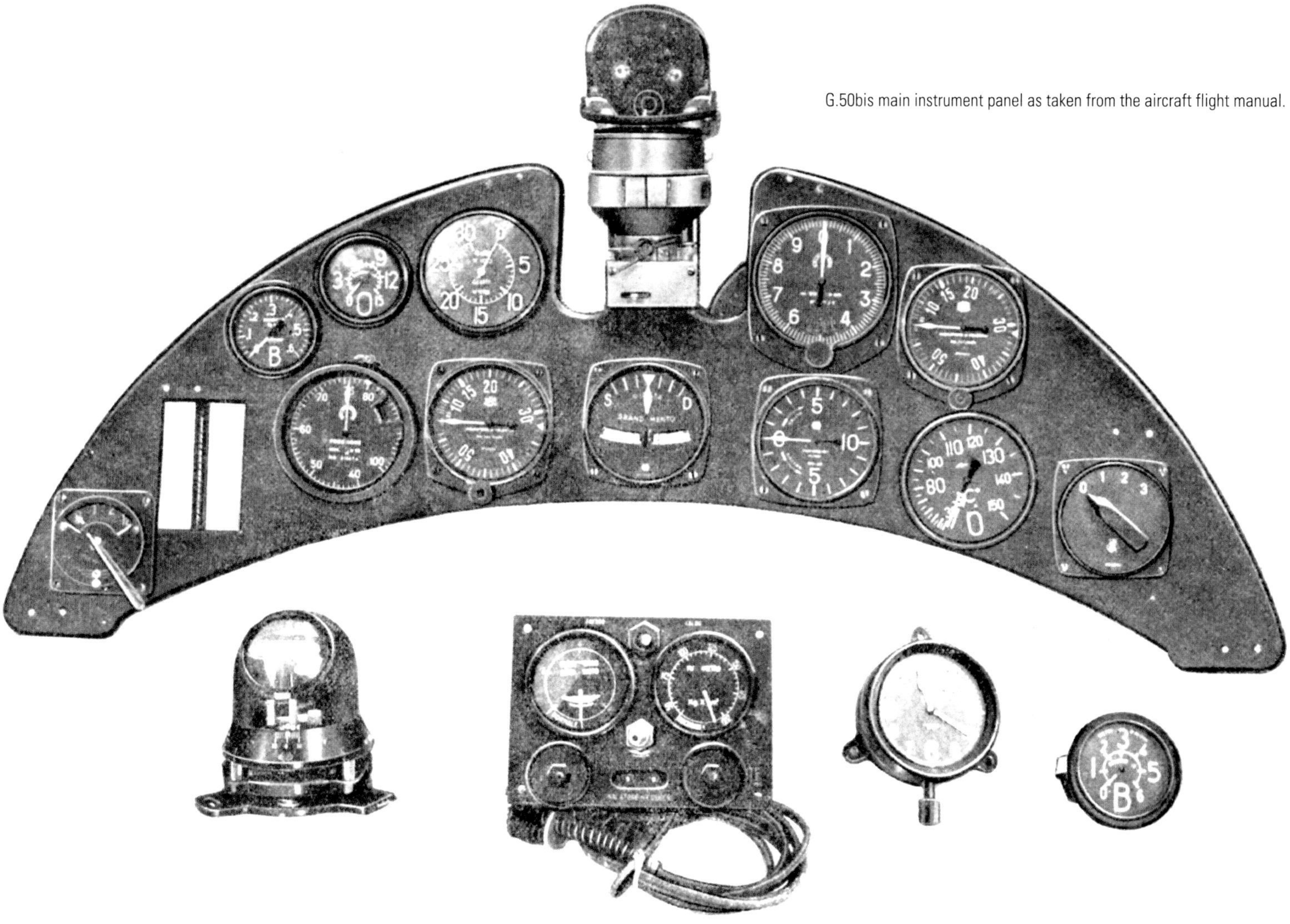

G.50bis main instrument panel as taken from the aircraft flight manual.

The G.50 in the Spanish Civil War

THE most modern monoplane fighter of the Regia Aeronautica was sent to Spain for reasons of prestige as well as to be evaluated, but this experience revealed some limitations in the new aeroplane.

In February 1939, equipped with twelve CMASA-manufactured I *Serie* G.50s, the *Gruppo Caccia Sperimentale G.50* was constituted, and was deployed to Spain under the command of *maggiore* Mario Bonzano. The fighters were embarked in the merchant ship *Tevere* and unloaded at the port of Tarragona. Still in their shipping crates, they were subsequently transferred to the airport at Reus. The assembly and flight-testing were performed by FIAT and Regia Aeronautica engineers, and was completed without any major issues, as confirmed in a report submitted by *maggiore* Bonzano to Roma on 29 March 1939.

> 'I am on the Madrid front, around 70 km behind the lines. Assembly of the aircraft required a relatively short time. I proceeded with the assembly cautiously to avoid unwelcome surprises that could have been derived from hurried work. The unloading operations were performed rapidly, and the transport of the aircraft to the airfield, around 12 kilometres away, was by truck. Redeployment from Reus to Escalona was completed in two stages, Reus-Zaragoza and Zaragoza-Escalona. A large part of the latter stage was conducted over Red territory at a height of 6,000 metres. No inconveniences of note during the transfer. We remained grounded at Zaragoza for four days due to bad weather. From the day of our departure from Reus until today a strong wind has been constantly blowing.'

Besides *maggiore* Bonzano, the *Gruppo Sperimentale* also included *capitano* Roveda, *tenenti* Del Prete, Trevisan, Martissa, Sant'Andrea, and David, *maresciallo* Marasco and *sergenti maggiore* Pongiluppi, Acerbi, Tassinari, D'Amico, Buvoli and Meneghini, while for opportune operational and political motives the unit was placed under the control of the XXIII *Gruppo Caccia 'Asso di Bastoni'* commanded by *maggiore* Aldo Remondino.

Once established at its final destination, the airfield at Escalona, some 70 km south-west of the capital Madrid, the G.50s took part, albeit with fairly limited participation, in the final phase of the Spanish Civil War, including maintaining an alert flight, as described in *maggiore* Bonzano's report:

> 'I have already completed seven combat missions, providing escort for the fighter *gruppi* cruising over the skies of Madrid at a height of 7,500-8,000 metres. Naturally, it is not possible to stay in the sky above the CR.32s

Above, below and opposite page right: The workshop of the G.50 of the *Reparto Sperimentale Caccia* (Experimental Fighter Unit) at Reus in Spain in February 1939. Experiments in Spain revealed a long series of flaws on the G.50, an aircraft that Italian pilots generally considered to be 'heavy, underpowered, poorly manoeuvrable, and dangerous.' (ASF)

*because of the existing speed difference.
I cruise slowly with the boost pressure at zero. Above 8,000 metres, the aircraft behaves well, it still climbs higher; in the cockpit, the pilot does not feel cold. Again, in this case it is necessary to manoeuvre delicately, because the speed value is always high, as is, consequently, acceleration in the turn. The guns fire magnificently, the engine is excellent, and the machine manoeuvres well. The already known faults still affect the undercarriage when it closes. The mechanical coupling is therefore indispensable so as to avoid the undercarriage opening once it is closed to some extent as a result of the imperfect sealing of the valves. The windshield has some failings, caused by its less then optimal manufacture. The transparent section has come away once again at an altitude of 8,000 metres.*

'I would propose, without hesitation, the adoption of an open cockpit for the pilot. Visibility from the G.50, despite being good, is, in comparison to the Messerschmitt or Rata, deficient towards the rear part of the aircraft. If this is added to the minimal downward visibility caused by the wings and the short time available for staying at altitude or to reach the enemy, the question of visibility becomes urgent.'

An interesting section of the report filed by Bonzano contains his suggestions regarding the modification of operational tactics. He suggests organising smaller combat formations, similar to those adopted by the Luftwaffe when the first fast monoplane fighters were introduced, and which would become the standard basic fighter tactic:

'Examining the methods of patrols along the front, we must move away from crossover flights with tight formations, as has happened with the CR.32. The formations should be reduced to pairs for greater efficiency and separated by at least 100 metres to enable better monitoring of the sky, coupled with the fact that at a reduced speed it is difficult to stay in formation. In regard to combat, it is preferable to fly in pairs, as it is more difficult to maintain a formation of three aircraft. This runs the risk of isolating the third aircraft of the formation, making it difficult for it to follow the actions of the commander. It is obvious that the flight leader must be well trained, and it is necessary to have a full briefing on the execution of the mission on the ground. In a following report I will better develop these concepts.'

Following Bonzano's report and further tests conducted in Italy, numerous modifications were made in an attempt to eliminate the reported drawbacks:

- a new type of jack to block the trolley;
- replacement of the cast metal air intake with a sheet metal one so that in the event of landing with retracted gear it does not cause the engine crankcase to break through as occurred in an accident;
- replacement of the anemometer with one of 560 km/h;
- shortening of the cloche by 3-4 cm;
- reduction of the collimator support to eliminate vibrations and the danger in the event of a rollover;
- radical modification of the pilot's seat to eliminate too many defects found.

As mentioned, the G.50s arrived in Spain as the war was reaching its conclusion and they were never able to enter into combat against Republican aircraft which, by then, had been reduced to a minimum and were almost inactive.

The first war mission was carried out on 16 March when six G.50s under command of *maggiore* Bonzano covered a formation of twenty-five Fiat CR.32s heading towards Madrid, from an altitude of 7,500 to 8,000 m. It was during this first mission that *sergente maggiore* Guido Pongiluppi, flying the G.50 coded 1-9, fainted due to gas fumes emanating from the engine which infiltrated the cockpit. Fortunately, he regained consciousness and made an emergency landing in a wheat field, some 20 km north of Toledo, the aircraft suffering only minor damage.

The next day, five G.50s again escorted CR.32s, while two pairs flew over Escalona airfield on a protection mission. On the 18th, the unit strength was reduced to ten aircraft following a landing accident involving a G.50 which suffered engine problems. The aircraft, which had been engaged in aerobatics, piloted by *tenente* Enzo Martissa, was forced to land on the bed of the Alberche river and was seriously damaged, although it proved possible to repair it at the Legion's workshops at Seville-Tablada.

On 21 March six G.50 escorted ten Savoia S.79 above the enemy airfield at Madridejos. The next day, it was *maggiore* Bonzano who escorted seven S.79 over Madrid.

After a few days of inactivity, the *Squadriglia Sperimentale* resumed its protection cover above Toledo, carrying out its last war flights on the 28th. That day ten G.50s provided air cover for Nationalist troops advancing on Madrid on the last day of the war.

On 1 April 1939, the Spanish Civil War ended without, as mentioned, the FIAT G.50s being able to engage in a single aerial combat. After the end of the bloody conflict, the G.50s, like all the other aircraft of the *Legion*, were handed over to the new Spanish Air Force. Despite being amongst the most modern fighters in service, the G.50s did not resonate particularly well with the Spanish pilots, and despite a series of impressive flying demonstrations provided by the Italians, FIAT never managed to sell any further examples. Becoming, to all intents and purposes, Spanish property, the G.50s, were assigned to *Grupo* 27, flying alongside former *Legion Condor* Heinkel He 112 Bs. The operational life of the Italian fighters was not overly long; they were operated in Spanish Morocco for a period, the last aircraft being withdrawn from service in 1943.

The twelve G.50s used in the Spanish Civil War came from the first order of forty-five production aircraft. Delivered by sea to Tarragona on 27 February 1939, they were reassembled in Reus and carried out their first patrol on 14 March.

Below: A FIAT chief technician (in white overalls) checks the rudder of a G.50 shortly before a test flight at Reus in March 1939.

The first series aircraft sent to Spain were notable for the cockpit being completely enclosed by a large rearward sliding canopy which was subject to deformation and breakage. It was later removed.

Some of the protagonists of the Spanish war photographed around a fighter of the *'Reparto Sperimentale Caccia G.50'*. From left: *maggiore* Remondino, commander of 23° *Gruppo Caccia*, the Spanish ace Joaquín García Morato (in cockpit) and *maggiore* Bonzano, commander of the small unit.

Above: For reasons of political expediency, Bonzano's unit became the fourth squadron of the 23° *Gruppo Caccia 'Asso di Bastoni'* commanded by *maggiore* Aldo Remondino. The insignia of the *Gruppo* was painted on the fuselage just aft of the cockpit.

Left and below: After the war the G.50s were assigned to *Grupo* 27 of the Aviacion Nacional. In the hands of Spanish pilots, the Italian monoplane fighters were plagued by a series of accidents, which put several of them out of action. However, the last was still flying in 1943.

A G.50 at Barajas airport before the Nationalists' Grand Parade on 12 May 1939. Five-hundred aircraft were on the field, including those captured from the Republicans. Note that the G.50s on these two pages of photographs are without undercarriage fairings.

The G.50 in the Second World War

As mentioned, the first G.50s of the I *Serie* were used to equip a *Reparto Sperimentale Caccia* based at Ciampino commanded by *maggiore* Bonzano and established to conduct training and operational evaluation. On 27 January 1939, three G.50s, piloted by *maggiore* Bonzano and *tenenti* Beretta and Marasco, flew an air display at Guidoniain in front of King Vittorio Emanuele III and Mussolini. After a low-level flypast, G.50 MM3571, flown by *tenente* Giovanni Berretta, crashed into a depot, killing its pilot and a mechanic on the ground. The probable cause of the accident was attributable to the aircraft entering a spin, one of the first such incidents – but, without doubt, not the last. The first *Squadriglia Sperimentale* was subsequently joined by another *squadriglia* equipped with modified G.50s and commanded by *capitano* Aldo Alessandrini.

* * *

Under 'Programma R' it was planned that the Regia Aeronautica would field two complete *Stormi* operating G.50s, the 51° and 52° *Stormo*. The first G.50s were delivered to the 20° and 21° *Gruppo* of the 51° *Stormo* CT, constituted officially on 1 October 1939, and subsequently to the 22° *Gruppo* of the 52° *Stormo* CT based at Pontedera, while the 24° *Gruppo* continued to operate the CR.32 from Sarzana airfield. These two *Stormi* were later paired under the newly formed 8ª *Brigata Caccia*, the units selecting as their emblem a black howling wolf on a red background with the motto *Ad Hostes Ululans* for the 52° *Stormo* CT, and a red wolf on a black background with the motto *Hostibus Terror* for the 51° *Stormo* CT.

The G.50 commences wartime operations

On 10 June 1940, the day of Italy's entry into the war, some 118 G.50s had been delivered to the Regia Aeronautica, of which 97 were operational and 21 under maintenance or awaiting collection. The FIAT fighter was in service with the two *gruppi* of the 51° *Stormo* CT commanded by *colonnello* Umberto Chiesa, more specifically the 20° *Gruppo* (351ª, 352ª, 353ª *Squadriglia*) led by *maggiore* Mario Bonzano and the 21° *Gruppo* (354ª, 355ª, 356ª *Squadriglia*) of *maggiore* Giovanni Buffa. The 51° *Stormo* CT was the only unit of the Regia Aeronautica to be completely equipped with the G.50, and operated from Ciampino Sud. The other G.50s in service were assigned to the 22° *Gruppo* (357ª, 358ª, 359ª *Squadriglia*) of *maggiore* Giovanni Borzoni, parented by the 52° *Stormo* CT commanded by *colonnello* Angelo Tessore and based at Pontedera. The other unit controlled by the 52° *Stormo* CT was the 24° *Gruppo* (360ª, 361ª, 362ª *Squadriglia*), commanded by *tenente colonnello* Eugenio Leotta, flying from Sarzana airfield, but still equipped with the FIAT C.R.32 biplane.

Both of these units were part of the 8ª *Brigata Aerea 'Lupi'*, placed under the control of the 3ª *Zona Aerea*, and on the outbreak of hostilities with France, the 20° *Gruppo* was tasked with providing air defence for Roma, while the 21° *Gruppo* was assigned the defence of Napoli, duties which were carried out until September with scrambles, patrol missions, and also night flights. Nevertheless, operational capability was somewhat limited, and activity was concluded without recording any events of note, apart from the tragic loss of *sergente* Loris Malagoli, who on 16 June 1940, crashed during a patrol mission

---

The emblem of the 51° *Stormo* CT

THE HOWLING WOLF EMBLEM (see opposite page) had only a short life with the 51° *Stormo* CT as the unit replaced it, following an event during training, with the famous black cat snatching three mice.

At the time, the 51° *Stormo* CT was sharing Ciampino airport with the 12° *Stormo* BT, equipped with the S.79, which proudly painted the celebrated three green mice emblem on sides of their aircraft. During their joint training, the S.79s had always got the better of the slower CR.32s. However, this was not the case during one exercise in the skies over the Italian capital, when the new G.50s of the 352ª *Squadriglia*, 20° *Gruppo*, managed to intercept and break up a formation of S.79s, this giving a victory to the fighters for the first time.

On their return, it is said that one of the pilots, visibly satisfied with the results of the flight, exclaimed the celebrated phrase, 'Finalmente quei signori dei Sorci Verdi han trovato il gatto che fa per loro…' ('Finally, those lords of the green mice have found the cat that does for them…').

From this ironic phrase *tenente* Vincenzo Sant'Andrea drew inspiration for the design of a new unit insignia featuring a black cat clawing at three grey mice. The new emblem was quickly and enthusiastically adopted to replace the original howling wolf insignia. It should be said that the original design featured the mice coloured, obviously in green, a clear allusion to the *Sorci Verdi* of the 12° *Stormo* BT, but following a compromise imposed by the highest levels of the Regia Aeronautica, who were intent on not diminishing the undertakings of the *Sorci Verdi*, the unit opted to paint the three mice in grey. Despite this, once they had arrived in Belgium as part of the C.A.I., the fiercely proud personnel of the 20° *Gruppo* decided to change the colours on their badge to green, and it has remained unchanged to the present day, as featured on the fins of the Eurofighter Typhoons of the *Stormo* at Istrana.

The insignia of the 'Gatto Nero' (Black Cat) of the 51° *Stormo* CT painted on the tail fin of a G.50 of 20° *Gruppo* in Libya.

Pilot's cloth version of the 51° *Stormo* CT emblem. (P.Monti)

51° *Stormo* CT emblem on the current Eurofighter Typhoons of the *Stormo* 20° *Gruppo* at Istrana.

A pilot of a G.50 belonging to the 359ª *Squadriglia* of 22° *Gruppo*, 52° *Stormo* CT operating from Pontedera in June 1940 sits on the edge of his cockpit with his feet resting on the entry/exit door.

Left: An early series G.50 belonging to the 351ª *Squadriglia* of 20° *Gruppo*, 51° *Stormo* CT photographed at Ciampino Sud airport near Rome. (F.Ballista)

Above: Early series Fiat G.50s belonging to the 351ª *Squadriglia* of 20° *Gruppo*, 51° *Stormo* CT in flight in the skies over Rome. Note the early camouflage scheme applied to the aircraft and their sliding canopies which pilots preferred to keep open. (F.Ballista)

An overfly parade for five G.50s of the 355ª *Squadriglia* of 51° *Stormo* CT at Ciampino Sud on 6 June 1940, a few days before the commencement of war for Italy. (R.Gentilli)

The insignia of the 8ª *Brigata Aerea* featuring the emblems of two of its units, the 51° and 52° *Stormo* CT, united by similar designs, but of differing colours. (P.Monti)

A pair of Fiat G.50s of the 356ª *Squadriglia* of 21° *Gruppo*, 51° *Stormo* CT on a reconnaissance flight along the slopes of Vesuvio volcano near Napoli.

This production series G.50, probably MM3570, was used by the *Centro Sperimentale* at Guidonia-Montecelio for flight evaluation.

A FIAT advertisement published in *L'Ala d'Italia* in 1941. (P.Monti)

Ground crew carry out maintenance work on a line-up of G.50s from the 361ª *Squadriglia* of the 24° *Gruppo Autonomo* CT at Tirana airfield. (P.Monti)

A G.50 of the 361ª *Squadriglia*, 24° *Gruppo Autonomo* CT photographed on a chilly day at Tirana. (P.Monti)

The engine runs up on this G.50 of the 355ª *Squadriglia*, 24° *Gruppo Autonomo* CT at Tirana. Note the fuselage riveting and access panels. (AM)

along the Tyherranian coast, probably due to adverse weather. It should be noted that on most occasions the fighters defending Napoli, in this early period of the war, never managed to impede British bombers which attacked the city on numerous occasions. During the first few days of the war, the 22° *Gruppo* also provided escort cover for S.79s on some of their bombing raids on ports and airfields in Corsica prior to the signing of the armistice with France.

The Balkans

In October 1940, at the beginning of the Greek campaign, another three *gruppi* were equipped with the G.50, and ready to enter action in the Balkans. Two *gruppi* were placed under the control of the *Comando Aeronautica Albania*, more precisely the 24° *Gruppo Autonomo* of *maggiore* Vincenzo Dequal at Tirana, formed by the 354ª and 355ª *Squadriglia,* and the newly formed 154° *Gruppo Autonomo*, commanded by *maggiore* Angelo Mastragostino with the 361ª and 395ª *Squadriglia*, operating from the airfields at Berat and Devoli.

Somewhat scuffed in appearance, these G.50s of the 354ª *Squadriglia*, 24° *Gruppo Autonomo* CT receive maintenance in a hangar at Tirana. (AM)

A good in-flight view of a well-worn G.50 of the 355ª Squadriglia, 24° *Gruppo Autonomo* CT while on patrol along the valleys of the Greek/Albanian border.

Also assigned to the 4ª *Squadra Aerea* was the 2° *Gruppo* of the 6° *Stormo* CT commanded by *maggiore* Giuseppe Baylon, parenting the 150ª and 152ª *Squadriglia* which were divided between the airfields at Bari, Grottaglie and Brindisi. The latter unit, together with its G.50s, was also operating CR.32s, and its mission was to assure the air defence of the important port of Taranto and the surrounding infrastructure. In total, between Albania and Puglia, the Regia Aeronautica had placed some eighty G.50s in the field, initially opposed by the similarly classed Gloster Gladiator and obsolete PZLs, P.24s and Bloch MB 151s.

Military operations took a path far different from that envisaged by the generals of the Regio Esercito, and inherently the fighters of the Regia Aeronautica became involved in the dangerous work of providing support to infantry as well as escorting bombers and standing defensive patrols to protect Italian airfields and positions.

The G 50s drew their first blood on 7 November 1940 when they shot down two Wellingtons of 70 Squadron over Valona, (CR.42s were also involved and claimed one victory). The first confirmed encounter between G.50s and the Greek Air Force occurred on 11 November when *capitano* Pier Giuseppe Scarpetta shot down a Blenheim of 32 *Mira*. Previously, on 3 November, 22 *Mira* had one of its PZL P24s shot down and another seriously damaged reportedly by G50s, but this action is not recorded in Italian documents.

The task of the Italian fighter pilots was very different when they faced the first RAF Gloster Gladiators and confirmation of this was recorded after a dogfight on 19 November when a mixed Italian formation of CR.42s and G.50s of the 160° and 24° *Gruppo Autonomo*, escorting Italian bombers, encountered a formation of Gladiators from 80 Squadron. By the end of the furious engagement the British had shot down three C.R.42s and a G.50 of the 355ª *Squadriglia*, while the Italian pilots claimed two victories. In fact, only one Gloster had been seriously damaged and its pilot wounded.

During November, the G.50s were also involved in strafing Greek and British targets, under escort from CR.42s, as occurred in the mission of the 27th, when twelve G.50s attacked the airfield at Kozani, strafing numerous Greek aircraft on the ground. The G50 continued to steadily shoot down British bombers, with three Blenheims of 84 Squadron falling on 22 December to the guns of pilots of 154° *Gruppo*.

On 6 January, an attack by Blenheims of 211 Squadron on Valona was repulsed by CR.42s of the 150° *Gruppo Autonomo* and G.50s of the 154° *Gruppo Autonomo*, which shot down three of them. After attacking and damaging a Blenheim, L1487, with his wingman, *tenente* Livio Bassi, managed to bring it down. The Blenheim ditched near the coast, and the Italian pilot was able to attract the attention of a Regia Marina destroyer by flying low past the ship and waggling his wings, directing it toward the wreck, where the survivors were recovered.

In the meantime, the British fighter force was reinforced with a new arrival of Gladiators as well as by the appearance of the first Hurricanes in mid-February 1941, the latter aircraft undoubtedly affecting the technical equilibrium established in combat at the end of 1940, in particular when set against CR.42s.

At the end of December, moreover, *maggiore* Baylon's 2° *Gruppo Autonomo* was withdrawn from the Balkan theatre and posted, with its two

G.50s of the 355ª *Squadriglia* of 24° *Gruppo*, 52° *Stormo* CT operating from Tirana.

Refuelling for a G.50 of the 355ª *Squadriglia* of 24° *Gruppo Autonomo* CT at Tirana. Note the worn paintwork on the dorsal edge of the fuselage aft of the cockpit and the unit emblem on the tail fin.

A member of the ground crew guides a G.50 of the 359ª *Squadriglia*, 154° *Gruppo Autonomo* CT at Devoli, February 1941. (AM)

squadriglie, to Libya for operations in North Africa. On 20 February, a major air battle occurred, when fifteen G.50s engaged in escorting a reconnaissance flight, were intercepted by a formation of Gladiators and PZL 24s. An intense dogfight ensued, at the end of which the Italian G.50 pilots claimed the destruction of ten enemy aircraft with no losses suffered. In reality, the aircraft of both sides returned to base with all aircraft, although the top Greek ace, Andreas Antoniu, of 22 *Mira* had to force-land his PZL P24 due to the damage suffered. On return, one damaged G.50 was forced to make a disastrous emergency landing and was written off.

A very different outcome resulted after an encounter fought in the afternoon of the same day when Blenheim bombers escorted by Hurricanes attacked Berat airfield. Twelve G.50s of the 154° *Gruppo Autonomo* CT were scrambled, and headed off towards the bombers, but were confronted by the Hurricanes, which having the advantage of height, pounced on the Italian fighters. It was not long before the G.50 of *tenente* Alfredo Fusco, hit by a burst of fire from a British fighter, exploded in mid-air, while after damaging a bomber, the G.50 of *tenente* Livio Bassi was attacked by a pair of Hurricanes and suffered serious damage. *Tenente* Bassi, despite being injured, returned to base with his aircraft in flames, but died a few days later from the serious burns he had received. The two valorous pilots were subsequently awarded the *Medaglia d'Oro al Valor Militare*. In return, only a Blenheim of 211 Squadron was forced to crash-land and was written off.

Intense air activity continued over the following weeks, with continuous air combat, in the course of which both sides claimed many victories.

Only eleven G.50s were lost or badly damaged in combat due to enemy action in this theatre, with five pilots killed. On the other hand, the FIAT monoplanes were able to shoot down or badly damage at least 45 Greek and British aircraft. Particularly outstanding was the performance of the two *Squadriglie* of 154° *Gruppo* which, in exchange for three FIATs lost in combat, were able to shoot down or damage up to 28 enemy aircraft. The FIAT fighter did perform most effectively, proving itself capable of conducting successful operations, often in less than optimal weather conditions. The G.50 was possibly the worst of the Italian first generation monoplane fighters but, in contrast to the C200, in Greece during the winter of 1940-41, it was available in sufficient numbers and with pilots sufficiently trained to make good use of it. The FIAT pilots managed to exploit their greater speed to regularly intercept the British and Greek light bombers, and were able to hold their own against the first Hurricanes I arriving in that sector thanks to their superior manoeuvrability. Indeed, on the relatively few occasions that the monoplanes clashed, four G.50s went down with the loss of the top ace, Livio Bassi, against the loss of three Hurricanes, two of them piloted by the aces, Charles Dyson and Richard Cullen. Paradoxically, for the FIAT pilots, the slower and older Gladiator proved as difficult a nut to crack as the Hurricane, because although the G.50s always endeavoured to turn air combat to terms more favourable for themselves, avoiding as much as possible the air combat manoeuvres in which the British biplane proved to be decidedly more agile, the RAF Gladiators were able to shoot down or heavily damage at least six of them. Six Glosters went down in exchange, but most of them were Greek machines. A factor which was much appreciated, was the robustness of the Italian aircraft.

In North Africa

North Africa saw the FIAT fighter particularly active in operations, with the first examples arriving on 23 December 1940 with the 358ª *Squadriglia*, which in late January 1941 was incorporated into the 2° *Gruppo Autonomo* CT, itself newly transferred into the theatre from the Balkans on 6 January. The G.50s were quickly deployed on patrol missions, to provide escort for motorised convoys and to strafe advancing British armour, although such operations were made particularly difficult by the problems caused by the local conditions, since the FIATs possessed no form of anti-sand protection. Towards the end of January, of the thirty aircraft present in Libya, only three were serviceable. Despite this, the pilots of the 2° *Gruppo Autonomo* CT struggled on with its

Two G.50bis of the 352ª *Squadriglia* in flight over the deserts of North Africa. The nearest aircraft is 352-3, MM5936.

Below: The first Fiat G.50s of the 2° *Gruppo Autonomo* CT under the command of *maggiore* Baylon arrived in Libya at the end of 1940. This G.50 was photographed while escorting what appears to be a Ju 88.

A member of the ground crew, wearing protective goggles over his tropical helmet in case of either a sandstorm or as protection when engines were run up and aircraft taxied, assists a pilot of the 20° *Gruppo Autonomo* CT with his parachute and harness. The pilot wears a fur-collared flying suit but a lightweight tropical white flying helmet for protection against the sun in the open cockpit.

few available aircraft, following the fate of retreating Italian forces.

On the few occasions in which they met the enemy fighters, the FIATs were able to hold their own, as, for example, on 25 January when a formation led by *capitano* Sterzi bounced and shot down or heavily damaged four Gladiators of 3 Squadron, RAAF. The situation improved slightly with the arrival on 25 January of the 155° *Gruppo Autonomo* CT (351ª, 360ª and 378ª *Squadriglie*), commanded by *maggiore* Luigi Bianchi.

Having conquered a large part of Tripolitania, the British advance came to a halt, and this situation, in advance of the Axis counter-offensive of April 1941, allowed the two G.50 *gruppi*, to reorganise at their bases, the 155° *Gruppo Autonomo* CT being located at Misurata and the 2° *Gruppo Autonomo* CT at Castel Benito. That month the units began to accept deliveries of the G.50bis, a variant equipped with anti-sand filters on the carburettor intakes and the oil radiators, together with a propeller spinner to protect the sensitive mechanics. The principal activities in this period involved numerous escort missions conducted on behalf of Axis fighter-bombers, in particular German and Italian Ju 87s, as well as patrol flights and escort for naval convoys arriving from Italy. The Stuka escorts were particularly onerous, especially during the attack dive, which required the planning of a specific mission profile that saw the G.50s fly along the Ju 87s' approach route, and then initiate a slight dive, followed by an elongated 'S' turn to rejoin the bombers at the critical moment of their pull-up, when they were particularly vulnerable. The German Stuka pilots, however, were very happy to have the escort of the relatively slow Italian fighters as they would protect them against all odds, if necessary. A particularly significant day for the 155° *Gruppo Autonomo* CT was 14 April 1941, when eight fighters engaged in a mission

Dust trails behind this G.50bis of the 352ª *Squadriglia* of 20° *Gruppo Autonomo* CT as it rolls out, probably from the strip at Sidi Rezegh.

escorting German and Italian Stukas attacking targets near Tobruk were intercepted by RAF Hurricanes which shot down two German Stukas and the G.50s of *tenente* Cugnasca and *maresciallo* Marinelli. Keeping up their record against the Hurricane, in return, the G.50s shot down the aircraft of 73 Sqn piloted by Sgt. Webster and by the ace F/Lt. J.D. Smith, who were both killed.

In the same period a certain number of aircraft was also modified in the field with the installation

A FIAT G.50bis of the 352ª *Squadriglia* of 20° *Gruppo Autonomo* CT photographed during a combat mission over the desert with the waters of the Mediterranean in the background.

Survivors of the *Squadriglie* from the disbanded CAI which had been deployed to Belgium in 1940, had to accustomise themselves to operating from coastal airstrips in North Africa when they were urgently transferred to Libya.

A G.50bis of 20° *Gruppo Autonomo* CT escorting Bf 110s of 2.(H)/*Aufklärungsgruppe* 14. Note the rod protruding from the ventral surface of the nacelle of the Bf 110 in which the photographer flies. This was a visual indicator for the pilot that the undercarriage was retracted (it lowered when the undercarriage was down).

of underwing shackles for two small bombs. This transformed the FIATs into fighter-bombers, an adjustment which enabled effective air support missions, especially in the area around Sidi el Barrani, where the G.50bis were particularly active, despite opposition from Hurricanes and Curtiss P-40s which were increasingly present in North African skies.

At the end of April 1941, the two *gruppi* were deployed to Derna, beginning a rotation of the units, as by then the few operational aircraft and their personnel were worn out from months of intense and problematic activity over the desert. For this reason the 2° *Gruppo Autonomo* CT was substituted by the 20° *Gruppo Autonomo* CT, posted into theatre from the Channel Front (151ª, 352ª and 353ª *Squadriglia*) and equipped with thirty G.50bis. The new units undertook considerable combat activity despite their limited assets and the problems linked to continual relocations. Missions included strafing British motorised units and positions, performing the routine escort role for Axis fighter-bombers and offensive patrols over the front line.

In June, the G.50s were involved in supporting operations in support of the capture of Tobruk and in the Side El Barrani area against the British Eighth Army. It was in the course of a mission over Sidi El Barrani that *capitano* Montefusco, commander of the 151ª *Squadriglia,* was lost. Having been hit by anti-aircraft fire, he attempted to return to base but probably seriously injured, crashed in the desert. For his bravery he was decorated with the *Medaglia d'Oro al Valor Militare*.

On 7 September the G.50s of 155° *Gruppo* with the C.200s of 153° *Gruppo* carried out a most successful strafing attack against the landing grounds around Sidi Barrani, where 1 and 2 Squadrons, SAAF, 33 Squadron, and an RNFS were based. At the end, the Commonwealth air forces admitted the loss of two P-40s and two Hurricanes as well as heavy damage to nine more Hurricanes. That same night the four squadrons left their bases and retreated. The Italians suffered no losses.

In the afternoon of 19 November, twenty G.50bis of the 20° *Gruppo Autonomo* CT, detached to the satellite airfield at Sidi Resegh, were attacked on the ground by a formation of Tomahawks of 112 Squadron and subsequently by a British armoured column. Only three G.50s managed to take off, while some nineteen G.50bis and a Caproni Ca 133 transport were destroyed or captured by British soldiers who overran the airfield. Fortunately, a large number of the Italian personnel, albeit with some scares and not a little luck, managed to evade capture, escaping in the few trucks available prior to the arrival of the British. In a few hours the 20° *Gruppo Autonomo*

The escort of Luftwaffe Ju 87s and Bf 110s over North Africa was often provided by FIAT G.50s of the 2° *Gruppo Autonomo* CT, seen here covering a Bf 110 of ZG 26 fitted with long-range tanks and a Ju 87 R of II./St.G 1.

had been practically eliminated. A small win was obtained by *capitano* Bonzano's pilots on the 4 and 5 December, when in a series of clashes over El Adem, they claimed the destruction of nine P-40 Tomahawks over the two days for the loss of just one G.50, whose pilot escaped by parachute.

The number of G. 50s operating in Libya was, however, never significant, ranging from a minimum of twenty in February to a maximum of eighty aircraft in October 1941, when their withdrawal from service commenced with the arrival of the AerMacchi C.200s as well as the more modern C.202 *Folgores*. In North Africa in December 1941, there were just 35 FIAT G.50bis operating with the 12° *Gruppo Autonomo* CT (159ª, 160ª and 165ª *Squadriglia*) from Tripoli-Castelbenito airfield, which had just replaced the exhausted 20° and 155° *Gruppo Autonomo* CT a few days previously.

In the spring of 1942, the 12° *Gruppo Autonomo* CT was joined by the 160° *Gruppo Autonomo* CT (375ª, 393ª and 394ª *Squadriglie*) equipped with a mix of CR.42s and G.50bis. Nevertheless, as 1942 progressed, the number of G.50bis in service gradually diminished to the point that in the summer, the 12° *Gruppo* and 160° *Gruppo* had a fleet of no more than fifty aircraft flying from the airfields at Castelbenito and Sorman. In August the 12° *Gruppo Autonomo* CT returned to Italy, transferring its remaining fighters to the 160° *Gruppo Autonomo* CT, which on the eve of the battle of El Alamein was equipped with little more than twenty G.50bis, operated essentially for ground attack, having passed its CR.42s on to other units in the sector. After the December repatriation of the 160° *Gruppo Autonomo* CT, at the moment of the abandonment of Libya in January 1943, the only unit still operational on the G.50bis was the 368ª *Squadriglia* at Sfax, with at least thirteen aircraft, these being used for numerous ground-attack missions in Tripolitania and Tunisia until the unit's withdrawal, on 13 May 1943, to the island of Pantelleria with just seven surviving G.50bis.

G.50bis, MM5949, coded '151-1', of the 151ª *Squadriglia* of 20° *Gruppo Autonomo* CT at Sidi Rezegh with unit emblem on the tail.

Maintenance for a G.50bis of the 352ª *Squadriglia* in Africa. (AM)

A G.50bis of the 20° *Gruppo Autonomo* CT, photographed moments before take-off, probably at Gambut airfield.

A G.50bis of the 151ª *Squadriglia* seen wrecked at Sidi Rezegh. Among those involved in the battles that characterised the second British offensive, the 20° *Gruppo* suffered the greatest losses at the hands of British ground forces in two events on 19 November – at Sidi Rezegh, following a deep infiltration by enemy armoured forces into the German-Italian line and then, on 22 December, when withdrawal had already been decided, as a result of a British commando raid on the field at Agedabia, the unit lost 18 and 5 aircraft respectively.

The other fronts: the Aegean and the Mediterranean

Following the end of hostilities with Greece, the 154° *Gruppo Autonomo* CT returned to Italy, operating for a few weeks from the airfields at Brindisi (395ª *Squadriglia*) and Lecce (361ª *Squadriglia*) before being disbanded. On 9 July, however, it was reconstituted at Grottaglie and equipped with a mixed fleet of G.50bis and CR.42s – the latter operated in the night fighter role – as well as with the AerMacchi C.200. In October 1941 it carried out important escort missions for naval convoys until May 1942, when it was transferred to the island of Rhodes to contribute to the defence of the Aegean sector together with the 161° *Gruppo Autonomo* CT, still equipped with a mixture of CR.32s and CR.42s. Despite delivery of the first C.202s to the 154° *Gruppo Autonomo* CT, the G.50bis, together with a handful of CR.42CNs, continued to be utilised extensively for all fighter roles, offensive patrols, ground-attack and assault missions until the Armistice, operating from Gadurra and Maritza airfields on Rhodes, and maintaining a detachment on the island of Kos. Following the Armistice, around thirty serviceable G.50s were captured by the Germans.

The G.50s were furthermore engaged in the defence of continental Italy, participating in some of the principal air/sea battles which were fought in the Mediterranean between 1941 and 1943. One unit equipped with the G.50bis was the 151° *Gruppo Autonomo* CT (366ª, 367ª and 368ª *Squadriglia*) which, with a fleet of 35 G.50bis, was transferred to Araxos airfield in Greece, mainly to provide an armed escort for convoys.

Operating from Sardegna were the few G.50bis of the 160° *Gruppo Autonomo* CT based at Venafiorita airfield near Olbia. They provided a modest contribution to the defence of the island against the daily Allied offensive against airfields and military installations, while also worthy of mention is the activity of the newly formed (in January 1943) 50° *Stormo d'Assalto*, placed under the command of *tenente colonnello* Ferruccio Vossilla. This was formed by the 158° and 159° *Gruppo Assalto* with a mixed fleet of G.50s, C.202s and C.R.42s. After the Allied landings in Sicilia, the unit was relocated to Crotone in Calabria, and conducted numerous attacks with G.50bis, striking landing ships, stores, and Allied columns, but suffering notable losses in combat and also on the ground, the latter due to the continuous Allied bombing of the airfields from where operations were conducted. By mid-July the unit was almost without aircraft.

A G.50bis of the 395ª *Squadriglia* overflies Rodi airport in 1942.

Some of the G.50s destined for the 162ª *Squadriglia* of 161° *Gruppo Autonomo* CT photographed during a stop at Pescara, home of a Scuola di Volo.

A FIAT G.50bis, MM6050, of the 162ª *Squadriglia*, 161° *Gruppo Autonomo* CT at Rodi.

Pilots of 154° *Gruppo Autonomo* CT photographed shortly before climbing aboard their aircraft for an armed reconnaissance mission over the Aegean.

Left: Fighters of 154° *Gruppo Autonomo* CT on an airfield in the Balkans.

The cloth flying suit insignia of the 154° *Gruppo Autonomo* CT. (P.Monti)

This G.50bis of the 163ª *Squadriglia* had seen better days. The photograph was taken at Grottaglie airfield after aircraft of the unit had returned from a patrol over the Aegean theatre of operations. The port main wheel has buckled outwards and the starboard wheel has collapsed, probably due to a ground loop. (F.Sanetti)

After the Armistice

ON the date of the Armistice, the majority of the G.50s still in service – around one third of the more than 700 aircraft constructed and of several versions – were mainly used by the flying schools, the *Gruppi complementari*, and various specialist schools.

Those aircraft still conducting combat missions numbered little more than fifty G.50bis. They comprised the twenty aircraft operated by the 50° *Stormo Assalto* which was undergoing reorganisation at Lonate Pozzolo airfield; a G.50bis in Corsica at Aiaccio belonging to the *sezione intercettori* of the 160° *Gruppo* CT; a pair of G.50bis at Sarzana airfield; seven aircraft in Albania with the 376ª *Squadriglia* CT and five with the 392ª *Squadriglia* CT at Tirana airport; three at Araxos in Greece with the 385ª *Squadriglia* CT and another thirteen examples with the 154° *Gruppo Autonomo* CT on Rhodes. It also seems that one or two G.50s were still at Centocelle.

Almost all of these aircraft were captured by German forces after 8 September and in part assigned to the Luftwaffe to be used for training duties with *Fliegerführerschule* (A) 123 at Graz-Thalerhof and *Jagdgeschwader* 107 and 108. The latter two units were the former *Jagdfliegerschulen* (JFS 7 and JFS 8) which had been transformed into fighter units in January 1943, but which also continued to perform training activities at Toul and Essay les Nancy in France where the G.50s, which arrived in February 1944, operated for some months. On 12 April 1944, JG 108 suffered eighteen Macchi C.200 either destroyed or with varying degrees of damage at Vöslau as a result of a bombing raid, along with six CR.42s and light damage to a single G.50.

Another small number of two-seat G.50Bs remained in Italy, utilised for a variety of subsidiary roles, while another batch of G.50bis were transferred by the Germans to the Croatian air arm, which had already acquired ten G.50s directly from Italy. Most of the other recovered aircraft were demolished or destroyed during the ongoing fighting. At least four aircraft were subsequently utilised for training duties by the Aeronautica Nazionale Repubblicana at the *Scuola di volo di I e II periodo* near Torino. Little is known about their use.

Only a few G.50s managed to fly to Allied-occupied southern Italy after the Armistice, and at the main Lecce/Galatina base just two G.50bis (MM.6322/6483) were serviceable. They were overhauled by the *Servizio Tecnico* of the *Raggruppamento Caccia* after having been modified with dual controls for use at the *Scuola Caccia* (fighter school) at Lecce Leverano together with another G.50B recovered from Sardegna. They operated with a mixed fleet of C.R.42s, C.200s and Nardi FN. 305s.

A G.50 of 154° *Gruppo Autonomo* CT undergoes maintenance amidst a grove of olive trees. Visible below the open cockpit access door is the emblem of the *Gruppo*.

This G.50, with its unit markings deleted, was assigned for a short time to 3° *Stormo* CT before that unit converted to the C.202 Folgore.

A G.50bis assigned to the Luftwaffe's 3./JG 108, possibly at either Bad Vöslau or Wiener Neustadt in July 1944

A pair of G.50s from the *Scuola Volo* at Rimini fly over the famous square known as La rotonda sul Mare at Rimini (below) and the surrounding countryside of Carpegna (left).

Two pilots walk along a line-up of six G.50bis at an airfield in Italy before transfer to an operational unit in North Africa.

Above: A G.50 of the 150ª Squadriglia, 2° *Gruppo Autonomo* CT.

Finland – The Suomen Ilmavoimat

The G.50bis, FA-19, of Lentolaivue 26 (LLv.26) taxiing at Helsinki-Malmi airport in the winter of 1941/42.

IN 1939 the Suomen Ilmavoimat, in expectation of a probable conflict with the Soviet Union, commenced a search for a modern fighter aircraft to replace its by then obsolete Bristol Bulldog IVs which equipped *Lentolaivue* 26 (LLv.26). The FIAT G.50 was identified as the possible fighter with which to modernise the Finnish front line combat fleet. This assessment led to a visit to Italy from a delegation of the Suomen Ilmavoimat. After various meetings with the leaders of the Regia Aeronautica and the management of FIAT, on 23 October 1939 a contract was signed for the initial supply of twenty-five aircraft. Deliveries were scheduled for the first weeks of 1940. This was to be achieved by including a good number of the fighters that had only recently entered service with the 51° *Stormo* at Ciampino. The clauses of the agreement required that the first two aircraft should be new-build machines at CMASA awaiting delivery to the Regia Aeronautica, and that another Finnish commission, formed of pilots and engineers, would return to Italy to accept the aircraft and embark upon a rapid cycle of training. This commission, led by *Majuri* (Major) Stahle arrived in Italy on 4 November 1939. In the course of one of the test flights on 14 November, while diving the aircraft from 3,500 metres, pilot Tapani Harmaja, suffered the loss of his aircraft's canopy as well as minor injuries, and damage to the

G.50bis, FA-17, MM3599, at Helsinki Malmi airport, August 1942.

fighter's tailplanes. A subsequent analysis of the flight revealed that the aircraft had reached a speed of around 830 km/h, an accomplishment which was considered as relevant as confirmation of the fighter's robustness.

Subsequently, the Finnish pilots conducted further flights at Furbara to test the armament. The G.50 provided a good impression to the point that on 17 November 1939, just two weeks prior to the start of Russian aggression against Finland, the order for the first twenty-five machines was ratified. The Finns baptised the G.50 the '*Fijiu*',

the Finnish language equivalent of '*Freccia*', the name used by the Italians for the fighter.

In conformity with the contract, the first machines were sent by railway to the small German port of Sassnitz on the island of Rügen and then transported by ship to Malmö, in Sweden, where they would be assembled and transferred to Finland. However, only two of the first batch of aircraft arrived by this route just prior to the end of November. The first G.50 destined for the Suomen Ilmavoimat was delivered on 18 December 1939, followed on 2 January 1940

G.50s of LLv.26 at Joroinen in June 1941. Note the worn wing marking on the aircraft in the foreground. (SA-Kuva)

A G.50 taxies out at Lunkula in August 1941. (SA-Kuva)

by the second aeroplane. The two aircraft were initially coded SA.1 (ex MM4738) and SA.2 (ex MM4740), and only towards the end of January, did they receive their respective final serials FA-1 and FA-2. The other six aircraft were despatched by rail in two shipments, one of two and one of four, on 4 and 7 December 1939 respectively. Unfortunately, they were held at Sassnitz following a protest by the Soviet Minister of Foreign Affairs, Vyacheslav Molotov, to his

Left: Pilots of 3/LLv.26 photographed at Kilpasilta on 14 August 1942. From left to right: Sgt Ilmari Pöysti, 2/Lt Nils Trontti, S/C Onni Paronen and 1/Lt Olli Puhakka, the unit commander. Behind them is the G.50 coded FA-29. Puhakka ended the war with 46 victories and was awarded the Mannerheim Cross. (SA-Kauva)

German equivalent, Joachim von Ribbentrop. It should be remembered that some months earlier the 'Molotov-Ribbentrop' pact had been signed in which there featured a secret agreement that Finland would return to the sphere of influence of the Soviet Union. For this reason the Germans decided to revoke permission for the aircraft to transit through German national territory, but the Italian government managed to obtain the release and return of the railway wagons carrying the aircraft and the essential logistics material necessary for their operation.

To avoid any further negative impact or problems of a political or diplomatic nature, the

FIAT FIGHTERS

A G.50 rolls out at Rautu airfield in September 1942. (SA-Kuva)

Right: G.50, FA-33, serving with 3/Le.Lv.26 at Kilpasilta on 3 September 1942. S/C Ponni Paronen is seen in the cockpit. The tail of the aircraft bears an '8' in yellow, the colour of this unit. (SA-Kauva)

A fine study of G.50, FA-32, with the pilot at readiness in the cockpit at Rautu, summer 1942. (SA-Kuva)

A pilot returns to Rautu following a successful flight in the summer of 1942. (SA-Kuva)

FIAT G.50, FA-11, was the aircraft often flown by Lt Nieminen, commander of 3 *Lentue* of Le.Lv.26. The aircraft enjoyed long service, as it was known to have flown as late as September 1946. (R.Gentilli)

A FIAT returns from a combat patrol, Rautu, summer 1942. Note the unusual polka dots sprayed on the spinner of the G.50 at left. (SA-Kuva)

Italian Government decided to deliver the fighters via sea from other Italian or European ports, to Sweden, where they would be reassembled and transferred by air to Finland. On 4 January, a steamer embarked seventeen G.50s plus four spare engines and ammunition, while on 21 January the consignment of six aircraft returned by Germany were sent via rail, passing through France to the port of Antwerp, where they were loaded onto a freighter for delivery to Sweden. In the meantime, driven by the necessity for equipment to confront a probable new crisis with the Soviet Union, the Finnish Government requested the supply of a further sixty aircraft for delivery between March and April. In response, the Italian Government only sanctioned the delivery of ten machines on the pretext that the remaining aircraft were required to complete the re-equipment of Italian units which were close to completing their conversion onto the monoplane.

These further ten aircraft were loaded onto the Norwegian cargo ship *Braga*, which sailed from the Italian port of Livorno on 28 January 1940, arriving in Sweden on 17 February. On arrival in Sweden, the fighters were assembled at Trollhattan and Gothenburg airports, and test flown by FIAT test pilot, Carlo Cugnasca, prior to being transferred by Swedish pilots to Västerås airport, north of Stockholm, where they were accepted by Finnish pilots for their delivery to Finland.

On arrival, they were assigned to LLv.26, the unit of the Ilmavoimat destined to operate the Italian fighter. Two of the aircraft were lost in accidents during these delivery flights. The first to be lost was FA-8 on 7 February, flown by *Kersantti* (Sergeant) Wallenius, while the second was FA-7, which disappeared on 8 February, probably in difficult weather conditions over the Baltic Sea while being flown by Hungarian volunteer pilot, Bekassy.

The Italian aircraft arrived in Finland as the first phase of the Finnish-Soviet conflict was drawing to an end. Despite repeated pressure and requests from the Chief of Staff of the Suomen Ilmavoimat, General Lundquist, it had not been possible to expedite the checking over of the aircraft and their subsequent flight-testing prior to sending them to operational units. This was a cause of considerable irritation to the Finnish commanders who were anxious to utilise the G.50s in support of Finnish forces who were fighting across the entire front. It should be noted that together with the aircraft, an Italian technical mission also arrived in Finland, led by *colonnello* Giuseppe Casero and deployed to offer technical assistance and training for Finnish personnel. Despite the technical difficulties and the slow delivery rate, the supply of 32 aircraft had been completed by mid-March 1940, while the final aircraft was delivered on 19 June 1940, probably following technical problems.

Some of the Finnish pilots managed to take part in the fighting before the end of the Winter War, obtaining notable results, above all *Kapteeni* (Captain) Ehrnrooth, a test pilot from the Tampere workshops, who on 13 January 1940 managed to shoot down an SB.2 twin, followed on 29 January by a DB.3 bomber.

Fighting had commenced in January, but only on 26 February, following a hasty conversion, did LLv.26 begin combat operations, these being interrupted after fourteen days by the armistice. The Finnish pilots had received tacit instructions to concentrate their efforts against Soviet bombers, avoiding as far as possible encounters with enemy fighters; this was a rewarding tactic, which resulted in numerous victories, despite the enormous disproportion of forces in the field.

In this first phase of their operation, the G.50s suffered from numerous problems, bringing to light significant defects, many of which were provoked by the low temperatures, in which the aircraft had not been foreseen to operate. Consequently, it became essential to switch to mineral oil and to change gaskets and other items unsuitable for severe climatic conditions. The maintenance of aircraft proved to be difficult and laborious, with problems in accessing components and with a generally poor quality of materiel. This resulted in a low rate of aircraft utilisation despite the efforts of pilots and ground crews who also complained of incomplete training. Nevertheless, it should be remembered that the fighters supplied belonged to the first construction

In Finland the G.50 was also known as the *'Fijiu'* ('Arrow'). Several Finnish aces flew the FIAT, and one of them, Oiva Tuominen, achieved 23 of his 44 aerial victories flying the type. (R.Gentilli)

In February 1942, the G.50, FA-33, MM4737, was tested with non-retractable snow skids of the type fitted to the Fokker D.XXI fighter. (R.Gentilli)

series, so they were not completely fine-tuned, and also that their entry into service in difficult environmental conditions was rushed.

Despite this difficult initial period, the FIATs, albeit with reduced availability, commenced operations with LLv.26 from 11 February 1940, and the G.50bis was also soon thrown into the mix, the type achieving its first victories as early as 26 February when an I-16 and a DB-3 were downed. The following day, however, the first combat loss was recorded, when at the end of a dogfight near Mankki with a Soviet I-153 biplane, the G.50bis, FA-12, flown by pilot Malmivuo, was shot down. On 11 March, on the eve of the armistice, Italian volunteer pilot, Dario Manzocchi, was injured in the course of a dogfight and was killed when he attempted to make an emergency landing on a frozen lake. His G.50bis, FA-22, overturned. The end of the 105-day conflict saw the Soviet Union emerge victorious, but at the price of heavy losses.

* * *

The period preceding the 'Continuation War', fought between 25 June 1941 and 19 September 1944, was used to identify and resolve the numerous technical problems that had arisen during the first weeks of operations, and also to apply all the improvements introduced to the second production series in Italy to the aircraft that had been delivered thus far. Problems connected to erroneous assembly and maintenance were overcome; enclosed cockpits on seven of the aircraft delivered were changed; modifications were made to the propellers with the adoption of new Swedish-built spinners intended to protect the variable pitch mechanism from freezing temperatures (although, ultimately, the solution to this problem was only possible through the use of a new type of lubricating oil). For operations from snow-covered ground, a fixed undercarriage with skis was fitted, similar to that used on the Fokker D.XXI.

With an improvement in the situation that had restricted activity during the first months of operations, faith in the Italian fighter increased considerably, to the point that, as already mentioned, a request was submitted to Italy for another batch of sixty aircraft. An initial demonstration of the effectiveness of the Ilmavoimat and the FIAT fighter occurred on 25 June 1941, the start date of the Continuation War, when a formation of fifteen Soviet SB-2bis bombers attacked Joroinen airfield in south-east Finland. In the space of a few minutes, eight G.50s already in the air for local patrol missions, intercepted the Soviet bombers and in a brief engagement claimed thirteen aerial victories. The Soviets, however, admitted the loss of nine SB-2 bis: but in any case, it was certainly a positive result for the Italian fighters.

After this first exploit, the Fiat G.50s continued to be operated with good results, conducting missions to intercept enemy bombers as well as mounting fighter sweeps and railway protection patrols, and engaging Soviet aircraft on numerous occasions. Indeed, of the 177 confirmed victories achieved by LLv.26 in the period 30 November 1939 to 4 September 1944, at least 100 were lodged by pilots flying the G.50, with just 41 overall losses suffered by the unit which included, alongside only three G.50 losses, those involving the Bristol Bulldog IIA, Fokker D.XXI, Gloster Gladiator and Brewster B-239.

On 28 June the unit was moved to Ratasalmi to support the combat operations of the Finnish Army north of Lake Ladoga, active in maintaining air superiority above the Finnish troops of the VI. and VII. Army Corps. These formations reached Lake Ladoga in mid-July. On 21 July, 2. *Lentue* and 3. *Lentue* (flights) of LLv.26 relocated to Joensuu. Three days later the VI. Army Corps reached Tuulosjoki, and on 29 July the 1. *Lentue* moved to the island of Lunkula, the base to which, at the beginning of August, the remaining two *Lentue* transferred, tasked with providing defensive patrols to counter highly active Soviet bombers. The area of operations thus became that of Aunus-Praasa-Hyrsyla and Pitkaranta.

Following a breakthrough achieved by the IV. Army Corps at Tuulkseny and an advance as far as Syvari, on 16 September LLv.26 relocated to Immola to fight in the eastern part of the Karelian Isthmus, conducting defensive patrols to protect the regional industrial centres and lines of communication, and the land forces which, having reached the preceding Finnish border had initiated a war of position. At the end of the year, 1. *Lentue* relocated to Malmi with the mission of defending the capital against the enemy offensive, while 2. *Lentue* remained at Immola. The balance of 1941 proved to be favourable for LLv.26, as with the loss of just two aircraft the unit had added some 52 victories to its combat record.

At the beginning of 1942, the second year of the war, LLv.26 was structured around just two *Lentue*: the 2 .*Lentue* was based at Immola and 1. *Lentue* at Malmi. In general, the first two months of the year passed relatively calmly, and towards the end of April the 3. *Lentue* was created, the entire unit continuing to provide the air defence and visual reconnaissance capability for the Karelian Isthmus, deploying its *Lentue* around the various airfields in the area to maintain proximity to the front line. In the course of the fighting, the Italian-built fighters delivered an excellent performance, not only in clashes with Russian-built fighter aircraft but also when confronting decidedly more capable aircraft, such as the Hurricanes and even Spitfires supplied to the Soviet Union by Britain. Indeed, on 17 August 1942 two out of six Hurricanes that were attacking boats on Lake Ladoga were shot down, while in the same area on 26 August, the Finnish fighters recorded another two victories against a pair of Soviet Spitfires. A further two Hurricanes were lost by the Russians on 14 October. Obviously, these were not the only Soviet losses in the course of the year, but these victories provide an understanding of how the G.50s, despite being inferior from a technical aspect, could achieve success against more powerful adversaries when well flown by Finnish pilots.

LLv.26 entered 1943 with nineteen fighters divided between its three flights, of which the 1. *Lentue* and 3. *Lentue* were based at Kilpasilta airfield and the 2. *Lentue* at Malmi. On 23 April, the 3. *Lentue* moved to the airport at Suulajjaervi.

The entire year was relatively quiet for the unit; the Russians, having suspended their activities in the eastern part of the Karelian Isthmus, had redeployed their aircraft to other sectors of the front. In the course of a dogfight on 2 May, a flight of the 3. *Lentue* shot down an I-15 bis and an I-153 fighter. These were the final victories achieved by the G.50, as they were now beginning to demonstrate their limitations, not just in terms of combat performance, but also technically, due to extensive use and a lack of spare parts. Even by the end of 1942 the daily availability of aircraft never exceeded six or seven aircraft. At the beginning of 1944 LLv.26 began to re-equip with the Brewster Buffalo, progressively transferring its remaining G.50s to LLv.30, which utilised them for a few months on reconnaissance missions, then passed them on at the end of the same year to the Kauhava flying school, where they concluded a more than honourable career in the Scandinavian skies.

In spite of the limited number of aircraft employed and the relative complexity of maintenance encountered during their careers, the Finnish G.50s made a valuable contribution to fight against the Soviet Air Force, demonstrating a fair degree of combat efficiency, with performance quite similar to that of American and Soviet aircraft operating in the Finnish theatre.

Aircraft delivered to the Suomen Ilmavoimat

I Series: MM3599, 3601, 3603, 3605, 3606, 3609, 3610, 3613, 3613.
II Series: MM4722*, 4724*, 4725*, 4726*, 4727*, 4730, 4731, 4732, 4733, 4734, 4735, 4736, 4737, 4738, 4740, 4743, 4745, 4750,
III Series: MM4939, 4940, 4941, 4942, 4943, 4944, 4946, 4947

*denotes aircraft delivered with enclosed cockpits and subsequently modified locally.

Combat victories recorded by Finnish pilots in the FIAT G.50

Pilot	Victories in the G.50	Overall total victories
Oiva Tuominen	23	43
Olli Puhakka	13	43
Nils Trontti	6	7
Onni Paronen	5.5	12.5
Urho Nieminen	4	11
Lauri Lautamäki	4	5.5
Lasse Aaltonen	3.5	12.5
Valio Porvari	3.5	7.5
Olavi Ehrnrooth	2	5
Klaus Alakoski	1	26
Ilmari Joensuu	1	5

Statistics

G.50 combat losses	3	
Victories claimed	88	
Victories confirmed	41	

Finnish aces

The G.50 pilot with the highest number of victories was Flight Master Sergeant Oiva 'Oippa' Tuominen. Of his 43 confirmed, 23 were obtained in the FIAT, one of which was claimed during the Winter War. On 17 August 1941 Tuominen shot down four Russian bombers in four minutes. He was the first Finnish pilot to be awarded the Mannerheim Cross. Another well-known FIAT pilot was Major Olli Puhakka; one of his victories was achieved without him firing a shot. A series of aerobatic manoeuvres at tree-top level caused an opposing Polikarpov I-16 to crash. Puhakka also achieved 43 victories, including twelve while flying the G.50.

Croatia – Zrakoplovstvo Nezavisne Države Hrvatske

AFTER the invasion of the Kingdom of Yugoslavia on 6 April 1941 and the country's occupation by Axis forces, the nationalist leader, Ante Pavelić, became the head of the new Independent State of Croatia (NDH). Consequently, on 19 April the Zrakoplovstvo Nezavisne Države Hrvatske (ZNDH) was created, the air force of the Independent State of Croatia, which turned to its Italian and German allies for the supply of military equipment. After a series of political and military evaluations, the Italian government agreed to the transfer of ten Caproni Ca.311 reconnaissance aircraft, twenty Avia FL.3 trainers, nine G.50bis (*serie* V) single-seat fighters and a two-seat G.50B. The aircraft supplied were fully complete, including radio apparatus and were accompanied by a good stock of spares and munitions, including four A.74/RC38 engines.

The military assistance package was delivered in June 1942. However, the fighters, which departed from Torino on 12 June flown by Italian pilots, were forced to stop over in Udine for some days due to the poor weather and a series of political and bureaucratic mix-ups which were finally resolved on 25 June, when the G.50s took off from Udine and flew to Zagreb Borongaj airfield.

On the following day the aircraft were officially presented to General Vladimir Kren, the Commander in Chief of the ZNDH, and some days later to the Head of State, Ante Pavelic, and the Chief of Staff of the Croatian armed forces, General Slavko Kvaternik and General Kren. The single-seaters wore Italian serials MM6203 to MM6211 and ZNDA serials composed of progressive numbers from 3501 to 3509 for the single seats, while the G.50B two-seat, constructed by FIAT's subsidiary CMASA, had Italian serial MM6477 and subsequently received Croatian serial 3510. In this four-digit numbering system,

the first digit identified the role that the aircraft was principally destined to perform); the second digit, the type of aircraft and the final two digits, the progressive individual numbers. An Italian pilot, *sottotenente* Guido La Ferla, who had previously ferried the G.50B to Croatia accompanied by local pilot, Captain Bosner, remained in Croatia to follow the training of the pilots destined to fly the G.50 together with two FIAT engineers, who were tasked with providing the corresponding training for the local technical personnel. Once the training of the personnel had been completed, the G.50bis were divided between the airfields at Zagreb Borongaj, Zagreb Lucko and Sarajevo Rajlovac, but were unable to enter into action rapidly as supplies of ammunition for the SAFAT guns had not yet arrived. By October, together with six BH-33, the G.50bis constituted the 16° *Lovacka Jato* (16.L), and were utilised in intensive anti-guerrilla operations, initially in Bosnia and Herzegovina, and then in Serbia, Dalmatia and Croatia at the end of the conflict.

After the Italian Armistice of 8 September 1943, Croatia obtained further examples of the G.50 from the Luftwaffe. These had been captured from the Regia Aeronautica in the Balkans, and it is estimated that 20-25 aircraft of this type were operated by the ZNDH. A Croatian report of late 1943 makes reference to around twelve G.50s being available, plus another three under repair, the type being used to defend Croatian airspace from a variety of airfields, including Agram, Banja Luka, Mostar, Zemonico, Bihac, and Grobnico. By 1944 the remaining G.50bis were decidedly outclassed and were replaced in their primary fighter role by Messerschmitt Bf 109Gs and Macchi C.202s. They were mainly relegated to training, although opportunities to undertake operational missions were not lacking. It was during one of these, conducted in conjunction with four MS 406 in early April 1944, that a G.50 was shot down by an American fighter, while numerous other G.50s were destroyed on the ground by various American bombing raids on Borongaj airfield.

Due to their obsolescence, the G.50bis could achieve little against Allied bombers. Moreover, the chronic shortage of fuel resulted in a significant reduction in flying, to the extent that by September 1944, only seven G.50s were still operational. On 2 September 1944 two G.50bis departed from the airfield at Borongaj for a patrol and reconnaissance mission along the Tito partisans' lines. One of the two pilots, Lieutenant Andrija Arapovic, taking advantage of the situation, and unbeknown to his flight leader, departed the formation in G.50 serial 3505 and deserted, landing on a strip on the island of Vis, which already housed aircraft of the Narodno Oslobokilacka Vojska Jugoslavije (NOVJ – the Yugoslav Popular Liberation Army), which took the aircraft on charge and used it in action on several occasions. In the course of the conflict other G.50s were captured by the NOVJ, but it seems that none of them were utilised. After the end of the conflict, those G.50bis still airworthy were retired and stored at Zemun airfield.

A G.50bis, coded '3504' of the 2 LJ of the Croatian ZNDH photographed at Borongaj, in the summer of 1944. What was probably a white fuselage band appears to have been overpainted and note the unit marking on the cowl and spiral spinner. (B. Ciglić)

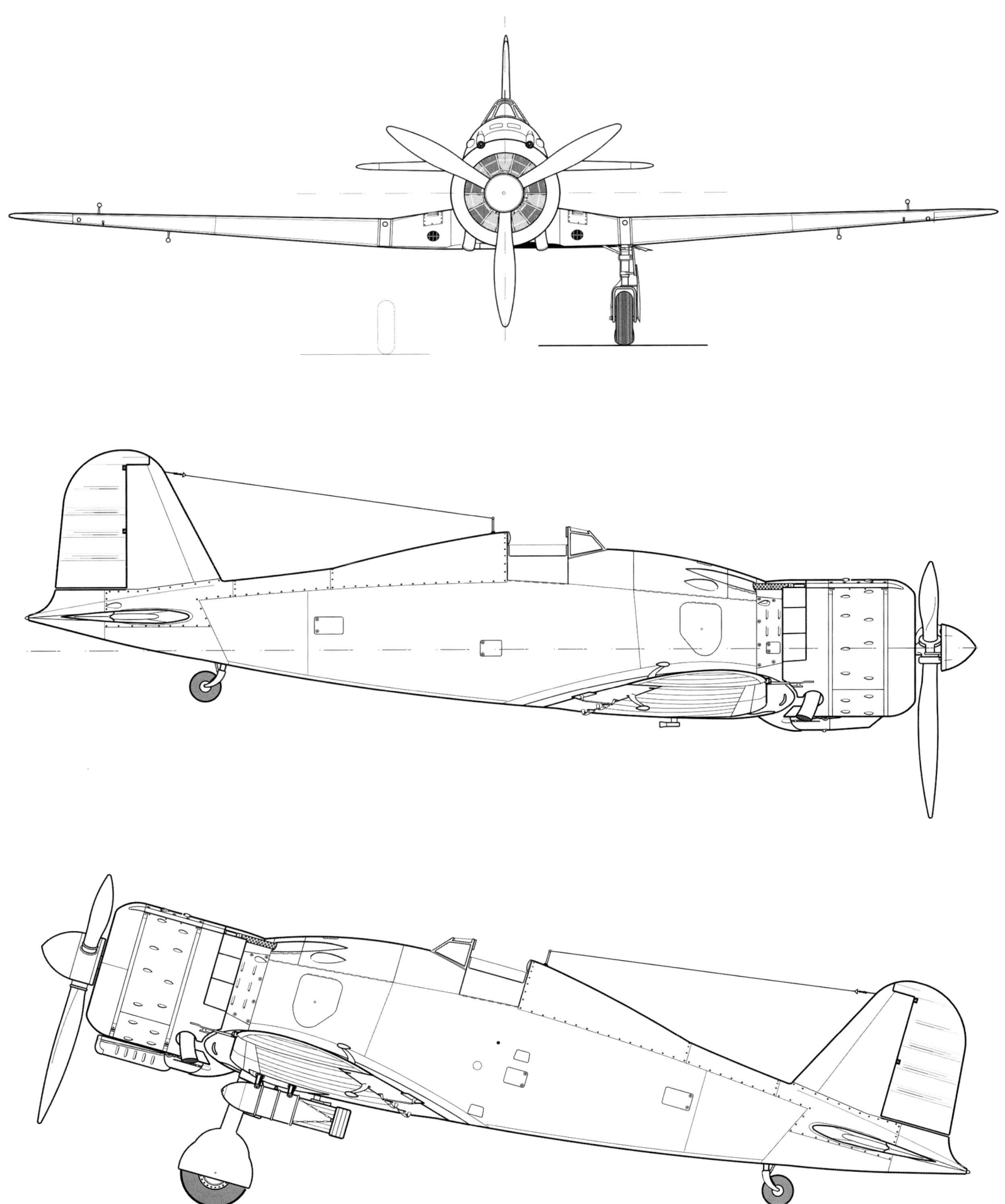

FIAT FIGHTERS

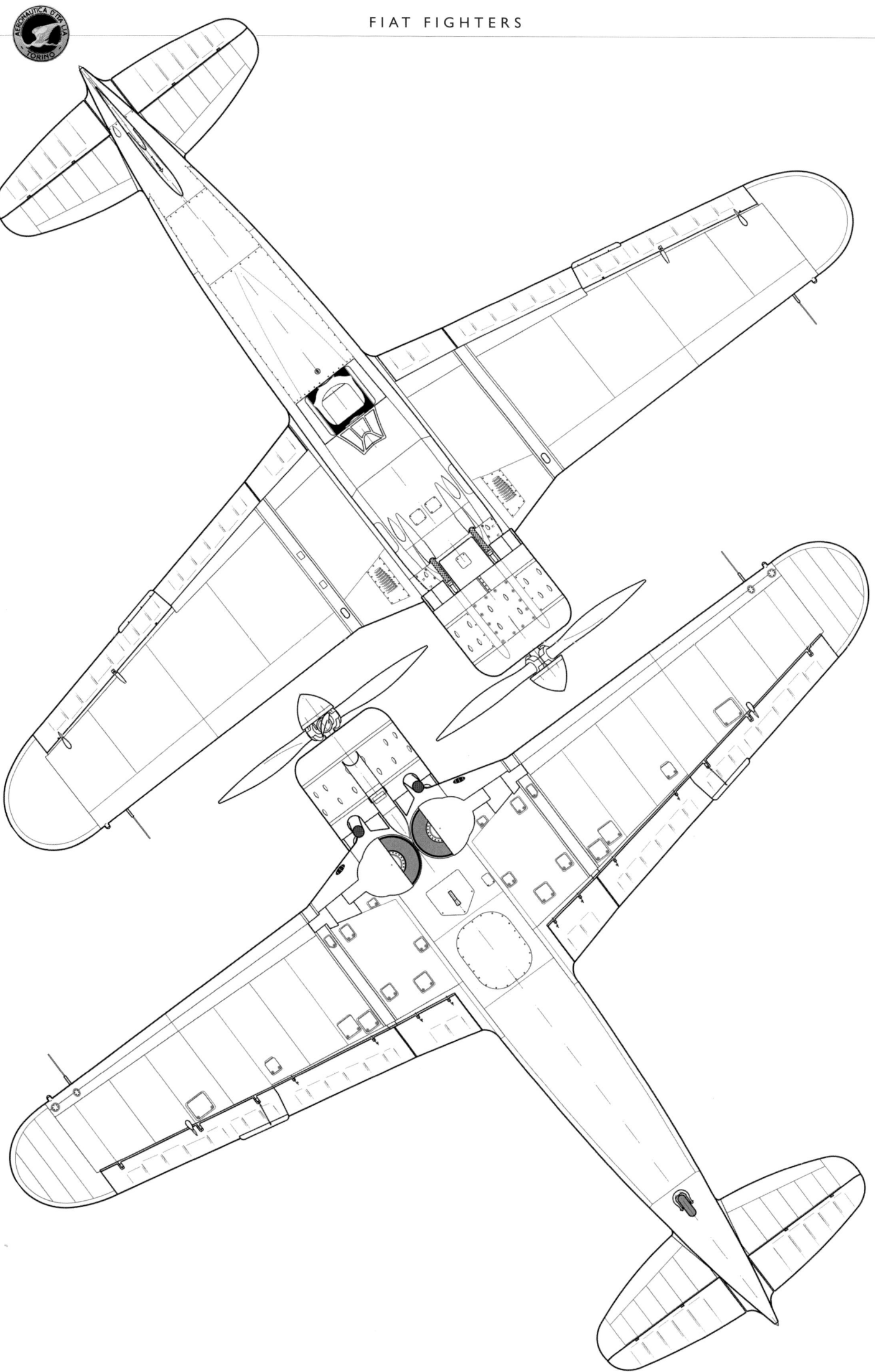

G.50, MM334, prototype at time of maiden flight, Caselle, February 1937

G.50, MM334, on display at 2° *Salone Internazionale Aeronautico*, Milan, October 1937

G.50, MM3594, '351-2', 351ª *Squadriglia*, 20° *Gruppo*, 51° *Stormo* CT, Ciampino, October 1939

G.50, '356-8', 356ª *Squadriglia*, 21° *Gruppo*, 51° *Stormo* CT, Napoli Capodichino, June 1940

G.50, '150-7', 150ª *Squadriglia*, 2° *Gruppo Autonomo* CT, Grottaglie, October 1940

G.50, personal aircraft of *maggiore* Mario Bonzano, commander of 20° *Gruppo*, 56° *Stormo* CT, *Corpo Aereo Italiano*, Maldegem, October 1940

G.50, MM5403, '352-13', 352ª *Squadriglia*, 20° *Gruppo*, 56° *Stormo* CT, *Corpo Aereo Italiano*, Maldegem, November 1940

G.50, 359ª *Squadriglia*, 154° *Gruppo Autonomo* CT, Devoli, February 1941

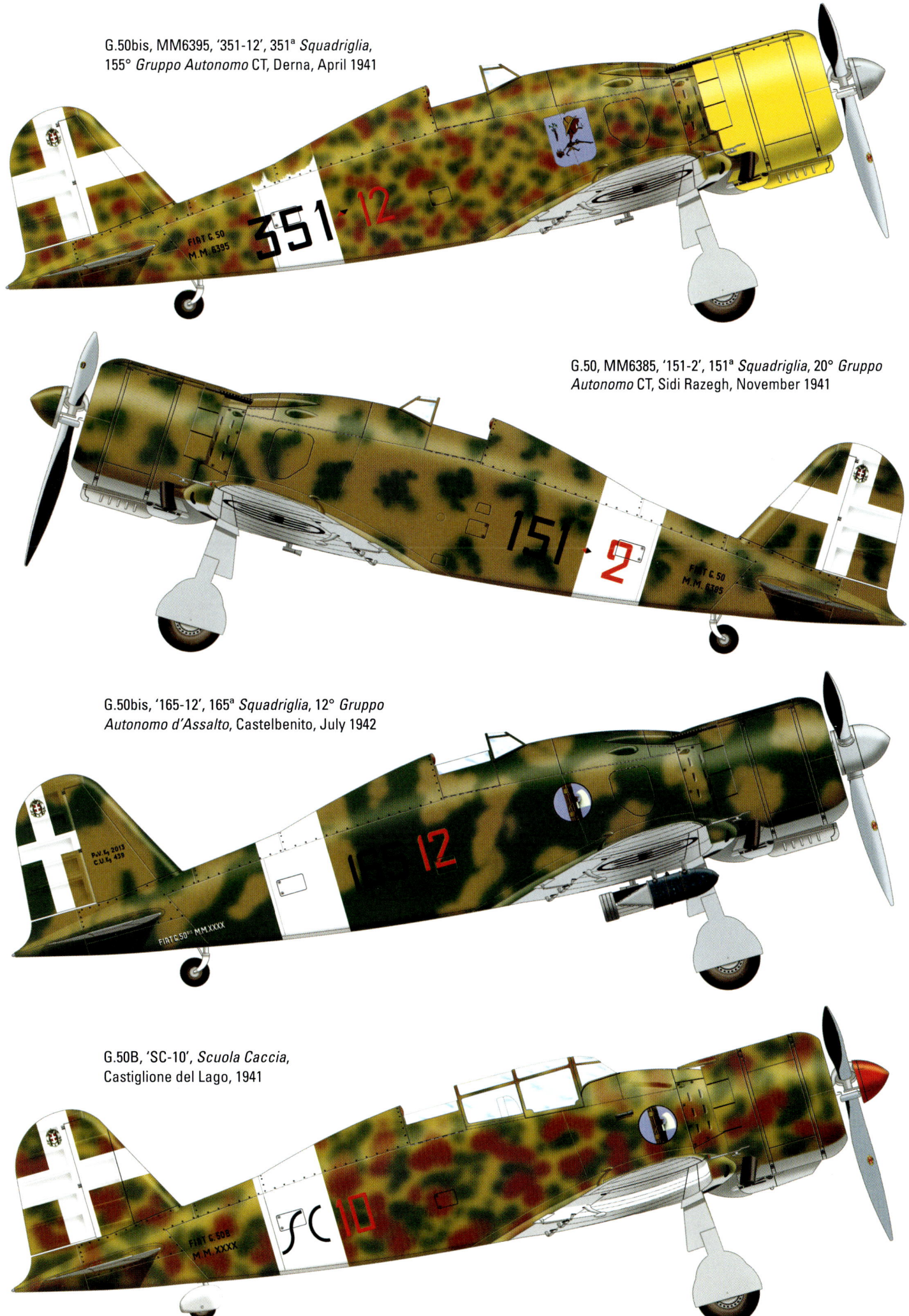

G.50bis, MM6395, '351-12', 351ª *Squadriglia*, 155° *Gruppo Autonomo* CT, Derna, April 1941

G.50, MM6385, '151-2', 151ª *Squadriglia*, 20° *Gruppo Autonomo* CT, Sidi Razegh, November 1941

G.50bis, '165-12', 165ª *Squadriglia*, 12° *Gruppo Autonomo d'Assalto*, Castelbenito, July 1942

G.50B, 'SC-10', *Scuola Caccia*, Castiglione del Lago, 1941

G.50B, MM6483, 'Black 1', 3ª *Squadriglia*,
2° *Gruppo Scuola Volo A.M.I.*, Brindisi 1946

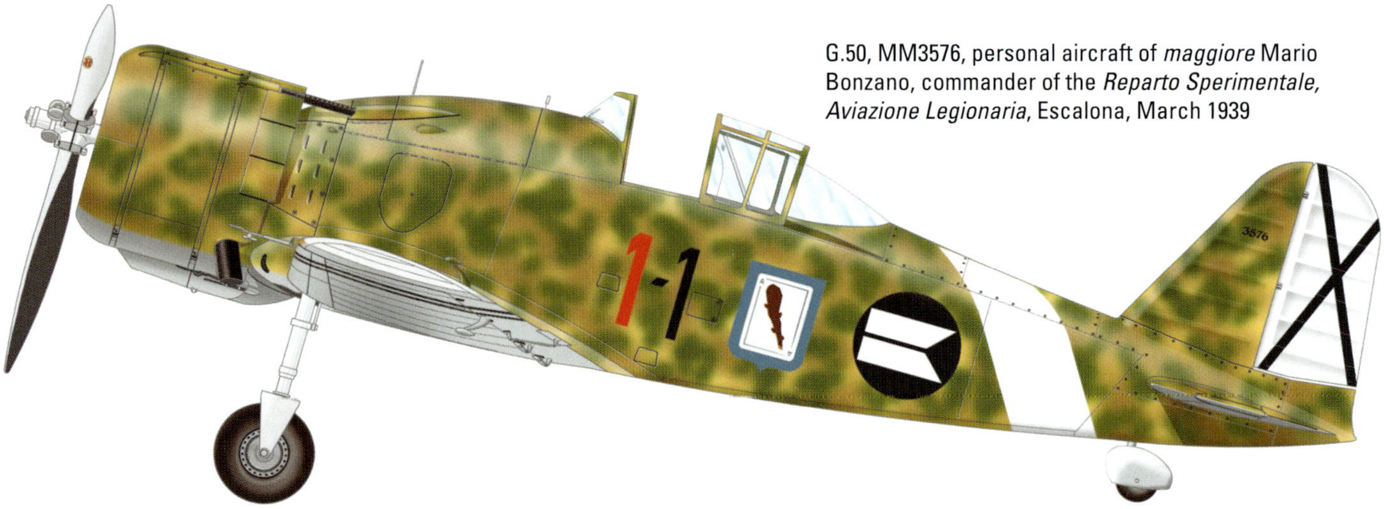

G.50, MM3576, personal aircraft of *maggiore* Mario Bonzano, commander of the *Reparto Sperimentale, Aviazione Legionaria*, Escalona, March 1939

G.50, 'FA-26', 1. *Lentue/Lentolaivue* 26, Suomen Ilmavoimat, Lunkula, August 1941

G.50bis, *Jagdgeschwader* 107, Toul, January 1944

CHAPTER SEVEN

Fiat G.55 CENTAURO
Production and Variant

Front view of the second prototype MM492 at Torino Caselle.

DEFINED by many as 'the best fighter produced in Italy during the war', in the course of its intense but brief operational use, conducted almost entirely under the banner of the Aeronautica Nazionale Repubblicana (ANR), the FIAT G.55 proved itself to be an extremely interesting and capable fighter. Unfortunately, like the other two Italian fighters of *Serie* 5 equipped with the DB 605, the AerMacchi C.205V and Reggiane RE.2005, the *Centauro* entered service when the outcome of the war had taken an irredeemable course. The few examples produced from the spring of 1943, around 164, when added to the more than 160 *Veltros* and little more than thirty *Sagittarios* constructed, were unable to make any significant contribution to the conflict.

In the words of its designer, Giuseppe Gabrielli, the origins of the G.55 can be traced back to the mid-1930s when:

'In the following years the Italian *Stato Maggiore* finally realised that air-cooled radial engines, such as the A.74, failed to deliver aircraft the necessary speeds, and reoriented themselves towards a liquid-cooled, higher power engine, thereby adhering to the concepts that in Germany and Britain had resulted in the production of the Messerschmitt [Bf 109], Hurricane and Spitfire. FIAT was requested to modify a G.50 by installing the German engine fitted to the Messerschmitt: the Daimler-Benz 601 developing 1,050 hp at altitude. Thus the G.50V was born; this was a test aircraft which was useful in addressing the problems connected with the installation of the armament and cooling system. It was evidently the prelude to a request, which came immediately after, to design a fighter aircraft fitted with the aforementioned engine, and with armament and protection characteristics that were far in advance of those of the G.50. An industry-wide competition was launched, and saw the

Pages published by the weekly magazine *ALI* in 1944 depicting stirring scenes of air combat with aircraft of the USAAF.
(P. Pesaresi)

FIAT FIGHTERS

participation of Macchi, with Castoldi's C.205V, while at FIAT we produced the G.55, which made its first flight on 20 April 1942. It was, demonstrably, an excellent aeroplane from all points of view, and was highly regarded by its pilots and mechanics for the simplicity of its construction and its high level of efficiency. We were in the midst of a war, and production of the G.55 was pushed to the maximum. FIAT was also entrusted, even though it was the aircraft's production leader, with the licence manufacture of the engine, but our industrial potential was relatively modest.'[1]

The evolution of the design

The studies for the final design of the G.55 date from summer 1939, reflecting the period in which the *Stato Maggiore* of the Regia Aeronautica expressed firm interest in the development of a new fighter equipped with a new Italian in-line, liquid-cooled engine then under development at the *Centro Motori* at FIAT. This new engine, the project manager for which was *Ingegner* Fessia, was the FIAT A.38 RC 13-45. With its sixteen inverted V (at 90°) cylinders and single-stage, two-speed compressor, the engine should have been able to develop a power output of 1,200 hp at an altitude of 4,500 m. Initially it was designed to be associated with contra-rotating propellers, but the excessive complexity of this concept led to the adoption of a three-bladed propeller being proposed. *Ingegner* Gabrielli set to work to integrate the powerful engine with a new fighter, believing that it would be capable of greatly exceeding 600 km/h, and for this reason would constitute an enormous step forward in comparison with the radial engine fighters then in service. Unfortunately, the development of the A.38, initiated in June 1940, just a few weeks prior to the first flight of the AerMacchi C.202, was protracted for many months, and was characterised by a series of technological problems which were difficult to resolve, in part connected to the use of less than

[1] From *Una vita per l'Aviazione* by Giuseppe Gabrielli, Bompiani Editore, 1982

VALENTINO CUS

BORN in Austria in 1901, Valentino Cus became an Italian citizen, and in 1923 obtained his military pilot wings, serving with several different fighter units. Taken on by FIAT in 1932 as a test pilot, he was a protagonist in the development and presentation of numerous aircraft constructed by the Torino-based company, including the conduct of the first flights of the G.8 trainer and the CR.42 fighter. Having been appointed to the position of test pilot responsible for the G.55 programme, he made the first flight of the prototype MM491 on 30 April 1942.

---

excellent quality prime materials, a problem that was also common to a major part of Italian industrial products. The Regia Aeronautica and FIAT, which had based many of their joint aspirations on the new aircraft, found themselves in a difficult situation. But, despite the various problems encountered, in April 1941 FIAT received an order sanctioning the preparation of three prototypes. However, following the technical issues that plagued the engine in the winter of 1940, FIAT was able to prepare only one example of the new aircraft, intended for static tests in the wind tunnel and which, in the meantime, had been designated the G.55.

To overcome this situation, and in conjunction with the request from the DGCA of the Regia Aeronautica for a new high-altitude interceptor fighter, *Ingegner* Gabrielli decided to redraft the G.55 design by opting for the German 1,475-hp (take-off) DB 605A in-line engine, which had become available following the acquisition by the Regia Aeronautica of a licence for its manufacture. Responsibility for production of the engine would be assigned to FIAT. This opportunity sealed the

The second FIAT G.55 prototype, MM492, ready for its first test flight at the Aeritalia airfield on 30 April 1942. The serial painted near the tail appears to have been 'censored'. Initially, the aircraft was finished in a 'lizard'-type camouflage scheme.

abandonment of development of the A.38 by FIAT which, in fact, had never even completed its qualification trials. Moreover, it was the same reason that led to the abandonment of the possibility of installing the 1,250-hp Isotta Fraschini *Zeta* engine, this also not having been perfected.

Meanwhile, *Ingegner* Gabrielli adapted the already graceful lines of the new fighter to accept the excellent German engine, which FIAT had assigned the company designation of RA 1050 RC 58 (RA signifying Regia Aeronautica) with a certificated power of 1,250-hp at 5,800 m. The German engine was a twelve-cylinder, inverted V (60°), liquid-cooled configuration, with a compressor and reducer, the configuration and dimensions of which were not too different from those of the FIAT A.38 RC 15-45. Consequently, it was relatively easy for Gabrielli to adapt the original G.55 design to accept the new engine.

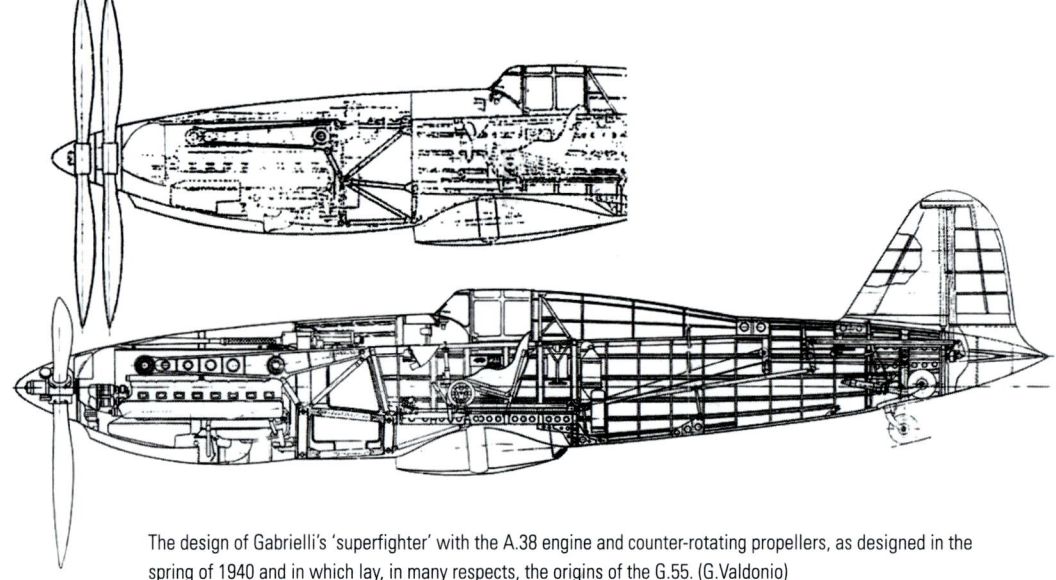

The design of Gabrielli's 'superfighter' with the A.38 engine and counter-rotating propellers, as designed in the spring of 1940 and in which lay, in many respects, the origins of the G.55. (G.Valdonio)

G.55 MM492 was slightly damaged in a forced landing while being flown by *maggiore* Borzoni at the Guidonia test centre in the summer of 1943. Note the construction of the extended flap.

Front three-quarter view of the second prototype being evaluated at Guidonia Montecello by the Centro Sperimentazioni Aeronautiche. The photograph highlights the impression of power and sturdy construction that was a feature of *Centauro*.

The first prototype, MM.491, was completed in early 1942 and made its first flight on 30 April of that year flown by test pilot Valentino Cus. This aircraft was followed by two further prototypes, MM492 and 493.

Gabrielli's design work resulted in an excellent fighter which united good handling qualities, especially at altitude, with potential for series manufacture. It also possessed heavy armament, concentrated in the nose of the aircraft and comprised of a 20 mm Mauser MG 151 cannon with a 200-round magazine firing through the propeller boss and four 12.7 mm Breda SAFAT machine guns with 300 rounds each, two of which were housed above the engine block and two laterally below the engine. Below the wings were hard points capable of carrying loads of up to 100 kg each, and suitable for either bombs or 125-litre supplementary tanks.

In September 1942 the G.55 prototype was sent to Guidonia for extensive evaluation, while the second prototype, MM492, flew in August and the third example, MM493, in February 1943. Flying of the prototypes was rotated around the

The G.55 prototype at the Furbara test centre (second from left) on 28 March 1943 on the occasion of the twentieth anniversary of the Regia Aeronautica.

other FIAT test pilots, Enrico Rolandi, Serafino Agostini and Vittorio Catella, as well as, naturally, *Comandante* Cus. The flight trials conducted by the test pilots of the *Centro Sperimentale* at Guidonia confirmed the excellent performance of the G.55 which, in the meantime, had been officially baptised with the name 'Centauro'; all the fighters of the so-called *Serie* 5 were named after constellations, such as the C.205N *Orione* and the RE.2005 *Sagittario*.

In comparison with the C.205V[2] and the RE.2005, the G.55 proved to be faster, well-built and more robust, possessing better handling qualities and with more modern installations and cockpit layout. It also became the most suitable of the Series 5 fighters for large-scale production thanks to its structural features, while it also was considered the simplest from the point of view of operational maintenance. These two very important aspects, irrespective of technical and performance considerations, undoubtedly impacted the final assessment of the aircraft in comparison with the other fighters evaluated at Guidonia, despite the fact that both the C.205V and RE.2005 were excellent aircraft with very distinctive characteristics, making it difficult to create a ranking table. The AerMacchi C.205V was assessed to be slightly superior to the other two fighters in operations at low to medium altitude, more specifically up to 6-7,000 m, but above these altitudes, particularly because of its shorter wingspan, it was decidedly disadvantaged, and required careful and precise piloting.[3] For their part, at higher altitudes, the G.55 and RE.2005 were decidedly more agile and faster – and practically equal, although the Reggiane fighter appeared to be slightly superior in performance, but structurally more delicate. The final judgement of the Guidonia test pilots' evaluation was published on 4 November 1942. It was favourable to the *Centauro*, assessing the fighter as better at high altitude, with a good rate of climb and sustained handling at altitude, and preferable to the other aircraft as a bomber interceptor. The *Centauro* also demonstrated good handling qualities whilst performing various aerobatic manoeuvres during evaluation, and without displaying any particular problems.

Further confirmation of the importance of the *Centauro* was provided by the favourable outcome of comparison flights conducted at Guidonia in the autumn of 1942 against German Bf 109 G and Fw 190 fighters. During the evaluations, however, some small defects were identified, but these were considered to be easily resolvable through factory modifications, while some issues were discovered in the ammunition supply to the machine guns, together with some difficulties in accessing the cannon which were identified by ground engineers. For this reason, the DGCA suggested to FIAT that the layout of the armament should be reviewed. This suggestion led to only the first two prototypes and the seventeen aircraft of *sottoserie* 0 (sub-series 0 – MM91053-91069) being built with the armament concentrated in the nose of the aircraft, while the third prototype (MM493) featured a new armament layout which subsequently became the standard for all the other G.55s produced. This comprised three Mauser MG 151 cannon, one of which fired through the propeller boss, while the others were installed in the wings, firing outside the propeller disc. Just two 12.7 mm SAFAT machine guns were mounted in the classic position above the engine, with their fire synchronised with the propeller. The two machine guns mounted below the engine were discarded. Photographic evidence reveals that, in the course of their operational service, some of the *sottoserie* 0 aircraft (MM91058 and 91060) were probably modified to accept wing cannon, while it is also evident that some of the early *Serie* 1 aircraft, (for example, MM91081), were not fitted with wing cannon.

The design of the G.55 was certainly easier to industrialise than those of the *Veltro* and the *Sagittario* and, benefitting significantly from FIAT's undoubted industrial and political weight, it had all the cards in play to provide the Regia Aeronautica with an opportunity to standardise the fighter force on a single aircraft. Again, however, this possibility remained only at the level of ambition. In fact, the DGCA also prescribed that the C.205V should be put into production. This was a choice which, in many respects, had its own logic when considering that production and subsequent availability to the units would require only a short time, as it was very structurally similar to the C.202 *Folgore* and therefore the already active production lines could be utilised with minimal modification. FIAT was therefore ordered to establish a production line for the AerMacchi fighter alongside that of the G.55. This opportunity was, however, never realised due to both the reluctance of the Torino-based company to manufacture an aircraft from another designer and, providentially for FIAT, the destruction of the *Veltro* production line at Torino by American bombing.

In the meantime, on 16 November 1942, the Regia Aeronautica placed an initial order for 600 G.55s. Production would be trusted to a series of connected manufacturers which would form three principal production rings of which the group leaders would be FIAT, SIAI, and CMASA. Utilising the output of the associated companies engaged in producing components for the aircraft could deliver a potential production rate of around 50/60 aircraft per month.

---

[2] Testing of the C.205N Orione was delayed several months after that of the other two Serie 5 fighters.

[3] It is worth underlining that the actual fighter proposed by AerMacchi as a *Serie* 5 contender was the C.205N *Orione*, the *Veltro* arising from a simple adaptation of the C.202 *Folgore* airframe to accept the DB 605 engine; it did, however, have a different operational utilisation than that intended for the *Serie* 5 fighters.

Despite the good intentions, the organisation of this series of production rings resulted in delays and defections, with SIAI abandoning the project and being substituted by AerMacchi and Piaggio. The Regia Aeronautica requested the individual group leader companies to deliver 600 fighters each, plus 1,200 from FIAT itself, a project that thus called for a utopian production plan of at least 3,600 fighters over the span of two years. The initial order also involved the construction of 34 aircraft in *sottoserie* 0 (effectively a pre-series production batch), which was later reduced to seventeen aircraft and their transformation into *Serie* 1ª fighters. Unfortunately, production of the *Centauro* encountered significant delay, created by the necessity to decentralise some of the production processes so as to avoid bombing raids on the Torino factory, but also because of delays in the fine tuning of the aircraft, to the extent that *generale* Fougier in person, the *Capo di Stato Maggiore* of the Regia Aeronautica, intervened to request that FIAT complete the aircraft with the two-wing cannon. The continued requests for modifications and new variants also contributed to the hiatus, none of these ever seeing the light, but wasting precious time and resources, such as the request from the Regia Aeronautica to produce a version armed with four wing cannon.

The aircraft's entry into service was the subject of continual procrastination. This resulted in the paradox that the G.55 which, from an industrial perspective, could have been produced in far greater numbers than any other *Serie* 5 fighter, saw the least operational use with the Regia Aeronautica before the Armistice of 8 September 1943. In fact, after construction of the first *sottoserie* 0 fighters, production of the definitive aircraft, the so-called G.55 *Serie* 1, only commenced in August 1943, and prior to the Armistice, the Regia Aeronautica had accepted delivery of just thirty G.55s from *Serie* 0 and *Serie* 1.

Among the various G.55 designs requested or proposed, the most interesting was a two-seat variant. This was derived because it was considered that the introduction of the new *Serie* 5 fighters would create training problems, in view of the fact that the flying schools were still equipped with decidedly obsolete aircraft such as the CR.42, G.50 or C.200. For this requirement, *Ingegner* Gabrielli drew up the G.55B (*biposto* – two-seat), an aircraft which retained, substantially, the same build and dimensions of the single-seater but featuring two cockpits in tandem fitted with duplicated flying controls. With the abolition of the two wing guns and the fuselage fuel tanks, the G.55B would be around 500 kg lighter than the operational aircraft. But again, delays and the progress of the war, resulted in work on the project being suspended. However, it was *suspension* rather than abandonment, as Gabrielli reworked the project in the immediate post-war period following interest from the newly constituted Aeronautica Militare.

German interest

At the beginning of 1943, a German technical commission visited Guidonia to conduct an evaluation of new Italian aircraft projects including the *Serie* 5 fighters, with particular attention devoted to the G.55 and the Re.2005. The aircraft were also tested by some German pilots with both the G.55 and the RE.2005 being viewed very positively. In the opinion of the German pilots, the G.55 was considered 'excellent' in all respects, to the point that it was felt to be in a class of its own. Despite being equipped with the same DB.605 engine as the Bf 109 G-6, the G.55 was considered to have superior technical characteristics, good lift and climbing capability, along with excellent armament, and much greater structural strength than the Messerschmitt fighter.

Particularly relevant in this regard is the record of a meeting held in Berlin on Monday, 22 February 1943, in the presence of *Reichsmarschall* Hermann Göring, *Generalfeldmarschall* Erhard Milch and other notable pilots and senior Luftwaffe staff officers, including *Generaloberst* Hans Jeschonnek (Chief of General Staff), *Oberst* Edgar Petersen (*Kommando der Erprobungsstellen*), *Generalmajor* Dietrich Peltz (*General der Kampfflieger*) and *Generalleutnant* Adolf Galland (*General der Jagdflieger*). They had gathered to discuss programmes for new aircraft to be introduced into service with the Luftwaffe:

Göring: I'm glad that the Italians, at long last, have produced a respectable fighter. And I can only say; let them build them to capacity.

Milch: We also should do something in that sphere. A disgrace to our own industry. It is indeed a disgrace to our industry.

Göring: The Italians have never built inferior aircraft and have always been competent in the construction of aircraft and engines. I remember the FIAT and Alfa. They have also held the world speed record. The ability of the Italian aircraft industry has always been of the best. They are unable to mass produce however, and there we must help them. We can consider ourselves lucky if they have produced a good fighter aircraft. It's one in the eye for our own people anyway.

Petersen: We must attend to this at once. The airframe of the FIAT G.55 can accommodate the DB 603 engine, while the Me 109 is unable to do so any longer. The G.55 with the DB 603 would be an ideal fighter aircraft.

Galland: From our experience the Italians have always forgotten something in their fighter aircraft, either the armour or guns.

Göring: It's to be hoped, however, that for the purposes of these comparison flights, they've been informed about this, otherwise it's a waste of time.

Petersen: The fighter specialist has flown the aircraft. With the exception of the radio, it carried complete equipment and fuel for one and a half hours, whereas we carried fuel for only one hour. We can't ignore the fact that the Italian aircraft has a performance equal to that of our latest types.

Milch: Then please obtain three Italian aircraft at once and fly them here, in Rechlin. I would have the DB 603 installed in these aircraft as we have been discussing this morning. It would mean a considerable advance towards the Me 209. I can't imagine the Fw 190 with the BMW 801 engine, as it is today, being sufficient for the next two and a half years. Especially as we don't know what the English and the Americans are building.

Göring: The Americans haven't so far produced a fighter that is anything to write home about.

Galland: For some time. The Typhoon has now emerged again, after a disappearance.

Göring: I'm also in favour of the proposal. However, I consider it more than likely that the English will effect an improvement with their own types. I would like to ask what is our best means of improving our fighters other than the jet propulsion business?

Milch: The Me 209 and especially its engine. The industry hasn't offered us anything in the aerodynamics field, which would enhance our position.

Galland: In the Me 209 we would have an aircraft capable of better take-off and landing, which would reduce the number of crashes.

Göring: If the Italian aircraft is good, then we won't deny the fact, and we'll mass produce them here. We don't want any false pride.

Milch: Thereby we could advance a year.

Galland: And it would also do our designers good.

Göring: On top of that perhaps, we could include the Italian pilots as well, in our complete programme. Anyway I'm very pleased to hear this about the Italians. But haven't they anything about bombers?

Petersen: They're very poor; I've seen them all….[4]

This generally positive outlook on the part of the Germans led to the suggestion to equip the G.55 with the DB 603 engine, thus giving rise to the G.56 project, with the certainty that the new engine could push the fighter to a speed of over 700 km/h and a possible ceiling of approximately 13,000 m. Contact between Italian and German

---

[4] Air Ministry A.H.B.6 translation, G223299/IF/3/49/35, 8 March 1946.

Aircraft built	c/n	Series	*Matricole Militari*
3	nc 1-3	Prototypes	MM491-492-493
17	nc 4-20	*Serie* 1 *Sottoserie* 0	MM91053-91069
144	nc 21-164	*Serie* 1	MM91070-91213

engineers continued. From this emerged the possibility of Italian industry building aircraft parts and spares for Focke-Wulf as well as the possible production of the DB 603 in Italy. Further contact made it possible to consider the firm possibility of FIAT supporting series production of the fighter and also of building it in Germany where some aircraft were transferred for test.

However, the worsening war situation, the devastating bombing suffered by FIAT, and critical assessment over mass production of the fighter as a result of its complex construction when compared to that of the German fighters, meant that the idea was abandoned. Thus, in September 1944, the *Reichsluftministerium* ordered the complete cessation of all production activity.[5]

Production versions

Based on the manufacturer's construction numbers prior to the end of the war, it is believed that a total of just 164 aeroplanes was completed (the highest known being nc 164), including the three prototypes and the 17 G.55 of *sottoserie* 0. It is also believed that of the initial order for 600 aircraft, those produced before the Armistice, and following the resumption of activity by FIAT in the autumn of 1943, numbered 144 aircraft belonging to production *Serie* 1. (see table at top)

Before the end of the war, however, further variants of the fighter were proposed, the majority of which progressed no further than the drawing board. The only variants actually produced were the G.55S, optimised for torpedo-attack missions, and the G.56 which, potentially, could have represented the definitive and most powerful version of the FIAT fighter, powered by the excellent DB 603 1,750-hp engine.

G.55s *Silurante* (torpedo-attack)

In 1942, in consideration of the fact that the *aerosiluranti* (torpedo-attack) units were still equipped by the outdated S.79 tri-motor, an idea was conceived that proposed the use of a fighter as the launch platform for a '*silurotto*', a smaller dimension torpedo with a weight reduced to 680 kg from the almost 1,000 kg of a standard torpedo. However, the idea was initially discarded following the development by Gabrielli of a similar design for an aircraft specialising in this mission, designated the G.57 which, in turn, was subsequently abandoned. The idea was proposed again in the early months of 1944 by A.N.R. commanders who were desperately searching for aircraft capable of effectively performing the torpedo-attack role. In this respect Giuseppe Gabrielli, when questioned over the development of such based on the G.55, responded with considerable scepticism:

> '*They proposed that I investigate a variant of the G.55 that would be able to carry a torpedo weighing 1,000 kg under the fuselage. Stefanutti, who had prepared some sketches of the configuration that such an aircraft would have assumed, was particularly convinced of the merit of a development of this nature. The variant required the significant lengthening of the tailwheel and the total reworking of the engine's liquid cooling radiator. I was not in accord with this proposal, and I refused to take responsibility for it. A heated discussion arose, which concluded with threatening words in my respect regarding a lack of cooperation.*'

However, *tenente colonnello Ingegnere* Sergio Stefanutti of the *Direzione Tecnica* of the A.N.R. received permission from Gabrielli to proceed with the project, independently progressing the studies to transform the *Centauro* into a torpedo-attack aircraft. A series of modifications was introduced to a production aircraft at the Venegono SRAM (a maintenance unit) with the idea that the *Centauro* could be capable, technically and practically, of being the only Italian fighter of the period to undertake this role. The final configuration of the fighter/torpedo-attack design, known as the G.55S, included the possibility of attaching a standard 987-kg torpedo, with the aircraft offering a radius of action of around 300/400 km, sufficient to

Two photographs of the G.55S, MM91086, at Venegono, showing details of the installation of a standard 987-kg torpedo. It should be noted that contrary to the original FIAT design, only the machine guns in the fuselage were removed and the wing cannon retained.

---
[5] In the first phase of initial production, the completion of a G.55 required around 15,000 working hours, significantly more than the 5-6,000 hours necessary to produce a Bf 109.

Three images of the G.55S prototype at Venegono during testing. The results of the trials were encouraging. Despite the cumbersome external load, performance was good and handling acceptable.

depart a coastal airfield and to penetrate deep into the Tyrrhenian or Adriatic seas in search of the Allied fleet that had disappeared.

One of the more practical aspects of the G.55S was that once a torpedo had been released, the aircraft became a standard fighter again, and so could be used for self-defence and similar operations. G.55 MM91086 was the aircraft selected for conversion, and after in-depth studies of the technical problems associated with the aerodynamics of torpedo launch, the fighter received modifications to the lower part of its structure to enable the attachment of the torpedo with a system comprised of two electro-mechanically operated pincer brackets. In order to mount the torpedo, it was necessary to divide and split the principal radiator located under the fuselage by 90 cm, to lengthen and reinforce the tailwheel shock absorber and create its new fairing, and to install the special electrical release control panel for the torpedo in the cockpit. A 5.46-metre-long Whitehead torpedo weighed 920 kg and so to lighten the aircraft, the two 12.7 mm SAFAT machine guns were stripped out, but the wing cannon were retained. The rear section of the torpedo was completed by the fitment of wooden directional surfaces which were positioned under the fuselage of the G.55, the aircraft's rear fuselage being capable of raising and lowering to the correct height as required. The tailwheel had three height settings, *retratto*, *allungato* and *massimo allungamento* (retracted, lengthened, and maximum length), which could be selected in accordance with the terrain from which the aircraft would operate. The torpedo was also fitted with a retarding parachute which enabled it to enter the water at a controlled speed and at the correct inclination, the parachute and tail surface assembly detaching automatically on contact with the water.

The prototype was completed in the autumn of 1944, and the task of testing the new aircraft was assigned to *capitano* Adriano Mantelli who, at the end of March 1945, transferred the aircraft to Lonate Pozzolo airfield for the conduct of flight trials using a dummy torpedo made from cement. A German technical commission visited Lonate Pozzolo to evaluate the project, and Mantelli performed an effective demonstration of the aircraft, even flying some basic aerobatic manoeuvres despite the heavy external torpedo load. This showed the sceptical Luftwaffe officers that the G.55S retained margins of manoeuvrability with a torpedo attached that were more than sufficient. At the end of the demonstration, Mantelli performed a dive from which he launched the torpedo accurately onto the target.

Given the positive results, the A.N.R. command quickly issued an order for a series of ten aircraft, but the deteriorating war situation did not allow the order to be fulfilled.

The G.55 prototype did, however, survive the war, being stored in the Agusta workshops at Cascina Costa. Recovered post-war, it became the first G.55 to be reconditioned by FIAT and delivered to the Aeronautica Militare in 1947 as a trainer.

G.56

As result of the G.55's good performance, the production line was not dismantled or destroyed after the Armistice. In the light of possible interest in the fighter on the part of the Luftwaffe and profiting from the availability of an example of a new DB 603A 1,750-hp engine delivered from Germany directly to FIAT, *Ingegner* Gabrielli decided to significantly shorten the time necessary to create a new design. He preferred to adapt the already excellent G.55 airframe to accept the new engine. Construction of two prototypes was initiated, the aircraft being designated FIAT G.56, and to which military serials MM.536 and MM.537 were assigned. On a dimensional level, the G.56 was virtually identical to the G.55, with the same height and wingspan, but with an increase in total length of eight centimetres. The empty weight rose from 2,730 kg to 2,900 kg, while the total weight rose to 3,854 kg. Armament comprised only three 20 mm MG 151 cannon with a supply of 600 rounds for the three weapons. The only obstacle to series production was the difficulty in obtaining a supply of engines for which, prior to commencing engine construction under licence, FIAT had to request a certain quantity to be delivered directly from Germany.

The first prototype, MM536, flew in German markings for the first time on 28 March 1944, with test pilot Valentino Cus at the controls. During its early flight trials, it revealed excellent speed performance characteristics in the order of 690/700 km/h. This aircraft, however, was badly damaged by the Allied bombing of 25 April 1944 which almost completely halted production at the Torino facility. It was only with the completion of the second prototype, MM537, that evaluation trials could be resumed. Nevertheless, with the Torino factories virtually destroyed and the unfavourable progress of the war, German officials issued the order to cease any further development of the fighter in September 1944.

In the aftermath of the war, the first prototype was recovered by FIAT, and after the company had returned it to flying condition, it was utilised as an armament trials aircraft and a flying engine test bed. Amongst the engines tested were the Isotta Fraschini Delta RC, the Rolls Royce Merlin 40, and the Packard V.1650.

The longitudinal section of the G.56 clearly shows how the large DB 603 engine could be accommodated in the fuselage of the G.55 without any particular problems, adapting different engine mounts along with the removal of the two fuselage guns. (G.Valdonio)

The first prototype of the G.56, MM536, photographed at Torino Caselle. The aircraft was heavily armed with three 20 mm cannon, two in the wings and one in a central position firing through the propellor hub. (P.Monti)

The first prototype of the G.56 was damaged as a result of Allied bombing in April 1944 and although development of the second prototype, MM537, continued, the *Oberkommando der Luftwaffe* terminated the project in September 1944. (G.Barbettai)

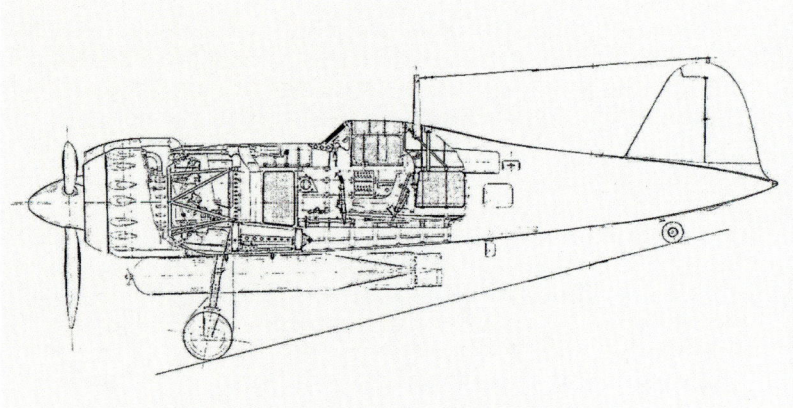

A drawing of the G.57 equipped with a FIAT A.83 RC24-52 radial engine of 1250 hp, and a proposed torpedo. A design that did not progress as the aircraft was not developed after the Armistice. (G.Valdonio)

G.57

This interesting project took shape in the second half of 1942 when the Regia Aeronautica requested a variant of the G.55 optimised for the fighter-bomber and torpedo-attack roles. For reasons of standardisation, it was decided to use as a base airframe that of the G.55, adapting it to be used with a radial engine, considered to be more reliable and less vulnerable than a water-cooled alternative for these types of mission. The engine selected was the 1,250 hp FIAT A 83 RC 24-52 'Vortice', at the time still under development, but which was expected to enter series production towards the middle of 1943. The design for the new aircraft, identified by the project designation G.57, was developed in Torino by the *Ufficio Tecnico* (Technical Office) of *Ingegnere* Gabrielli, but its subsequent production was to be handed to *Ingegnere* Stiavelli of the CMASA *Ufficio Tecnico*, the company that would be involved in construction of the aircraft.

The armament planned for the aircraft comprised the two 20 mm MG 151 cannon and the two classic 12.7 mm Breda-SAFAT machine guns coupled with the ability to attach a Whitehead 680-kg *silurotto* (small torpedo) or an equivalent weight in bombs. The predicted performance was a speed of around 600 km/h with performance optimised for operational missions conducted at low to medium altitudes. The protracted development of the A.83 engine prevented completion of the aircraft prior to the Armistice, and consequently the project was abandoned.

G.58

At the end of 1942, in response to an unannounced Regia Aeronautica competition for a long-range, twin-engine heavy fighter which included participation from SIAI with the SM.91 and 92, Caproni with the CA.380, and FIAT-CANSA with the FC.20, Gabrielli proposed a design for a twin-engine, single-seat, twin-fuselage fighter, with the cockpit positioned on the left fuselage. In reality the G.58, which was the design designation, was none other than the combination of two G.55 fuselages attached to a wing centre section (similar to the Twin Mustang), thereby potentially obtaining, with appropriate design and industrial effort, a fast and heavily armed fighter, equipped with four 12.7 mm machine guns and six 20 mm cannon. The project was finalised in the spring of 1943, and it was predicted that a possible production site could be that of FIAT-CANSA at Cameri. In July 1943 the first aerodynamic evaluation of a wind tunnel model commenced, but the Armistice brought an end to any activities relating to the project.

The FIAT G.58 was a long-range fighter project, heavily armed with four 12.7 mm machine guns and six 20 mm cannon, and formed by combining two G.55 fuselages with a common wing centre section. The study dates from April 1943 with construction entrusted to CANSA, but the Armistice prevented any development of the project. (G.Valdonio)

G.58

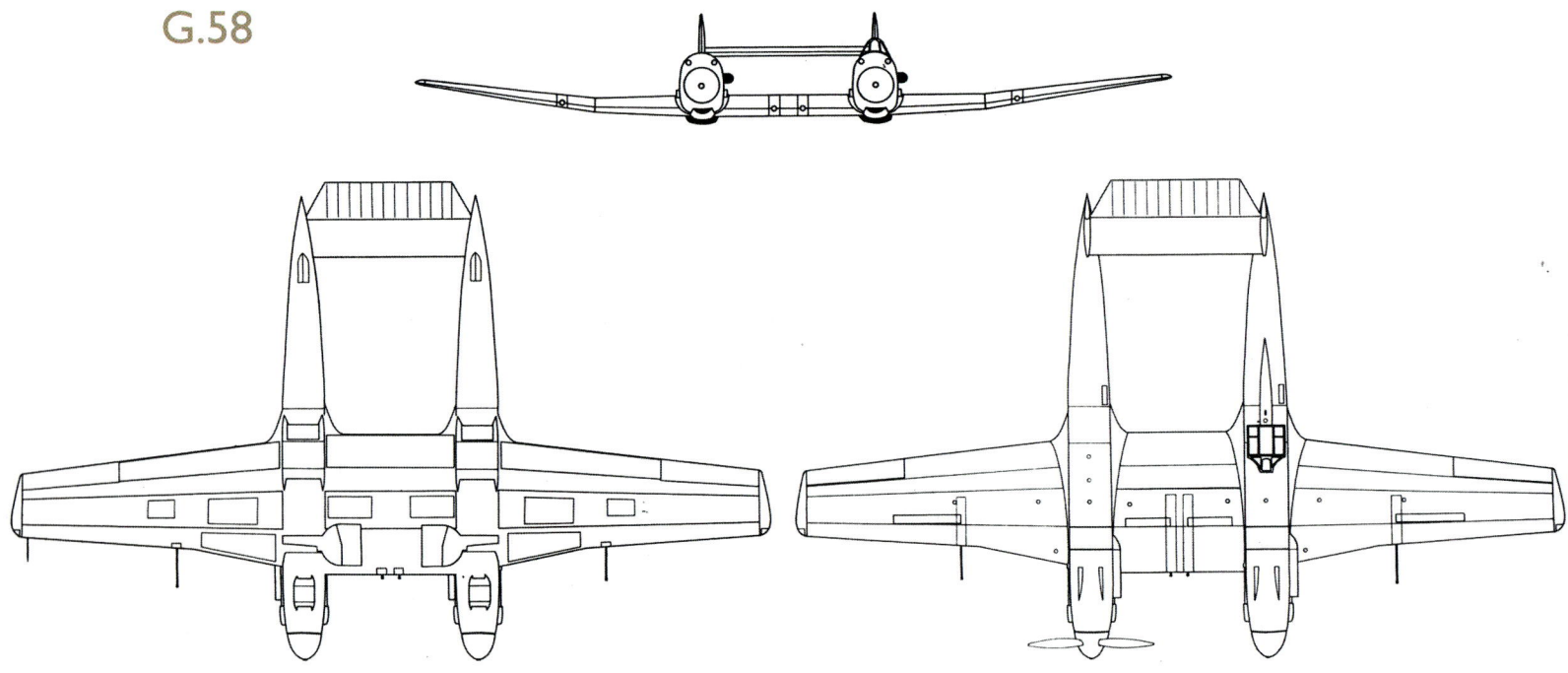

FIAT G.55 Technical Data and Description

THE G.55 was a low cantilever wing, single-engine, single-seat monoplane, entirely metal in construction with an elliptical fuselage section in duralumin, a semi-monocoque forward fuselage structure and full monocoque fuselage rearward from the ninth frame. The airframe was clad in super-avional.

The two-spar cantilever low wing was all-metal with cladding in worked duralumin. The ailerons were a duralumin structure clad in fabric, while the flaps extended along the length of the trailing edge as far as the ailerons. The tailplanes, formed by fixed horizontal stabilisers to which were attached hinged elevators and a vertical tail, were completely metal in structure with duralumin cladding apart from the mobile sections, which were fabric covered.

The main undercarriage was fully retractable with inward rotation and fitted with FAST oleo-pneumatic shock absorbers, while the tailwheel, also retractable, was steerable.

Fuel was stored in each wing in two tanks containing 120 and 60 litres respectively, positioned between the spars, and two fuselage tanks containing 80 and 130 litres, the larger of which was located under the cockpit and the smaller behind the pilot's seat. The total fuel tank capacity was around 570 litres, increasing to 770 litres with supplementary tanks.

The aircraft's electrical system was 24 Volt, powered by a Marelli GR 1200 generator and two accumulator batteries. The oil tank was located behind the engine close to the firewall, while the water tank, horseshoe in shape, was positioned between the engine and propeller.

Refuelling for a G.55 at Venaria. (Garello via Ballista)

A FIAT RA 1050 RC 54 engine powered the fighter, which in reality was the German Daimler-Benz DB 605 A engine manufactured under licence, an inverted V-12 1,350-hp water-cooled, 12-cylinder inverted V motor which drove a Piaggio P.2001 3.05 m-diameter, three-bladed metal propeller with pitch automatically variable in flight. The large radiator was positioned in the fuselage below the cockpit, while the oil radiator was under the engine in a lower fairing.

The cockpit was protected by an armoured windscreen capable of withstanding strikes from 12.7 mm ammunition, and the central part of the canopy hood opened laterally to the right and

Technical Data*

Length	9.39 m
Height	3.13 m
Wingspan	11.85 m
Wing area	21.1 m²
Empty weight	2,700 kg
Max weight	3,672 kg
Powerplant	FIAT RA 1050 RC.58 *Tifone* (licence-built DB 605A-1)
Power at 3,800 m	1,350 hp
Max speed at 7,000 m	625 km/h
Cruising speed	490 km/h
Minimum speed	163 km/h
Climb to 1,000 m	53"
Climb to 4,000 m	4' 20"
Climb to 7,000 m	8' 44"
Ceiling	12,700 m
Range	1,200 km
Take-off run	300 m
Armament	2 x 12.7 mm machine gun; 3 x 20 mm MG 151 cannon

* Data extracted from *Manuale Istruzione e Norme di Montaggio, Regolazione e Impiego del velivolo G.55*, 1943

A close-up photograph of the front of a 'Serie 0' G.55 of the 1ª *Squadriglia*, 2° *Gruppo Caccia* at Bresso in April 1944. To be noted are the *Squadriglia* emblem and the configuration of the lower cowling with a channel for the lower machine gun.

could be detached in an emergency if a bail-out was required. The pilot sat on a seat armoured with 8 mm thick steel. Behind the pilot's headrest was a tubular metal frame offering protection in the event of a roll-over. There was a luggage compartment in the easily accessible fuselage 'hump'.

Behind the cabin was a radio bay containing a B.30 transceiver and a BG 42 ADF radio direction finder, the antenna for which was fixed to the underside of the fuselage.

The principal armament in the production series fighter was provided by two Breda SAFAT 12.7 mm machine guns mounted on top of the engine cowling on shock-absorbed supports. This enabled both their vertical and horizontal adjustment, with the guns synchronised to fire through the propeller disc: the magazines held around 300 rounds per gun. A 20 mm Mauser MG 151 cannon was installed in the forward part of the aircraft, firing through the propeller boss and had a 250-round magazine. Two further Mauser MG 151s were installed in the wings firing outside the propeller disc with each gun's magazine containing 200 rounds. Hardpoints were installed under the wings, capable of supporting external munitions stores or supplementary fuel tanks.

For gun-aiming, the pilot utilised a San Giorgio C 1 reflector gunsight bolted onto a dedicated support above the central upper instrument panel.

Seen here from clockwise from top left, the G.55 engine installation, air filter and liquid-cooled radiator. (Pagliano via GAE)

A pilot of the 51° *Stormo* CT during conversion training to the G.55 at Foligno airfield. Note the non-fixed directional sight, the sighting device with the reflex collimator graticule and the armoured glass. Note that the sight in the cockpit is offset to the right as with Luftwaffe fighters. Interestingly, the pilot is wearing a Luftwaffe LkpN101 summer flying helmet and Nitsche & Gunther flying goggles. From the outset, the Luftwaffe supplied the Italians with a variety of flight clothing and life vests.

This page and following page: Cockpit from a '*Serie* 0' G.55. The main instrument panel included an O.M.1/03 compass, S.Giorgio reflector sight, lockable gyroscope horizon, turn indicator, course repeater, climb/descent indicator, speed indicator, tachometer, clock, pitot and venturi gauges, and control column with firing button and the three ammunition round counters.

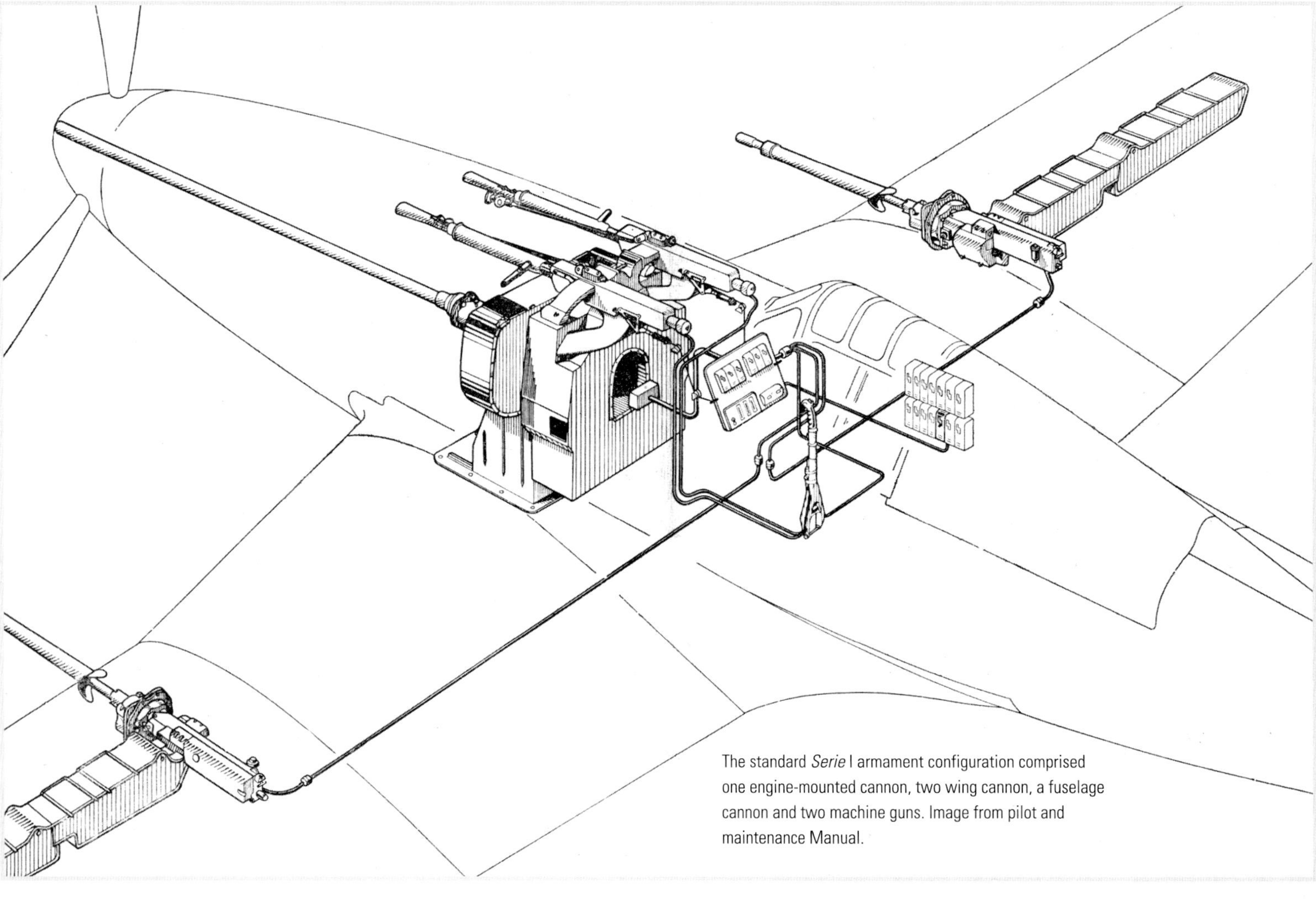

FIAT FIGHTERS

The standard *Serie* I armament configuration comprised one engine-mounted cannon, two wing cannon, a fuselage cannon and two machine guns. Image from pilot and maintenance Manual.

Left and below: Detail of 20mm wing gun fairings and barrel. (Pagliano via GAE)

The G.55 in service with the Regia Aeronautica

THE third prototype (MM493), having been utilised for weapons trials, was assigned to the 353ª *Squadriglia* of the 20° *Gruppo*, 51° *Stormo* at the end of March 1943, where it was flown by *maggiore* Riccardo Roveda. While in the process of being reorganised and re-equipped with the C.205V at Ciampino airport, the *Squadriglia* was transferred to Sardegna in May 1943 with the rest of the 51° *Stormo*, operating from Capoterra airfield with its *Veltros*, *Folgores* and the single *Centauro*. From mid-May 1943 the fighters of the 51° *Stormo* CT conducted frequent interception missions, targeting Allied aircraft and recording numerous combat encounters. From the little information available, it seems that on 5 June 1943 the sole G.55 performed its first combat operation, contributing, together with a *Folgore* and a *Veltro*, in the downing of a B-26 Marauder, one of twelve which had attacked Capoterra airfield. Also in June, the *Centauro* was used in another two interception missions. In a further dogfight, on the 28th, flying with ten *Veltros* and seventeen *Folgores*, it was involved in an important series of clashes along the eastern and western coastlines of Sardegna, at the end of which the Italian pilots claimed eight Allied aircraft as destroyed.

In the same month, twelve G.55s of *sottoserie* 0 were assigned to the 4° *Gruppo Complementare Caccia* at Foligno. The *gruppi complementari* mostly supported activities by depot units or provided advanced pilot training for three fighter *Stormi* and two bomber *Stormi*. There were four such *Gruppi Complementari Caccia* within the Regia Aeronautica, three for bomber units and two for reconnaissance and transport. The 4° *Gruppo Complementare* supported the 51° and 52° *Stormo* CT and the CLXI° *Gruppo Autonomo*. Prior to receiving its first G.55s the *Gruppo* operated mainly AerMacchi fighters, namely the C.200, C.202 and C.205.

Ciampino: one of the first series examples, MM91059, assigned to the 353ª *Squadriglia* of the 20° *Gruppo Caccia*, 51° *Stormo* CT. The aircraft livery is the standard Regia Aeronautica dark olive-green colour on the fuselage and upper surface, with grey undersides

The pilots of the 4° *Gruppo Complementare* commenced flying in June 1943, but at the beginning of July the order arrived tasking the personnel of the 353ª *Squadriglia* to convert onto the *Centauro*, the unit having recently returned to the mainland from Sardegna where it had run out of aircraft. The 353ª *Squadriglia* consequently received nine G.55s, nearly all from *Serie* 1, and completed its fleet with another four C.205Vs. Following the bombing of Roma on 19 July 1943, the unit was relocated to Ciampino airport, from where it performed some interceptor missions and scrambles prior to returning to Foligno at the end of the month. There it rejoined the other *squadriglie* of the 20° *Gruppo* (351ª and 352ª) which were waiting to be re-equipped with the *Centauro* in advance of a return to Sardegna. However, the 353ª *Squadriglia* remained at Foligno only for a few days, as on 7 August it was sent back to Ciampino to defend Roma from daylight attacks by American bombers, although it only performed a limited number of such interceptor missions because of a series of limitations placed on operational activity following the declaration of Roma as an 'open city' as announced on 15 August 1943.

In early September further scrambles and defensive patrols were conducted. The final combat mission was performed on the fateful morning of 8 September 1943, the day on which the Armistice was announced, when some G.55s took off to intercept American bombers heading for Frascati. On that day the 353ª *Squadriglia* had a force of ten (or possibly twelve) G.55s on charge, although the number of serviceable aircraft was

Photographs of the FIAT G.55 in Regia Aeronautica useage are rare. Here is one such machine, void of any unit markings and the identities of the pilot and aircraft are not known.

probably no more than half. All were captured by German troops which occupied Ciampino airfield the following day.

Towards the end of August, after the FIAT production lines had begun to roll out the *Centauros* of *Serie* 1, a few G.55s were assigned to the 372ª *Squadriglia* of the 53° *Stormo* at Mirafiori airfield, but there is no information available on operational activity.

On the date of the Armistice, besides the handful of aircraft with the 353ª *Squadriglia*, it is believed that, officially, the Regia Aeronautica had little more than thirty G.55s on charge. After the Armistice, no G.55 flew in the colours of the Regia Aeronautica in Allied-occupied Italy with the exception of G.55 MM.91150. On 4 April 1944, one of the FIAT test pilots, Serafino Agostini, profiting from the task of test-flying a *Centauro* prior to delivery to the A.N.R., used the aircraft to flee to southern Italy together with Allied agent, Francesco Gentile. The escape had evidently been pre-planned, and the *Centauro* landed at Piombino escorted by some American P-47 Ds. Subsequently, the fighter was transferred to Guidonia (Roma) and then to Napoli. It was later shipped to the Central Fighter Establishment at RAF Tangmere in England where it was unpacked on 7 April 1945. It received RAF roundels and was allocated the serial VF201 on 27 April. Never flown, it was eventually placed into storage at RNAS Ford where it slowly decayed until it was finally scrapped.

Two photographs of a G.55 of the 353ª Squadriglia, 20° *Gruppo*, 51° *Stormo* CT during a visit to the Scuola Caccia at Castiglione del Lago. The only Regia Aeronautica unit equipped with the G.55, the 353ª *Squadriglia* received most of its aircraft in August 1943. Like the example shown here, the fighters were thus devoid of the Fascist insignia which was abolished in late July 1943 after the downfall of the regime.

The G.55 in service with the A.N.R.

AFTER the Armistice and the ephemeral use of the G.55 by the Regia Aeronautica, in September 1943 FIAT Aeritalia, like the other major Italian industrial concerns, entered a difficult period, subjected to the control of the German R.U.K.. It endeavoured to survive through a precarious game of equilibrium: it had to retain work in order to avoid the sequestration of its manufacturing equipment and the deportation of the workforce, but it had to do so without seeming to establish a form of collaboration that might ferment more energetic clandestine activity within its factories and so consequently lead to reprisals from the Germans. Provision was therefore made for a reorganisation of the original production line to focus on aircraft which could be of interest to the German war effort, and in light of the establishment of the Aeronautica Repubblicana in October. In the case of the latter, this would apply mainly for the fighter units, which would be engaged principally in the defence of Italian cities against Allied bombing. Such reasoning justified the conduct of the company.

It was not by chance, therefore, that of the five production lines existing in September 1943, only those for the G.12 transport and, incredibly, the CR.42 were retained, together obviously with that for the G.55, for which authorisation was quickly received for the production of 128 fighters, followed in the spring by a further possible order for the manufacture of 500 aircraft. No limitations were placed on the licence manufacture of the DB 605 engine, but it was hoped to rationalise the production of the engine together with the other licence-holding firms.

Agreements were signed in October 1943 between the *Sottosegretario dell'Aeronautica Repubblicana*, Ernesto Botto, and Luftwaffe headquarters in Italy. These specified that the structure of each new arm of service in the newly constituted Aeronautica Repubblicana would comprise an operational *gruppo* and a *squadriglia complementare* to train pilots. All the available G.55s and new build examples were, meanwhile, assigned to the emerging air force, and at the end of 1943 the structure of the Aeronautica Repubblicana was as follows:

- **1° *Gruppo Caccia*** based at Mirafiori e Caselle (Torino) with three *squadriglie* – '*Larsimont*', '*Bobba*' and '*Occarso*' equipped with AerMacchi C.205Vs

- ***Squadriglia Complementare Caccia 'Montefusco'***, based at Venaria Reale (Torino) equipped with G.55s and C.205Vs

- ***Gruppo Aerotrasporti 'Terracciano'*** equipped with SIAI S.81 and SM.82 tri-motor transports

- ***Squadriglia Complementare Aerosiluranti*** equipped with S.79s

The initial decision to deploy both the 1° *Gruppo Caccia* and the *Squadriglia Complementare Montefusco* in the Torino area was based on significant logistical and military requirements. These were founded on the fact that the principal Italian industrial centres as well as the production lines for the modern G.55 and AerMacchi C.205V fighter aircraft were concentrated in Piemonte and the western part of Lombardia. Moreover, the proximity of FIAT Aeritalia and AerMacchi facilities assured the continuous assistance of a specialised workforce and the widespread availability of spare parts. Despite this, 1° *Gruppo Caccia's* stay in Piemonte was of a brief duration, despite the positive outcome of its first actual combat, fought in the sky above Torino on 3 January. On 12 January the unit received the order to relocate to a new base at Campoformido (UD), this as a consequence of operational decisions taken by the Luftwaffe high command, aimed at reinforcing the defences of the southern sector of the Reich. For this reason, and because of the increasing intensity of Allied bombing of the industrial cities of north-west Italy, from early February 1944 an alarm section was created within the *Squadriglia Montefusco* using both G.55s and C.205Vs. With the availability of new-production G.55s, in the same period, the constitution of a 2° *Gruppo Caccia* was authorised, to be based at Bresso airfield on the outskirts of Milano, thereby concentrating the G.55s of the so-called *sottoserie* 0 mainly with the

G.55s of the *Squadriglia Complementare 'Montefusco'* and a C.205V. In the background is the royal estate (bottom photograph) adjacent to Palace of Venaria and airfield. On *Centauro* Nrs 8 and 13 the national insignia are of the first 'wide fringed' version. (Garello via F.Ballista)

G.55, MM 91097, '5', with the name of the commander Giovanni Bonet on the nose. The signature of the fallen commander survived briefly as unit insignia on the *Centauro* of the 3ª *Squadriglia* after its incorporation into the 1° *Gruppo Caccia* at Reggio Emilia.

Capitano Bonet and *sergente* Arrigoni in conversation in front of a G.55 at Venaria. *Capitano* Bonet was shot down on 29 March 1944 while Arrigoni fell in action over the Tuscan-Emilian Apennines on 26 June 1944, shot down by a Spitfire of No. 238 Squadron, RAF. (Garello via F.Ballista)

Squadriglia Complementare Caccia 'Montefusco'. Constituted in November 1943 at Venaria Reale airfield, and commanded by *capitano* Giovanni Bonet, this *squadriglia* was named in memory of *capitano* Mario Montefusco, who was killed in action on 4 July 1941 in North Africa.

Operated alongside the G.55s was a small element of AerMacchi C.205Vs, used to train those pilots destined for posting to the 1° *Gruppo Caccia*, which was completely equipped with the *Veltro*.

Of particular interest is the comparison made between the two fighters operated from Venaria as reported by *tenente* Biron:

'7 January 1944: first flight in the G.55 in service as a pilot of the Aeronautica Repubblicana. We found the aircraft, brand new, lined up at Caselle airfield, ready for use. After a certain number of training flights, we began to mount our first real alert service. During a test flight, along with commandant Bonet, we flew a climb-rate comparison test in the two aircraft. I was flying a Macchi C.205V, he was in the G.55. Up to four or five thousand metres the Macchi climbed magnificently, and then it began to run out of breath. With a struggle, I reached 11,000 metres. At this altitude the Macchi, short of wing area, was an ironing board. It could barely hold on and seemed to ask for speed to recover the air that it was lacking. The G.55, on the other hand, still manoeuvred fairly well.'

It should be stressed that the G.55s delivered to the Aeronautica Repubblicana were characterised by the installation of an inverted throttle, similar in function to those fitted to German and Allied fighters, together with the potential to utilise auxiliary fuel tanks. They also featured complete cannon armament. Deliveries of these new aircraft, which commenced at the end of 1943, increased in parallel with increasing output from FIAT. In the early months of 1944, the company had produced more than fifty aircraft prior to the fateful USAAF bombing raid of 25 April 1944, which resulted in the cessation of production following the damage caused to the Aeritalia facilities, and in destruction and damage to numerous G.55s either newly completed or awaiting collection on the adjacent airfield.

As mentioned above, after the departure of the 1° *Gruppo Caccia* for Friuli, the '*Montefusco*' organised its own alarm section which was called into action for the first time on 21 February 1944. Six G.55s attempted, unsuccessfully, to intercept a formation of American bombers. Following another pair of interceptions, again with no result,

Right: FIAT-Aeritalia's final assembly line in Torino seen in the aftermath of the American bombing attack of 25 April 1944.

Above: The G.55, MM91118, severely damaged by daylight bombing on 25 April 1944 by B-17s of the USAAF 301st Bomb Group on the FIAT-Aeritalia workshops. The action resulted in the destruction of three assembly lines and about forty aircraft.

The sad remains of a new G.55 destroyed by American bombs on 25 April 1944. The air raid resulted in 37 civilian deaths and the destruction of at least fifteen *Centaurs*. (P.Pesarcsi)

on 17 March *sottotenente* Mazzei, flying a C.205V, attacked the SIAI SM 92 prototype in error. This mistake occurred because of the SM 92's similarity to the American P-38. Despite the damage suffered, the pilot managed to recover the aircraft, albeit with some difficulty, and land at Lonate Pozzolo airfield. In the meantime, in March 1944 at Venaria, where FIAT had dispersed the majority of the G.55s produced, some examples were prepared for the 2° *Gruppo Caccia,* which was officially constituted on 1 March 1944 and based at Bresso airfield with the following composition:

- 1ª *Squadriglia* 'Gigi Caneppele'– 'Gigi tre osei' insignia

- 2ª *Squadriglia* 'Nicola Magaldi' – 'Diavoli Rossi' insignia

- 3ª *Squadriglia* 'Giorgio Graffer' – 'Gamba di Ferro' insignia

On 29 March 1944 one-hundred bombers from the American 2nd Bomb Group attacked the railway and industrial infrastructure of Torino. Four of the six pilots of the *squadriglia* 'Montefusco' who had scrambled engaged the B-17G formation, launching a head-on attack from above and damaging some of the bombers on their first pass. *Capitano* Bonet attacked B-17G 42-97152, already damaged by anti-aircraft fire, and with the assistance of *sergente maggiore* Lucio Biagini, forced it to crash some ten kilometres from the town of Cairo Montenotte. However, at that point the Italian pilots became the prey of the escorting P-47 D Thunderbolts which fell on the four G.55s. Overcome by the more numerous enemy, *capitano* Bonet was fatally injured by machine gun fire from the Thunderbolt of Major Herschel Green, commander of the 317th Fighter Squadron. Bonet crashed in his G.55 near the city of Alba, while *maresciallo* Jellici managed to take to his parachute with his aircraft in flames. The loss of *capitano* Bonet, the highly respected commander of the *Squadriglia* 'Montefusco', was particularly felt by the personnel of the unit and to commemorate him they decided to rename the *Squadriglia* after him and to paint the noses of their G.55s with his signature, adopting it as the unit insignia.

The increasing combat operations of the *Squadriglia Complementare Caccia* 'Montefusco-Bonet' fighter section resulted in a reorganisation of the unit, which elevated the section to the status of a *Gruppo Complementare Caccia,* commanded by *tenente colonnello* Tito Falconi. It comprised the *Squadriglia Allarme* 'Bonet' based at Venaria, commanded by *capitano* Giulio Torresi, and two other training units, the *Squadriglia Addestramento* and the *Scuola Caccia,* based respectively at Cervere and Casabianca. The *Squadriglia Caccia* 'Bonet' was in a very unique position, as although it undertook exclusively operational duties, it was subordinate to the control of the headquarters of a training unit and not the *Comando Caccia*, as was the case with the 1° and 2° *Gruppo Caccia*. In the first weeks of April, *capitano* Torresi was engaged in the reorganisation of the unit and the raising of its morale, sorely tested by the loss of the former, much-loved commander Bonet. Torresi obtained new aircraft and pilots and towards the end of April there were 28 pilots and at least 11 FIAT G.55s on charge, together with two residual C.205Vs:

FIAT G.55 fleet with *Squadriglia Allarme Bonet*, 24 April 1944

MM91110	2
MM91060*	3
MM91111	4
MM91097	5
MM91075	6
MM91064*	7
MM91101	8
MM91116	10
MM91072	11
MM91073	12
MM91117	13

* G.55 *sottoserie* 0

After a fruitless scramble on 19 April 1944, on the 25th, the '*Bonet*' fighters were widely engaged in confronting heavy American attacks targeting the AerMacchi and FIAT aeronautical factories and the Austrian airfield of Wiener Neustadt, the home of a

Pages published by the weekly magazine *ALI* in 1944 depicting stirring scenes of air combat with aircraft of the USAAF. The fighters shown here are Macchi's. (P. Pesaresi)

Bf 109 production line. On that day the bombing of the FIAT Aeritalia factories at Torino was conducted by at least 117 B-24 Liberators of the 304th Bomb Wing, accompanied by 45 P-47s of the 325th Fighter Group, while the bombers sent to attack AerMacchi were escorted by P-38s of the 82nd Fighter Group. Seven G.55s took off from the airfield at Venaria to confront the American bombers, plus two C.205Vs of the '*Bonet*' and despite their numerical inferiority, they launched an attack, diving down onto their targets. However, a handful of Italian fighters could do little against such a large number of American aircraft and consequently the result of the mission was merciless for the Italian pilots. Despite their best efforts, the raid was particularly violent with the FIAT factories heavily bombed. Three G.55s were shot down. *Sergente maggiore* Lucio Biagini was killed, and *Capitano* Torresi and *maresciallo* Ennio Tarantola managed to bail out of their damaged fighters.

Over the following days there were further scrambles, but none were productive as the fighters, probably poorly directed by the ground detection stations, never managed to reach the bomber formations in time.

On 12 May 1944 the *Squadriglia d'allarme* '*Bonet*' engaged in its final air combat in the skies above Piemonte as two weeks later the entire *squadriglia* was amalgamated with the 1° *Gruppo Caccia*, which was in extreme need of new personnel and aircraft. On that day the US Fifteenth Air Force had planned a series of missions against the lines of communication, bridges, railways, and airfields in the north, in prospect of a resumption of the Allied land advance along the peninsula following a pause in combat operations. The 301st Bomb Group sent thirty-four B-17Gs to bomb Piacenza San Damiano airfield, but as it was under cloud cover, the bombers switched to their alternate target – the railway station at Chivasso, near Torino. Seven G.55s scrambled from Venaria and made repeated attacks on the bombers and they all returned undamaged to their base in Puglia. *Tenente* Biron describes the engagement:

> '12 May 1944: Third dogfight for the squadriglia. I took part as formation leader of seven aircraft, later reduced to five due to technical faults. The engagement was fought against a formation of 31 B-17s, without any escorting fighters. The engagement was carried out in a relatively calm manner and was well managed. I saw the starboard engines of the aircraft that I had machine-gunned burning, but I had to break off because of the clouds. No losses on our part.'

The 2° *Gruppo Caccia* goes into action

On 30 April 1944 the first operational sortie was recorded by the G.55s of the 2° *Gruppo Caccia*, flown from Bresso airfield, where the unit had received its first G.55s a few weeks earlier. This first combat mission was certainly dramatic as of the four G.55s scrambled to intercept a formation of B-24s escorted by P-38s, the fighter flown by *tenente* Nicola Manzitti failed to return, although he was also credited with the destruction of an enemy fighter. Despite their efforts, the Italian pilots failed to prevent the heavy bombing of the airfield and adjacent Breda aircraft factory

The 2° *Gruppo Caccia* marked its aircraft with conspicuously large numerals, as with 'Yellow 5', MM91089, photographed at Bresso near Milano in April 1944. (Pagliano via GAE)

A G.55 of the 2° *Gruppo Caccia 'Diavoli Rossi'* is readied for take-off at Bresso in April 1944.

A G.55 of the 2° *Gruppo Caccia 'Diavoli Rossi'* landing at Bresso in April 1944.

Right: A detail photograph of the nose and forward fuselage of a G.55 of 1ª *Squadriglia*, 2° *Gruppo Caccia* at Bresso. Note the wing cannon with long shrouds, underwing racks and the *'Gigi Tre Osei'* unit emblem on the nose.

Below: Bresso was a busy airfield in March and April 1944, with several ANR aircraft operating from there, including fighters, bombers and transport machines. (Pagliano via GAE)

Two fine in-flight studies of G.55, MM91058, 'Yellow 1' of the 2° *Gruppo Caccia* flown on this occasion by *tenente* Ancillotti. The aircraft flew with 353ª *Squadriglia* of 51° *Stormo* CT before the Armistice of 8 September 1943. (Pagliano via GAE)

which, given the level of damage suffered, was forced to suspend its activities.

On 9 May 1944, the 2° *Gruppo Caccia* was relocated to the Cascina Vaga airfield near Pavia, and after a few days spent settling in, on 25 May sixteen G.55s took off to intercept another large formation of B-24s escorted by P-38s. In the encounter that followed, *maggiore* Feliciani was credited with one four-engined bomber destroyed, while *sottotenente* Orsolan, who failed to return from the mission, was credited with the shooting down of a fighter. Nevertheless, following the limited production of aircraft authorised by the Germans, and the Allied bombing that slowed and eventually led to the suspension of fighter and spare parts production, the operational efficiency of the 2° *Gruppo Caccia* was so low that with the agreement of the senior German commanders in Italy, A.N.R. headquarters decided to re-equip the unit with the Bf 109 G-6 and transfer the residual G.55s to the 1° *Gruppo Caccia* at Reggio Emilia.

A G.55 of 2° *Gruppo Caccia 'Diavoli Rossi'* photographed moments after take-off, probably from Bresso. (Pagliano via GAE)

The 'open air alert dispersal' of 2ª *Squadriglia* of 2° *Gruppo Caccia* at Cascina Vaga complete with unit shield, hooks and bench for flight gear and helmets, as well as a blackboard showing aircraft status and formation composition. (D'Amico & Valentini via GAE)

The pilots of 1ª *Squadriglia* at readiness at Cascina Vaga, near Pavia, with their G.55s in the background. (Pagliano via GAE)

The G.55 'Yellow 7' was a distinctive aircraft of the 2° *Gruppo Caccia* having received a camouflage scheme of a brown wave-mirror pattern. (D'Amico & Valentini via GAE)

Although the light from the sky makes it difficult to see, the G.55 shown here is finished in the earliest available example of a three-tone splinter pattern. The photograph was taken on 23 April 1944 and shows an aircraft flown by *sergente maggiore* Cavagliario. (D'Amico & Valentini via GAE)

G.55 'Yellow 8' of the 1ª *Squadriglia*, 2° *Gruppo Caccia* shows off an experimental three-tone splinter camouflage. Only aircraft of the 1ª *Squadriglia* tested experimental colour schemes. The rear fuselage panel aft of the cockpit appears to be a replacement in a different colour.

G.55 'Blue 5' of 1ª *Squadriglia*, 2° *Gruppo Caccia*, in another variation of a three-tone splinter camouflage. The photograph was probably taken at Reggio Emilia in April 1944. (D'Amico & Valentini via GAE)

G.55 'Blue 2' of the 3ª *Squadriglia*, 1° *Gruppo Caccia* at Reggio Emilia. Traces of Bonet's signature can still be seen on the nose; most of the signature insignia were erased after the unit's assignment to the 1° *Gruppo Caccia*.

A pair of G.55s of 2° *Gruppo Caccia* on patrol in the Milano area. (Pagliano via GAE)

The *Squadriglia* 'Bonet' merges with the 1° *Gruppo Caccia*

The assignment of the *Squadriglia* 'Bonet' to the 1° *Gruppo Caccia* and the G.55s of the former 2° *Gruppo Caccia* which, since 24 April 1944, had operated from the airfield at Reggio Emilia and the satellite field at Cavriago, occurred in a period of real crisis for the unit, in terms of personnel and aircraft. To the eighteen C.205Vs then on charge were added at least twenty-two G.55s; these were divided between the 1° and 3ª *Squadriglia*, while the 2ª *Squadriglia* remained equipped exclusively with the *Veltro*. On 4 June, the first interceptor mission was conducted by eleven *Veltros* and fourteen *Centauros* with no positive results being recorded, but with the loss of *sottotenente* Mazzei who crashed in unknown circumstances, possibly because of the poor functioning of his oxygen system. On 9 June, *capitano* Giuseppe Robetto and *sergente maggiore* Chiussi each claimed victories during an attack against B-24 bombers flying their return leg from Germany, while on 13 June, in the course of another combat mission, *sergente maggiore* Luigi Di Cecco was forced to make an emergency landing.

On 15 June a twenty-aircraft formation comprising a mix of C.205Vs and G.55s patrolling northern Tuscany, encountered a formation of Spitfires. Despite being injured, *sottotenente* Fausto Morettin managed to jump from his G.55, MM91087, but would later die from his injuries, his leg having been riddled by rounds from an enemy fighter. By the end of the dogfight, another two Italian fighters had been shot down, but their pilots, Saieva and Gorrini, managed to survive. On 26 June a formation of fifteen Spitfires bounced a formation of six G.55s and seven C.205Vs carrying out a patrol flight, but at the end of the brief clash, the *Veltro* of *sergente* Arrigoni had been shot down. On 27 June Spitfires attacked Reggio Emilia airfield, managing to destroy two G.55s ready for take-off on the ground, and severely damaging another. As the Allied attacks against Reggio Emilia intensified, it was decided to move the 1° *Gruppo Caccia* on 2 July to Vicenza airfield.

On the previous day, 1 July 1944, the unit suffered a heavy blow with the death of *capitano* Torresi, who was shot down by a P-47 D just after taking off in his G.55. It was not the only loss recorded that day, as of the five *Veltros* and six *Centauros* to get airborne, another four aircraft failed to return, with the death of *sergente maggiore* Boscaro, the other three pilots managing to save themselves. The events of that day were recorded by *tenente* Giuseppe Biron:

'*1 July 1944: at the airfield at Reggio Emilia, we are not really "living" now. There are continuous attacks by Thunderbolts and Spitfires to the extent that the alarm never goes off. We pilots live in trenches next to our aircraft. While taking off for a patrol mission, my friend and the Squadriglia commander, Giulio Torresi, a fierce fighter, was shot down... We relocated entirely to Vicenza airfield, given the impossibility of operating from Reggio Emilia. Command of my Squadriglia was assumed by tenente Guido Bertolozzi, more senior than me.*'

Two other G.55s were lost, together with C.205Vs, on 20 July, when a mix of twenty *Veltros* and *Centauros* were scrambled to intercept a formation of B-24s in the skies above the Veneto. They were bounced by the bombers' P-51 D and P-38 escorts. In the encounter, *maggiore* Guglielmo Arrabito, who had only recently been nominated as commander of the 1° *Gruppo Caccia*, was killed, along with *sergente maggiore* Ugo Sgubbi of the 2ª *Squadriglia*. *Tenente* Biron managed to exit the cockpit of his G.55, MM91101, but as he left his fighter, he struck the tailplane and suffered severe injuries. More fortunate was *maresciallo* Romano Spazzoli, who

Vicenza, July 1944. The nose of this G.55 bears the emblem of the *'Asso di Bastoni'* (Ace of Clubs). A tarpaulin appears to have been placed over the aircraft's aerial mast. (D'Amico & Valentini via GAE)

A G.55 of the 1° *Gruppo Caccia* parked in a blast pen off the apron at Reggio Emilia. (Pagliano via GAE)

Tenente Vittorio Pignatti jokes with *sergente maggiore* Carlo Cavagliano. They were pilots of the 1ª *Squadriglia 'Gigi Tre Osei'* of the 2° *Gruppo Caccia*. Note both are wearing Luftwaffe-supplied Schwimmweste 10-30-B-2 life vests. Vittorio Pignatti is also holding a Luftwaffe *Flieger-Leuchtpistole* L double barreled flare pistol. (Pagliano via GAE)

managed to bail out without any problems, while *tenente* Sandro Beretta was forced to make a disastrous emergency landing, destroying his *Veltro* in the process. Biron recalled those dramatic moments:

'20 July 1944: The Gruppo scrambled on its first flight from Vicenza to attack a powerful formation of four-engine bombers returning from a raid on Germany, escorted by numerous fighters. In all, perhaps five-hundred aircraft. Commandant Visconti, on a short leave, had been replaced by maggiore Arrabito, who quickly took off in his Macchi. In our G.55s, we quickly lost contact with him because of the speed difference. At around 9,000 metres I attacked a formation of twin-engine Lockheed fighters, but I didn't prolong the attack so as not to become too distanced from the rest of my formation. Nevertheless, these Lightnings were no longer those that we had encountered some months previously at Napoli. To me they seemed more powerful and faster, as they chased me and caught up with me. I tried in vain to disengage by turning and I realised that I was alone. I turned, and the nearest Lightning began to fire. I saw the red flashes illuminate the mouths of its numerous cannon. I persisted with the hope that I could reach my two wingmen, who were ahead, to warn them of the danger. I didn't manage to. I pushed down into a dive but forgot the overspeed. When I remembered, it was too late. The engine was screaming and began to fail at around three thousand metres, after I had descended from six thousand metres in a controlled spin, during which I had lost my pursuers. I considered landing but, at around one thousand metres, the engine began to run roughly and caught fire. The American fighters had definitely hit me, but I never understood whether the engine was on fire because of the hits received or because I had mismanaged it during the attack. I decided to jump and, letting go of the controls, the aircraft, perfectly balanced, began to sink in a gentle glide. I climbed out of the cockpit and sat on the fuselage behind the seat, with both legs on the left-hand fuselage side and my right hand gripping the radio antenna mast. I felt no wind, as I was in aerodynamic shadow. Paying close attention to the tailplanes, I tried to slide off and underneath them, but I didn't manage to, and was hit by the elevator on the right-hand side of my chest. The pain made me pass out, but probably a guardian angel woke me, just in time for me to open the parachute (for some time, in fact, I had stopped attaching the automatic parachute opening chord to the fuselage in order to avoid the laceration of the parachute canopy in the event of a high-speed bail-out). I opened my eyes and saw my two boots hovering above me in the sky. I operated the parachute cord which opened normally. After the jerk, the belt tightened around my chest, preventing me from breathing and resulting in unspeakable pain. Gasping, I fell into a vineyard in Ponte di Piave, near a farmhouse. They came out and gathered me up. A painful and embarrassing detail: they believed that I was an Italian pilot fighting with the Americans and assured me that they would manage to hide me before the arrival of the Germans. Half an hour later, a German car, rushed me in a hurry to the civilian hospital in Oderzo.'

Following other engagements that achieved no particular results, on 1 August *sergente* Balduzzo was forced to jump from his G.55 for a second time, having been hit after a formation of nine G.55s and six C.205Vs was bounced by the Thunderbolt escorts. The Italian pilots had intercepted a formation of American twin-engine medium bombers near Mantova which had attacked a bridge at Canneto sull'Oglio. On this occasion the Italians claimed a bomber and a Thunderbolt fighter shot down. This was the final operational mission flown by the G.55s of the 1° *Gruppo Caccia*. A few days later, the unit was forced into inactivity following a block on the supply of fuel initiated as part of Operation *Phönix*, the plan conceived by *Generalfeldmarschall* Wolfram von Richthofen, commander of *Luftflotte* 2, with the intent of transforming the A.N.R. into a '*Legione Aerea Italiana*' under the direct operational and administrative control of the Luftwaffe.

However, the German plan, supported only by a limited number of pro-Nazi officers within the A.N.R., was doomed to fail, as the majority of the personnel assigned to the units refused to adhere to it. With their aircraft grounded due to lack of fuel, they preferred to destroy the tens of *Veltros* and *Centauros* rather than hand them to the Germans. Operation *Phönix* was subsequently cancelled personally by Hitler, who had been pressurised by a decisive personal intervention by Mussolini, who had been kept in the dark about the plan that had been orchestrated by von Richthofen.

These sad historical events form the conclusion of the wartime career of the G.55. The fighter units of the A.N.R., following some months of reorganisation, returned to combat operating Messerschmitt Bf 109 G aircraft supplied by the Germans.

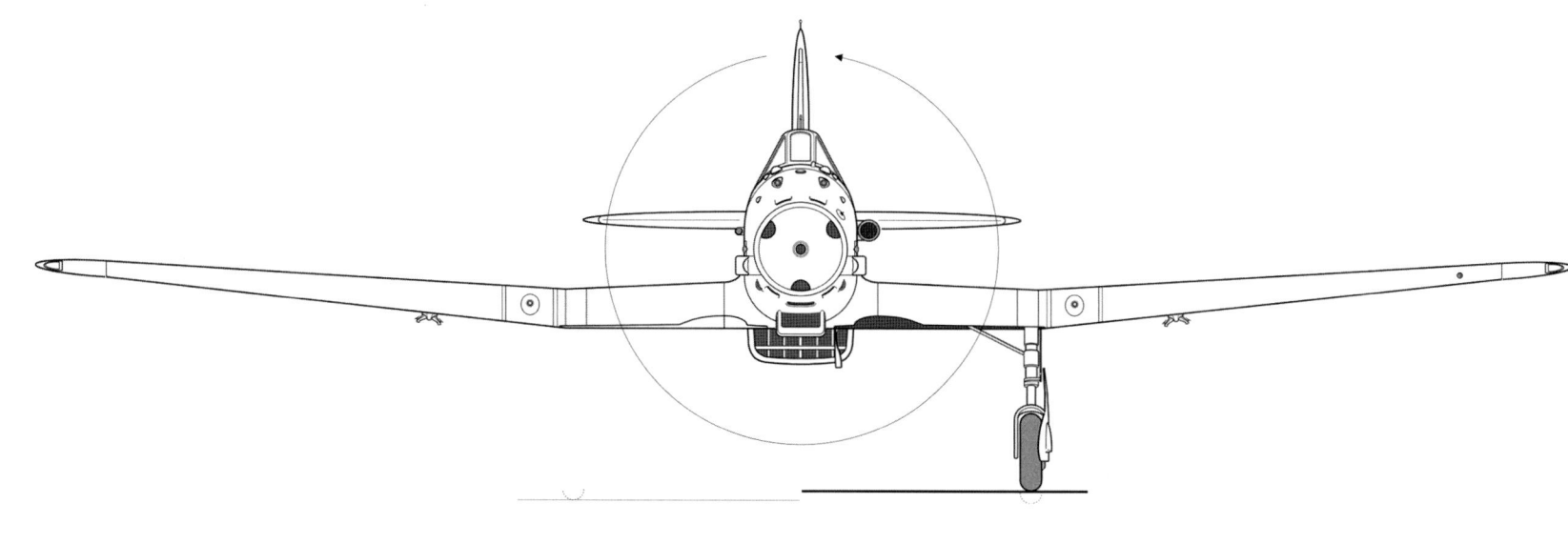
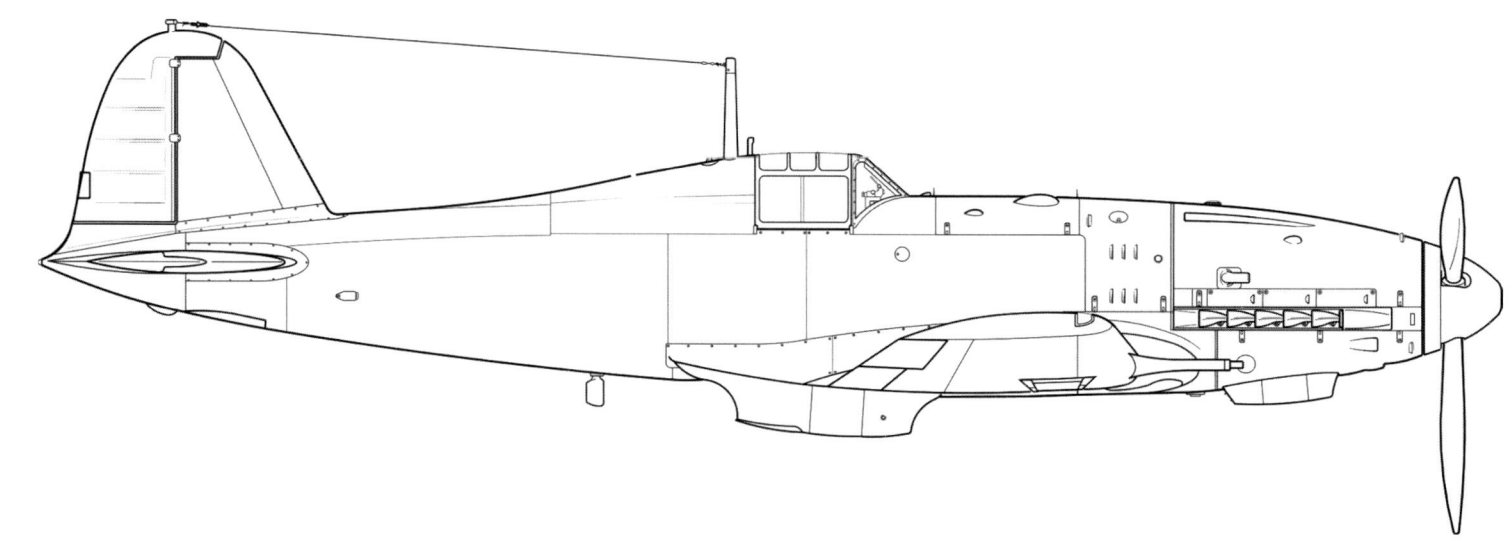
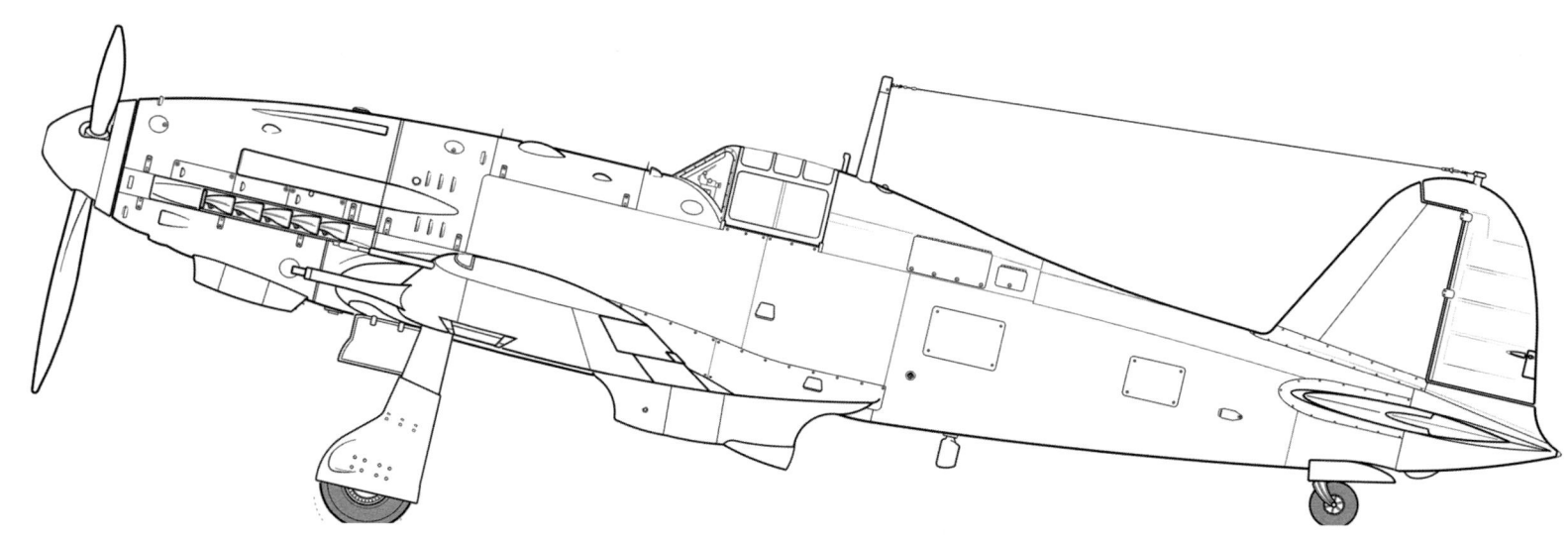

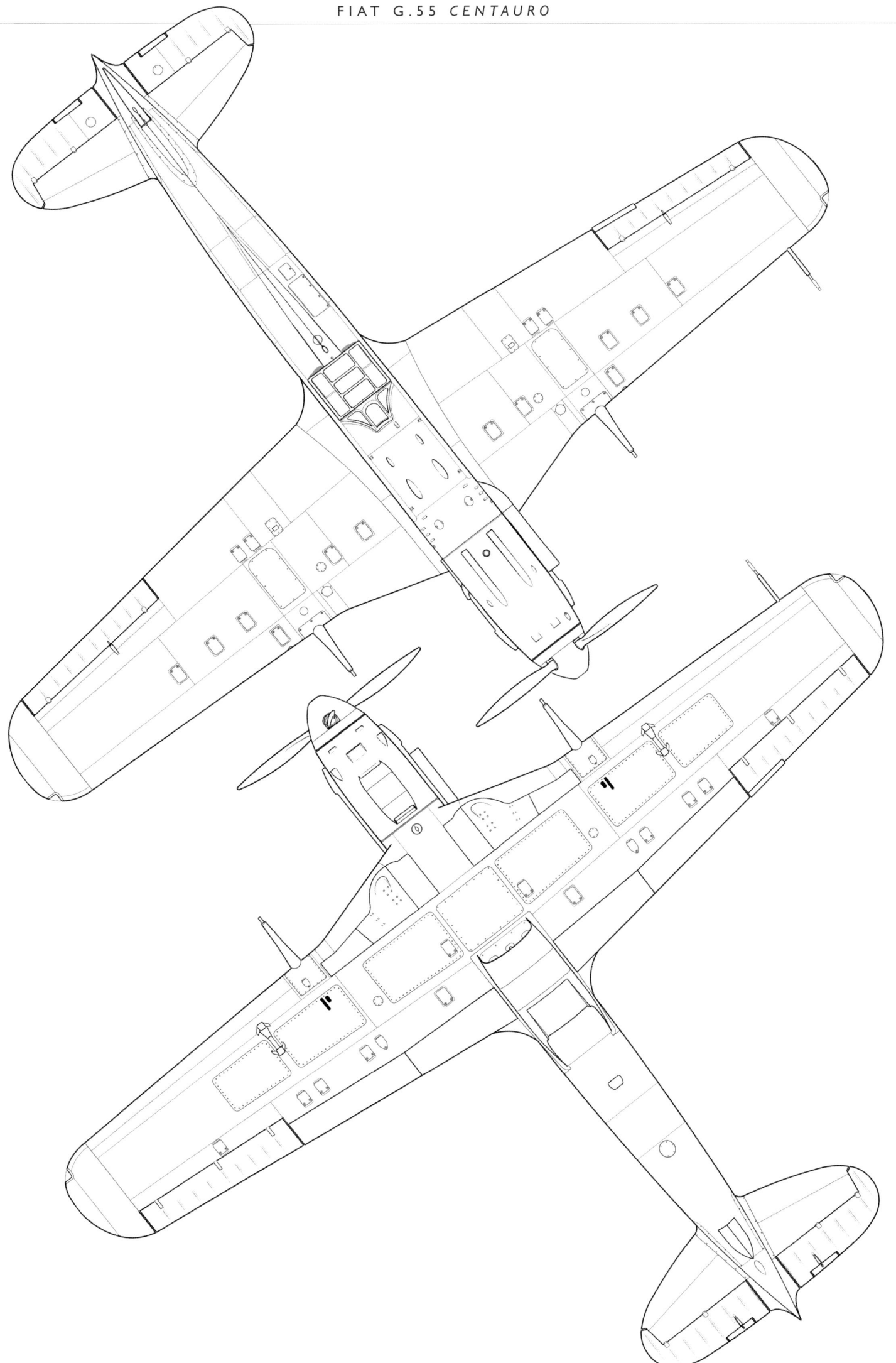

G.55, MM91059, 353ª *Squadriglia*, 20° *Gruppo*, 51° *Stormo* CT, Ciampino, August 1943

G.55, MM91058, 'Yellow 1', 2ª *Squadriglia*, 2° *Gruppo Caccia*, Bresso, March 1944

G.55, MM91077, 'Black 7', 1ª *Squadriglia*, 2° *Gruppo Caccia*, Cascina Vaga, May 1944

FIAT G.55 CENTAURO

G.55, 3ª *Squadriglia*, 2° *Gruppo Caccia*, Cascina Vaga, May 1944

G.55, 2ª *Squadriglia*, 2° *Gruppo Caccia*, Cascina Vaga, May 1944

G.55, 3ª *Squadriglia*, 1° *Gruppo Caccia*, Reggio Emilia, June 1944

G.55, MM91086, torpedo-bomber conversion, Venegono, March 1945

CHAPTER EIGHT

The *Corpo Aereo Italiano* (C.A.I.)

Ground crew roll a FIAT CR.42 of the 85ª *Squadriglia*, 18° *Gruppo* CT back towards its camouflaged netting shelter at Ursel. (R.Gentilli)

A few months after the campaign against France in 1940, Mussolini decided to send an air corps to the English Channel sector to operate alongside the Luftwaffe. He believed that Britain was on its knees and he was convinced that for reasons of prestige and political opportunity, it would be beneficial for Italy to provide its own contribution and support to German forces operating against Great Britain in what would become known as the 'Battle of Britain'. This decision was, undoubtedly, a choice connected to his political ambitions, as in the summer of 1940, at the height of the Battle of Britain, and with the RAF apparently heading for defeat, he dreamt of a place at the victor's table alongside his German ally. It would be testimony to the phrase he had pronounced some months earlier: 'Nothing more than blood shed in common, and commonly supported sacrifices, can create a solid and lasting relationship between peoples when they are animated by absolute loyalty and by an identity of interests and ideals.'

Mussolini's decision was not motivated by genuine opportunity or military necessity. It was opposed by the commanders of the Regia Aeronautica who were conscious of a lack of preparedness and a state of technical inferiority on the part of the aircraft in service. Above all, they were fearful of opening up another front in the war which could well prove to be a move that would push the already stretched forces of the Regia Aeronautica to crisis point. Nevertheless, despite their objections, Mussolini would not listen to reason and as a consequence, on 10 September 1940 the *Corpo Aereo Italiano* (C.A.I.) was established, comprised of two *stormi* of FIAT BR.20M, considered to be the bomber aircraft most suitable for the new operational theatre, and a newly formed fighter *stormo* equipped with FIAT CR.42 and G.50 fighters. The *Corpo* would be based at several airfields in Belgium.

Generale Rino Corso Fougier was appointed to command the C.A.I. Having conducted a reconnaissance of the operational theatre, he

Colourful and dramatic wartime propaganda postcard 'celebrating' the Regia Aeronautica's participation in operations over England. (P. Monti)

GENERALE RINO CORSO FOUGIER

Generale Rino Corso Fougier (centre with coat over arm) was the commander of *Corpo Aereo Italiano* (CAI). At far right is *tenente colonnello* Riccardo Hellmuth Seidl, a member of *Generale* Fougier's staff. The German officers are believed to be, at left (in leather overcoat), *Oberst* (promoted to *Generalmajor*, 1 July 1940) Stefan Fröhlich, *Kommodore* of KG 76, and second from right, *Generalmajor* Hans Jeschonnek, Chief of the Luftwaffe General Staff. (P.Monti)

CONSIDERED the father of formation aerobatics in Italy, Rino Corso Fougier was born in Bastia in Corsica on 14 November 1894. In June 1916 he joined the *Battaglione Aviatori*, obtaining his military pilot's license on 4 February 1917. After initially serving with the 113th Reconnaissance Squadron, having switched to fighter units in August 1918 he was appointed commander of the 83ª *Squadriglia Caccia* based at Poianella. At the end of the war, in April 1919, he served with the 87ª *Squadrigli 'Serenissima'* before being assigned, after the establishment of the Air Force in 1923, to a position on the General Staff of the 2ª Z.A.T.. Promoted *tenente colonnello* in July 1927, he was appointed commander of the 1° *Stormo Caccia* at Campoformido on 1 June 1928, a command he held until 1 June 1933 when he assumed command of the 3ª *Brigata Aerea*. Assigned to the Government of Tripolitania, from July 1935 to December 1937, he commanded the Regia Aeronautica in Libya.

After being promoted to generale *di Divisione Aerea*, he held command positions in the wars in Ethiopia and Italian East Africa, as well as participation in the Spanish Civil War. He became inspector of schools in 1937 and, after being promoted to generale *di Squadra Aerea* on 14 April 1939, he assumed command of the 3ª *Squadra Aerea* on 1 September 1939. Between September 1940 and January 1941, he was in command of the *Corpo Aereo Italiano* in Belgium, while from 15 November 1941, he held the position of Undersecretary of State for the Regia Aeronautica and then *Capo di Stato Maggiore* on 28 October 1942, ending his long and honoured military career after the armistice of 1943. He died on 24 April 1963.

(*Ricognizione Strategica Terrestre* – land-based strategic reconnaissance).

In total, the overall strength of the entire contingent was in excess of 4,500 personnel, with the logistics and technical material transported to the theatre in 1,000 railway wagons between 11 and 24 September 1940. The *Stato Maggiore* headquarters of the C.A.I. was installed in a villa at Espinette, near Brussels.

Together with the fighters and bombers, a certain number of Caproni Ca. 133 transports and Caproni Ca. 164 two-seat liaison aircraft were also sent, as well as a militarised Junkers Ju 52/3m made available by the civil airline, Ala Littoria, for the commanders of the C.A.I. to enable direct communications between Italy and Belgium.

For the short-range movements of *Generale* Fougier, the Germans made a Fieseler *Storch* available which, thanks to its short take-off and landing capability, could operate from the grass directly outside the C.A.I.'s headquarters at Espinette.

Given the short endurance of the Italian aircraft, the decision to operate from poorly suited airfields in Belgium was derived from the fact that almost all the airfields located in France, close to the English Channel, were occupied by the Luftwaffe. The position of the Italian units was consequently further away from England and, in reality, this restricted the potential target area for bombing raids to a sector south of the Thames, limited to the north by the 53rd parallel north, and to the west, by the meridian of longitude 1° west of Greenwich.

Again, the Italian fighters did not possess sufficient endurance to undertake operations similar to those flown by the Germans, who could count on spending around half an hour over British territory, including combat. It was estimated that the CR.42s and G.50s would be able to stay for a maximum of ten minutes over eastern Kent or south-east Sussex, and that prolonged combat would risk impeding return to their point of departure. As a consequence, the fighters would be principally reserved for alert duties in the defence of Belgium and the southern part of the Netherlands, as well as defensive patrols over convoys and for the escort of the BR.20s.

returned to Italy and proposed that Italian participation should be limited to the despatch of personnel alone, as the Germans would be able to provide aircraft better adapted to operations over the Channel Front than those available in Italy. This sensible suggestion also fell on deaf ears, and so in mid-September 1940, *Superaereo* assigned fighters and bombers to the units of the Italian contingent. The fighter force was united under the command of the 56° *Stormo* CT formed by the 18° *Gruppo* of the former 3° *Stormo*, with fifty CR.42 biplanes and the 20° *Gruppo* of the 51° *Stormo* equipped with the FIAT G.50.

The bomber force was formed from the FIAT BR.20M of the 13° and 43° *Stormo* BT and the CANT Z 1007s of the 172a *Squadriglia* RST

The mottle-camouflaged Caproni Ca.133 assigned for transport duties to the 95ª *Squadriglia*. (R.Gentilli)

One of the five Cant Z.1007bis of the 172ª *Squadriglia Ricognizione Strategica Terrestre* photographed at Chievres airport in Belgium in the winter of 1940/41. (F.Ballista)

A BR.20M of the 5ª *Squadriglia 'La maledetta'* of 43° *Gruppo* BT, 13° *Stormo Bombardamento Terrestre* while taxiing at Melsbroek airfield in November 1940.

The Fieseler Fi 156 Storch, TH+AB, donated to *generale* Fougier by *Generalfeldmarschall* Albert Kesselring, commander of *Luftflotte* 2. After the CAI returned to Italy, the Fieseler accompanied the *Corpo* and received the Italian code I-THAB.

FIAT FIGHTERS

The insignia of the 18° *Gruppo* CT. (P. Monti)

Left: and above: The CR.42s of the 18° *Gruppo* CT photographed after their departure from Torino Caselle while on a stopover at Darmstadt in Germany during the unit's transfer from Italy to Belgium. (AM)

To ensure the operational readiness of the Italian units, logistics aspects were assigned to the headquarters of the Luftwaffe's *Luftflotte* 2 which would provide installations and equipment, while the Italians would be responsible for their units' operational management. German efficiency proved to be remarkable, and the Italian personnel discovered airfield infrastructure to be of the highest level, including wooden hangars in which to house their aircraft and dispersals with hard standings that were protected by blast walls and hidden by camouflage netting. The only negative aspect of the Belgian airfields, with the exception of Melsbroek, was that they did not possess cement or asphalt runways, limiting operations on the ground especially in regard of the imminent winter season.

The C.A.I. arrives in Belgium

The transfer of the two bomber *Stormi*, which departed Italy on 27 September 1940, proved to be decidedly difficult and in some respects it was traumatic. Awful weather conditions en route together with some technical issues, coupled with

Right: Pages from the logbook of *maresciallo* Guido Fibbia of the 95ª *Squadriglia*. The pages show the date of the stopovers made by the CR.42s during the journey from Italy to Belgium. (F.Ballista)

the nature of the route, forced a number of BR.20Ms to make emergency landings at a variety of airfields in central Europe.

Despite a transfer planned to include multiple stops, the fighters also suffered during a journey that was somewhat complicated due to continual flight cancellations arising from the adverse weather, and because of several accidents. The CR.42s of the 18° *Gruppo* were only able to depart on 6 October because of the weather, with the engineers supporting the fighters during the trip following in three Ca 133s assigned to the *Gruppo*, while the remainder travelled by train. The first leg took the biplanes to Munich, but even here they were forced to stop over for some days due to the persistent poor weather conditions, resuming their flight only on 18 October when the CR.42s landed in Brussels. Finally, on 9 October the Italian biplanes made the short flight to Ursel airfield, their final destination.

The G.50s of the 20° *Gruppo*, however, left Treviso airfield on 22 September, followed by six Ca 133s. They arrived at their destination of Maldegen airfield only on 18 October 1940, after a trip which was heavily affected by weather along the route.

Ciampino Sud airfield. The FIAT G.50s of the 20° *Gruppo* are seen in front of the hangar prior to their transfer to Belgium. In the foreground is the personal aircraft of *maggiore* Mario Bonzano, commander of the *Gruppo*, identifiable by the unit number and commander's pennant applied to the fuselage. (R.Gentilli)

Left: The G.50s of 20° *Gruppo* CT. After arrival at Maldegem, a large, white, diagonal band was applied to the fuselage of *maggiore* Bonzano's aircraft. (AM)

Below and bottom: The G.50s of the 20° *Gruppo* photographed in Germany during the transfer flight to Belgium. (AM)

Order of Battle – *Corpo Aereo Italiano* (C.A.I.)
October 1940

C.A.I. HQ, Espinette, Brussels
Generale S.A. Rino Corso Fougier

56° *Stormo Caccia Terrestre*, Maldegem
Colonnello Umberto Chiesa

18° *Gruppo Caccia Terrestre* (83ª, 85ª and 95ª *Squadriglia* with 50 FIAT CR.42, combat-ready at Ursel under *Maggiore* Ferruccio Vosilla

20° *Gruppo Caccia Terrestre* (351ª, 352ª and 353ª *Squadriglia* with 42 FIAT G.50, combat-ready at Maldegem under *Maggiore* Mario Bonzano

15ª *Brigata Aerea da bombardamento*, Beloil near Chievres
Generale B.A. Ruggero Bonomi

13° *Stormo Bombardamento Terrestre*
with 31 FIAT BR 20M at Melsbroek under *Colonnello* Carlo De Capoa

11° *Gruppo Bombardamento Terrestre* (1ª and 4ª *Squadriglia*) under *Maggiore* Giuseppe Aini
43° *Gruppo Bombardamento Terrestre* (3ª and 5ª *Squadriglia*) under *Tenente Colonnello* Giulio Monteleone

43° *Stormo Bombardamento Terrestre*
with 30 FIAT BR 20M at Chievres under *Colonnello* Luigi Questa

98° *Gruppo Bombardamento Terrestre* (240ª and 241ª *Squadriglia*) under *Maggiore* Mario Tenti
99° *Gruppo Bombardamento Terrestre* (242ª and 243ª *Squadriglia*) under *Tenente Colonnello* Giovan Battista Ciccu

172ª *Squadriglia* R.S.T. (*Ricognizione Strategica Terrestre*) with 5 Cant Z 1007bis at Chievres under *Tenente Colonnello* Carlo Perrelli Cippo

interaction with Luftwaffe pilots. It should be stressed that the German pilots were particularly supportive, providing detailed aeronautical charts and vital information on the tactics used by the RAF. They also distributed life jackets and more appropriate flying clothing to the Italian air crews in further evidence of the Regia Aeronautica's amateur organisation. Thanks also to German assistance, all the CR.42s were fitted with a 25-kg armoured plate which was mounted on the back of the seat in order to protect the pilot. The supplementary fuel tank, installed under the seat to facilitate the transfer from Italy, was removed as it was considered to be potentially dangerous in combat.

Another critical factor was the minimal training provided for the theatre of operations, as the Italians were not used to flying on instruments, an ability that was indispensable in meteorological conditions that were very different from those typically encountered in the Mediterranean. In fact, over the Channel, the autumn weather conditions were extremely variable, with frequent showers alternating with fog and low cloud. Added to all this was the constant risk from ice formation in flight, as the Italian aircraft were not fitted with anti-icing systems on their wings or windscreens. Despite an attempt to adopt some remedies, particularly for the bombers, the only solution to the icing problem was to reduce altitude! The ice also represented a danger for the various external instrument sensors, and it is likely that some of the accidents were caused by the formation of ice in instrument probes and pitot tubes. Efforts to provide a remedy through modifications to heating systems and the replacement of Italian pitots with German alternatives did not have a major effect. The seasonal meteorological conditions also created significant problems for ground operations

Continues on page 214

Summing up, some three weeks had been necessary to complete the deployment from Italy, at the end of which, on 19 October 1940, the total loss of some four BR. 20s and two G.50s had been recorded, with three crewmen fatally injured, one badly injured, and damage to a third G.50.

On arrival the Italian airmen were amazed to discover the perfect form of camouflage adopted by the Germans to hide their airfields, and that their fighters could be housed in hangars camouflaged as farmhouses or hidden while on dispersal aprons. Nevertheless, even on their first familiarisation flights the Italian aircraft began to demonstrate their deficiencies, the fighters in particular, as their open cockpits meant that their pilots suffered terribly from the cold. Moreover, the fighters did not possess adequate instrumentation for navigation in an environment that was very different from the sunny blue skies of the Mediterranean.

The lack of radio transmitter/receivers in most aircraft, with the mediocre ARC-1 equipment usually fitted to just those machines on alert, or used by *Gruppo* or *Squadriglia* commanders, further limited coordination between the fighters and between fighters and bombers, as well as

A BR.20M parked in a sandbag revetment under camouflaged netting. Each parking area included an ammunition depot. The Genio Aeronautico also provided for the construction of wooden barracks for the personnel attending to airfield services and also large fuel depots, consisting of underground tanks from which fuel could be dispensed directly to the aircraft. (AM)

A BR.20M with its lower and side surfaces covered with black, washable paint for night operations. The first ever CAI night action over England was that carried out by sixteen BR.20Ms over Harwich harbour. (AM)

Below: A FIAT CR.42 of the 18° Gruppo CT being refuelled at Ursel before a mission. The ground technician uses the typical Italian-built 'Emanuel pump' that survived in service within the Aeronautica Militare until the early 1950s. (AM)

A camouflaged hangar disguised as a farmhouse at Ursel airfield. (AM)

Right: The dispersal areas at Ursel were paved with wood to facilitate the movement of the aircraft in bad weather when the ground was soft and/or muddy. (AM)

On a grey autumn day, a mechanic of the 83ª *Squadriglia* conducts a pre-flight inspection of the engine of a CR.42. (AM)

Right: A last-minute mass briefing for the CR.42 pilots of 18° *Gruppo* CT tasked with a bomber escort mission over Great Britain. (R.Gentilli)

This photograph shows clearly the insignia of the 18° *Gruppo* CT painted on one of the unit's CR.42, MM5666. At left is *sergente* Felice Longhi, while the other pilot appears to be *sottotenente* Bordoni.

A CR.42, 85-13 of the 85ª *Squadriglia* in flight over the flat Belgian countryside.

A line of armourers feed a belt of 12.7 mm rounds into the SAFAT machine gun ammunition bay of an 18° *Gruppo* CR.42. Note the pilot's parachute harness resting on the port wing rear strut.

The CR.42 of the CAI had brown upper surfaces with green mottles and light blue-grey lower surfaces. Upon their arrival in Belgium, the three squadrons of the 18° *Gruppo* CT were also distinguished by the colours of their propeller spinners: red for the 83ª *Squadriglia*, green for the 85ª and white for the 95ª.

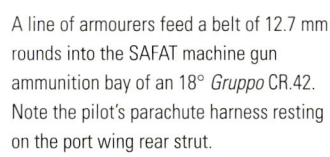

CR.42s of the 85ª *Squadriglia* at Ursel airfield in Belgium flank one of the Fokker G.Is captured when the Germans occupied The Netherlands. The aircraft was later used by the Luftwaffe as a trainer. The CR.42, MM6976, 85-16 at right is the aircraft destroyed in an emergency landing close to Coulton railway station, near Lowestoft in Suffolk on 11 November 1940. The pilot *sergente* Antonio Lazzari was unhurt. See pages 272-273. (R.Gentilli).

Far right: Humorous drawing of Winston Churchill painted on the walls of the 18° *Gruppo* pilot's accommodation at Ursel. (R.Gentilli)

Pilots of the 18° *Gruppo* CT relaxing on the snow-covered field at Ursel in the winter of 1940/41.

CR.42, 85-12, of the 85ª *Squadriglia*, piloted by *sergente* Cavallar, was damaged during a crash-landing after a training sortie from Ursel. (R.Gentilli)

as the frequent and heavy rains transformed airfields into quagmires, while the low temperatures created problems with heating aircraft engines. To overcome this issue the Germans provided the engineers with special stoves to warm engines and associated liquids prior to take-off.

Another important aspect was the change in the military situation in autumn 1940 when compared to that which had inspired the decision to despatch the C.A.I. to Belgium. The planned invasion of England (Operation *Seelöwe*) had recently been cancelled and the Luftwaffe's plan to destroy the RAF and British military infrastructure had, to all intents and purposes, failed. The RAF, moreover, had managed to emerge from its critical moment, and its pilots were more than ever combative and motivated.

The C.A.I. goes into action

Despite the operational environment being so different to what had been envisaged in the summer, and despite the unfavourable weather conditions, over the night of 24 October 1940 seventeen BR.20Ms conducted their first bombing mission, attacking the port installations of Harwich and Felixstowe. Twelve aircraft from the 13° *Stormo* and four from the 43° *Stormo* had been assigned for the mission, but it commenced in the worst of ways. BR.20M MM21928, piloted by the commander of the 5ª *Squadriglia*, *capitano* Pagani, suffered an engine failure and crashed shortly after take-off from Melsbroek with the loss of the entire crew. Another two aircraft were subsequently forced to return to base due to a variety of faults. The remaining bombers did, however, manage to reach their objective and dropped their loads of 100-kg bombs despite the intense anti-aircraft fire which damaged one aircraft. The return of the formation was hampered by poor weather conditions which caused radio failures, resulting in two BR.20Ms, MM21895 and MM22601, diverting from their route to such an extent that their crews had no alternative but to take to their parachutes and leave their aircraft to their destiny. Another BR.20M was forced to land at Lille airfield having become lost and reaching the limit of its endurance. After this first night mission and its disappointing outcome given that, so it seemed, the damage caused was minimal, it was decided to evaluate the use of the bombers on daylight sorties.

Wartime propaganda postcard.
(P. Monti)

A view of Melsbroek airfield, home base of the Italian BR.20M fleet. The aircraft are parked in the open air under camouflage netting. (R. Gentilli)

A formation of BR.20Ms during a daylight bombing mission over Harwich.

A detail photograph of BR.20M, MM22253, '3-8' of the 3ª *Squadriglia*, the fuselage of which was painted with its mission markings. These represented four missions over Harwich, two over Ipswich and one over Great Yarmouth. (R. Gentilli)

The following morning, some CR.42s of the 18° *Gruppo* performed their first operational mission, flying a patrol between the northern Belgian cities and the French coastline as far as Boulogne. On their return, CR.42 MM5664, flown by *sergente* Angelo Bonelli, overturned on landing due to the soft ground of the landing strip. Having been engaged in further patrol missions along the Belgian coast, on the evening of 27 October the Italian fighters were tasked with participating in their first combat sortie over England. Taking off at dusk in less than optimal weather conditions, the 38 CR.42s of the three *Squadriglie* of the 18° *Gruppo*, led by *maggiore* Vosilla, never managed to rendezvous with the BR 20s they were planning to escort, and the bombers diverted back to base because of a lack of fighter cover. The fighters, however, continued their mission and flew above the designated target, subsequently returning to Ursel. On landing, the CR.42 piloted by *capitano* Giulio Anelli of the 85ª *Squadriglia* was damaged in an accident caused by the appalling condition of the runway which was illuminated by searchlights. Thirty-six G.50s of the 20° *Gruppo* led by *maggiore* Bonzano, airborne from Maldegem, failed again to locate the bombers, and returned to their base after little under an hour in the air. The G.50 flown by *tenente* Vittorio Merlo was damaged on landing due to the poor nocturnal visibility.

On 29 October however, 39 CR.42s of the 18° *Gruppo*, 13 aircraft from each *Squadriglia*, together with 34 G.50s of the 20° *Gruppo*, of which 12 were drawn from the 351ª and the remainder from the other two *Squadriglie*, were assigned the task of protecting 15 BR.20s sent to attack targets near the town of Ramsgate. This mission went well, and the Italian fighters, having joined up with the bombers above the city of Bruges, managed to assure air cover for the attack formation, which was molested only by anti-aircraft fire that damaged some of the bombers. Of note is the fact than on the same day another 24 G.50s, divided into flights of four aircraft, provided air cover for an important Wehrmacht troop-landing exercise in the area between Dunkerque and Gravelines.

On 1 November, 36 CR.42s and a similar number of G.50s were sent to conduct several free fighter sweeps close to the British coastline, returning at dusk without making contact with any British aircraft.

On the morning of 5 November, two British fighters flew over the Ghent area, pursued in vain by three G.50s which, having scrambled, never managed to intercept. On the same day, eight aircraft from the 13° *Stormo* bombed Ipswich and Harwich at night, dropping 32 100-kg and 12 250-kg bombs, returning to their base without any

FIAT FIGHTERS

Extract from the logbook of *maresciallo* Guido Fibbia of the 95ª *Squadriglia*. Note the mission report of 29 October 1940 (written in red) when Fibbia carried out a bomber escort mission over Ramsgate and had a dogfight with a Spitfire, firing 350 rounds of 12.7 mm machine gun ammunition. He had another encounter with a Spitfire on 11 November on a mission to Harwich. Other missions took him to Dover and Folkestone. (F.Ballista)

Curious German personnel examine a FIAT G.50 of the 352ª *Squadriglia* as it undergoes maintenance under camouflage nets. (E.Leproni)

particular problems despite the anti-aircraft artillery reaction.

Over the following days, the weather conditions impeded the operations of the Italian fighter force, at least until 8 November, when 22 G.50s, flying an offensive mission over southern England, spotted RAF fighters but were not able to engage them. During the encounter, a pair of British fighters manoeuvred into a position from where they could attack some of the Italians but desisted from their plan when they spotted that other G.50s had adopted a more favourable position. In the course of a coastal patrol between Ostend and the Hook of Holland, some CR.42s of the 85ª *Squadriglia* spotted a British reconnaissance twin, and set off in pursuit, but once again they were unable to catch it.

On 9 November some 30 CR.42s and G.50s took off to escort a bombing raid, but when the biplanes had been in the air for an hour, over the English Channel they were ordered to return to Ursel as the bombers had been forced to interrupt their mission due to bad weather. The following day some four biplane sections from the 18° *Gruppo* carried out defensive patrols along the Belgian coast, and two CR.42s took off in response to an alert in order to intercept an aircraft which, however, was later identified as German.

'Operation Cinzano'[1]

On 11 November 1940, the C.A.I. recorded one of its most negative days. A complex mission

This photograph, taken at Maldegem during maintenance work on FIAT G.50s of the 20° *Gruppo* CT, clearly shows the deterioration of the paint applied to the fighters which was due to the very different environmental conditions in north-west Europe compared to the climate of the Mediterranean.

had been organised, termed by the Italians as 'Operation Cinzano' It would be a joint operation with the Luftwaffe which had as its objective the city of London and a departing naval convoy. The mission, which the Italians codenamed 'Operation Cinzano', was planned to involve the use of ten aircraft from the 43° *Stormo* and five CANT Z.1007Bis. These aircraft were to be escorted by 40 CR.42s and 24 G.50s and along with the bombers, they would be tasked with conducting a daylight raid on Harwich. The plan required a diversionary attack to be flown by the CANT Z.1007 Bis, under the protection of the G.50s, on objectives in southern England with the intention of diverting the British defenders away from the German aircraft and BR 20Ms, which

A G.50 belonging to 20° *Gruppo* CT, well camouflaged between moveable pine trees and nets at Maldegem. (E.Leproni)

---

[1] 'Operation Cinzano' was named after a popular Italian aromatised, fortified wine used as an aperitif or cocktail ingredient.

Two FIAT G.50s of the 352ª *Squadriglia* in front of the camouflaged hangar at Maldegem. (E.Leproni)

Wartime propaganda postcard. (P. Monti)

Humorous drawings painted on the walls of the 18° *Gruppo* pilot's accommodation at Ursel.

would head towards Harwich. The meteorological forecast was fair, and the operational plan was conceived and evaluated jointly by German and Italian commanders, with timings that were tight and well calculated. For the Italians, the rendezvous point was selected as above the coastal city of Ostend, where the fighter formations would subsequently divide and provide separate escorts for the CANT Z.1007Bis and BR.20M bombers. Unfortunately, due to the arrival of an intense blanket of cloud, the G.50s never managed to arrive at the rendezvous, forcing the CANT Z.1007Bis to conduct their mission without an escort. This left the CR.42 biplanes flying at different altitudes having, not without difficulty, established contact with the bomber formation, and having the task of providing the sole protection for the BR.20M formation. Thus, it was with only the CR.42 escort that the Italian bombers arrived at the English coast with the defences already alerted by preceding air combat. As they approached Harwich, the Italian formation was soon attacked by British fighters. The CR.42s led by *maggiore* Vosilla promptly intervened to defend the BR.20Ms, and despite being inferior to the British Hurricanes, they engaged in a bitter duel. Again, on this occasion the RAF pilots praised the performance of the Italian airmen, as evidenced by Lt. Wells of 41 Squadron:

> *'I began to follow two CR.42s flying in close formation, but shortly after they turned very tightly, and I was left speechless. As they rolled out of the turn they even managed to get on the tail of my aircraft, opening fire…'*

It was later confirmed, however, that three Italian CR.42s had been brought down by the British fighters. Two were certainly shot down, that flown by *sergente* Enzo Panichi of the 83ª *Squadriglia* (MM6978), which disappeared over the English Channel, and that of *sergente maggiore* Antonio Lazzari of the 85ª *Squadriglia* (85-16, MM6976), which was forced to make an emergency landing by Corton railway station to the north of Lowestoft in Suffolk. The aircraft was effectively destroyed and the pilot captured.

A third CR.42 (95-13, MM5701), piloted by *sergente* Pietro Salvatori of the 95ª *Squadriglia*, made an emergency landing near Orford Ness in Suffolk, concluding its landing run with its nose buried in the sand.[2] The account of the commander of 603 Squadron, George Denholm, is particularly revealing:

> *'The Italian biplanes seemed almost to be toy aeroplanes, painted in bright colours to the point that it seemed a pity to shoot down such pretty aircraft. However, I could not do anything else, and having seen six (!) go down, I have to say that I had watched a great spectacle. I should nevertheless report that the Italian pilots fought against us in a way that I have never seen the Germans do.'*[3]

The bomber force also suffered the loss of two BR.20Ms (242-3, MM22267 and 242-10, MM22260), which were shot down over the sea with the loss of four of the five crew members, while a third aircraft (243-2, MM22621), badly damaged, had to make a forced landing in England near Bromeswell in Suffolk. Of the initial formation of ten bombers, only three managed to return to base, as another four had to make emergency landings in the Belgian countryside. Moreover, following a navigational error caused by strong gusts of wind, the Italian bombers dropped their bombs well outside the target area. The troubles continued until their return when, due to bad weather and fuel shortage, almost half the aircraft were forced into making emergency landings at various locations in France and Belgium. They suffered significant damage and at least two aircraft were destroyed. One of them was CR.42 MM5576, piloted by *sergente* Mario Sandini, who was forced to land near a parade

---

[2] The aircraft is on display today at the RAF Museum at Hendon.

[3] *The Falco and Regia Aeronautica in the Battle of Britain*, H. Gustavsson.

FIAT CR.42, 95-13, MM5701 – RAF serial BT474

The precise reason for the emergency landing of *sergente* Petro Salvatori's CR.42 near the beach at Orford Ness in Suffolk following the aerial battle of 11 November 1940, has never really been clarified. However, it is likely that following a dogfight, Salvatori became disorientated and, short of fuel, elected to land on the beach.

After being recovered, the aircraft was transferred to RAF Martlesham Heath for repair, and resumed flying on 27 November at the RAE Farnborough wearing British roundels and bearing RAF serial BT474. Subsequently, the aircraft was transferred to the AFDU (Air Fighting Development Unit) at Duxford on 28 April 1941 which used it for evaluation flights until 1943 when it was placed into storage as a potential museum exhibit. After being subjected to some degree of restoration at Biggin Hill in the mid-1960s, which saw it returned to colours resembling the original scheme, it remained in the RAF Museum Store at RAF St. Athan until 1979, when it was placed on display in the RAF Museum at Hendon in north London.

The FIAT CR.42, MM5701, 95-13, of *sergente* Salvatori that was forced to land on the shingle beach at Orford Ness, Suffolk, following a possible engine overheating.

Bottom right: At the time of writing, *sergente* Salvatori's biplane is at the RAF Museum at Hendon in north London.

Below: The captured CR.42 with RAF serial BT474 as used when the aircraft was operated by the Air Fighting Development Unit at Duxford. This is the aircraft flown by Lt. Eric 'Winkle' Brown.

ground in Amsterdam, while the other destroyed aircraft was CR.42 95-6, MM5662 of *tenente* Pasquale Tacchini, which crashed near the town of Cassel, some 20 km from Dunkerque.

From this unfortunate mission, only the Cant Z.1007bis returned to base without issues, while the Fiat G 50s did not participate in the operation, as they were forced to return to their own base at Maldegen because of fuel shortage following their delayed arrival at the rendezvous point and bad weather. The same problems also affected some of the Bf 109 Es of the Luftwaffe which had been scheduled to provide high-altitude top cover escort.

The final balance of 'Operation Cinzano' was negative for the C.A.I.. The 43° *Stormo* BT, after suffering aircraft lost and damaged, found itself with just 17 bombers available out of its pre-mission fleet of 22, while the 18° *Gruppo* paid a much heavier price, dwindling from 46 serviceable fighters to just 33 aircraft. In respect of claims, at the conclusion of the combat, which lasted for more than fifteen minutes, the Italian fighter pilots claimed nine British fighters shot down and another four probable kills. However, RAF Operational Record Books report no losses of aircraft on that day, and merely damage to two Hurricanes, both of which managed to return to base.

A vivid testimony of the dogfights is provided in two mission reports prepared, respectively, by *tenente* Cesare Giuntella and *sottotenente* Giuseppe Re of the 85ª *Squadriglia*:

'*Close to the objective, as the bomber formation assigned to us to escort had stretched out, we detached from the rest of the formation to maintain direct escort over a group of six BR.20s. Towards 15.05 capitano Anelli, who commanded the squadriglia, spotted that the bomber formation to our left was under attack by enemy aircraft, and turned rapidly towards them, followed by his wingman, myself and my wingman, and a pair that followed. A fight commenced with the enemy aircraft, in which I lost contact with the formation leader. Shortly after I noticed a Spitfire which, followed by a CR.42, was looking to avoid its fire by turning left. Finding the Spitfire in front of my guns, I opened fire, tightening the turn. The enemy aircraft stayed under the fire of my guns for around ten seconds, after which it dived away quickly to the right. In the subsequent turn, it entered a spin and disappeared towards the sea. Continuing the combat, I was able to machine-gun another Spitfire, which was turning and trying to reach my altitude. In the following manoeuvre the Spitfire, in a long dive, disappeared from my sight. Subsequently, I noticed that to my right, our aircraft and enemy aircraft, the latter in the majority, were engaged in combat. Entering the battle, I performed some dives and climbs but was never able to fire a shot. At around 15.15, finding myself isolated at an altitude of 3,000 metres, I turned onto my return course of 150° with 100 litres of fuel remaining. During the dogfight I had seen a vast fire with a thick plume of smoke. There were flames of around eight burning aircraft. A convoy of seven ships was following the coast, heading south-west. The dogfight had lasted eight minutes. I landed at Ursel at 15.45. During one engagement my wingman lost contact with me in the tight combat manoeuvring. Rounds fired – 130 7.7 mm calibre.*'

The mission report submitted by *tenente* Giuntella corresponds with that submitted by *sottotenente* Re:

'*Wingman in a flight led by tenente Giuntella, during a mission to escort our bombers, I arrived over the east coast of England at 14.40, where the second bomber formation was attacked by British fighters. My flight leader quickly turned left and I, despite my engine at full power, could not manage to follow him, and entering cloud I lost sight of him. Once back in the clear, I was forced to engage in combat with a Spitfire which was close by me. The aircraft I had attacked escaped shortly afterwards, so I attempted to rejoin my companions, but was forced to desist from the attempt as I was attacked from above by three enemy fighters of the same type as the previous one. During the dogfight I managed to machine-gun two of these aircraft many times, while the third remained above them as a look-out. During this engagement, I saw a British fighter plunge almost vertically downwards from above, probably a Hurricane. Remaining alone with two Spitfires, during a very tight turn, I fell into a spin and I recovered to a normal attitude just beneath a British fighter that was crossing, but not attacking; I joined him in an almost head-to-head fight until the enemy aircraft, after one last, furious burst, did not turn back towards me and departed the area, hiding in the clouds below. It was at that moment that I thought it best to check my fuel level and I realised the need to turn back home. I joined up with sergente maggiore Lazzari, who took the lead position ahead of me on my left. Immediately after getting myself into position as his wingman, I noticed that an enemy fighter was manoeuvring to attack our formation from above: I warned my flight leader with a burst of gunfire and, with me following, he turned to the left. During the dogfight that followed, all three of us flew into cloud, and on breaking out a few moments later, I found myself alone. I began the return leg at an altitude of 2,000 metres, having lost around 5,000 metres during the engagement. Eventually I spotted the ground in a gap in the clouds, and having run out of fuel, I glided down to land. I touched down near Denderleeuw at around 15.50, but once my wheels hit the soft ground, I rolled for a few metres and then turned over. My aircraft suffered damage to a propeller blade, its rudder, and minor damage to the right wing, which had already been holed during the battle. Also hit in combat was the left wing, holed in two places. Rounds fired: 115 7.7 mm calibre and 214 12.7 mm calibre.*'

Despite the unfavourable weather conditions, the personnel of the C.A.I. managed to complete other bombing raids on British targets, such as that conducted on 18 November 1940, when six BR.20Ms of the 43° *Stormo* once again attacked the port of Harwich, while on the night of 20/21 November 12 BR.20Ms of the 13° *Stormo* bombed the port of Ipswich. In this last mission, however, a BR.20M was lost in unknown circumstances, although it was suggested that it was due to the accretion of wing ice, a problem that had afflicted other aircraft in the formation that night. The fighter units were, however, engaged in defensive and patrol missions over the coasts of Belgium and the southern Netherlands, as well as offensive patrols over the channel and bomber escort missions.

Towards the end of November an order was issued to constitute a six-aircraft alert section at Vlissingen, with fighters drawn alternately from the 18° and 20° *Gruppo*; those from the latter unit quickly commenced their deployment, but a few days later a G.50 overturned on landing due to the excessively soft ground and was written off. On 19 November three CR.42s were added to the section, tasked with conducting night fighter operations.

All the operations performed from Vlissingen were overseen by the German regional *Luftgaukommando Holland* and the fighters allocated to that organisation did not participate in the defence of the zone assigned to the 56° *Stormo*, which was the area enclosed by the Belgian coast, the Belgium/Dutch border from the coast to the River Scheldt, and from this river as far as Ghent, and then a line joining Ghent to Ostend. The operational directives assigned to the *Sezione* at Vlissingen established that:

- Four aircraft of the *Sezione* should be ready to take off at any time of day within three minutes of receiving the order

- Two CR.42s should be ready to intervene against possible enemy raids from dawn to dusk, and taking off or landing at night wherever necessary.

During a night training and area familiarisation flight, however, the two pilots who had taken off were unable to see each other due to the darkness, and had to land individually at first light. As a consequence, it was decided that if an alarm was raised, only one fighter would be scrambled.

On 21 November two CR.42s, airborne from Vlissingen on a patrol, spotted a Bristol Blenheim which was flying in cloud near Walcheren Island. The two Italian pilots, *tenente* Specker and *maresciallo* Giuseppe Ruzzin, tried in vain to follow the aircraft, as described in the official post-mission report:

Maresciallo Giuseppe Ruzzin of the 85ª *Squadriglia* photographed in the cockpit of CR.42 '85-09' shortly before a mission. (R.Gentilli)

'*After five minutes of unfruitful patrolling, I resumed my circuit of the island, and after three-quarters of the circuit, the radio announced a report of a British aircraft south-west of Vlissingen. Together with maresciallo Ruzzin, I set off to hunt it down and spotted it east of Walcheren island at an altitude of around 300 metres, heading south to north around 1,000 metres away from me. The visibility was already poor, and reduced to less than 100 metres, forcing me to fly at wave-top height until the point when I saw the enemy disappear into the clouds. The compass had gone mad, so I reached the land with the aid of the waves, following their direction. I saw an airfield, which I then realised was a dummy airfield. I had no more than 60 litres of fuel left, and I did not recognise the area. I therefore elected to make a forced landing, which occurred without issue at 13.05, despite the sandy terrain, the strong wind, and the almost zero visibility. The nearest town was Ouddorp. I requested the German Ortskommandantur for 200 litres of benzene to return to base.*'

The aircraft of the 56° *Stormo* that remained at their respective bases of Ursel and Maldegem were, to the contrary, required to undertake three patrols of two to four aircraft each in the zone between Ostend and Bruges on a daily basis, one at first light, one around midday, and the last towards the end of the day, weather permitting. Additionally, they provided a local alert service, with two or one pairs respectively, on alternate days between the two bases.

A second clash with the RAF

The second and final clash with British fighters occurred on 23 November, when 24 G.50s departed at 12:50 to conduct an escort patrol alongside 29 CR.42s of the 18° *Gruppo* and a *Staffel* of Luftwaffe Bf 109 Es on behalf of a German bomber mission transiting the skies above the Channel between Dunkirk and south-eastern England. In the sky above Dungeness the G.50 pilots spotted four Hurricanes flying at a lower altitude, and without hesitation, *maggiore* Bonzano, the formation leader, manoeuvred to attack the British fighters. However, the Hurricanes declined to engage and quickly hid inside a bank of cloud. In the course of the attempted attack, the two *Gruppi* became separated and lost visual contact with each other. On regaining altitude, Bonzano recovered the G.50 formation at Calais and subsequently returned to Maldegen short of fuel. During the landings, the G.50 piloted by *sergente* Otello Bonelli was badly damaged while attempting a dead stick landing because of fuel exhaustion.

Now isolated south-east of Folkestone, the CR.42s entered combat with a dozen Spitfires of 603 Squadron, which were later joined by more from 74 Squadron. Benefitting from their greater approach altitude, they launched an attack on the Italian biplanes. The Italians, unintimidated, accepted the challenge, and fought hard against the British, trying to exploit to the maximum the handling qualities of the CR.42 to counter the more powerful and potent RAF fighters. The engagement, with all the participants at the limits of their endurance, was concluded in just a few minutes. Despite the courage demonstrated, once again on this occasion, the technical superiority of the British fighters overcame the efforts of the Italian biplane pilots. Caught by the attack from above, CR.42s MM5694 and MM5663, flown respectively by *tenente* Guido Mazza of the 83ª *Squadriglia* and *sergente maggiore* Giacomo Grillo of the 95ª *Squadriglia*, were hit and crashed into the English Channel, with neither pilot able to survive. Another three pilots, *maresciallo* Felice Sozzi, *sergente maggiore* Franco Campanile and *sergente* Pietro Melano (83-2, MM6974), despite being injured, managed to recover to dry land in France, while numerous other CR.42s returned to their base with various levels of damage.

At the end of this engagement the Italian pilots claimed at least five kills, but British documentation reveals that all the RAF aircraft returned to base, albeit that one Spitfire, P3789, piloted by Lt. Winskill of 603 Squadron, was seriously damaged by Italian machine gun fire, but still returned successfully.

In late November and early December bad weather prevented the execution of further operational missions apart from some patrol flights along the Continental coastline of the English Channel and some unsuccessful scrambles. One of the patrol missions saw 25 CR.42s depart on a fighter sweep on a route linking Calais, Margate, Eastchurch, Folkestone, and Calais. The appalling weather conditions encountered in the Eastchurch area forced the formation to return to base. The operation should also have included the participation of eight G.50s of the 20° *Gruppo*, but due to the poor weather, the two Italian formations never managed to link up. Another twenty G.50s, led by *maggiore* Bonzano, were engaged in a fruitless attempt to intercept a formation of Spitfires, but due to the enemy's height advantage they were unsuccessful. For their part, on 29 November, the bombers conducted another raid on Lowestoft, Harwich and Great Yarmouth. On their return, BR.20M MM21908 crashed into a house at Diegem while on approach, with the loss of all six members of the crew. Despite the fact that the campaign known as the Battle of Britain had concluded, even for the Italian contingent, the bombers vainly attempted some further missions, but these were hampered by the weather. However, the Italian crews did manage to complete some other flights prior to the end of the year, albeit without achieving any significant results.

On 30 November six CR.42s took off in the morning on a patrol mission. Surprised by unforecast fog, they attempted to return to the airfield and *tenente* Romolo Artina, flying CR.42 95-10, hit a hangar at Maldegem while attempting a landing. He was forced to divert to Knokke Le Zoute airfield where he managed to execute a perfect landing, minimising the damage to his aircraft. Twenty-five G.50s moved to the forward airfield at Gravelines on 6 December, as the closer departure point would offer more time over the target. However, poor weather conditions dogged their operation and the fighters returned to their base at Maldegem. The bad weather that continued until mid-December permitted only a few local patrol flights and on 14 December, a raid on the port facilities at Harwich by eight BR.20s, although results were limited given the difficulty in identifying the target area because of the clouds.

At the end of a series of patrol flights on 21 December, two CR.42s (MM5664, *sergente* Luigi Morellato, and MM5696, *sergente* Mario Lingua) were damaged following crash-landings caused by fuel shortage. On the following night, 22 December, six BR.20Ms again bombed the port area of Harwich. Once more, ice formation and

Armourers reload the two 12.7 mm Breda SAFAT machine guns that made up the armament of the FIAT G.50. Note the protective walkway strips laid over the surfaces of the inner wing.

Engine maintenance at Maldegem for a FIAT G.50 of the 352ª *Squadriglia* of 20° *Gruppo* CT under protective camouflage netting. Note the pilot's parachute and harness placed at readiness on the aircraft's port wing. (N-Malizia)

Metal lapel shield with the emblem of the 20° *Gruppo* CT. (P.Monti)

bad weather proved to be equally as dangerous an enemy as the anti-aircraft fire; a BR.20M became lost, and given the impossibility of making an emergency landing, the commander, *capitano* Machieraldo, ordered his crew to take to their parachutes. The final bombing raid performed by the BR.20Ms was conducted by four aircraft of the 13° *Stormo* on 2 January 1941, the target once again being the port of Harwich. Only two of the four bombers managed to reach the target and release their bombs, as the other two BR.20Ms had to return to base shortly after take-off due to technical problems.

Return to Italy

In an environment and a technical situation that was proving so difficult for the crews, the inevitable order arrived instructing the personnel and equipment of the C.A.I. to return to Italy. Following a first attack on the night of 19/20 December on Ursel airfield by a solitary Blenheim, on 21 December the order was received for the withdrawal of the 18° *Gruppo*, with the suspension of all activity from the following day prior to the transfer of the unit's CR.42s to North Africa. On 10 January, 29 CR.42s (a thirtieth aircraft having crashed on take-off), left Ursel airfield for Frankfurt airport, accompanied by seven Ca.133s and five Cant Z.1007bis of the 172ª *Squadriglia* R.S.T.. After pausing for a day, the aircraft departed for Italy in the early afternoon, but shortly after take-off, Cant Z.1007bis MM22148, piloted by *tenente* Samperisi, crashed into a wood a few hundred metres from the airport due to an engine problem, resulting in the death of an NCO and injuries to other members of the crew. At the conclusion of this tragic return trip, 18 CR.42s landed at Torino and 11 at Verona, while three Cant Z.1007bis' descended into Treviso, the final aircraft landing at Ronchi dei Legionari. Of the seven Ca.133 which landed at Frankfurt, five arrived in Italy the following day, one was forced to divert back to Ursel for urgent repairs, and the seventh was delayed by a mechanical fault, only arriving in Italy on 18 January.

At the end of this period of operations, the CR.42s of the 18° *Gruppo* had conducted 278 patrol missions, two scrambles, 93 attempted escort missions and 79 escort flights, achieving an overall total of 454 missions. Three aircraft were shot down in combat, two were forced to land in British territory due to engine failure, two more were destroyed and another seriously damaged in forced landings due to combat damage, resulting in injuries to their pilots. Furthermore seven CR.42s were badly damaged in forced landings after running out of fuel or encountering bad visibility (and also because of a cyclone that struck the area), ten suffered minor damage in combat, and another five suffered accidents because of the condition of the landing field or poor visibility. Three pilots were killed, three were injured in combat, three were injured in flying accidents, and two were taken prisoner.

For the 20° *Gruppo* – the operations of which, by the end of 1940, had amounted to 303 patrols missions, 26 scrambles, 34 escort missions and 26 attempted escorts, a total of 493 operational missions – its destiny was very different. Following an agreement made with the German commanders, the Italian Command decided to withdraw only a part of the personnel and aircraft of the *Gruppo*, leaving the 352ª and 353ª *Squadriglia* in Belgium to operate autonomously under the control of the Luftwaffe's II. *Fliegerkorps*. The agreements dictated that the G.50s would be utilised mainly for protective patrols and scrambles with the intention of intercepting enemy bombers during their incursions, and being tasked with guarding a limited stretch of coastline to the east of Walcheren Island and to the west of the city of Ostend. As such operations could be effected directly from the base at Maldegem, the alert section at Vlissingen was to be withdrawn to enable intensification of the protective patrols, which were to be performed from dawn to dusk.

In compliance with the accord made with the Germans, it was envisaged that the 20° *Gruppo* would receive a replacement for its G.50s in the shape of the Messerschmitt Bf 109 E, or even the F model, and in advance of this potential opportunity, from December the training activities of an initial group of Italian pilots commenced, conducted by personnel of the *Ergänzungsgruppe* of JG 51 at Cazaux in southern France, while the first of two such aircraft had been delivered to the Italian unit.

As part of the conversion syllabus, besides general familiarisation with the Bf 109 and its operations, flights at Cazaux involved some machine gun attacks against fixed targets. In parallel, training of the remaining mechanics and civilian staff of the technical section detached to Maldegem airfield would be conducted by the Erla and Daimler-Benz firms at Antwerp. When equipped with the new German fighter, it was intended that the 20° *Gruppo* would be controlled by JG 51, commanded by *Oberstleutnant* Werner Mölders, and would have the same duties as the German fighters – vigilance patrols between Boulogne and Calais in less than good weather conditions, and interdiction sorties along the French coast when the weather was favourable.

Italian pilots of the 20° *Gruppo* CT pose with Luftwaffe pilots, probably of the *Ergänzungsgruppe* JG 51, during the transition course to the Messerschmitt Bf 109 E at Cazaux.

Despite the efforts of the Italian pilots, now tasked with patrols in the Flemish skies still in their G.50s and aimed at confronting incursions of RAF bombers, they never managed to enter into contact with British aircraft.

On 5 February 1941, another unfortunate episode was recorded involving *sergente maggiore* Felice Pecchiari, who, while innocently flying G.50 MM5458, became the target of friendly fire. He was fired at in error, initially by a Bf 109 E and subsequently by German anti-aircraft fire. Fortunately, Pecchiari was able to return to base with his aircraft damaged. Not so lucky was *tenente* Mario Roncali who, on 13 February, after starting to chase an enemy aircraft flying at low level over Flanders, crashed in unknown circumstances in his G.50 (possibly MM5457), and lost his life. By the end of February, another three G.50s had been seriously damaged in a variety of landing accidents. These unfortunate events commenced on 17 February with *sergente maggiore* Bruno Baldacci, followed on the 21st by *sergente maggiore* Ersio Caponigro, and *tenente* Giuseppe Calamai on the 26th. The latter incident was the only one from which the aircraft emerged as repairable, but it also saw the pilot severely injured and requiring sixty days of recovery. The final accident to involve an Italian aircraft occurred on 3 April 1941, when the G.50 piloted by *sergente maggiore* Renato Meneghini crashed near Desvres in unknown circumstances.

At the end of March 1941 the 20° *Gruppo* was relocated to the airfield at Desvres with 22 G.50s, four Ca. 133s and two Ca.164s. This transfer was due to the distance from the airfield at Maldegen to the most important operational area over the English Channel, which often forced the Italian pilots to fly to the limits of their endurance and to divert to Luftwaffe airfields to refuel. On 4 April, *Generalfeldmarschall* Kesselring, commander of *Luftflotte* 2, visited the unit, but unfortunately he poured cold water on the expectations of the Italian pilots, for despite previous agreements made, the unit would no longer receive the promised Bf 109 E. Rather, the plan was to re-equip the unit with C.202s or Re. 2001s that Italian commanders had indicated would be sent to Belgium. Despite this, on 14 April the commanders of the 20° *Gruppo* received the order to return to Italy in expectation of a transfer to the Balkans.

On 16 April the remaining 22 G.50 and four Ca.133 departed for Italy via Frankfurt, taking with them the indispensable equipment necessary for operations in Greece. At the conclusion of their time in Greece, it was planned that the unit should return to the Channel, to Desvres, which would be held available. On 17 April the unit reached Neubiberg (near Munich), from where it should have continued on to Vienna and then onwards to Greece. However, at the German airfield, following the collapse of the Greek front, the unit received an order to relocate to Gorizia, and then to Roma Ciampino, where it would be reorganised and re-equipped with the new G.50bis prior to subsequently transferring to the North African theatre.

Incredibly, during the course of its operational activity in Belgium (over 660 missions flown), the pilots of the 20° *Gruppo* never had an opportunity to enter into combat with British aircraft, losing one fighter in an accident and damaging seven others. Then, in its few months of activity as a *Gruppo Autonomo* under the operational control of II. *Fliegerkorps*, following the return of the other C.A.I. units to Italy, the *Gruppo* conducted another 693 combat operations, again never confronting British opposition, but losing four aircraft in accidents, with the death of two pilots.

CHAPTER NINE

FIAT fighters to the training schools

Some CR.30B two-seaters were still operated in the early months of the war by the *Scuola Caccia* based at Castiglione del Lago. (M.Amatiello)

THE entry into service of monoplane fighters, the piloting of which required a different approach in comparison with that of 'easier' biplanes, coincided with a requirement to equip Italian military flying schools with more formative training aircraft that had technical characteristics as similar as possible to the performance of those on the front line.

The training syllabus

At the end of their theoretical studies, student pilots were trained for the award of their *brevetto di 1° period* (first-level licence), corresponding to the private pilot licence, flying for around ten hours, four of which were under dual control. The student had to be able to safely demonstrate the ability to land within a predefined field, to climb to 3,000 metres in a minimum time, and to perform a series of 'figure eights', always maintaining the same height. This period of training was conducted on aircraft such as the Caproni Ca.100, Avia FL.3 and IMAM Ro.41.

Having obtained his *brevetto*, the new pilot transferred to a *Scuola di 2° Periodo* (second-level school), where around 45 hours would be flown, of which at least twenty were on single-engine types with a minimum speed of at least 150 km/h, (Breda 25 or similar), twelve hours of which would be dual control and eight solo. At the end of this instructional period the student had to depart and land at four different airfields, climb to 5,000 metres and perform a series of turns and at least thirty minutes of level flight. After this, five hours of aerobatics were planned using aircraft with fighter-like characteristics, of which three would be dual control and two solo. Subsequently the cadet would transfer to a specialisation school to prepare to fly fighters or bombers.

If the student demonstrated an aptitude for fighters, he would be transferred to an advanced flying course on the CR.30 or CR.32, at the end of which the student would be capable of ably handling the biplane and to perform a repertoire of solo aerobatics. The schools that delivered these

FIAT FIGHTERS

courses did not have a rigid programme, and the number of flying hours involved varied as a function of the capabilities of the student. Subsequently, the cadet began to fly the CR.30 and CR.42, with solo and formation flying, and also exploring the methods of attacking enemy formations.

At this point the student was ready for the final phase of training which was undertaken initially with operational units, but subsequently with a unit's own *Gruppo Complementare*, where the new pilot perfected instrument flight training, night-flying, and formation flying.

FIAT fighters with the *Scuole Caccia* (Fighter Schools)

Meanwhile, at the start of 1940 the *Scuole di Volo di 2° Periodo* began to receive their first CR.42s, which were then followed by C.200 and G.50 monoplanes. As a two-seat version of the CR.42 had never materialised (although during the war it was planned to produce such a version), the flying schools continued to utilise the dual control CR.30DC, still considered to be formative, and reserved the single-seat CR.42s for the final phases of advanced training. The situation regarding training on monoplanes was different, and for this requirement more than 100 two-seat G.50Bs were built, these being assigned to the main *Scuole Caccia* (fighter schools), based at Gorizia Merna, Castiglione del Lago, Foligno, Rimini, and Campoformido during 1942.

One negative aspect of Italian pilot training was the limited scope for live weapons firing, which was reduced to a few flights attacking ground targets and some flights firing against balloons anchored to the soil! Very often, especially after the initial phase of the war, the limited resources and fuel available did not permit the execution of the number of hours comparable with those flown by the pupils in the RAF or USAAF. Another negative aspect of the syllabus was the undervaluation of the importance of instrument flight training, the results of which became clearly apparent with the unfortunate experiences of the C.A.I. over the English Channel.

In 1941 a reorganisation of the training sector resulted in the *Scuole di Volo di 1° Periodo* using Avia FL.3, Saiman 200/202 and Ro.41 aircraft for fighter pilot training with a requirement that the student had to fly them for around fifty hours. The *Scuole di Volo 2° Periodo* syllabus however, called for conversion onto the two-seat CR.30DC followed by training in the CR.32 and CR.42, which were considered to be transitional fighters. The cadet then moved on to the single- and two-seat G.50 and the single-seat C.200. Again, in this case another fifty hours were programmed, and subsequently new pilots were posted to their units or to one of the *Gruppi Complementari* for the final phase of their training. Following this reorganisation, the old identification style of applying the acronyms of a school's base airfield to the sides of the fuselages disappeared and in its place numbers appeared, but maintaining the use of wide, white recognition bands on aircraft fuselages and on wings.

At the end of 1941 the specialist fighter *scuola di 2° periodo* numbered a fleet of fewer than 400 aeroplanes which were divided into more than 100 CR.42s, 185 G.50s, of which 90 were two-seaters, and the remainder being C.200s. To these aircraft should be added another 120 CR.32s and thirty CR.30DC, which brought the total of aircraft in service with *Scuole Caccia* and *Gruppi Complementari* to over 500 machines. In the early months of 1942, the *Scuole* for *Assalto, Bombardamento a Tuffo* and *Caccia Notturna* (Ground-Attack, Dive-Bombing and Night Fighting), also began to receive CR.42s and C.200s to reinforce their existing fleets thanks to a greater availability of aircraft.

The establishment of the *Gruppi Complementari* in 1941, initially for final fighter specialisation training for students destined to fly with 1°, 2°, 4° and 52° *Stormo*, subsequently doubled with the inclusion of other *Stormi* and *Gruppi* CT. The CR.42 was the most used aircraft in these units, at least until mid-1942 when the *Gruppi Complementari* began to be issued with more effective types which were still serving with operational units, such as the single- and two-seat G.50, the C.200, as well as the C.202 and RE.2001.

Some CR.42s were also used by the *Scuole di Volo Senza Visibilità* (Instrument Flying Schools) at Malpensa and Villafranca, while others, suitably modified, were operated as glider tugs by the *Scuola di Volo senza Motore* at Cameri and Orio al Serio, where they were equipped to tow the DFS.230 assault glider and even the large AL.12/P developed by Aeronautica Lombarda. In this

The remaining CR.32s in the Regia Aeronautica inventory were used widely during the war by the various *Scuola Caccia*. This example was operated by the school at Castiglione del Lago for advanced training alongside several other aircraft types.

FIAT FIGHTERS TO THE TRAINING SCHOOLS

Two CR.42s operated by the *Scuola Caccia* at Rimini finished with different camouflage applications.

Below: A view of the flightline at the *Scuola Caccia* at Castiglione del Lago showing a range of biplanes and monoplanes. Visible in the distance is Lake Trasimeno.

CR.42AS, MM6882, of the *Scuola Caccia Assalto* based at Ravenna. (F.Ballista)

A young student pilot wearing a 'Salvador' parachute along with the canine mascot of his school. (P.Monti)

A CR.42 of an unknown *Scuola Caccia*. Aircraft assigned to the schools normally carried a wide white band over wings and the fuselages. After the reorganisation of the flying schools in 1941, the aircraft adopted large individual numbers instead of the initials of the school.

Two photographs of a G.50bis of a *Scuola Caccia* trailing balloons intended to aid trainee pilots in machine-gun fire.

respect, worthy of note was the ferry flight which towed a glider along the long route from Venegono to Guidonia, as performed by a CR.42 piloted by *maggiore* Erardo Fruet.

The *Gruppi Complementari* of the Regia Aeronautica

In the first half of 1941, exactly one year since the outbreak of the war for Italy, *Superaereo* realised that there was a requirement to rearrange the training programme, having identified that pilots arriving at front line units from the flying schools did not possess the essential technical and operational knowledge to integrate fully into fighter and bomber units. In fact, as mentioned, until that time, operational training for a new pilot had been entrusted to the final front line unit, with the young pilot being assigned an experienced mentor who could pass on *his* experiences in combat. This system impacted significantly on the activities of a unit which was forced to dedicate expert pilots – already precious in a challenging staffing environment – to assisting newcomers to fill the gaps in their knowledge. The constitution of the *Gruppi Complementari* therefore had the dedicated role of providing new pilots with this *pre-operational* training, together with re-qualifying personnel returning to their unit after prolonged absence or having been posted to other non-operational duties. The *Gruppi Complementari* were usually located at the principal bases of the units, and generally provided training for multiple operational units, using excess or reserve aircraft, or those of the *Stormo* which had been repaired or reassigned.

A group of young pilots and technicians pose for a snapshot in front of a FIAT G.50B. (R.Gentilli)

Student pilots gather around a G.50B. Note the wide white band under the wing to identify a flying school aircraft.

Rare colour photograph of G.50s and G.50bis of a *Scuola Caccia*. Some sources suggest they were taken at the Rimini school.

G.50s and G.50bis of *Scuola Caccia* with student pilots running up their engines.

Right: The Aeronautica Lombarda AL-12P transport and troop-carrying glider prototype, and in the background, the CR.42 used to tow the glider.

The CR.42 tug at work with an Aeronautica Lombarda type AL.12 cargo glider in tow piloted by test pilot Valsania.

The tow hook on the CR.42 glider tow aircraft. This device was designed and fitted by the Aeronautica Lombarda for towing the gliders of the S.V.S.M. *(Scuola Volo Senza Motore)* in Cameri.

CHAPTER TEN

FIAT fighters in post-war service

FIAT CR.42

A SMALL number of CR.42s were still in service at the end of the war, and at least fifteen airframes were sent to the Caproni workshops at Gardolo (Trento) for overhaul. After the war, with a requirement for new training aircraft and the need to give work to the aeronautics industry, Aeronautica Militare decided to refurbish these aircraft, converting most of them into two-seat dual-control aircraft for assignment as trainers to the 3ª *Squadriglia* of the *Gruppo Scuola Volo di 2° periodo* at Lecce Galatina.

Identified examples of the converted two-seat aircraft are MM6282/8485/8986/7020/8972/8911. In 1946 at least three further aircraft underwent a similar two-seat conversion. Subsequently, they were transferred from Lecce to Brindisi in conjunction with the relocation of the *Scuola di Volo*, and some were distributed to the *Sezione Autonoma Collegamento* (Autonomous Communications Section) at Centocelle. A limited number of aircraft were operated for some months on weather reconnaissance duties by the *Squadriglia Autonoma Unità Aerea* based at Venezia Lido San Nicolò. They were equipped with a meteorograph, a portable recorder configured for the simultaneous recording of

A CR.42 two-seater (above) and single-seater (top) of the 3ª *Squadriglia* of the *Scuola di Volo* based at Brindisi after the war.

A CR.42 with the markings of the *Scuola di Volo* but operated by the *Centro Addestramento al Volo* of the 1ª *Zona Aerea Territoriale* at Milano-Linate as a trainer and fast liaison aircraft.

Above and opposite page top: One of the two-seat trainer CR.42s converted after the war by Agusta. The 'Z1-6' code denotes a machine of the 1ª *Zona Aerea Territoriale* at Milano-Linate.

Some single-seater aircraft, such as 'Z1-2', were still in service after the war with the *Centro Addestramento al Volo* of 1ª *Zona Aerea Territoriale* at Milano-Linate airport.

atmospheric pressure, temperature, and relative humidity. The Venezia CR.42s usually flew two missions each day, the first in the early morning and the second in the late afternoon, but already by early 1947, the biplanes had been replaced by more modern aircraft such as the Reggiane 2001.

With the delivery of new, two-seat training aircraft such as the G.55B and N.A. T-6 Texan/Harvard, the surviving single- and two-seat CR.42s were reassigned as liaison aircraft and for continuation training of non-operational pilots to the I Z.A.T. (*Zone Aeree Territoriali* - Territorial Air Zone), based at Milano Linate. Assigned to the C.A.Vs. (*Centro Addestramento al Volo* – territorial Flight Training Centres) these aircraft were identified by the application of fuselage code prefixes commencing with the letter 'Z', followed by the Roman number of the Z.A.T., and then an individual two-digit identifying number, the aircraft flying in the skies around Milan at least until the early 1950s.

The only twin-seat FIAT G.50B to survive the aftermath of 8 September 1943. The aircraft was active until 1948 with the Scuola di Volo at Lecce Galatina. (F.Ballista)

FIAT G.50

At the end of the war the newly created Aeronautica Militare still had a single two-seat G.50B in service; the fate of the other aircraft is not known, but the most probable explanation is that they were destroyed or rendered unusable in accidents at the schools. The lone G.50B was operated until at least 1948 by the 3ª *Squadriglia* of the 2° *Gruppo Scuola Volo* at Lecce Galatina, later transferred to Brindisi. The aircraft, MM6483, had been adapted by the *Squadra Riparazione Aeromobile* at Lecce by modifying the last flyable single-seat G.50bis. However, the student who sat in the rear cockpit, did not have flap, brake, or undercarriage retraction controls, as these were only installed in the forward cockpit reserved for the instructor.

FIAT G.55

From the devastated airfields in northern Italy at the end of the war, the Regia Aeronautica managed to recover some fifteen G.55s. The airframes were in reasonable condition, sufficiently so to enable them to be returned to flying condition after refurbishment. Amongst the accords reached with the Allied Control Commission was the authorisation for their overhaul on the condition that they be utilised as advanced trainer replacements for the older aircraft still in service and, by then, no longer suitable to undertake this fundamental role. Meanwhile, in the light of a requirement to contribute to the rebirth of the shattered Italian aviation industry, FIAT was charged with the task of reconditioning the recovered fighters to G.55A standard by removing the armament and armour and converting five aircraft from single-seaters to two-seat G.55Bs. This was in accordance with a project conceived by the designer Gabrielli in 1944, but which never came to fruition because of the prevailing war situation. Amongst the first aircraft to be overhauled by FIAT was the former G.55 torpedo-attack aircraft which was assigned serial MM91096. After the work the aircraft received an all-over silver colour scheme, but retained the peculiarity of its dual radiator configuration, which had been necessary to enable the carriage of a torpedo. It was retained by FIAT for a series of trials with new systems before being delivered to the Aeronautica Militare in August 1948, however not before seeing the installation of a central radiator to bring it in line with the other aircraft produced.

In the meantime, following the signing of the peace treaties, Italy was permitted to manufacture new aircraft. FIAT, in consideration of the fact that it possessed other usable airframes and engines that had been held in store since the halting of the production lines following the bombing of April 1944, decided to reactivate the FIAT G.55 assembly line. This was to satisfy a request for an advanced training aircraft for the Aeronautica Militare and for an order that come from Argentina for a total of 45 examples, 30 of which were to be single-seat G.55As and 15 two-seat G.55Bs. Also influencing this decision was the Aeronautica Militare's desire to relaunch work in the Italian aeronautical industry by providing it with the minimum number of orders sufficient to ensure its vital survival, and enabling the start of production of a large part of what the firms had ready, or almost ready, even at the risk of finding itself with a fleet of aircraft that were far from the desired optimum.

Following this initiative, and still holding stocks of components and RA 1050 engines[1], FIAT commenced production of a further 12 G.55As (which were assigned serials MM91214-91220 and MM91225-MM91229) and four G.55Bs (MM91221-91224), as commissioned by the Aeronautica Militare. This order was, however, cancelled to enable FIAT to honour an order for 19 G.55s received from Egypt (15 single-seaters and four two-seaters), which was followed by a further order for 16 G.55s for the Syrian Air Force.

---
[1] This was the German DB 605 engine constructed under licence by FIAT.

The G.55S, MM91086, survived the war thanks to the fact that it operated from the Agusta facilities in Cascina Costa. After the war it was recovered and, although lacking its external armament, it retained the double radiators fitted during the war to accommodate a torpedo. It was used for a certain period as a test aircraft by FIAT and was then brought to G.55 standard and probably sold to Egypt.

The first post-war G.55, MM91167, was completed in 1947 with the transformation of an existing I *Serie Centauro* into a training aircraft and given the designation G.55A. The first flight of this variant, with no armament installed, was performed in September 1947.

The only unit of the Aeronautica Militare to operate the G 55As and Bs, albeit for a limited period prior to their return to FIAT for conversion into G.59s, was the 5ª *Squadriglia* of the 3° *Gruppo Addestramento, Scuola Caccia* based at Lecce Galatina airfield.

FIAT G.55A/B delivered to Aeronautica Militare

MM	C/N	Version	MM after conversion to G.59	
91086	37	G.55A	53037	former G.55S (torpedo variant)
91155	106	G.55B	53030	
91167	118	G.55A	53027	
91170	121	G.55B	53033	
91174	125	G.55A	53031	
91176	127	G.55A	53026	
91177	128	G.55A	53029	
91178	129	G.55A	53036	
91179	130	G.55A	————	crashed before delivery
91180	131	G.55A	53032	
91181	132	G.55B	52038	
91182	133	G.55B	53035	
91183	134	G.55B	53034	

Additional photographs of the first post-war G.55, MM91167 as seen on the previous page.

Two Italian Air Force G.55As in flight. The aircraft in the foreground is MM.91167, c/n 144, and in the background the former G.55S, MM91086, delivered to the *Scuola di Volo* at Lecce Galatina in 1948.

G.55B, MM91174, c/n 125, photographed before delivery to the flight schools of the AMI. The thirteen G.55s recovered after the war in northern Italy were transformed into seven G.55A single-seaters and six G.55B two-seaters, and assigned to the *Scuola di Volo* at Lecce Galatina.

This G.55, without a serial and MM, was probably the first example of the G.55B two-seater, the former MM91176, built by FIAT/Aeritalia in 1946. The aluminium livery was the standard colour scheme of the Aeronautica Militare after the war.

G.55B, MM91170, c/n 121. The construction of the trainer version of the G.55 had not much altered its general appearance.

FIAT FIGHTERS

FIAT fighters in post-war service abroad

FUERZA AEREA ARGENTINA

After the end of the Second World War, as part of a plan to renew the Fuerza Aerea Argentina (FAA) fleet, in 1946 the General Staff of the FAA initiated negotiations with Italy concerning the acquisition of a batch of 70 two-seat FIAT G.46-2B primary trainers, powered by the Gipsy Queen 30 engine. These were to be delivered at the beginning of 1947. This was a source of finance that would benefit the Torino-based manufacturer, which was struggling in the severe post-war crisis. It transpired that the FAA also elected to acquire a batch of two-seat G.55s to be used for the advanced training of its pilots. This would provide an excellent opportunity for trainees to gain experience in a high-performance aircraft from which the FAA could then select the best students for assignment to the fighter force. The negotiations also included the possibility of acquiring the G.59, but instead the FAA formalised an order for 30 single-seat G.55As (assigned serials C01 to C30) and 15 two-seat G.55Bs (serials C31 to C45). To satisfy this order, it was decided that the first single-seat aircraft would be drawn from the fleet of the Aeronautica Militare, while the remaining single-seaters and all the two-seaters would be new-build aircraft manufactured post-war.

In the course of 1947 a group of five Argentine pilots and a similar number of mechanics were sent to the base at Lecce Galatina to train on the fighter, after which they accompanied the first batch of aircraft to Argentina, alongside some Italian pilots and engineers, amongst whom was FIAT test pilot, Valentino Cus. The first nine G.55As arrived in the Latin American country in June 1947, delivered to the El Palomar base, where they were assembled and flight-tested prior to their official presentation on 21 July 1947, when five aircraft performed a flypast during the celebrations of the *Día de la Independencia*. The first four G.55s to be assigned to a unit, Grupo 1 *de Caza* of the *Agrupacion Aerea de Combate* based at El Plumerillo near Mendoza, were the aircraft serialised C10, C11, C12 and C13, these being followed on 10 September by the first two G.55Bs (C31 and C32) and another single-seater (C14). Another three single-seaters were delivered on 3 December (C01, C02 and C03).

At the beginning of 1948 the *Agrupacion Aerea de Combate* was disbanded and its fighters reassigned to the *Regimiento 2 de Caza*, subsequently reorganised into the *Grupo 1 de Caza* on 9 January 1951. The frequent accidents, and more importantly, the complex maintenance requirements, combined with a shortage of spares, limited the operational availability of the G.55 to the point that, in 1952, only 20 single-seaters were in the fleet, of which at least five were in storage or under repair, and of just 11 two-seaters only eight were in flying condition. The residual aircraft

Italian FIAT and Argentinian technicians photographed in Buenos Aires in 1947-48.

The Fuerza Aerea Argentina was the largest user of the FIAT G.55 and numbered thirty single-seat and fifteen two-seat aircraft. The Argentine machines were equipped with two 12.7 mm machine guns and were used as advanced training aircraft. (Santiago Rivas)

The G.55A, C-09, belonging to *Grupo* 1 of the *Agrupación Aérea de Combate of Grupo* 5 photographed at the air show organised by the Aeroclub Mar del Plata in February 1948. (Santiago Rivas)

The FIAT G.55A C-25 of the *Regimento* 2 *de Caza* remained in service until the end of 1954 and was discharged from active service only in early March 1955. (Santiago Rivas)

Below: A FIAT G.55A in service with the 5th Squadron of the Royal Egyptian Air Force. Note that Egyptian aircraft were equipped with wing guns. The camouflage was made up of two shades of brown.

continued their flying activities for a couple of years until the final retirement of the last operational aircraft, little more than ten, at the end of 1954, after just seven years' service.

In terms of the possible supply of new G.59s, negotiations were not concluded, despite a G.59-1A (MM91116, FAA serial C-46) being donated by the Italian government to Argentina for evaluation. Named '*Aguila*', the single-seater was assigned to the *Grupo* 1 *de Caza* of the IV *Brigata Aerea* at El Plumerillo, being utilised for a period as the personal aircraft of *Comodoro* Mario Donadei, the commander of the *Grupo* 1 *de Caza*. It was withdrawn from service after suffering damage on 12 September 1952 during an emergency landing.

EGYPT

In the immediate post-war period the Royal Egyptian Air Force (REAF) proved to be a good customer for the Italian aviation industry. Having finalised the acquisition of batches of AerMacchi C.205Vs, the Egyptian government signed a contract for the supply of a batch of 17 single-seat FIAT G.55As and two G.55B two-seaters, with the option to purchase 20 G.59s. This option, however, was never exercised and Egypt finalised the acquisition of another eight single-seaters and two two-seaters, along with 29 DB.605 engines, and a batch of 116 Breda 12.7 mm SAFAT machine guns. The aircraft supplied had, in the main, been overhauled by FIAT, after the Aeronautica Militare had handed back a series of fuselages and aircraft to FIAT in late January 1948 – probably thirteen fuselages in all. It should also be borne in mind that it was possible to supply aircraft to Egypt only after the Aeronautica Militare had cancelled a previous order placed for sixteen G.55s (12 G.55As and 4 G.55Bs) that were under construction at FIAT.

With this move, the Aeronautica Militare contributed to the rebirth of the Italian aviation industry, offering the precious possibility of employment for the FIAT workforce and optimising the potential of the company to obtain vital export orders in the difficult post-war market. In exchange, FIAT would provide the Aeronautica Militare with an equivalent number of G.59 aircraft, also offering to supply another 13 G.59s to replace the returned G.55s, thereby enabling the Aeronautica Militare to renew the fleet of the *Scuola Caccia* at a decidedly favourable cost.

The supply of the aircraft to Egypt was, however, characterised by delivery delays, as the first aircraft only arrived towards the end of 1948. The fighters were assigned to the 5th Squadron, based at Al Ballal. It is not clear whether they arrived in time to be utilised during the final phases of the Arab-Israeli conflict of 1948, as at the end of that year the unit was still undergoing conversion training. As was the case with the AerMacchi C.205Vs, the G.55s were operated as front line fighters until the arrival of the first Gloster Meteors, and then subsequently used as advanced trainers. The aircraft were delivered in natural metal finish, but in service were painted in an RAF Desert Air Force camouflage, composed of two tones of brown and a white identification band with black edges around the fuselage and above and below the wings.

Another FIAT G.55A in service with the 5th Squadron of the Royal Egyptian Air Force.

SYRIA

Between 1949 and 1950 the air arm of this Middle Eastern nation received 30 G.55s and G.59-2A/Bs. It seems that at least 12 single-seat G.55As and a single G.55B, obtained from a batch initially intended for the Aeronautica Militare, were used to satisfy the order. These aircraft were characterised by armament comprising four Breda 12.7 mm SAFAT machine guns, two fuselage-mounted and two in the wings, and wings pre-fitted with shackles capable of carrying bombs up to 100 kg or 125-litre supplementary fuel tanks. Other substantial modifications introduced were the adoption of armour for the seat and protection for the fuel tanks. It is presumed that all the aircraft were camouflaged in a scheme similar to that worn by the Egyptian aircraft, but using brown and green colours with sky-blue undersurfaces and identification numbers applied on rudders, the sequence of which is not known. The aircraft were probably operated from the base at Al Mezze, near Damascus, as front line fighters, at least until the arrival in 1952 of the first Meteor jet fighters. They were later assigned to advanced training duties.

Right and below: The G.55As destined for the Syrian Air Force were delivered to Damascus airport. The Syrian fighters were armed with two 12.7 mm SAFAT machine guns in the wings and were camouflaged with bands of two colours, probably shades of brown and green.

CHAPTER ELEVEN

From G.55 to G.59 – a brief, but intense story

FIAT G.59-1A, MM53018, was a single-seater of *Serie* II production. It was modified as the G.59-3A as a prototype trainer for advanced navigation and the calibration of ground equipment, but it proved too expensive and was not progressed.

IN the immediate post-war period, a requirement for an advanced training aircraft induced the *Direzione Tecnica* of the *Divisione Aviazione* of FIAT to identify alternative engine solutions for the available G.55 airframes, given the difficulties in obtaining original Daimler-Benz engines. Among the options proposed, and also in a reflection of the limited economic resources available, the simplest solution was the adoption of Anglo-American produced engines which, at the time, powered aircraft such as the Spitfires that had been assigned to the newly formed Aeronautica Militare, a factor that held technical and logistical advantages.

The ideal engine was the Rolls-Royce Merlin, which was available in quantity, with no shortage of spares. Consequently, the Aeronautica Militare loaned to FIAT two Spitfire Mk IX (MM4082 and MM4091) to enable their engines to be installed in the airframe of a G.55. Following a series of in-depth evaluations which took account of acquisition costs and availability of engines and spares, *Ingegner* Gabrielli selected the Rolls-Royce Merlin 500-20, V-12 engine with a two-speed supercharger developing around 1,420 hp at take-off and driving a four-bladed Fiat/Hamilton Standard 3.40 m diameter propeller with right-handed rotation. Adaptation of the British engine did not present any particular problems apart from an obvious requirement to completely redesign the forward part of the aircraft and the fitment of a four-bladed propeller.

The designation initially proposed for the model, G.55BM (*Biposto* Merlin), was quickly replaced by that of G.59B, and the first prototype G 59B (NC1), which was assigned serial MM53010, made its inaugural flight on 4 March 1948. The aircraft was displayed at the Paris Salon between 29 April and 15 May 1949 carrying civil registration I-TORO. It featured an interim engine cowling configuration which was later modified slightly in production aircraft. In view of the pleasing results derived from the installation of the British engine, the Aeronautica Militare returned

A FIAT advertisement published in *ALATA* aviation magazine in September 1949.

A FIAT G.59-2B, 5-77, MM53281, of 5° *Aerobrigata* used as a fast liaison and instrument flight trainer.

This FIAT G.59-2A, MM53253, was one of the few of this type to be used for a short period by the AMI flying school.

Left: G-59-1A, MM53266, assigned as fast liaison aircraft to the 5th ATAF. (C.Valenti)

the seven G.55As which it had in service (one aircraft MM91179, NC130, having been lost prior to conversion), together with six G.55Bs. For this reason, the G 59s of the first production series retained the construction numbers allocated to them originally as G 55s, and later were also identified by the designations G.59-1A and G.59-1B. The first modified example of the *Serie* I to be delivered, on 14 February 1950, was G.59A MM 53026 (ex G.55A NC 127 MM91176), followed shortly after by the first two examples from *Serie* II, which comprised new-build aircraft.

An important aspect was that the single-seat G.59As were equipped with two Breda SAFAT 12.7 mm machine guns, installed in the wings, and while the early G.59Bs delivered were unarmed, from MM53277 of the *Serie* IV the aircraft had the option to carry a Breda SAFAT 7.7 mm machine gun in the starboard wing, albeit at the cost of a small reduction in fuel capacity. They also featured two hard points under the wings which could hang training bombs of up to 100 kg or 125-litre supplementary fuel tanks. Moreover, all the G.59s, single-seat or two-seat, and also unarmed aircraft, could be fitted with a S. Giorgio C 1 reflector gunsight and a gun camera for training purposes.

From *Serie* IV, again commencing with G.59B MM53277, the main pilot's aircraft handling controls were switched to the rear as until that moment, if a two-seater was being flown by a solo pilot in the front cockpit, it was essential to stow around 85 kg of ballast in the rear. *Serie* V introduced a particularly important structural modification to both the single-seat and two-seat versions which involved the introduction of new, rearward-sliding teardrop canopies intended to improve access and visibility. Over the years the aircraft of the early series were brought up to *Serie*

The G.59-4B production line at FIAT Aviation at Torino Caselle. The first conversions with the new bubble canopy began with the production *Serie* V.

Below: The only G.59-2A example purchased by the Fuerza Aerea Argentina (FAA) was nicknamed *'El Aguila'*. At that time the FAA did not need such an advanced single-seat trainer. (Santiago Rivas)

V standard with the new canopies, while the series following the V series introduced only minor modifications and detailed refinements.

Before production concluded in 1954, FIAT had produced 174 new-build G 59s including the converted 12 G 55As and Bs into the new model, while new-build production had been divided into ten series. In total the Aeronautica Militare received 161 new-build Fiat G 59s.

A single G.59-1A (NC2) was sold to Argentina in 1951. Coded C-46 and name *Águila*, it was operated by *Grupo 1 de Caza* of the *IV Brigata Aerea* based at El Plumerillo, while another fifteen aircraft were delivered to Syria (see Chapter Ten).

Service with the Aeronautica Militare

In the early 1950s training activity within the newly constituted Aeronautica Militare was divided into three distinct phases known as '*Periodo*'. Operations were concentrated on several airfields in the Puglia region. Basic instruction was conducted by the *Scuola di 1° Periodo*, formed from the *1° Gruppo di Volo* at Gioia del Colle and equipped with Stinson L-5 light trainers. Activity was aimed at providing students with their '*brevetto di pilota d'aeroplano*' (pilot licence) after thirty flying hours. Subsequently students transferred to the *2° Gruppo di Volo* at Brindisi, flying for fifty hours in the FIAT G.46 to complete the 2° *Periodo* before being admitted to the *Scuola di Volo di 3° Periodo* at the 3° *Gruppo Scuole di Lecce*. The school was equipped with the G.55A and G.55B, and the residual AerMacchi C.205V, which were used until their replacement, commencing from early 1950, by the first G.59A/B, which remained in service until the end of 1957. At the Lecce school students flew sixty hours to obtain their *brevetto di pilota*

A G.59 single-seater S3-146, (left) and a two-seater S3-142, ready to leave the parking area at Lecce Galatina, home of the *Scuola di Volo*.

A G.59-2B, S3-09, of the AMI Flying School fitted with the Rolls-Royce V12 Merlin 500-20 engine with a two-speed supercharger developing around 1,420 hp. The photograph shows clearly the redesigned forward cowling with the supercharger air scoop and the four-bladed Fiat/Hamilton Standard propellor. The '09' on the wing leading edge identifies the aircraft's individual airframe number as S3-09, allowing easy identification for ground personnel, pilots and trainees.

The elegant and functional lines of the G.59-4B, MM53616, c/n 159, the twenty-third of the twenty-five aircraft belonging to the *Serie* VIII production.

The main feature of the G.59-4B was the adoption of a 'bubble' cockpit hood. With its introduction, both pilots were given improved visibility over the -2B variant.

Below: The single-seater G.59 was also modified with a bubble canopy, receiving the designation G.59-4A. In this photograph, G.59-4A, MM53365, is on the ramp at FIAT Torino Caselle together with, at left, a G.59-4B ready for delivery to the AM.

A G.59-4A, S3-19, warms up its engine before a training sortie from the *Scuola di Volo* at Lecce Galatina. Note the fairings for the two 12.7 mm SAFAT machine guns used for pilot training.

A G.59-4A, S3-29, of the *Scuola di Volo* at Lecce Galatina banks to port.

An interesting line-up on the tarmac in front of the 'Savigliano' hangars at the *Scuola di Volo* at Cagliari Elmas. The aircraft no longer have the 'S3-B' code painted on their fuselages, but rather these have been replaced by the new 'SE' code denoting *'Scuola Elmas'*. Unusually, the flightline includes various types of G.59 two-seaters, single-seaters and a pair of F-51Ds, a Beechcraft Model 18, and a C-47 in the background. (G.Baschirotto)

Two photographs of G-59-4B, SE-23, of the *Scuola di Volo* at Cagliari Elmas. (R.Paolich)

militare, commencing their course on the two-seat G.59B and then switching to the single-seat G.59A before completion of training with a few missions in the F-51D Mustangs on charge of the *Scuola di Volo*.

With an increasing requirement for pilots, at the beginning of 1952 the *Comando Scuole di Volo della Sardegna* (Sardinia Flying Training Command) was created at Cagliari-Elmas, along with the constitution of the *Scuola di Volo di 3° Periodo* at Elmas (202° and 203° *Gruppo*) and the 2° *Periodo* school at Alghero Fertilia (211° *Gruppo*). The aircraft utilised initially was the North American T-6 Harvard, but these were joined later by FIAT G.59A/Bs, F-51D Mustangs and a few Beech C-45s.

As a consequence, the fuselage code prefixes of the G.59A/B fleet were revised. Previously, these aircraft were marked using the 'S-3B' code prefixes followed by the individual aircraft number. Following the creation of the Cagliari Elmas training school, aircraft with 'SL-' code prefixes identified those in service at Lecce Galatina, while those with an 'SE-' prefix identified those used by the *Scuola* at Cagliari Elmas.

The entry into service of American T-6 trainers in 1950 and the new training syllabus essential to support the arrival of the first jets in the early 1950s, resulted in a further revision of the training programmes. After an initial phase in which student pilots gained their *brevetto di pilota* flying Macchi M.416 or Piaggio P.148, they subsequently flew around 150/160 hours on the T-6, continuing on to another sixty hours split between the G.59A/B and T-33A jet. This was the policy until at least 1958 when the syllabus for new pilots was further revised. Of the approximately 280 hours required to train a new pilot, 200 were flown in the T-6 and the remainder conducted in the T-33A. This new programme no longer included any conversion onto the G.59A/B and facilitated the

transfer of the remaining aircraft to various operational and second line units.

The majority of the G.59A/B fleet was consequently assigned to the *Centri Addestramento Volo* (C.A.V. – Flight Training Centres) of the *Zone Aeree Territoriali* (Z.A.T. – Territorial Air Zones, later becoming air regions – *Regioni Aeree*) and to operational units, where they were utilised for liaison, the maintenance of pilots' minimum flying hours, and instrument training by the *Squadriglie* V.S.V. (*Volo Senza Visibilità* – Instrument Flight/Blind Flying). These subsequently became *Squadriglie Collegamento* (Communications Flights), while some G.59A/Bs were also issued to the 56ª T.A.F. (Tactical Air Force, later Vth ATAF) operating from Vicenza. Serving with these second-line units, the G-59s became extremely popular as they were frequently placed into the hands of highly skilled pilots, many of them Second World War veterans, and were the protagonists in memorable aerobatic demonstrations at numerous air displays staged in the post-war period.

The final official flight of a G.59 was conducted on 26 November 1968, undertaken by G-59-4B MM53772 (NC179) of the *Reparto Sperimentale* (Test Unit) *di Volo* at Pratica di Mare.

Summary of Built Versions

G.59-1A – single-seat version / converted from G.55A
G.59-1B – two-seat version / converted from G.55B
G.59-2A – single-seat version
G.59-2B – two-seat version
G.59-4A – single-seat version fitted with a bubble canopy
G.59-4B – two-seat version fitted with a bubble canopy

Variant	Serie	M.M.	Number Built	Note
G.59-1A/1B	I Serie	MM53026 to MM53035	13	6 single-seater / 7 double-seater. Former G.55A/B converted to G.59
G.59-1A/1B	II Serie	MM53010 to MM53025	16	12 single-seater / 4 double-seater *
G.59-1B	III Serie	MM53133 to MM53142	10	10 double-seater
G.59-2A/2B	IV Serie	MM53253 to MM53266	30	14 single-seater / 16 double-seater
G.59-2B/2B	IV Serie	MM53267 to MM53282		
G.59-4A/4B	V Serie	MM53363 to MM53372	20	10 single-seater / 10 double-seater. Bubble canopy
G.59-4B/4B	V Serie	MM53373 to MM53382		
G.59-4A/4B	VI Serie	MM53509 to MM53513	10	5 single-seater / 5 double-seater. Bubble canopy
G.59-4B/4B	VI Serie	MM53514 to MM53518		
G.59-4A	VII Serie	MM53519 to MM53531	25	8 single-seater / 17 double-seater. Bubble canopy
G.59-4B	VII Serie	MM53532 to MM53543		
G.59-4B	VIII Serie	MM53594 to MM53618	25	25 double-seater. Bubble canopy
G.59-4B	IX Serie	MM53681 to MM53690	10	10 double-seater. Bubble canopy
G.59-4B	X Serie	MM53767 to MM53781	15	15 double-seater. Bubble canopy
		Total built	**174**	(13 G.55 modified and 161 G.59 built with RR Merlin

* MM53018 nc10 later modified as G.59-3A as navigation trainer

Data from: *situazione matricolare* G.59, Aeronautica Militare Historic Office

The G.59-4A of the 51ª *Aerobrigata* used by *maresciallo* Antonio Mascellani for several demonstrations during the mid-1950s. Note the wartime 51° *Stormo* CT emblem on the rudder. The rear fuselage was painted red.

CHAPTER TWELVE

Camouflage and Markings

by Paolo Waldis

Colours and Camouflage Schemes

FIAT CR.32

THE first CR.32s entered service in early 1935 wearing the same overall silver livery which characterised all Regia Aeronautica fighters of the time. National insignia consisting of three green-white-red bands were applied to the vertical rudder, which extended to the horizontal tailplanes, in addition to unit codes painted on the fuselage sides. All aircraft of the first production batch left the factory with this finish, achieved by painting any fabric surfaces matt aluminium, with metal nose panels and undercarriage fairings left in natural aluminium. All wing struts were painted glossy black according to a typical FIAT practice of the time. (**1**)

From February 1937, when the final production batch of CR.32bis was being manufactured, the aluminium scheme was abandoned in favour of a new, experimental camouflage finish consisting of a disruptive three-colour 'splinter' scheme featuring broad bands of yellow, green and brown camouflage. (**2**) Since no official instructions have emerged to date prescribing the use of such a scheme, we can only imagine it was simply a company venture intended to replicate similar disruptive schemes then starting to see widespread use in other countries in the same period, particularly in Germany and the United Kingdom. It should be noted, however, that many other Italian aircraft manufacturers were starting to experiment with similar styles of camouflage with large contrasting areas of three or even more colours. The splinter scheme should have been tested in Spain during the Civil War, where the first aircraft in camouflage finish started arriving in early 1937. However, it was quickly discarded and deemed totally inappropriate for the arid climate of Spain and for the type of scrubland from where the Italian fighters actually operated. A more appropriate camouflage scheme of small, soft-edged blotches of two or three colours (usually green on sand or, more frequently, green and brown on sand) had already been successfully tested and this was invariably applied to any aircraft arriving in Spain in 'silver' livery and also to all those later machines arriving from Italy finished in the new splinter scheme. The only exception was the CR.32s based in the Balearic Islands which, due to a lack of any real enemy air threat, always retained their factory finish: overall

1 CR.32, personal aircraft of *maggiore* Fernando Zanni, commander of 22° *Gruppo*, 52° *Stormo* CT, Ghedi, March 1937

2 CR.32, MM3211, 357ª *Squadriglia*, 22° *Gruppo*, 52° *Stormo* CT, Gorizia, August 1937

FIAT FIGHTERS

aluminium for those which arrived in 1936, or wide, disruptive bands for those arriving in 1937.

The experimental camouflage schemes used during the Spanish Civil War were later evaluated positively by the Italian Air Ministry and they later formed the basis of the first official painting regulations regarding camouflage of Italian aircraft. However, the initial experimental splinter camouflage scheme was condemned to a premature death. In fact, a regulation of September 1937 issued by the General Air Staff prescribed the use of the same, soft-edged, mottled camouflage used in Spain for all newly built aircraft. The same regulation ordered the application of camouflage to the lateral and upper surfaces of the aircraft, while expressly prohibiting its use on the ventral surfaces, which had to retain their matt aluminium finish. As a consequence, the CR.32quaters in production at the end of 1937 began to leave the factory in a green and brown soft-edged, mottled scheme on a sandy yellow background. The colours were officially named '*Verde Mimetico*' (Camouflage Green*)*, '*Marrone Mimetico*' (Camouflage Brown) and '*Giallo Mimetico*' (Camouflage Yellow). The photographic evidence also indicates that the early production machines wearing this scheme featured larger blotches and lighter colour shades (possibly the same colours of the previous splinter scheme), while later production batches had the definitive camouflage with a smaller, soft-edged mottling of darker colours. This was a finish that would have remained unchanged on all FIAT fighters until the camouflage reforms introduced in 1941, by which time production of the CR.32 had long since been terminated. (**3** / **4**)

FIAT CR.42

Except for the prototype, painted aluminium overall, the whole production run of the CR.42 received the three-colour, soft-edged, mottled scheme prescribed by the official instructions issued in 1937 and confirmed in 1938. This was officially designated as a '*reticolo di macchie*' ('grid of blotches'). (**5**) The shape of the green and brown blotches varied on aircraft of different production batches, resulting in variations in both size and density, a probable consequence of the 'hand' of each painter and of different production times.

Despite the fact that the use of aluminium-based paints had been forbidden since at least 1939, in order to avoid reflection which compromised the effectiveness of camouflage, it

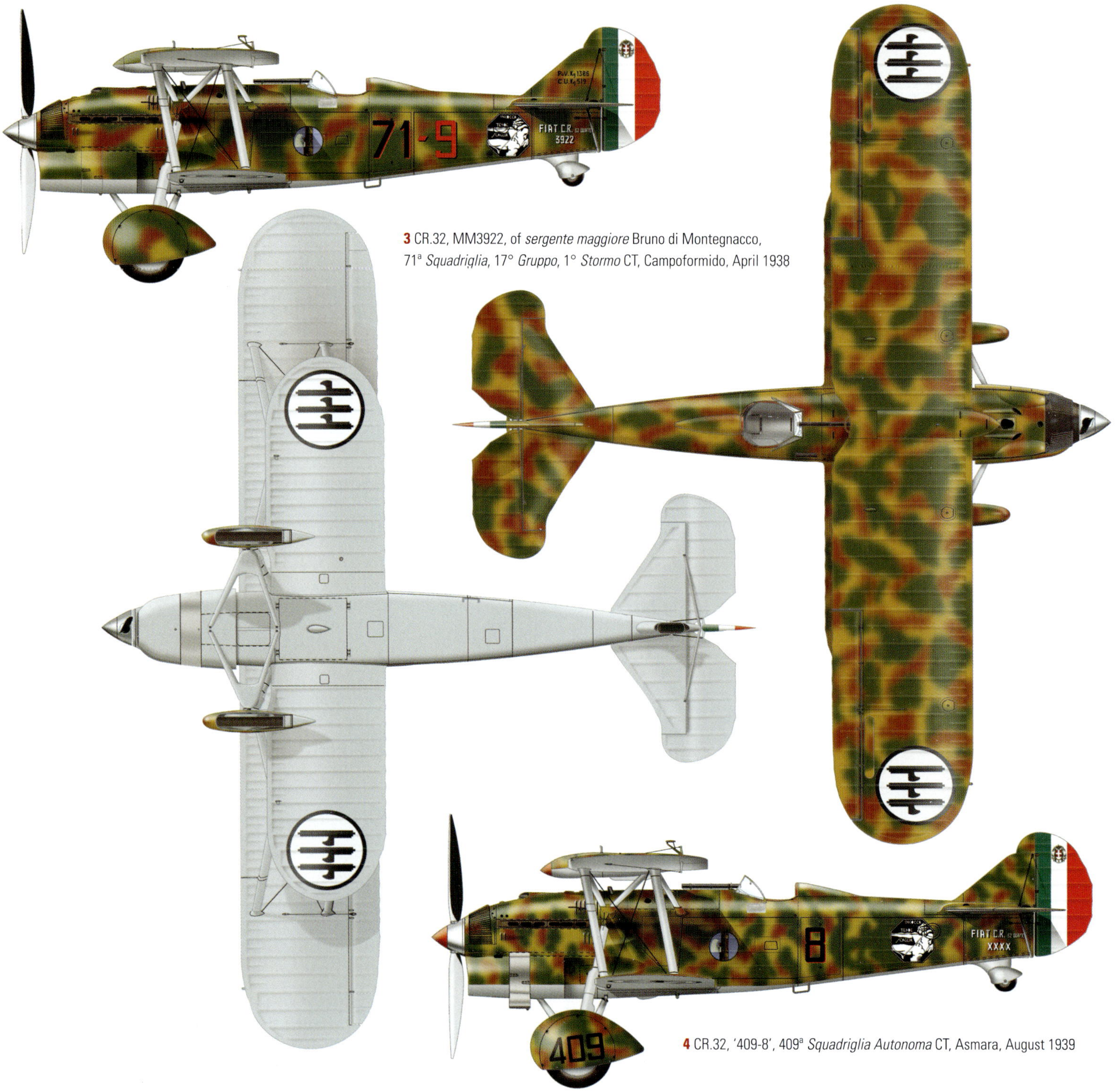

3 CR.32, MM3922, of *sergente maggiore* Bruno di Montegnacco, 71ª *Squadriglia*, 17° *Gruppo*, 1° *Stormo* CT, Campoformido, April 1938

4 CR.32, '409-8', 409ª *Squadriglia Autonoma* CT, Asmara, August 1939

CAMOUFLAGE AND MARKINGS

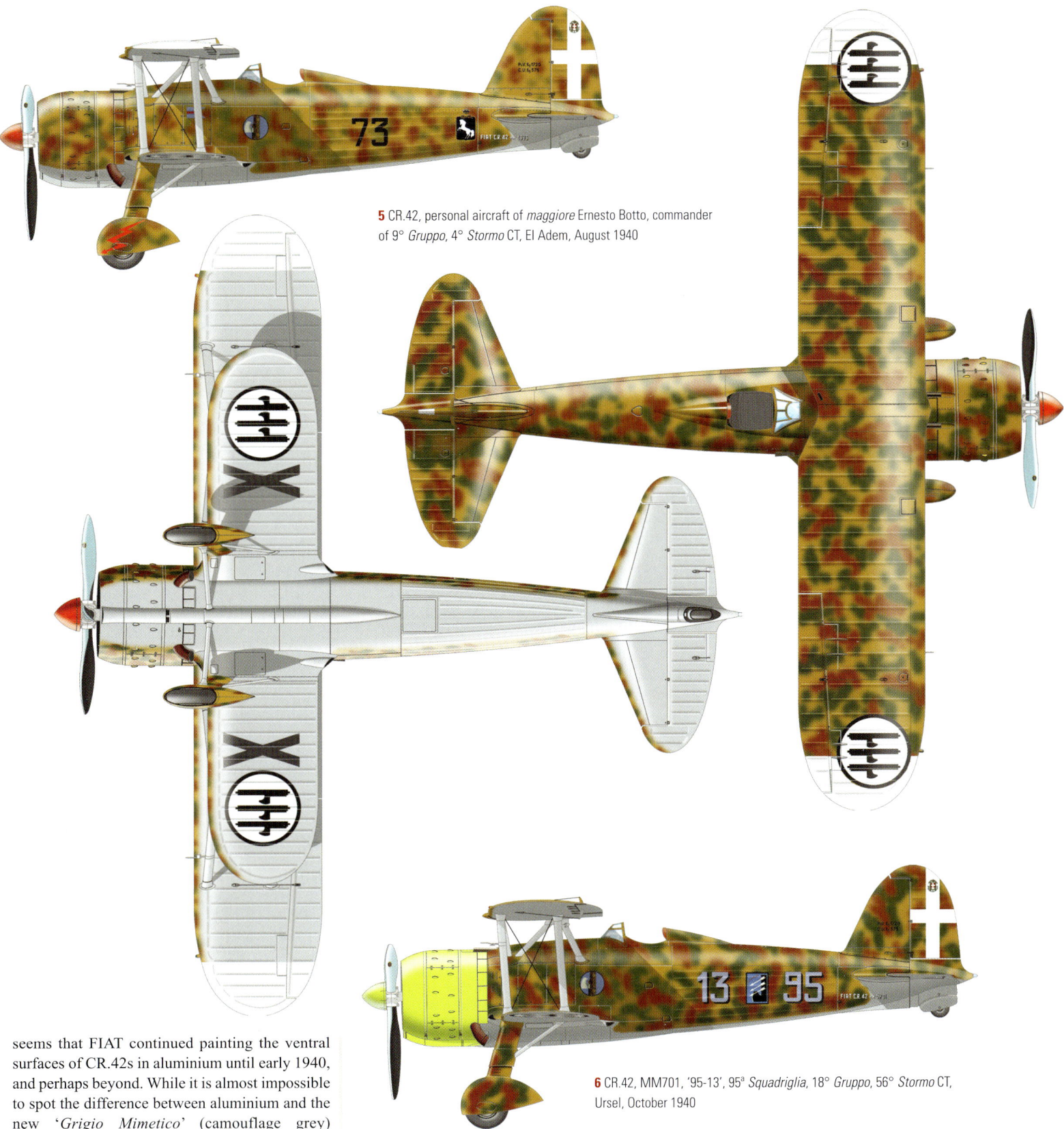

5 CR.42, personal aircraft of *maggiore* Ernesto Botto, commander of 9° *Gruppo*, 4° *Stormo* CT, El Adem, August 1940

6 CR.42, MM701, '95-13', 95ª *Squadriglia*, 18° *Gruppo*, 56° *Stormo* CT, Ursel, October 1940

seems that FIAT continued painting the ventral surfaces of CR.42s in aluminium until early 1940, and perhaps beyond. While it is almost impossible to spot the difference between aluminium and the new '*Grigio Mimetico*' (camouflage grey) prescribed by the official instructions in black and white photographs, because Italian paints had a distinct satin finish, some records report CR.42s as still having silver lower surfaces well into the early war period. However, in the absence of official documents to support this, we can only assume that, exceptionally, FIAT avoided using the new grey colour in order to exhaust existing stocks of old paints. The military serials and type designators were painted white under the tail planes and were highlighted in black according to a FIAT practice inherited from the CR.32. (**6**)

With the camouflage reforms of summer 1941 which prescribed new, simplified camouflage schemes instead of the traditional three-tone types, from October all newly produced aircraft were finished in a new scheme known as '*Schema Metropolitano*' ('home scheme'). This comprised recently introduced official colours: overall '*Verde Oliva Scuro*' (dark olive green) on the side and upper surfaces, and '*Grigio Azzurro Chiaro*' (light blue grey) for lower surfaces. (**7**) However, since, at that time, CR.42s were operating mainly in North Africa and the Mediterranean, the vast majority of production aircraft actually received the overseas scheme conceived for the North African theatre. This was formed of blotches of '*Nocciola Chiaro*' (light hazelnut brown) added to the same basic camouflage, creating a simplified mottled scheme when compared to the previous applications. In practice, just two colours were used for the upper surfaces, instead of three.

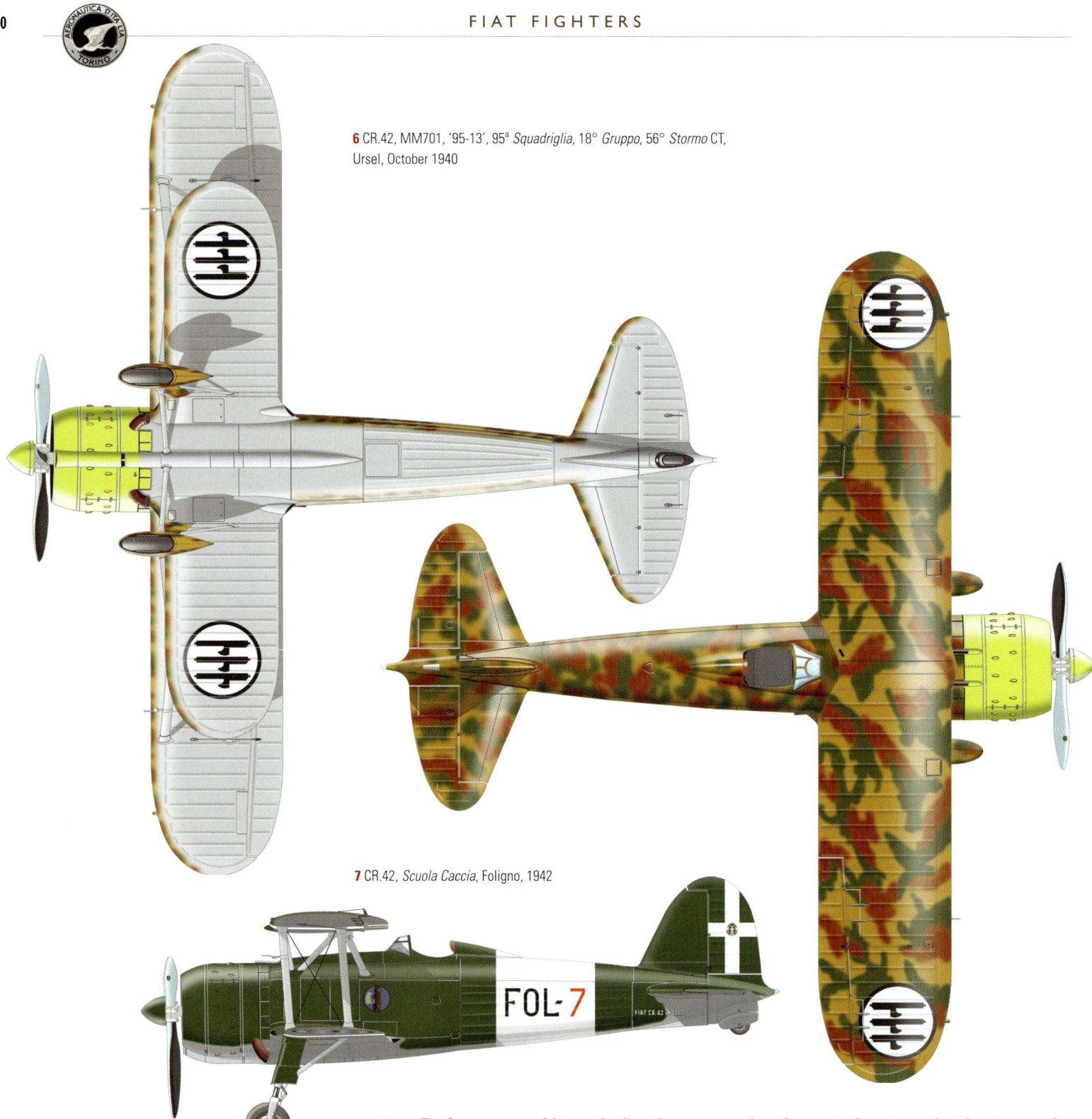

6 CR.42, MM701, '95-13', 95ª *Squadriglia*, 18° *Gruppo*, 56° *Stormo* CT, Ursel, October 1940

7 CR.42, *Scuola Caccia*, Foligno, 1942

Of note is that in the absence of official instructions regarding the shape and dimensions of the blotches, FIAT invariably applied rather sparse and rounded hazelnut blotches, introducing a camouflage pattern which was informally, and improperly, known as the '*ramarro* (lizard scheme)' of *Verde Oliva Scuro and Nocciola Chiaro (olive green and light hazelnut)*. It became recognised as a kind of factory trademark for any FIAT fighters produced in the final stages of war. (**8**)

Furthermore – and interestingly – these new colours were almost the same as the equivalent German colours RLM 70 *Schwarzgrün*, RLM 79 *Sandgelb* and RLM 76 *Lichtblau*, possibly the result of a certain sharing of experiences between the Regia Aeronautica and the Luftwaffe after more than a year of war. No further change would be introduced until after the Italian armistice, when some aircraft in a standard 'lizard' scheme used by the Luftwaffe until 1944 were over-sprayed in the field with irregular blotches and different shapes of the three German greys, RLM 74, RLM 75 and RLM 76. On the contrary, the few surviving aircraft operated by the Regia Aeronautica in the period of co-belligerence, being used only for communications and training duties, did not display any particular change of colours. Surviving aircraft operated post-war by the Aeronautica Militare – many of which were converted into two-seaters and used only within non-operational units – eventually received the typical overall aluminium finish of the period.

FIAT G.50

With the exception of the prototypes, all G.50 production aircraft left the factory in the standard camouflage scheme featuring the usual, soft-edged mottled scheme of the official three colours of the '*mimetico*' series. The only exception worthy of note was that the aircraft of the first production batch were painted with lighter colours, similar to those already seen on the CR.32s, with very

CAMOUFLAGE AND MARKINGS

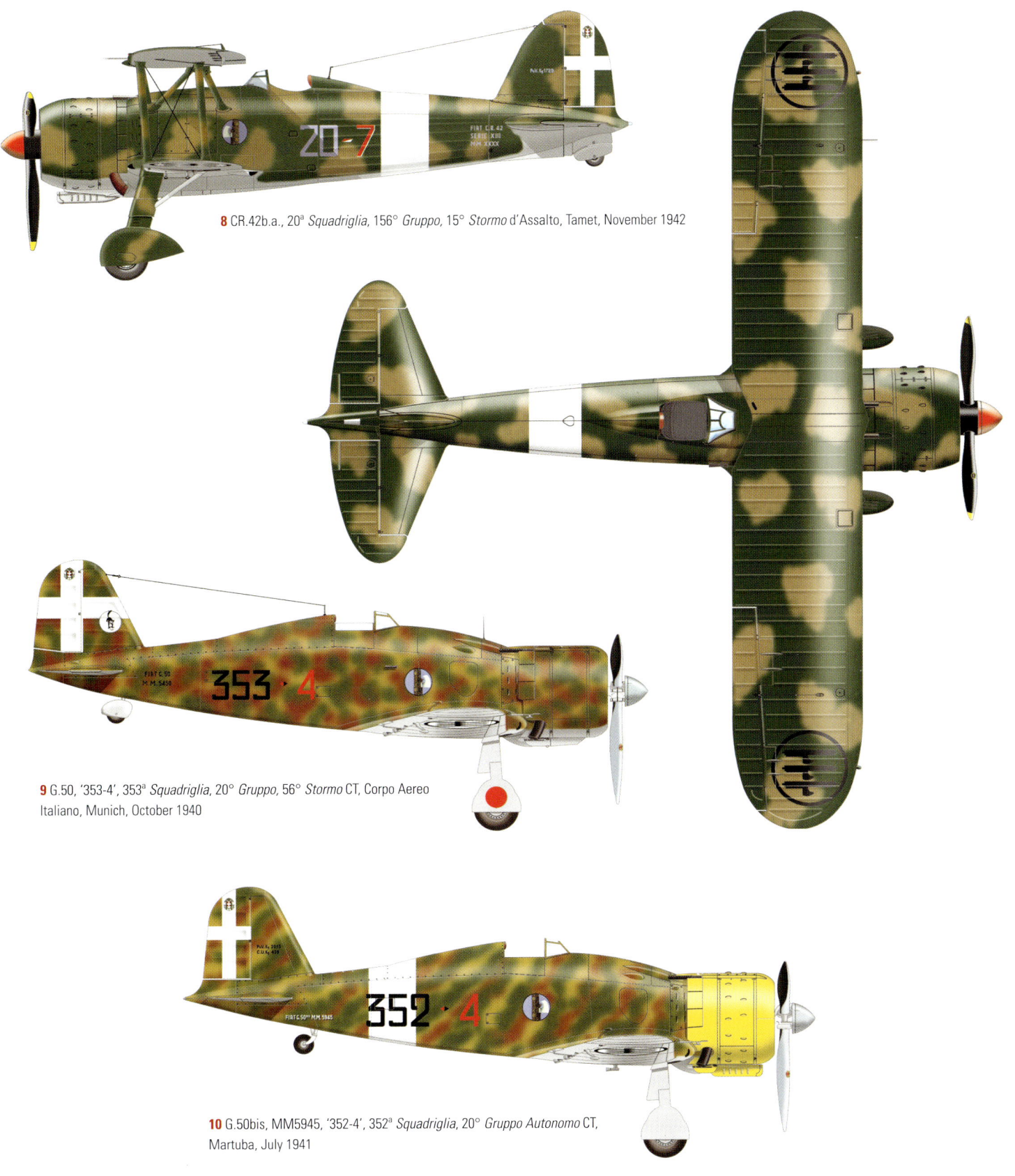

8 CR.42b.a., 20ª *Squadriglia*, 156° *Gruppo*, 15° *Stormo* d'Assalto, Tamet, November 1942

9 G.50, '353-4', 353ª *Squadriglia*, 20° *Gruppo*, 56° *Stormo* CT, Corpo Aereo Italiano, Munich, October 1940

10 G.50bis, MM5945, '352-4', 352ª *Squadriglia*, 20° *Gruppo Autonomo* CT, Martuba, July 1941

subdued *Verde Mimetico* and *Marrone Mimetico* blotches on a *Giallo Mimetico* background. (**9**) The ventral surfaces were probably *Grigio Mimetico* but, once again, it cannot be excluded they may still have been aluminium. Later production batches displayed darker tones of the same green, brown and yellow, like the colours used on the final CR.32s, all CR.42s, and any aircraft produced by FIAT until 1941. (**10**) Only with the introduction of the camouflage reforms, after the summer of 1941, when the last aircraft of *Serie* VII were being produced, was there a switch to the new uniform *Verde Oliva Scuro* scheme or frequently – with the addition of some *Nocciola Chiaro* blotches – to the so-called 'lizard' scheme. Ventral surfaces were finished in *Grigio Azzurro Chiaro*. (**11 / 12**) The very few aircraft operated by flying schools after the armistice of 1943 were left unchanged, until they were painted overall aluminium after the war.

10 G.50bis, MM5945, '352-4', 352ª *Squadriglia*, 20° *Gruppo Autonomo* CT, Martuba, July 1941

11 G.50, MM5452, '82', *Scuola Caccia*, 1942

12 G.50bis, personal aircraft of *maggiore* Antonio Giachino, commander of 151° *Gruppo*, Torino Caselle, March 1942

CAMOUFLAGE AND MARKINGS

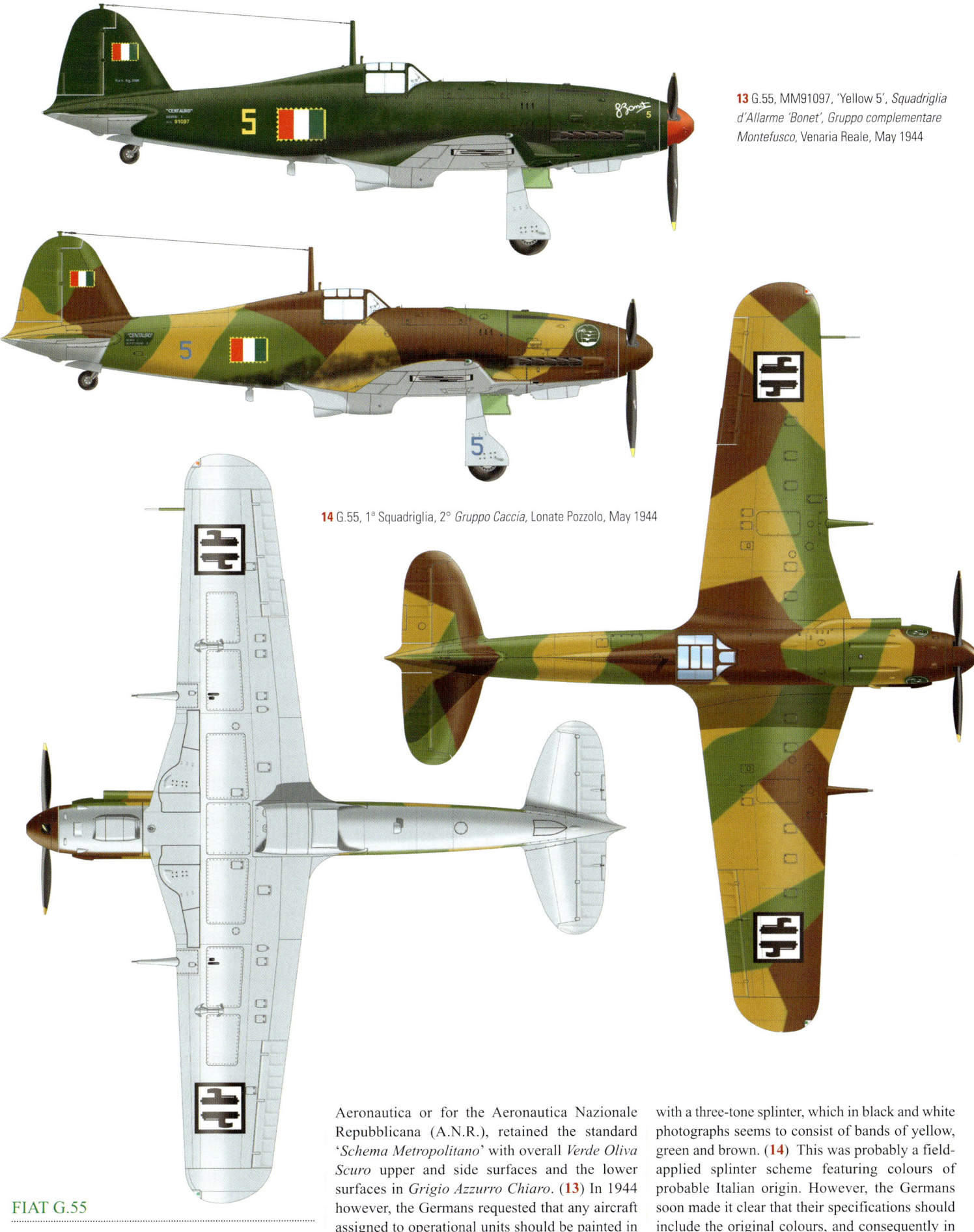

13 G.55, MM91097, 'Yellow 5', *Squadriglia d'Allarme 'Bonet', Gruppo complementare Montefusco*, Venaria Reale, May 1944

14 G.55, 1ª Squadriglia, 2° *Gruppo Caccia*, Lonate Pozzolo, May 1944

FIAT G.55

The prototype was the only G.55 camouflaged in the '*ramarro* camouflage scheme'. All those manufactured successively, whether for the Regia Aeronautica or for the Aeronautica Nazionale Repubblicana (A.N.R.), retained the standard '*Schema Metropolitano*' with overall *Verde Oliva Scuro* upper and side surfaces and the lower surfaces in *Grigio Azzurro Chiaro*. (**13**) In 1944 however, the Germans requested that any aircraft assigned to operational units should be painted in a Luftwaffe style splinter camouflage. The initial effect of this order was that in April the G.55s of the 1ª *Squadriglia* at Bresso began to be painted with a three-tone splinter, which in black and white photographs seems to consist of bands of yellow, green and brown. (**14**) This was probably a field-applied splinter scheme featuring colours of probable Italian origin. However, the Germans soon made it clear that their specifications should include the original colours, and consequently in May aircraft began to be repainted in the standard German RLM 74/75/76 greys. (**15**)

15 G.55, 2ª *Squadriglia*, 2° *Gruppo Caccia*, Cascina Vaga, May 1944

Concurrently, the factories had received the same instructions to adopt the German colour scheme but, strangely, at the FIAT factory, new G.55s were painted, once again, in camouflage colours seemingly of Italian origin, possibly after having obtained an exception from the rules which aimed to use up paints in stock. However, no official documents have emerged to confirm this assumption. Regardless, such a camouflage is photographically well documented on the G.55s awaiting delivery at the manufacturer's airfield on 25 April 1944, where a wide variation in styles of application can be observed, displaying various shapes and sizes of two-colour bands, probably in the usual green and brown colours. (**16**) The use of Italian colours was also indirectly confirmed when one of the last aircraft produced was delivered to the Allies in August by a defecting test pilot who was persuaded to cross the lines by an enemy agent. His aircraft was described in the British intelligence report as having a camouflage with green and brown bands. After the war those aircraft still on charge with the flying schools adopted the overall aluminium scheme.

16 G.55, MM91147, 3ª *Squadriglia*, 1° *Gruppo Caccia*, Vicenza, July 1944

CAMOUFLAGE AND MARKINGS

Insignia and Markings

Regia Aeronautica

The primary national insignia carried by the first CR.32s entering service in 1935 in silver livery, were the green, white and red stripes applied to rudders, which extended above and below horizontal tailplanes. The official emblem of Italy was applied on the white stripe, usually as a decal, consisting of the symbols of the Royal House of Savoy. From 1935, two small 'fasci littori' (fasces) were applied additionally. In addition the national tail insignia, a polychrome 'fascio' was carried on both fuselage sides, applied just forward of the cockpit in accordance with an official instruction dated February 1927. (**17**) Despite the regulations requiring the fuselage 'fascio' to be enclosed in a 35 mm dark lead-grey disc, the disc applied to any FIAT-produced aircraft was, typically, of a decidedly bright shade of light blue. Subsequently, another directive of July 1936 added four wing roundels to the national insignia: two on the upper wing and two under the lower one. This new insignia was formed of three parallel black fasces, with their blades always facing outwards, painted inside a 940-mm white disc, the size prescribed for fighters.

Besides national insignia, each aircraft carried its unit codes on both sides of the fuselage. These consisted of a black *squadriglia* number with the individual aircraft number, usually in red, and often completed by the *gruppo* emblem. Indeed, a directive dated 5 April 1927 put an end to a well-established practice dating back to the First World War: that of painting the *squadriglia* badge on the fuselage. However, the application of the *gruppo* emblem was to be short-lived, being subsequently replaced by the *stormo* badge in October 1937 for 'reasons of uniformity'. This basic set of insignia was left unchanged even when, in 1937, aircraft began to leave the production line in the three-colour disruptive camouflage. Also, in the following year, the first soft-edged mottled schemes were introduced; as the sole modification, this saw the removal of the tricolour bands from horizontal tailplanes, a measure taken in order not to compromise the overall effectiveness of the new camouflage schemes. In 1939, the entry into service of the new CR.42s and the first G.50s was marked by all such aircraft displaying the new factory-applied mottled scheme, and no further change to the national insignia was recorded, even the unit markings resulted unchanged.

Two days after Italy entered the war, on 12 June 1940, the Italian tricolour bands were ordered to be removed from rudders to avoid possible identification errors with similar tail markings carried by British and French aircraft, which although of different colours, resulted in some confusion. The tricolour was consequently replaced by a white 'Savoy' cross, which retained the Italian emblem of state within. At the end of 1940, FIAT fighters, like all other Italian aircraft, adopted a further identification marking consisting in a white band around the rear fuselage. This was

17 CR.32, MM2981, '73-1', 73ª *Squadriglia*, 9° *Gruppo*, 4° *Stormo* CT, Gorizia, November 1936

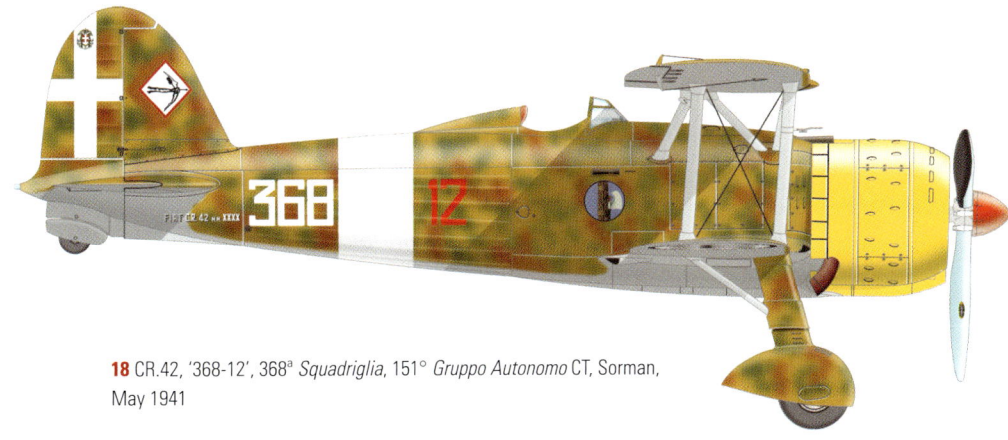

18 CR.42, '368-12', 368ª *Squadriglia*, 151° *Gruppo Autonomo* CT, Sorman, May 1941

19 G.50bis, '353-9', 359ª *Squadriglia*, 20° *Gruppo Autonomo* CT, Martuba, July 1941

retained as a standard visual recognition marking for all Italian aircraft until the Armistice of 8 September 1943. Under the instructions issued with the camouflage reforms of summer 1941 however, new orders were released relating to national insignia. In June 1941, confirming an order of the previous spring, a new regulation prescribed the application of a 60-cm-wide yellow band around the nose of all operational aircraft. The order also provided detailed designs for the different positions of the bands on aircraft with radial or inline engines, even detailing their position in respect of the exhaust collector. It was also ordered that the yellow colour should be extended to the propeller spinner, if one was present. Quite often, however, in conflict with the regulations, the yellow colour was added to the whole engine cowling. (**18** / **19**) However, (limiting our survey to FIAT fighters), the yellow noses were only applied to CR.42s and G.50s; in fact, by 1941 all CR.32s had been transferred to training units and relegated to non-operational duties. The yellow band was subsequently cancelled by an order of 22 October 1941, for reasons which remain unclear at the time of writing.

Finally, a directive of 25 August established that the background of the disc containing the wing *fasci* had to be of the same camouflage colour as the surrounding area, instead of white as generally observed previously. Furthermore, it was standard practice to identify the personal machine of unit commanders by the use of special command pennants, generally painted close to the cockpit. These pennants were formed of a red band on a blue background, triangular in shape for a *squadriglia* commander, swallow-tailed for a *gruppo* commander, and rectangular for a *stormo* commander.

The Co-belligerent Regia Aeronautica

No FIAT fighter served within operational units throughout the period of co-belligerence, as the few residual CR.42s and G.50s were only assigned to liaison units and flying schools, where they usually displayed only individual aircraft numbers. Moreover, as from 20 September 1943, the Regia Aeronautica adopted a totally new and different national insignia, adopting tricolour roundels on wings and fuselage, with the green in the centre and the red outside. The original camouflage colour schemes were usually retained until war's end.

A.N.R.

At an early stage the G.55s operated by the Aeronautica Nazionale Repubblicana invariably retained German insignia, but from January 1944, Italian fighters began to adopt new national insignia. These comprised two opposing black *fasci littori* painted inside a square in four standard wing positions. The *fasci* applied at the factory were painted on a white background above and below the wings, but those painted at unit level more often had a neutral background under the wing. On the fuselages an Italian tricolour flag was completed by a yellow post and fringe, which was repeated, smaller in size, on the tail fin. Individual numbering followed different rules depending on each unit: the *Squadriglia Complementare 'Montefusco'* had yellow codes, while within 2° *Gruppo Caccia* each *squadriglia* had a different colour: 1ª *Squadriglia* initially used blue numbers, and later black ones; the codes of the 2ª *Squadriglia* were yellow, while 3ª *Squadriglia* had white codes. *Squadriglia* assignment was also evidenced by the *squadriglia* badge often painted on the nose of an aircraft. Finally, when the *Squadriglia 'Montefusco'* was later incorporated into the 1° *Gruppo Caccia*, it eventually adopted blue fuselage codes outlined in white.

CHAPTER THIRTEEN

The Survivors

Above, below right and following page: The HA-132-L C.1-328 (Spanish-built CR.32) of the *Museo Storico* of the Aeronautica Militare at Vigna di Valle in Roma. It has the markings of the CR.32 coded 3-6 of the 24ª *Squadriglia* of the 16° *Gruppo 'Cucaracha'* during the Spanish Civil War. The engine in the foreground is the FIAT A.30 RA V-12 aero engine as used in the CR.32.

FIAT CR.32 / Hispano HA-132

ONLY two CR.32s survive intact today, one preserved at the Museo of the Aeronautica Militare Italiana and another in its Spanish equivalent. A common characteristic of the aircraft is that neither was originally constructed by FIAT but were manufactured under licence in Spain by the Hispano Suiza company with the local designation of Hispano HA-132-L '*Chirri*'.

Museo Storico dell'Aeronautica Militare, Vigna di Valle, Roma
HA-132-L   C.1-328

This aircraft was donated to the Aeronautica Militare by the Ejercito del Aire in 1955. Initially the fighter was restored in the colours of the 92ª *Squadriglia* of the Regia Aeronautica, but a subsequent external restoration of the aircraft by the GAVS (*Gruppo Amici Velivoli Storici* –

THE SURVIVORS

The Friends of Historic Aircraft Group) in the early 2000s saw the application of an appropriate livery for an aircraft of the *Aviazione Legionaria*, with the code 3-6 of the 24ª *Squadriglia* of the 16° *Gruppo* 'Cucaracha'. On the tail, the original Spanish construction number, 328, has been retained at the time of writing.

Below: HA-132-L C.1.262 on display at the *Museo del Aire Y del Espacio* of the Ejercito del Aire at Cuatro Vientos, Madrid.

Museo del Aire Y del Espacio, Cuatro Vientos, Madrid
HA-132-L   C.1.262

This aircraft is the result of a reconstruction performed by the Maestranza Aerea of Madrid, using parts from several original aircraft, amongst which are the vertical stabiliser, rudder and tailplane from the CR.32 coded 3-51, which was involved in the fatal crash of *comandante* Joaquín Garcia Morato.

FIAT CR.42 *Falco*

Museo Storico dell'Aeronautica Militare, Vigna di Valle, Roma
J-11 2539 cn917

This aircraft was rebuilt with the central fuselage of Swedish example, Fv 2539, united with components and materials sourced from various museums and collections. Originally the aircraft was assigned to the 1st Division of F 9 and identified by the code 9-8. It was damaged after a ground loop while taxiing on 6 July 1943. Subsequently, it was passed to Svensk Flygtjänst AB, assuming the civilian registration SE-AOP, having flown 310 hours in 540 flights with the Flygvapnet.

The Italian GAVS (*Gruppo Amici Velivoli Storici* – see previous) had recovered a FIAT A.74 engine from a lake in France, complete with a propeller, and this was restored by the Torino section of the GAVS in 1991-92, while a FIAT CR.42 wing section in German colours had been held by the Vigna di Valle museum for several years.

The remaining missing parts were constructed thanks to original drawings provided by FIAT and by the members of AREA (*Associazione Restauro Aeronautico*) of Varese who, in collaboration with the GAVS, proceeded with the complete reconstruction of the aircraft, reproducing it with the code 162-6, MM5643, as belonging to the 162ª *Squadriglia* CT based at Rhodes in 1941. The aircraft was delivered to the Museo Storico dell'Aeronautica Militare at Vigna di Valle for display on 12 May 2005.

Above and following page: CR.42 of the *Museo Storico* of the Aeronautica Militare at Vigna di Valle in Roma. It carries the code of the CR.32, MM5643, '162-6', belonging to the 162ª *Squadriglia* CT based at Rhodes in 1941. The aircraft is a former Swedish J.11, rebuilt with components recovered from different Flygvapnet aircraft.

THE SURVIVORS

FIAT FIGHTERS

Royal Air Force Museum, Hendon, London
CR.42   95-13   MM5701

The CR.42 on display at Hendon is the original aircraft flown by *sergente* Pietro Salvatori, who was forced to land in a field near the beach at Orford Ness in Suffolk on 11 November 1940 (see page 218).

Above and following two pages: The CR.42, MM5701, '95-13', of the 85ª *Squadriglia* on display at the Royal Air Force Museum in Hendon, London. It is the former *Corpo Aereo Italiano* fighter that crash-landed on the coast of Suffolk, England, on 11 November 1940.

THE SURVIVORS

THE SURVIVORS

Flygvapenmuseum (Swedish Air Force Museum), Linkoping
J-11 2543 cn921

The J-11 conserved in the Swedish Museum is *'Falco'* Fv 2543, c/n 921, which was operated in 1941-1942 by the *Kungliga Göta Flygflottilj* F 9 from Gothenburg Säve airfield. The fighter is currently displayed in the *Flygvapenmuseum* at Linkoping with the code F9-9, the last code applied during its operational career with *Flygflottilj* F 9 prior to its withdrawal from service on 13 March 1945.

The J-11, 2543, c/n 921, at the Flygvapnet Museum in Linkoping, Sweden. It is displayed in the markings of *Flygflottilj* F 9.

THE SURVIVORS

The former Flygvapnet J 11, Fv2542, coded F9-10, that crashed near Tårdnatjåkko on 13 April 1942 belonging to The Fighter Collection at Duxford in England. At the time of writing, it is under restoration to flightworthy status.

THE SURVIVORS

The Fighter Collection, Duxford
J-11   2542   cn920

This Swedish Air Force J 11 (Fv 2542 coded F9-10) crashed near Tårdnatjåkko, in the north of Sweden, on 13 April 1942 with the death of its pilot, Sergeant Bertil Klintman. It is reported that the meteorological conditions induced the pilot to misjudge his height above the ground.

The wreckage of the fighter was recovered in the early 1980s and acquired by The Fighter Collection in the United Kingdom in 1995. Following a long restoration with Vintage Fabrics at Audley End airfield, the aircraft, still not in flying condition, was displayed statically at the 2018 Flying Legends air show. The biplane was restored in the colours of CR.42 85-16, MM.6976 of the 85ª *Squadriglia, 18° Gruppo* which operated from Ursel airfield in Belgium. That aircraft was destroyed in an emergency landing close to Coulton railway station, near Lowestoft in Suffolk on 11 November 1940. The pilot, *Sergente* Antonio Lazzari, had evaded three Hawker Hurricanes until the variable pitch gear of the propeller jammed, leaving one of the three blades at a different pitch to the rest. Lazzari decided to land. Upon landing, he ran over the railway line which caused the aircraft to crash into an adjoining field, Lazzari was unhurt (see pages 214 and 217).

At the time of writing, its return to flying condition is still being completed in a hangar of The Fighter Collection at Duxford.

The CR.42, MM6976, 85-16, of the 85ª *Squadriglia*, 18° *Gruppo* following its crash-landing close to Coulton railway station, near Lowestoft in Suffolk on 11 November 1940. This aircraft can also be seen on page 214 prior to its loss.

FIAT G.50 *Freccia*

Muzejvazduhoplovstva Beograd (Aeronautical Museum Belgrade)
G.50bis MM6197/3505

The only FIAT G.50 surviving to this day is that in which Lieutenant Arapovic deserted to the island of Vis on 2 September 1944. After the war, the aircraft was stored in a depot at the Zemun base, and extracted, in 1951, for display on the occasion of the tenth anniversary of the popular insurrection as a symbol of the defeat of fascism. It was painted in false Regia Aeronautica *fasci* markings. In 1961 the Belgrade Aviation Museum recovered the aircraft. At the time of writing, it is in a precarious state of conservation and is awaiting restoration.

Archivio Storico Federighi, Pisa
G.50. MM ??

At the *Archivio Storico Federighi* at Pisa is the conserved wreckage of a FIAT G.50 that crashed in Belgium. Given its recovery location, it is extremely likely that the wreckage is that of the G.50 piloted by *tenente* Mario Roncali of the 352ª *Squadriglia*, who crashed at 12.45 on 13 February 1941 while returning after a scramble from Ursel to intercept an enemy aircraft flying at 300 m above eastern Flanders. The interception was unsuccessful, and while returning, the pilot lost control of the aircraft in unknown circumstances, crashing near Steenbrugge in Belgium.

The FIAT G.50bis preserved at the Aeronautical Museum Belgrade. (M. Gueli)

The *Archivio Storico Federighi* in Pisa curates a collection of rare parts of a G.50 that crashed in Belgium. They are probably from the G.50 flown by *tenente* Mario Roncali of the 352ª *Squadriglia*, who crashed on 13 February 1941. However, the wing is taken from another aircraft which was recovered in Italy.

FIAT G.55 *Centauro*

Museo Storico dell'Aeronautica Militare, Vigna di Valle, Roma
FIAT G.55 (reconstruction of former G.59A MM53265)

As no original examples of the FIAT G.55 survived the war, the idea of providing the *Museo Storico* at Vigna di Valle with an example of the *Centauro* stemmed from the availability of an original DB 605 engine held in an Aeronautica Militare store, coupled with the possibility of recovering the airframe of a G.59A (IV *Serie*, MM53265 c/n 74), conserved in poor condition in the *Parco della Rimembranza* in Novara.

The airframe and engine were taken to Lecce where, in 1990, the first intervention work commenced by the personnel of the 10° RMV (*Reparto Manutenzione Velivoli* – Aircraft Maintenance Unit). This work continued for around a year but was then suspended. The major Italian aerospace company, Alenia Aeronautica, offered to continue restoration, and in 1992 the partially restored fuselage and engine was moved to the Torino facilities of the *Divisione Aeronautica*. A subsequent period of crisis afflicting the Italian aerospace industry brought a further suspension of the work. Fortunately, however, the task was assumed by the Torino section of the GAVS, the work being brought to a conclusion thanks to the passion and technical competence of its members and the technical and financial support of numerous companies and the *Ministero dell'Università e della Ricerca*.

Some twelve years after work started, on 12 April 2002, the aircraft was officially displayed at the Velo pavilion (so named after the company that constructed it), reserved for the historic aircraft of the Aeronautica Militare that participated in the Second World War. It was finished in the colours of 'Yellow 5' of the *Squadriglia Complementare 'Montefusco Bonet'* of the A.N.R., based near Torino in 1944.

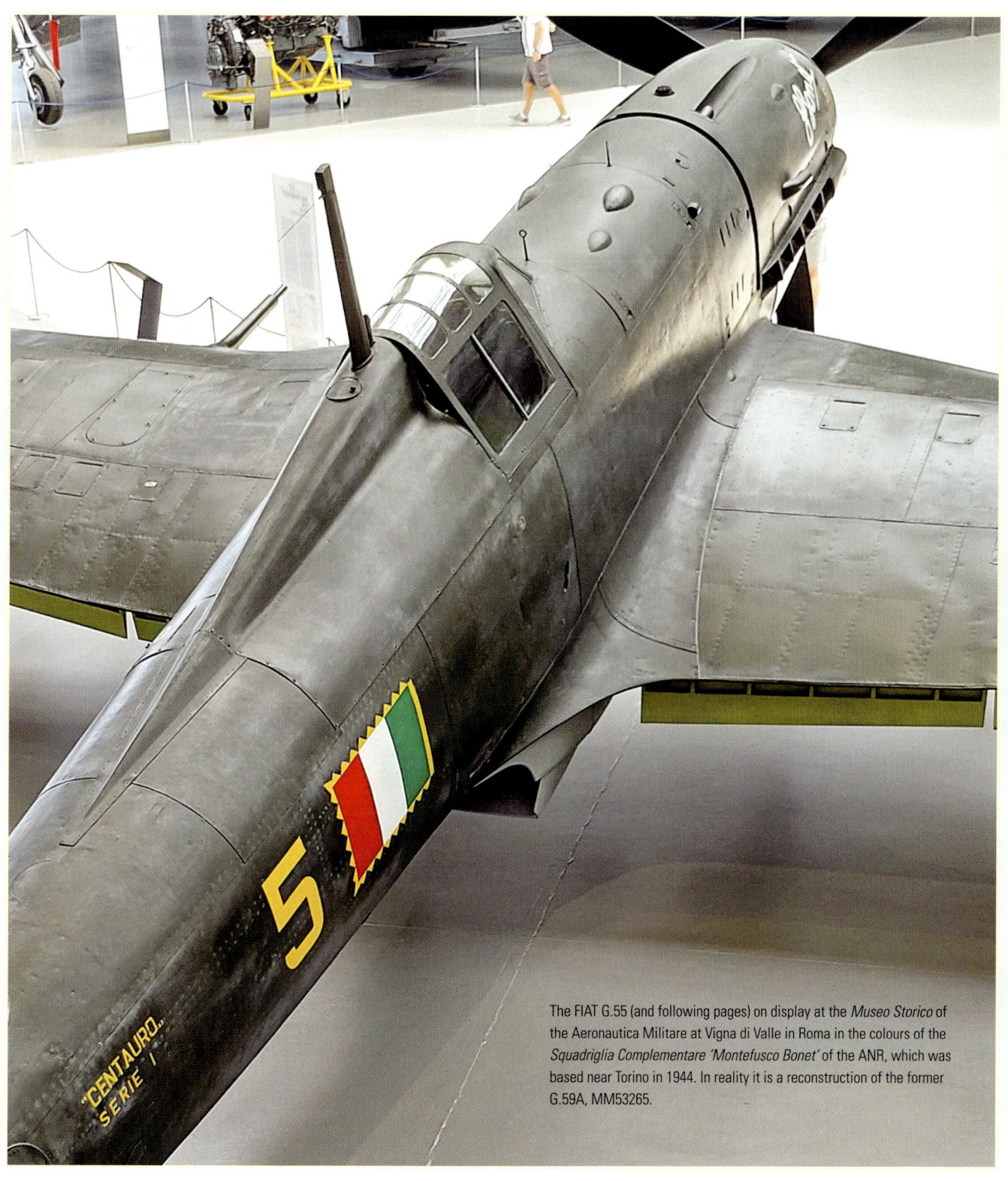

The FIAT G.55 (and following pages) on display at the *Museo Storico* of the Aeronautica Militare at Vigna di Valle in Roma in the colours of the *Squadriglia Complementare 'Montefusco Bonet'* of the ANR, which was based near Torino in 1944. In reality it is a reconstruction of the former G.59A, MM53265.

FIAT FIGHTERS

THE SURVIVORS

THE SURVIVORS

FIAT G.59

Museo Storico dell'Aeronautica Militare, Vigna di Valle, Roma
FIAT G.59-4B MM53276

This recently restored G.59 is preserved at the Museo Storico dell'Aeronautica Militare at Vigna di Valle. It was the sixty-first G.59 produced by Fiat Aviazione and constructed initially as a G.59-2B 4 series, subsequently being updated to the G.59- 4B version with a sliding bubble canopy.

The fuselage carries the code SE-7 of the *Scuola di Volo di Elmas* (Cagliari) where this aircraft served from the early 1950s until April 1961. Subsequently it was assigned to the *Centri di Addestramento* of the *Regioni Aeree* of Bari and Milano until it was retired and displayed at the Torino museum from 1962. In the mid-1970s, it arrived at Vigna di Valle where it was displayed until 2013. After two years under restoration, in November 2015, the aircraft was placed back on display by the *Museo* in its original livery of blue grey, wearing the insignia carried when it flew with the *Scuola di Volo di Elmas*.

Aeronautica Militare
Base Aerea San Damiano (Piacenza)
FIAT G.59-4A MM53526 cn131

After many years on display at the '*Città della Domenica*' theme park in Spagnolia (Perugia), this single-seat G.59-4A, coded RR-80, was recovered by the Aeronautica Militare in 1995 in a precarious condition and stored at the Torricola depot. The aircraft has recently been stored in the hangar of the *Sezione Valorizzazione Patrimonio Storico Aeronautico* on the Piacenza AM base.

Museo Storico dell'Università degli Studi di Palermo
FIAT G.59-4B MM53530

This FIAT G. 59, *Matricola Militare* 53530, was built at the end of 1952, and was operated firstly by the *Regione Aerea di Bari*, coded RB-40, and then by the *Regione Aerea di Roma* with the code RR-73. Having concluded its operational service with the Aeronautica Militare, in 1964 it was acquired by the former *Istituto di Aeronautica* of the Università degli Studi di Palermo. Today it is one of only five complete surviving examples, as well as one of the most important pieces in the *Museo Storico dei Motori e dei Meccanismi*, which has completed its restoration and is responsible for its conservation.

The perfectly restored FIAT G.59-4B, MM53276, in the markings of the *Scuola Volo* at Cagliari Elmas and displayed at the *Museo Storico dell'Aeronautica Militare* at Vigna di Valle.

The FIAT G.59-4B, MM53530, restored and preserved at the *Museo Storico dell'Università degli Studi di Palermo.* (via GAVS)

Military Aviation Museum, Virginia Beach, USA
FIAT G.59B-4B MM.53778

Meier Motors GmbH has been tasked by the Military Aviation Museum of Virginia Beach to convert this aircraft into a G.55 *Centauro* as soon as a DB 605 engine or its Italian counterpart becomes available.

Private owner
FIAT G.59-4B c/n 181 MM53774 I-MRSV

This aircraft, originally in service with the Aeronautica Militare as G.59-4B MM53774, belongs to the X *Serie* and is a two-seater with a sliding teardrop canopy. Of its service with the Aeronautica Militare, it is known to have been operated until 1968 by the *Scuola at Tiro di Guidonia* with the code RR-76. It featured a red spinner, the colour that identified the unit operating the aircraft. In fact, this machine, like the others of the series, originally had the option to be fitted with a Breda SAFAT 12.7 mm machine gun in a wing, and for small exercise bombs to be carried under the wings. No other details of the units that operated the aircraft during its military service are known, but it was acquired, after languishing in a hangar at Guidonia airfield by *Sig*. Pino Valenti, an enthusiastic pilot from Parma. Thanks to the support of a group of volunteer engineers from *Officine Aeronavali* of Venezia and to his friend, Sergio Arban, a former technical officer with the Aeronautica Militare who, based at Guidonia, was familiar with the aircraft, having worked on it for many years, after eight years of work, on 25 May 1992, the G.59 returned to grace Italian skies. It was piloted by Guido Zuccoli, previously an owner of the same type of aircraft in Australia. In 1999, the aircraft, camouflaged in Luftwaffe

Continues on page 287

Views of the FIAT G.59-4B, c/n 181, MM53774, 'I-MRSV', that was operated until a few years ago in Italy by aviation enthusiast Pino Valenti. It was perfectly restored to flying condition and displayed regularly at major air shows in Italy. It was recently sold to a German operator after the death of the owner and pilot.

FIAT FIGHTERS

Forward cockpit of FIAT G.59-4B, c/n 181, MM53774, 'I-MRSV'.

colours, took part in some scenes of the film *U-571*. In 2001, it was involved in an emergency landing, with its undercarriage retracted, and this kept it in the repair shop until 2006.

For many years the aircraft was managed by the *Nucleo Acrobatico Parmense*, owned by Pino Valenti, an organisation which manages other historic aircraft, including a FIAT G.46. Unfortunately, after Valenti's death in 2021, part of the collection was disposed of, and in the course of 2023 the G.59-4B was sold to a civilian operator in Germany.

Private owner
FIAT G.59-4B MM53772 D-FIAT

Of its period of service with the Aeronautica Militare, it is known that this aircraft served with the *Reparto Sperimentale Volo* with the code RS-25, and was also flown by the celebrated test pilot, *capitano* Riccardo Peracchi, on numerous occasions during air displays. Following its retirement from active service, the aircraft was placed into storage and subsequently sold to Guido Zuccoli, an Italian pilot and aviation enthusiast, resident in Australia. The G.59 was sent to the USA for restoration in 1984, the process being completed in 1987. At the conclusion of the work, the aircraft was registered NX59B and named '*Ciao Bella*' in homage to the pilot and the machine. Zuccoli used the G.59B to participate in the National Championship Air Races of 1987 and won the 'Lindbergh Prize' at the Oskhosh meeting prior to moving the aircraft to Toowoomba in Australia in 1988.

The following year, the G.59B was painted in an imaginary ringed camouflage colour to represent an Italian fighter of the Second World War, carrying the emblem of the 51° *Stormo*. It was placed on the Australian civil register as VH-LIX.

In 1994 the G.59-4B was converted into a single-seater but was converted back to a two-seater some years later when it was again restored, this time for its appearance in the remake of the film *Sahara* with James Belushi. After the death of Guido Zuccoli, in October 2015, the aircraft was acquired by a private individual through Meier Motors Aircraft, a company that was engaged to undertake a further restoration. The aircraft returned to the air in November 2017. At present it is preserved and managed from the Meier Motors Aircraft hangar at Bremgarten and displays a 'bare metal' livery with the German registration D-FIAT, c/n 185, ex MM53772.

INDEX

Aaltonen, Lasse, 165
Abello, *S.Ten.* Oscar, 86
Acerbi, *Serg.Magg.*, 144
Agnelli, Giovanni, 22, 128
Agostini, Serafino, 135, 177, 189
Aini, *Magg.* Giuseppe, 210
Alakoski, Klaus, 165
Alessandrini, *Cap.* Aldo, 148
al-Gaylani, Rashid Ali, 106
Anelli, *Cap.* Giulio, 215
Anselmi, *Cap.* Mario, 112
Antoniu, Andreas, 152
Arapovic, *Lt.* Andrija, 166, 274
Arban, Sergio, 281
Arrabito, *Magg.* Guglielmo, 198-199
Arrigoni, *Serg.*, 198
Artina, *Ten.* Romolo, 220
Assolant, *Cap.*, 79
Aurili, Giuseppe, 46
Baldacci, *Serg.Magg.* Bruno, 222
Baldi, *Cap.* Osvaldo, 30
Balduzzo, *Serg.*, 199
Baschirotto, *Serg.* Gianlino, 46
Bassi, *Ten.* Livio, 151-152
Baylon, *Magg.* Giuseppe, 151
Beccaria, *Ten.* Giuseppe, 87
Bellini, *Serg.*, 104
Benedetti, *Ten.* Mario, 86
Benjumea, *Cap.* Julio Diaz, 46
Beretta, *Ten.* Sandro, 148, 199
Berretta, *Ten.* Giovanni, 148
Bertolozzi, *Ten.* Guido, 198
Biagini, *Serg.Magg.* Lucio, 192-193
Bianchi, *Magg.*, Luigi, 153
Biron, *Ten.* Giuseppe, 191, 193, 198-199
Blenner Plunkett, P/O Reginald Patrick, 81
Blomberg, GFM Werner von, 60
Bobba, *Cap.* Guido, 93
Bocconi, *Serg.Magg.* Renzo, 86
Bonelli, *Serg.* Angelo, 215
Bonelli, *Serg.* Otello, 220
Bonet, *Cap.* Giovanni, 191-192
Bonola, Gen.*DA.* Augusto, 38, 47
Bonomi, *Gen.BA.* Ruggero, 210
Bonzano, *Magg.* Mario, 131, 144-145, 148, 155, 210, 215, 220
Borzoni, *Cap.* Giovanni, 60, 148
Boscaro, *Serg.Magg.*, 198
Bosner, *Cap.*, 166
Bottalla, Giovanbattista, 21, 25
Botto, *Cap.* Ernesto, 44, 46, 62, 85, 86, 190
Brach Papa, Francesco, 22, 30, 33, 64
Buffa, *Magg.* Giovanni, 30, 109, 148
Burges, F/Lt George, 86
Busoni, *Col.*, 84
Buvoli, *Serg.Magg.* Aldo, 144
Calafiore, *S.Ten.*, 111
Calamai, *Ten.* Giuseppe, 222
Calistri, *Cap.* Pietro, 93
Calvani, *Ten.*, 111
Campanile, *Serg.Magg.* Franco, 220
Canaveri, *Ten.Col.* Aldo, 43-43
Caponigro, *Serg.Magg.* Ersio, 222
Cappa, *Gen.BA.* Umberto, 47, 102
Caproni, Gianni, 66
Caputo, *Ten.*, 83
Carancini, *Ten.* Mario Gaetano, 99
Casero, *Col.* Giuseppe, 43, 163
Cassinelli, *Gen.BA.* Guglielmo, 30, 38, 47
Castellani, *Serg.Magg.*, 40
Catania, *Ten.*, 111
Catella, Vittorio, 177
Ceccherelli, *Ten.*, 40
Cenni, *Magg.* Giuseppe, 46
Chang, Gen. Kai-Shek, 49
Chiappa, *Serg.* Domenico, 105
Chiesa, *Col.* Umberto, 148, 210
Chiodi, *Cap.* Antonio, 86

Chiussi, *Serg.Magg.*, 198
Ciccu, *Ten.Col.* Giovan Battista, 210
Cippo, *Ten.Col.* Carlo Perrelli, 210
Contaldi, *Ten.* Bruno, 106
Corsi, *Serg.* Ugo, 91
Cugnasca, *Ten.* Carlo, 153, 163
Cullen, Richard, 152
Cus, Valentino, 37, 64, 70, 136, 174, 176-177, 181, 236
D'Agostini, *Ten.* Mario, 102, 104
D'Agostinis, *Cap.* Giuseppe, 41-43
D'Amico, *Serg.Magg.*, 144
Da Barberino, *Col.*, 30
Daffara, *M.llo.* Vittorino, 46
David, *Ten.*, 144
de Bernardi, Mario, 57
De Briganti, Giovanni, 130
De Capoa, *Col.* Carlo, 210
Dellanay, *Serg.* Roger, 116
Del Prete, *Ten.*, 144
de Mérode, *Lt.* Werner, 116
Denholm, George, 217
de Prato, *Cap.* Tullio, 131
Dequal, *Magg.* Vincenzo, 39, 41, 150
Desideri, *Serg.Magg.*, 109, 111
Di Cecco, *Serg.Magg.* Luigi, 198
di Montegnacco, Bruno, 46
Donadei, *Com.* Mario, 237
Dornier, Claude, 13
Dyson, Charles, 152
Ehrnrooth, *Kap.* Olavi, 163, 165
Fagnani, *Magg.* Tarcisio, 42
Falconi, *Ten.Col.* Tito, 86, 93, 192
Feliciani, *Magg.*, 195
Ferrarin, Arturo, 57
Fessia, *Ing.* Antonio, 128, 174
Folcherio, *S.Ten.*, 83
Fougier, *Gen.* Rino Corso, 27, 57, 59, 178, 205-206, 210
Franchino, *Ten.*, 99
Franco, *Gen.* Francisco, 39, 44
François, Armando, 46
Frascadore, *Ten.* Mario, 99
Fruet, *Magg.* Erardo, 226
Fusco, *Ten.* Alfredo, 152
Gabrielli, *Ing.* Giuseppe, 13-14, 18, 128, 130, 134, 136, 173-174, 176, 178-179, 181-182, 232, 239
Galland, *Gen.Lt.* Adolf, 178
Garcia-Morato, *Cap.* Joaquín, 41-42, 46, 260
Gardner Keeble, F/Lt Peter, 86
Gatti, *Ten.*, 99
Gentile, Francesco, 189
Ghiacci, *Ten.* Piero, 105
Giardinà, *Serg.Magg.* Antonio, 83
Gismondi, *Serg.*, 99
Giuntella, *Ten.* Cesare, 219
Göring, GFM Hermann, 62, 178
Graffer, *Cap.* Giorgio, 99, 108, 111
Green, Maj. Herschel, 192
Grillo, *Serg.Magg.* Giacomo, 220
Guerra, Ezio, 136
Harmaja, Tapani, 160
Hartley, F/O, 86
Incerti, Enrico degli, 46
Jannello, *S.Ten.* Pietro, 99
Jellici, *M.llo.*, 192
Jeschonnek, *Gen.Obst.*, Hans, 178
Joensuu, Ilmari, 165
Kármán, Theodore von, 128
Kesselring, GFM Albert, 222
Klintman, *Serg.* Bertil, 273
La Ferla, *S.Ten.* Guido, 166
Lamarche, *Maj.*, 116
Larrazabal, *Cap.* Angel Salas, 41,46
Lautamäki, Lauri, 165
Lazzari, *Serg.Magg.* Antonio, 217
Le Gloan, *Adj.*, 79

Leotta, *Magg.* Eugenio, 43, 148
Lingua, *Serg.* Mario, 220
Locatelli, *Ten.Col.*, Plinio, 38
Longo, *Gen.* Ulisse, 102
Lundquist, *Gen.*, 163
Lusardi, *S.Ten.*, 83
Machieraldo, *Cap.*, 221
Magaldi, *Cap.* Nicola, 99
Majone, Giuseppe, 46
Malagoli, *Serg.* Loris, 148
Malavolta, *S.Ten.* Ildebrando, 83, 84
Mancini, *S.Ten.*, 132
Mantelli, *Cap.* Adriano, 46,180
Manzitti, *Ten.* Nicola, 193
Manzocchi, Dario, 164
Marasco, *M.llo.*, 144, 148
Marcellini, Romolo, 46
Mari, *Serg.Magg.* Guglielmo, 105
Marinelli, *M.llo.*, 153
Marsan, *Cap.* Simeone, 62
Martissa, *Ten.* Enzo, 144-145
Mastragostino, *Magg.* Angelo, 150
Mazza, *Ten.* Guido, 220
Mazzei, *S.Ten.* 92, 198
Mecozzi, *Col.* Amedeo, 39
Meille, *Magg.* Enrico, 105
Melano, *Serg.* Pietro, 220
Meneghini, *Serg.Magg.* Renato, 144, 222
Merlo, *Ten.* Vittorio, 215
Micheli, *Cap.* Mario De, 80
Milch, GFM Erhard, 62, 178
Mölders, *Obstlt.* Werner, 222
Molinari, *Magg.* Oscar, 51, 60
Montefusco, *Cap.* Mario, 154, 191
Montoloono, *Ten.Col.* Giulio, 210
Monti, *Ten.* Ezio, 87
Morellato, *Serg.* Luigi, 220 Morettin, *S.Ten.* Fausto, 198
Moscatelli, *Cap.* Antonio, 60
Mosso, *Ing.* Giacomo, 17
Mottet, *M.llo.*, 84
Mussolini, Benito, 62, 87, 148, 199, 205
Neri, *Ten.* Ariosto, 58
Nieminen, Urho, 165
Nobili, Col. Guido, 46
Odero, Attilio, 13
Oliviero, *Ten.* Dante, 41
Orsini, *Ten.* Luciano, 105
Orsolan, *S.Ten.*, 195
Pacini, *Serg.*, 99
Pagani, *Cap.*, 214
Panichi, *Ten.* Enzo, 217
Parmeggiani, *S.Ten.*, 111
Paronen, Onni, 165
Patriarca, *M.llo.* Vincenzo, 111
Pecchiari, *Serg.Magg.* Felice, 222
Pegna, *Ing.* Giovanni, 128
Pellegrini, *Gen.SA.* Aldo, 47
Peltz, *Gen.Maj.* Dietrich, 178
Penna, *S.Ten.* Paolo, 99, 109, 111
Peracchi, *Cap.* Riccardo, 287
Petersen, *Obst.* Edgar, 178
Piaggio, Rinaldo, 13
Pinna, *Ten.* Maria, 86
Pinna, *Gen.DA.* Pietro, 47
Pongiluppi, *Serg.Magg.* Guido, 144-145
Porro, *Gen.SA.* Felice, 47
Porta, *M.llo.* Alfredo, 112
Porvari, Valio, 165
Pratelli, *Cap.* Rolando, 43-44
Presel, *Serg.Magg.* Guido, 46
Pricolo, *Gen.* Francesco, 106
Puhakka, *Maj.* Olli, 165
Questa, *Col.* Luigi, 210
Raffi, *Cap.* Antonio, 81-82
Ranza, *Gen.SA.* Ferruccio, 47
Re, *S.Ten.* Guido, 219
Remondino, *Magg.* Aldo, 44, 60, 62, 144

Rengel, *Cap.* Garcia Lopez, 46
Ricci, *Cap.* Corrado, 46, 83, 107, 111
Richthofen, GFM Wolfram von, 199
Rigatti, *Ten.* Mario, 86-87
Ritegni, *Serg.*, 99
Roatta, *Gen.* Mario, 42
Robetto, *Cap.* Giuseppe, 198
Rolandi, Enrico, 64, 133, 177
Rommel, GFM Erwin, 88, 95
Roncali, *Ten.* Mario, 222, 274
Rosatelli, *Ing.* Celestino, 10, 13-14, 21-23, 25, 30, 33, 57, 63-64
Rossi, *Magg.* Mario, 44
Roveda, *Magg.* Riccardo, 144, 188
Rovere, *Ten.* Mario, 102, 104
Ruzzin, *M.llo.* Giuseppe, 219-220
Sacchi, *Ten.Col.*, 57
Sagatizabal, *Cap.* Manuel Vasquez, 46
Sala, *Serg.Magg.* Arnaldo, 87
Salvatori, *Serg.* Pietro, 217-218, 264
Samperisi, *Ten.*, 221
Sandini, *Serg.* Mario, 217
Sant'Andrea, Vincenzo, 144, 148
Santoro, *Cap.* Corrado, 80
Scagliarini, *Cap.* Giovanni, 111
Scaglioni, *Serg.* Giuseppe, 91
Scapinelli, *Ten.* Pietro, 30
Scarpetta, *Cap.* Pier Giuseppe, 151
Sforza, *Cap.* Francesco, 105-106
Sgubbi, *Serg.Magg.* Ugo, 198
Smith, F/Lt. J.D., 153
Sozzi, *M.llo.* Felice, 220
Spazzoli, *M.llo.* Romano, 198
Specker, *Ten.*, 219
Squassoni, *Serg.Magg.* Felice, 111
Stahle, *Maj.*, 160
Stefanutti, *Ten.Col. Ing.* Sergio, 179
Stiavelli, *Ing.* Manlio, 21, 182
Tacchini, *Ten.* Pasquale, 219
Tarantola, *M.llo.* Ennio, 193
Tassinari, *M.llo.* Federico, 127, 144
Taylor, F/Lt., 86
Tedeschini Lalli, *Gen.SA.* Gennaro, 47
Tenti, *Magg.* Mario, 210
Tessari, *Gen.* Arrigo, 44
Tessore, *Ten.Col.* Angelo, 39, 148
Torre, *Ten.Col.* Pier Luigi, 64
Torresi, *Cap.* Giulio, 192-193, 198
Trevisan, *Ten.*, 144
Triolo, *Ten.* Alberto, 99
Trontti, Nils, 165
Tuominen, Oiva, 165
Valenti, *Sig.* Pino, 281, 287
Valentini, *Ten.* Lucio, 106
Velardi, *Gen.DA.* Vincenzo, 38-39, 42-44, 47
Vespignani, *Gen.DA.* Ottorino, 47
Visconti, *Com.*, 199
Visintini, *Ten.* Mario, 80, 82, 84
Vosilla, *Ten.Col.* Ferruccio, 44, 93-94, 156, 210, 215, 217
Wallenius, *Ker.*, 163
Waters, F/O John Lawrence, 86
Webster, *Serg.*, 153
Winskill, Lt., 220
Zerbi, *Ing.* Tranquillo, 30, 35, 128
Zotti, *Magg.* Andrea, 43, 46
Zuccoli, Guido, 281, 287